Since the Meiji Restoration, labor in Japan has moved from virtual serfdom to a position of great organization and power. No nation in Asia, and few in the West, has a record of labor advancement equal to that of Japan. This amazing development has been accomplished in the midst of conflicting pressures of democratic awakening, cultural traditions, nationalism, socialist philosophies, and various religious polarities.

If Japan has emerged as the leading industrial nation in Asia, so has its organized labor emerged as a kind of model for the Orient. Ayusawa's book is a history of this emergence from the mid-nineteenth century to the mid-twentieth century. What will be the role of Japanese labor in the years ahead as Japan seeks to increase her exports and as labor seeks to share more in the fruits of Japan's great success? The key to the next hundred years may be found in the first hundred.

As a compendium of historical material on Japanese labor, Ayusawa's definitive book fills a void which until now has existed in English translation. It is particularly useful to have a book written from the perspective of a Japanese, and his brilliant work may well become the standard reference in this field.

❀ *A History of Labor in Modern Japan*

A HISTORY OF LABOR IN MODERN JAPAN

by Iwao F. Ayusawa

EAST-WEST CENTER PRESS   HONOLULU

To the memory of DR. THEODORE RICHARDS
and MRS. MARY ATHERTON RICHARDS
FOUNDERS OF FRIEND PEACE SCHOLARSHIPS

this book is gratefully dedicated

Preface

The present study is the result of advice, encouragement, and help from many kind individual friends and institutions, particularly Dr. Robert Hall of the University of Michigan, director for many years of the Asia Foundation in Japan; the *Mainichi* newspapers of Tokyo; and, finally, the East-West Center, University of Hawaii.

The writer came to Hawaii first in 1911 as recipient of the *Friend* Peace Scholarship for study at the Mid-Pacific Institute in Honolulu. It was a pleasure and privilege to be invited exactly fifty years later, in 1961, to Honolulu as a Visiting Scholar at the East-West Center, where this study was finished. It is hoped that it will contribute to the ultimate realization of the lofty aims—better understanding and peace among nations—shared by the *Friend* Peace Scholarship and the East-West Center.

The work is divided into two parts: (I) historical development and (II) analysis of current problems. During the period devoted to the study, interrupted only slightly by a few occurrences of interest to labor, the writer was able to finish the writing of Part I in September, 1962, before returning to Tokyo. Chapter I, Introduction, was written last, before the manuscript was submitted for publication. Unavoidable circumstances delayed publication almost three years. In the interval, developments, both within Japan and in her international relations, have modified the picture somewhat. Revision of the text in the light of these developments was considered impractical. In other words, this book represents the history of labor in Japan up to 1962. Part II, "Analysis of Current Problems," will appear in due course.

Part I shows that the industrialization and modernization of Japan was hastened greatly by the stimuli supplied by foreign nations. The United States played a particularly crucial and dramatic part in the development of this phase of Japanese civilization. Some valuable contributions made by American scholars in the field of labor and industrial relations are acknowledged in this study. Incidentally, there is a singular dearth of material in English written by Japanese scholars and giving the viewpoint of the native Japanese. This study may perhaps begin to shed some light on this area, since the present writer, within the past forty or forty-five years, has had the privilege of meeting in person many of the great personalities, Japanese, American, and European, named in these pages. He was present at conferences where momentous decisions affecting the course of labor movements or their vital interests were made. It is hoped that the narration of somewhat anecdotal or personal incidents, not ordinarily encountered in governmental or official records, will be leniently accepted rather as enrichment of history than as impermissible digressions.

The emergence of the International Labor Organization (ILO) after World War I was an event of tremendous significance, especially for Japan. Its impact on the Japanese government's policy on labor, labor administration, and legislation; on the working-class movement; and on the general employer-employee relationship was, and continues to be, something impressive and far-reaching. The story of the impact of the ILO on Japan has not been told fully, except in two ILO publications which are now outdated. We trust that the efforts made in this study to trace the effects of the ILO on Japan's labor situation will meet with general approval, though what is given here is still largely sketchy and is only part of a study pursued by the writer on a larger scale.

The writer takes this opportunity to express his heartfelt appreciation of the invaluable help which Mrs. Kazuko Kuboniwa, his assistant at International Christian University, gave at every stage in the preparation of this book.

IWAO F. AYUSAWA

Honolulu
December, 1963

Contents

Chapter

Involved; The Shock of the Washington Conference of 1919; Impact of the ILO on the Labor Movement in Japan; Impact of the ILO on the Government's Policy; Change in Method of Selecting Workers' Delegates

Metamorphosis of Yuai Kai; Rise of Syndicalism and the First May Day in Japan; Conflict between Syndicalism and Bolshevism; First Split of Sodomei; The Second Split of Sodomei and After

Splits of Trade-Unions Resulting from Japan's Politics in the Far East; Spread of Trade-Unions and of Labor Disputes; The Peasants' Movement; Suihei Sha or the Levelers' Movement; Impact of the ILO on Labor Administration in Japan; Creation of a Permanent Delegation Office in Geneva; Impact of the ILO on Labor Legislation in Japan; The Special Countries Committee at Washington, 1919

Improvements in Protective Labor Laws; Application of Factory and Mining Labor Laws; Special Conditions of Labor in Japan; Rules on Wage Payment; Paternalism versus Workmen's Compensation

Origin—the Unemployment Problem; Ratification of the ILO Conventions; Privileges under Employment Exchange System; Special Exchanges for Seamen

Health Insurance; Post-Office Insurance

The Crucial Year of 1926; The Labor Disputes Mediation Act, 1926; The Trade-Union Bills

The ILO Tokyo Office Established; Albert Thomas' Visit; The Mission of Fernand Maurette

Tables

Charts

❀ *A History of Labor in Modern Japan*

CHAPTER I
Introduction

JAPAN IN WORLD HISTORY

Japan, whose real historical origin is lost in mythological antiquity, is perhaps unparalleled in world history in the way she continues to prosper and perform a role of no small importance in world affairs, despite the vicissitudes of war, history, and Nature. The date assigned by official tradition to the foundation of the Japanese Empire by Jimmu, the first emperor, is 660 B.C., although the scientific accuracy of this date is a matter of historical controversy. Be that as it may, a nation with a recorded history of more than two thousand years, ruled over by a single line of monarchs "unbroken for ages eternal," might well be considered unique in the present world.

Valuable contributions to the knowledge of Japan's antiquity, to her art, literature, political institutions, industry, and so on, have been made by eminent foreign scholars, historians, and men of letters, in addition to studies by native Japanese writers. One can think at once of a dozen or more classic works by British, American, German, and other foreign students of things Japanese. The Japanese turn to the amazingly comprehensive studies of these foreign scholars and learn from their penetrating observations. Nor is there any need to be ashamed of this growing practice in an age of increasingly intensive international interchange if, almost by habit, we turn to studies by non-Japanese authorities on Japan, studies which are often edifying and sobering for us. It is true that in the United States, also, among the most valued standard works on the political, economic, and social institutions of America, are volumes written by scholars, diplomats, professors, and scientists from England, France, Germany, and elsewhere.[1]

By the same token, if we seek, for example, authoritative information on Japanese art, art history, architecture, and antiquities, we turn to the classic works of an Englishman, Sir George Sansom.[2] There are several studies in English on politics and the political complexities of modern Japan. We may look up the works of American scholars such as, say, H. S. Quigley, C. Yanaga, or H. Borton. And for a comprehensive and yet lucid account of the transition of this nation from feudalism to democracy through the drastic and dramatic reforms attempted by the Allied Powers, the admirable work of the learned American Ambassador, formerly Professor at Harvard University, Edwin O. Reischauer,[3] is recommended to foreign and Japanese student alike. Few people nowadays may care to dip into the ponderous classic works of English or American writers of the early Meiji era, describing or extolling the uniqueness of the empire of the Mikado,[4] although, for the charms of life in the isles of Nippon, Lafcadio Hearn may never cease to be read with affection and appreciation.[5] Finally, in the field of labor and industrial relations, there are now several studies by American and other scholars that have shed light on the peculiarities of Japanese practices, resulting in a fairer view of the nature and formation of industrial relations in Japan.[6] What need is there, then, for another study of Japanese labor at this date? Are there matters of sufficient world interest to warrant this effort?

Apropos of these questions, an eminent American economist, a scholar specializing in the field of Japan's economy and trade, commenting recently on Japan's part in world development, says:[7]

Japan's rapid and successful industrialization, after being opened to foreign contacts in the mid-nineteenth century, is today a subject of renewed interest. The more we learn of the difficulties of economic development elsewhere, the more we find ourselves turning to Japan for possible answers. Japan is still the only Asian country to have developed an industrial, urban, middle-class society that in many ways is similar to Western industrial societies. At present China and India are making tremendous efforts to develop their economies and are having important successes—Rostow says they are taking off.[8] But Japan remains the only completed success story of a non-white, non-Western nation.

Does Japan deserve these words of praise? How true is it that Japan's is a "completed success story" in industrialization? Is she "developing an industrial, urban, middle-class society," as is stated here, like those of communities found in the industrialized countries of Europe and America?

To the extent that these are words of eulogy, we feel diffidence in accepting them. On the other hand, we are aware of the fact that, despite the wide divergence of climatic, demo-graphic, political, and economic conditions existing among the forty-two African and Asian nations that have acquired independence and gained admission to the United Nations since World War II, there is one feature common to all: they are awakening to new ideals of nationhood in an interdependent world. They are conscious of the common and equal responsibility falling on the new and young nations in shaping the world of tomorrow. For this reason, they are all seeking the techniques of industrialization, which they invariably regard as the key to rapid progress. And they are turning to Japan in many instances for information or guidance, assuming, rightly or wrongly, that Japan is one country of the non-white, Asian world that has achieved some success in industrialization.

It is this generous assumption that creates our feeling of diffidence or embarrassment, for, while it is true that Japan has succeeded in some respects, it is also true that she is failing in others. The present study is intended to tell the story, not only of the failures, but of the achievements, if any, of industrialization in Japan.

JAPAN IN THE WORLD ECONOMY TODAY

At the close of World War I, the role played by Japan as one of the Big Five at the Paris Peace Conference was of conspicuous importance. In the League of Nations, created by the Treaty of Peace in 1920, Japan occupied one of the five permanent Council seats until she withdrew from the League in 1933. In the International Labor Organization (ILO), Japan continued to play a prominent part as one of the "eight states of chief industrial importance," holding a permanent seat on its Governing Body. Further, Japan was one of the three major shipping nations (along with Great Britain and the United States) with the highest merchant marine tonnage. Her exports on the world market were even regarded at one time as a "menace" to the older manufacturing powers in Europe that had hitherto dominated world commerce.

It was this same Japan, successful and self-confident, that was defeated and that surrendered unconditionally in 1945. When General Douglas MacArthur landed in Japan in August, 1945, Tokyo, the capital city, and Osaka, the industrial center, as well as

most other cities and towns of any importance, were distressing
scenes of devastation, scorched and in ruins. With 80 per cent or
more of her industrial, mining, and transportation capacities
destroyed, the nation seemed destined to decay, never to rise
again. Who could have imagined then that this thriving country
which had "crumbled into dust," as it were, could rise to her
prewar stature within less than ten years? The occupation authorities computed that the industrial production of Japan, which had
fallen in 1945–1946 to 18.3 per cent of the prewar
(1932–1936 = 100) figure, was restored to 82.4 per cent in three
years (1946–1949); and her industrial activity (including mining,
manufacturing, and utilities) was restored from 32.5 per cent in
January, 1946, to 100.5 per cent in December, 1949. (See Table
1.)

Even more impressive is Japan's industrial recovery compared with that of other major industrial nations of the world.
Germany, after World War I, surprised the Western nations by
recovering her former industrial capacity within ten years after
she had succumbed in 1918. From the end of World War II to
1954 (see Table 2), Germany led the world's industrial powers in
the rate of recovery of industrial production, with an index
(1953 = 100) of 112 for Germany as against 94 for the United
States, 108 both for Japan and for the United Kingdom, 110 for
France, and 101 for the whole world. Germany was called the
"miracle of Europe" until then, but in that year the U.S.S.R.
overtook her and even went beyond her, with an index of 114.
Soviet Russia's leadership, however, did not last long; in 1956
Japan overtook and surpassed both Germany and the U.S.S.R.,
with an index of 144 against 138 for Germany, 141 for the
U.S.S.R, and 117 for the world. Since 1956, Japan has steadily
kept the top position, and in 1959, when the figure for the world
was 130, for India 143, Germany 162, and the U.S.S.R. 191, that
of Japan was 208.

To understand how this happened, we must examine more
closely a few of Japan's industries, especially during the years
after World War II. The loss of shipping tonnage that Japan
sustained in the last war was mentioned earlier.

The war dealt a lethal blow to Japanese shipyards and
shipbuilding facilities, which, subjected to reckless operation
during the war, had been left in a state of disrepair. Shipbuilding

TABLE 1

INDICES OF JAPANESE INDUSTRIAL ACTIVITY AND PRODUCTION
(1946–1949) (1932–1936 = 100)

	1946 Jan.	1946 July	1947 Jan.	1947 July	1948 Jan.	1948 July	1949 Jan.	1949 July	Dec.
Industrial Production (Mining & Manufacturing)	18.3	36.7	33.9	42.0	42.7	60.2	67.2	80.7	82.4
Industrial Activity (Mining, Manufacturing, & Utilities)	32.5	52.9	51.6	63.3	56.9	76.8	84.6	96.5	100.5

SOURCE: Supreme Commander of the Allied Powers (SCAP), GHQ, Economic and
Scientific Section, *Japanese Economic Statistics Bulletin* (November, 1949), Sec. 1.
Quoted by Robert A. Fearey in *The Occupation of Japan. Second Phase: 1948–1950*,
p. 217.

TABLE 2

INDICES OF INDUSTRIAL PRODUCTION OF THE MAJOR POWERS
(1938–1961) (1953 = 100)

Year	France	Germany	Italy	U.K.	USSR	U.S.	Canada	India	Japan	World
1938	75	77	61	75	30	34	38	76	96	51
1953	100	100	100	100	100	100	100	100	100	100
1954	110	112	109	108	114	94	100	107	108	101
1955	118	128	120	113	128	106	110	116	116	112
1956	130	138	128	114	141	109	120	126	144	117
1957	140	147	137	116	156	110	120	130	167	121
1958	146	151	142	114	172	102	118	132	168	118
1959	156	162	158	122	191	115	128	143	208	130
1960	174	180	180	127	—	119	130	161	261	145
1961	184	190	200	128	—	120	134	172	237	150

SOURCE: ILO, *Year Book of Labour Statistics, 1961* (Geneva: International Labor
Office, 1961).

technology was in a state of stagnation. Management and labor, however, were determined to update obsolete techniques and bring them up to international standards. They adopted new welding techniques, automatized the whole building processes, adopted the block system, and replaced outmoded and inefficient metal-working machines with the newest models. A rationalization program was pushed through, and by about 1955, when the shipping boom came, Japanese shipyards were ready to build the newest ships of all types. Foreign shipbuilding companies that had known the Japan of prewar days had confidence in the industry, skill, and technical proficiency of Japanese shipbuilders. The defeat in the war proved a blessing in disguise for shipbuilding, as in fact it did for practically every other industry, in that there was a complete shift from war industry to export business involving all types of goods, even huge Japanese-built ships. In the six-year period from April, 1955, through March, 1961, Japanese shipyards received orders from foreign clients for 439 ships totaling 7,167,000 gross ton, valued at nearly $3 billion. More recently, Soviet Russia placed with Japan's shipbuilders in August, 1962, one of the biggest single orders for ships ever received by Japan. In any case, during the five-year period 1956–1961, "Japan has been the biggest shipbuilder in the world in terms of launchings. From January through September, 1961, vessels launched in the world totaled 5,760,000 gross ton; of this total, Japan accounted for 1,250,000 GT, compared with 900,000 GT for the United States and 760,000 GT for West Germany."[9] From these figures, it seems likely that Japan will remain the foremost shipbuilder of the world for some time to come.

No less impressive is the way Japan has forged ahead to win world position in the manufacture and sale of steel and metal machines. A country notoriously deficient in necessary raw materials, Japan must import a great deal before exporting. For iron and steel manufactures she must import iron ore, scrap iron, and coking coal. By carefully selecting high-priced coking coal and manganese and iron ore, she has managed to restore and expand iron and steel manufactures; in 1960 she produced twelve million tons (metric) of pig iron and twenty-two million tons of crude steel, becoming the fifth largest steel producer in the world. The United States, the U.S.S.R., West Germany, and the United Kingdom are ahead of her, but it is expected that in little time she will edge out the United Kingdom and take fourth place in steel production, despite her lack of raw materials.

Traditionally, Japan is known to the world as a nation of textile mills. The upsurge of the textile industry in the newly developing countries has affected the position of Japanese export slightly, but in 1960, among all the export items of this country, textiles and apparel constituted the biggest single item ($879,-000,000), ahead of machinery and transportation equipment ($603,000,000). Before the war she led the world in textile exports. Today, fifteen years after the war, she still does. How did Japan manage to attain that position when she had to depend entirely on importation of cotton, wool, and other materials from abroad? This point will be discussed later, but in passing we may note that Japan will be gradually leaving the textile and other light industries for fuller exploitation by the newly developing nations and turning more to heavy and chemical industries, in which Japanese technical proficiency is likely to be employed with more benefit to all parties concerned. In the new long-range economic plan for Japan, covering a ten-year period (1961–1970), worked out by the Economic Planning Agency, a 10.5 per cent annual increase is called for in the export of heavy and chemical products, including machinery and transportation equipment, metals and metal products, and medical and chemical products, while textile goods, including apparel, will increase annually by only 5.3 per cent. Light industrial products for export will continue to include textiles as the chief item, but food, beverages and tobacco, light machinery, and miscellaneous articles (toys, cigarette lighters, and sundry articles) are included, and in their case, the annual increase in production will be only 8.2 per cent as against 10.5 per cent for heavy and chemical industries. (See Table 3.)

Without going into further details of the phenomenal economic and industrial recovery of Japan, it is fairly obvious that Japan's part in the world economy in the coming years will be one of considerable weight. It is estimated that her population will reach 100,000,000 within a few years, putting her among the top five countries in population. Having voluntarily abolished large armed forces, and solemnly relinquished the right of belligerency, she may never be one of the big five in the United Nations as she was in the League of Nations, but she is again one of the ten

TABLE 3

JAPAN'S ECONOMIC GROWTH PLAN

| Indicator | Actual average for fiscal year 1956–1958 | Targets for fiscal year 1970 | |
		Total	Annual increase (%)
Population	91,100,000	102,200,000	0.9
Gross national product	27,100,000,000	72,200,000,000	7.8
Gross national product per capita	297	707	6.9
Mining and mfg. production, index	100	432	11.0
Agriculture, forestry, & fishery prod. index	100	144	2.8
Imports	3,126,000,000	9,891,000,000	9.3
Food stuffs	539,000,000	804,000,000	3.1
Raw materials	1,439,000,000	3,789,000,000	7.7
Mineral fuel	476,000,000	1,863,000,000	11.1
Semifinished products	276,000,000	1,093,000,000	11.2
Finished products	393,000,000	2,230,000,000	14.7
Machinery	304,000,000	1,735,000,000	14.3
Other	89,000,000	595,000,000	15.7
Other	4,000,000	12,000,000	8.8
Exports	2,710,000,000	9,320,000,000	10.0
Heavy and chemical products	2,402,000,000	8,859,000,000	10.5
Machinery and transportation equipment	603,000,000	3,450,000,000	14.3
Metals and metal products	292,000,000	1,040,000,000	10.2
Medical and chemical products	120,000,000	493,000,000	11.5
Light industrial products	1,387,000,000	3,875,000,000	8.2
Textiles and apparel	879,000,000	1,723,000,000	5.3
Food, beverages, and tobacco	206,000,000	547,000,000	7.8
Light machinery	56,000,000	400,000,000	16.3
Miscellaneous	246,000,000	1,206,000,000	13.0
Other	299,000,000	461,000,000	3.4

NOTE: The Japanese fiscal year begins April 1 and runs to March 31 of the following year. All values are in fiscal-year 1958 prices.

SOURCE: Japan. Economic Planning Agency. *New Long-Range Economic Plan of Japan (1961–1970): Doubling National Income Plan* (Tokyo: The Japan Times, 1961), pp. 11, 77, 80.

instead of the eight states of chief industrial importance in the ILO and holds a permanent seat on the Governing Body. She is not yet a member of the Organization for Economic Cooperation and Development (OECD), although, since OECD is primarily an Atlantic grouping, her nonmembership is no immediate cause for worry. Japan, however has been a regular participant in the OECD's Development Assistance Committee (DAC), and the day may come when she will be officially invited to join, in recognition of her growing economic importance,* although we know that this is not the sole qualification for membership. Japan has been a full member, since September, 1955, of the General Agreement on Tariffs and Trade (GATT); here, however, she is encountering a form of discrimination. Some fifteen member states are applying the so-called "Escape Clause" (Article 35) against Japan and depriving her of most-favored-nation treatment.[10] However, advanced opinion in both Japan and abroad regards this discrimination as a blemish, not on Japan, but on the nations that are despoiling GATT of its *raison d'être* and of its ultimate utility. The situation will be rectified eventually by those nations belonging to GATT, not by Japan.

However, the situation in GATT does remind us of the need for disseminating more correct information abroad on Japan's industry and economy. In this connection another passage may be quoted from Warren S. Hunsberger, the American authority quoted earlier. In a report submitted to Congress by the Joint Economic Committee, after pointing out that Japanese goods are more competitive with America's domestic production that goods imported from Canada (which consist mainly of forest and mineral products and other basic commodities), he says:

> The long list of Japanese products sold here is headed by manufactures of rubber, steel, cotton, and wool. These are followed by radios, fish, plywood, ceramics, silk goods, and toys. And behind them come cameras and chemicals, pearls and paper, sewing machines, scientific instruments, and every year more products.
>
> These Japanese goods are not just the output of tiny factories making do with antiquated machinery and much hard labor. Such plants still exist, but little shops and small farms are losing labor nowadays to large, ultra-modern factories, whose trained labor force, numerous technicians and late model machinery are managed by highly competent executives.

* Since April 28, 1964, Japan has been a regular member of OECD.—*ed.*

Japan is now a different country from what it was in the 1930's or in World War II or in the days of the post-war occupation.[11]

THE CHARACTER OF THE PEOPLE AS A FACTOR IN ECONOMIC GROWTH

The next item is one that is apt to be overlooked or treated only casually by conventional economic writers. It is the character of the people of a country as a factor in economic growth.

Japan, deficient in the basic necessities for industrial or economic growth, has to support an enormous population on small mountainous islands with not even 18 per cent of their area arable for food crops. Moreover, she suffered vast devastation in the last war. The question as to how such a crowded island nation with all these handicaps can earn a living is one that cannot be answered with the physical or material and measurable data of conventional economics. Immeasurable or "imponderable" data are required to explain adequately Japan's economic strength or to plan properly for her growth. And among the imponderables, as a factor in economic growth, must be considered the character or quality of the people.

We noted above that the population of Japan will soon reach the 100-million mark, which will place her among the five most populous nations on earth. So large a population in the extremely limited land area would be none other than a liability were it not offset with some qualities which can be regarded as assets. The Japanese people are noted, as indeed are other races of man, for certain qualities which cannot be weighed or measured, bought or sold, or acquired overnight in a short drill course. To mention some of the more outstanding characteristics of the people: they tend to be industrious, agile, intelligent, and alert; skillful, ingenious, inventive, and enterprising; determined, patient, painstaking, and meticulous; obedient and amenable to discipline, even regimentation. They are capable of united action, though occasionally one encounters some who are egocentric and selfish, as one does in any community. Of course, these qualities are not peculiar to the Japanese people. The same can be said of the British, Scotch, German, Scandinavian, and many other races thriving today in the countries of the temperate zone. In addition to these inborn qualities, the Japanese people have learned to be self-assertive, even aggressive, since the opening of the country in 1868. They have, rightly or wrongly, considered it necessary for security or survival. Furthermore, they have had training since Meiji in modern industrial undertakings, and have acquired skill in mechanics and in the advanced techniques of Western nations; their experience of success in the various lines of technology has given them ample self-confidence.

In brief, these may be taken as the "imponderabilia" that account for the rise of the crowded island nation to the rank of a major industrial power before World War II.[12] As to the phenomenal recovery of Japan after World War II, it will be discussed in due course.

A land devoid of natural resources, if it is to expand as an industrial power and export much, will have to import much. That is precisely what Japan has done and will continue to do. To become the top textile-exporting nation, but producing no cotton, no wool, no jute, she has gone to the United States, to Brazil, to India, to Egypt in search of the cotton and wool best suited to the kinds of fabric she wanted to manufacture. To become one of the biggest steel manufacturers, she has had to depend on the ores transported from the United States, India, and China. If she is to continue to supply the world's need for shipping, she must collect materials from twenty-odd countries all over the world. A list of her export items shows how widely she has to depend on imports. Japan imports all the cotton and wool for her textile industry; bauxite for the light metal products; petroleum and oil for fuel; sugar, salt, wheat, and soybeans for food; phosphate rock, iron ore, scrap iron, and rubber for such products as ships and cars. Using these materials, she exports a long list of items, primarily manufactured products, such as cars, transistor radios, tape recorders, television sets, sewing machines, microscopes, telescopes, cameras, and the like, as well as textiles, still her principal export item.

Foreign exchange movements and the composition of Japan's foreign trade should also be examined closely for their implications; however, there is not time or space here for this, except to refer the reader to the economic growth plan of this country shown in Table 1, and to state that Japan today is determined to achieve national progress and prosperity through the exports and imports outlined there. It should be emphasized that, in carrying out the plan, the basic need is the *human* resource—which means the Japanese people and their character traits as enumerated earlier.

We have learned from history that it is not necessarily the nations favored with abundant natural resources that achieve progress or power and contribute to the world of man. The abundance of natural resources in a territory has, by inviting invasions from outside, brought disaster to a nation instead of serving as an asset. More important is the capacity of the people to exploit and make full use of those resources. In short, the factor which plays the decisive role in the ascendency of a nation is the character of its people.

THE JAPAN–UNITED STATES RELATIONSHIP

It must be noted at the outset that the full significance of the relationship between Japan and the United States is not appreciated as yet.

In her history of more than two thousand years, Japan has undergone momentous and critical changes on three occasions, each change opening a new era in her history. The first change occurred in A.D. 645, with the reforms called *Tai-Ka* (Great Change), boldly carried out by Prince Shōtoku. A new period, that of the "Civilization of Nara," was ushered in, largely as a result of the influx of Buddhism, which brought in its train the art and literature, architecture and sculpture, and new concepts of the state and government administration of the Asian continent. With the flourishing of the Nara Civilization, more than a thousand years passed without another critical change. In the latter part of this interval, thanks perhaps to the policy of complete isolation vigorously pursued by the Tokugawa Shogunate after A.D. 1600, Japan was saved from the perils of the colonial imperialism of the Western nations that had been engaged in the conquest of the non-European world since the early sixteenth century. A long internal peace, undisturbed by any Western power, reigned in the island empire.

The second great change came in 1853, with the advent of Commodore Matthew C. Perry, an American. It would not be accurate to place all credit or blame on Perry for what happened in Japan after the visit of the "Black Ships" under his command. Nevertheless, the fact remains that the appearance of Perry's ships in Yedo (now Tokyo) Bay coincided with the end of 700 years of feudalism under the shoguns—the end of a period for Japan which was, to quote a noted American scholar, a "prime symbol of the forbidding and medieval East," and seemed "to presage the phenomenal explosion of energy, productivity, and power [of that nation] that actually occurred."[13] The modernization of Japan, which has few parallels in history, may well have begun as a consequence of that incident. The Japanese people became zealous and ardent followers of the West, and tried to take in everything Western. They largely succeeded, until they found themselves upon the road which the Western nations had agreed among themselves not to travel any more. The road that Japan stumbled upon was an aggressive war, called the War of Greater East Asia (*Dai Tōa Sensō*)—a type of war common in the West up to the nineteenth century, but not after that. Japan was penalized for the transgression.

The third great change came when another American, General Douglas MacArthur, landed in Japan in August, 1945, in the capacity of Supreme Commander for the Allied Powers. The reforms introduced by this American in an effort to turn Japan from a nation of militarism and feudalistic traditions into a peace-loving and democratic country were of such historic significance that we refer to them appreciatively as the "MacArthur Revolution." As a consequence of the revolutionary measures introduced by the occupation forces under his command a new Japan is emerging. Precise knowledge about this third great change in Japan and a fair and unbiased appraisal of it are now necessary, since they will inevitably affect the future relations of the two nations facing each other across the Pacific Ocean.

Of the three revolutionary changes that radically altered the course of Japanese history, the United States was involved in two, and it does not seem likely that America will be able to return to the traditional isolationism of the eighteenth and nineteenth centuries and be freed from all involvement with Japan any more than Japan will be able to return to the blissful seclusion of the pre-Perry days and have nothing to do with America. This is obvious. For the opening of Japan and for the kindly guidance given her from the early Meiji period by the far-sighted Townsend Harris and other great American diplomats, missionaries, and educators, Japan remains sincerely grateful to America. There was a period in the course of the Japan–United States relationship when the relations of the two countries became strained, and finally a war came, but on both sides people are beginning to realize that there is growing between the two nations a bond of friendship. It is an imponderable, more deep-rooted than economics, more subtle than politics, and, though in our discussion we are apt to bring out more tangible and measurable statistical data as if we assumed they were of primary importance, they are not. Nonetheless, certain striking facts in the economic relations between Japan and the United States must be kept in mind.

When World War II ended, Japan's trade with the United States was non-existent. From that beginning, Japan's trade rose to great prominence in the postwar period. During the five-year period after surrender, Japan's share in U.S. foreign trade was only 1.7 per cent. Table 4 shows how rapidly Japan's position in U.S. foreign trade rose. She was only sixth in 1951, but ten years later, in 1961, she had risen to second place—second only to Canada. In U.S. imports, she rose from seventeenth place in 1951 to second in 1961, and in U.S. exports from fifth to second.

There is no more striking statistical data on the relationship of the two countries than that in Table 4, which shows the vital importance of one country to the other, growing more intense year by year. This may be accounted for in several ways.

Carthago delenda est was Rome's (and not merely Cato's) watchword, and no doubt the Carthaginian war cry was *Roma delenda est!* In the present state of tension between the two power blocs, i.e., the free nations led by the United States and the Communist nations led by the U.S.S.R., the tragic thing is that each seems to be seeking to destroy the other.[14] In the mounting hostile mood, little middle or neutral ground is allowed, with the result that the statistics of the kind we see here will be interpreted by the two sides in diametrically opposite ways. The preponderance of the United States in Japan's exports and of Japan in the United States's imports will be taken, by the Communists at any rate, as a sign of Japan's subservience to the United States and hostility toward Communist nations. The U.S. replies to those charges are trade limitations on exports with the long lists of COCOM and CHINCOM.[15] The government of Japan is vigorously pursuing its ten-year plan of economic growth, which will intensify rather than slacken Japan's trade with the United States. This can be regarded only with suspicion by the Communist nations, although Japan is seeking no less actively than at any previous period a closer and more realistic economic relationship with both continental China and the U.S.S.R.

On this matter, both the United States and the rest of the world need to understand the cumulative forces that operated in

TABLE 4

JAPAN'S PLACE IN UNITED STATES FOREIGN TRADE
(1951–1961)

Year	U.S. exports		U.S. imports		Total trade	
	Japan's share (%)	Japan's rank	Japan's share (%)	Japan's rank	Japan's share (%)	Japan's rank
1951	4.0	5	1.9	17	3.1	6
1952	4.1	4	2.1	13	3.3	7
1953	4.3	2	2.4	10	3.5	6
1954	4.5	3	2.7	8	3.8	6
1955	4.2	4	3.8	6	4.0	5
1951–55	4.2	4	2.6	9	3.5	6
1956	4.7	3	4.4	5	4.6	3
1957	5.9	2	4.6	6	5.4	4
1958	4.7	3	5.2	4	4.9	4
1959	5.5	2	6.8	3	6.1	3
1960	6.5	3	7.8	2	7.1	2
1956–60	5.5	2	5.9	4	5.7	3
Jan.–Aug. 1961	8.7	2	7.1	2	8.0	2

SOURCE: U.S. Congress. Joint Economic Committee. *Japan in United States Foreign Economic Policy,* by Warren S. Hunsberger. 87th Cong., 1st sess. (Washington, D.C.: GPO, 1961), p. 15.

the postwar period and practically impelled Japan to take its present position, especially after the Peace of San Francisco, and the subsequent Security Pact that led to the eventual rearmament of Japan. The political position Japan was obliged to take after 1952 automatically and inevitably reduced the possibility of expansion of Japan's trade with the continent of Asia, particularly with China and the U.S.S.R. Friends of Japan in the United States and elsewhere counsel her to expand in the newly developing area of Southeast Asia. It happens that this is the area that the Japanese troops ravaged in the last war. There is the barrier of the still smarting enmity—though that is diminishing appreciably— and the question of reparations. The latter is also proving less thorny year by year, but it will take time before the road is smoothed for normal and active trade, since the inhabitants of the area have to acquire both the habit and techniques of trade relationship. This is the chief explanation for the pre-eminent position which the United States (and Canada, incidentally) occupies in Japanese exports and imports at present. (See Table 5.)

On the other hand, the Japanese must, and do indeed, remember that among the factors that helped Japan's rapid industrial recovery after the war was the tremendous economic help afforded by the United States, both in the form of expenditures of the U.S. forces in Japan and adjacent areas, and in their procurements. In the period from the surrender in 1945 through

TABLE 5

JAPAN'S FOREIGN TRADE BY CONTINENTS
(1960)

Continents	Imports (%)	Exports (%)
United States and Canada	39.1	29.1
Asia	31.3	37.0
Europe	10.1	12.2
Australia and Oceania	9.0	4.9
Latin America	6.9	7.5
Africa	3.6	8.7
Total	100.0	99.4

SOURCE: Bank of Japan, *Economic Statistics of Japan, 1960*, pp. 245–248. Also Hunsberger, *op. cit.*, p. 11 (see note, Table 4).

the end of 1960, U.S. exports to Japan rose to approximately $10 billion and imports to $6 billion. The deficit of $4 billion was met by U.S. aid of over $2 billion during the occupation, and military procurement and troop expenditures estimated at more than $5½ billion; in addition, there were outlays for shipping and other services. In other words, it was not industry, will power, and other "imponderable" items alone that enabled Japan to perform her miracle of recovery.

However, at the same time, the United States must be reminded of the aspirations of the Japanese people, quite aside from their physical needs; this leads to the last major item of this introduction, which has to do with the mission which Japan and the United States must shoulder together.

THE CHALLENGE

Among the more industrially advanced nations in the world belonging to the United Nations and to GATT, some are seeking to protect their own industries against the inroads of goods manufactured in the so-called "low-wage countries." The motive is legitimate and justifiable. The regulations of GATT allow discriminatory treatment of goods exported from countries so classed. The wages of the countries in question may or may not actually be low. If they are in fact low, the countries in question are no doubt anxious to raise them to a higher level; perhaps they need help. Mere rejection or exclusion of the goods of those countries is no real solution. History has shown us that discrimination without compensatory help leads to unfortunate consequences.

In the Japan–United States relationship, which is politically, economically, and morally unique, it has been noted that except for Canada, Japan is the principal buyer of U.S. goods, particularly of textile raw materials. A fraction of the fabrics manufactured in Japan using the materials imported from the U.S., representing but a small fraction of the total textile goods consumed in America, has been exported to that country. This has led to complaints among textile manufacturers in the U.S. and to the adoption of measures to restrict textile imports rather severely. More recently, a quota system has been adopted to regularize the restriction, and it is hoped that such measures will help to minimize the friction, since Japan considers herself the best customer for U.S. goods, and expects American consumers to accord her the same courtesy. Moreover, Japan has adopted a program of "liberalization," calling for removal by the end of September, 1962, of all controls on 90 per cent of her imports on the basis of the fiscal year 1959. Japan is doing this despite the difficulty in balancing payments under increasing competition from imported foreign goods. With Japan venturing to adopt such a bold program, there is all the more need for more correct information in foreign countries on the improvements made in Japanese industries.

Another matter of significance in the Japan–United States relationship that constitutes a challenge is the emergence in postwar Japan of the trade-union organization as a new democratic force. America had a definite part in this matter. With the rise to power of organized labor in this country, Japan is no longer the same nation she was before World War II. Whichever way Japan turns politically, this fact must be borne in mind. In that connection, still another matter of history that America with her noble traditions cannot afford to lose sight of is the part she played in the adoption of Japan's new Constitution. It is a Constitution which guarantees freedom of speech, of thought, and of religion; assures the basic human rights; and relinquishes the right of belligerency by abolishing all arms and seeking peace and security, not in arms, but in justice and faith among the peace-loving nations of the world. The Constitution was adopted with the support and blessings of General Douglas MacArthur in his capacity as Supreme Commander for the Allied Powers. The people, particularly the intelligentsia, the student class, and the trade-unionists, have been converted to the new faith enunciated by the Constitution. Knowing the danger of Japan's reverting to the militarist ideology of the prewar days, they are distrustful of any move that tends to restrict the present course. It was because of this that the famous "Four Peace Principles" were adopted: (1) Over-all peace, that is, peace not only with the United States and the Western nations but the U.S.S.R. as well; (2) absolute neutrality, that is, taking no side in the conflict of the two power blocs; (3) no military bases in Japan, of either Japanese or foreign air, sea, or land forces; and (4) no rearmament under any excuse whatever.

Most unfortunate in this situation was the fact that only a few years after the Constitution came into force, the outbreak of war in Korea compelled the U.S. to invite Japan to reconsider the basic principles of that Constitution. Some faithful and ardent, if naive, followers of the Constitution still fail to see why Japan must suddenly rearm and resume the course of militarism which brought disaster and downfall of the nation. Incidentally, among those naive defenders of the Constitution are the trade-unionists. In the United States, under the tension that goes on between the two hostile blocs, organizations and individuals who oppose armament or armed resistance against aggression are apt to be suspected and treated indiscriminately as "Communists." Consequently, because of the position they take on the question of rearmament, trade-unions in Japan are apt to be confused with Communists. We will have to learn to draw distinctions between momentary and tactical expediency and true and lasting principles, because we are likely to find in Japan that those extremely naive men upholding the Constitution and opposing rearmament were truer friends of America than those asked to take the sword.

The few questions mentioned above are sufficient indications of the need for a more judicious approach to the problems of industrial relations and of organized labor in Japan. Above all, there is the need for more information. This study is designed to satisfy that need.

CHAPTER II

From the Meiji Restoration (1868) to the Russo-Japanese War (1904–1905)

THE RESTORATION OF MEIJI

A Fivefold Revolution

The feudal government, which had lasted for 265 years[1] under the Tokugawas, came to an end in the year 1867. The new regime under Emperor Meiji, who was sixteen when he ascended the throne, began in that year. To him were restored the power and the functions of reigning over Japan, hence the term "Restoration." In the Japanese calendar, that year was officially proclaimed as *Meiji gan-nen* or Year One of the Enlightened Reign (Meiji).

In that the political power hitherto usurped and held by the Shogunate was restored to the Emperor, the change that occurred is commonly referred to in English as a "restoration," but the changes that came over Japan were not confined to the political domain. What happened was, in fact, revolution simultaneously in political, economic, social, cultural, and ideological domains—a fivefold revolution, one might say.

The downfall of the feudal system of government that the Restoration entailed was accompanied by the decline and gradual disappearance of the old economic systems, loss of the authority of the absolute ethical codes, abandonment of time-honored but impractical social customs, and, finally, the adoption by the government and the people of a new policy designed to bring about under the new regime a complete modernization of the nation.

It is obvious under these circumstances that the term "restoration," widely used in describing the changes that occurred in and after the year 1868, is misleading, though not completely a misnomer. Far more adequate and fitting would be the word "revolution," although that word is shunned by the Japanese scholars of the old school. To those old-time royalists, or imperialists, who had wished Japan to be "a country reigned over by a line of Emperors unbroken for ages eternal,"[2] the word "revolution" was naturally odious and reprehensible.[3]

Forces that Contributed to the Decline of the Feudal Regime

There were diverse forces that contributed to the decline of the feudal regime that it is useful to recall here. The ruling class under the Shogunate, consisting of the feudal lords, the daimyo, and their retainers, the samurai, whose function was to fight in battles under the orders of their respective lords, had lost their prestige in the long period of domestic peace lasting more than two centuries. The feudal lords began to reveal their incompetence in administering their estates. The periodic trips, the *sankin kotai*, which the feudal lords were required to make to Yedo, the seat of the shogun, had gradually drained their resources. They were required to make these trips to pay homage and renew their allegiance to the shogun. While these trips impoverished the feudal lords and the retainers who accompanied their masters in the travels, they enriched the low and formerly despised class of merchants, the *cho-nin* (townsfolk), trading in the town. The *cho-nin* took advantage of the extravagances that the feudal lords and their retainers indulged in during their periodic travels to and from Yedo. Gradually the *cho-nin* gained the power and the wealth that the daimyo and samurai were losing.

The feudal economy of Japan was basically agrarian, similar to that which prevailed in medieval Europe. For the continuity of the feudal economy, it was essential to ensure stability and prosperity among the farming population. But in the latter part of the Tokugawa Shogunate, most farmers were suffering from extreme poverty. Increasingly high taxes levied by the feudal lords had led to misery and discontent among the farming population. Originally regarded as the only real producers of wealth, the farmers had been the most honored class among the common people, and were higher in the hierarchical order than the artisans and the merchants. The merchants occupied the lowest position among the common people, and were despised as parasitic people producing nothing, but profiting by the labor of others. Farmers, therefore, were nominally the most appreciated people in the feudal society of Japan, where there existed a theory akin to that of the physiocrats in eighteenth-century Europe. But as the feudal lords exacted heavier and heavier taxes from the farmers in order to meet the financial needs of the feudal estates, resentment rose among the farmers until it led to serious riots. The Shogunate experienced serious difficulties in suppressing the uprisings of the desperate peasants. It is clear that toward the end of the Tokugawa Shogunate, agrarianism, as the basic economic system of this country, was approaching a collapse.[4]

In addition to the deterioration of the political and economic systems, there were also powerful forces at work in the realm of ideas which contributed to the breakdown of feudalism. The complex nature of these forces requires a separate discussion.

Sonnō Jōi and What It Really Meant

Among the ideas that served to quicken the pace of revolution, none seemed to exert so powerful an influence as did the ideas embodied in the slogan *Sonnō Jōi.*

Literally, *sonnō* meant "loyalty to the emperor," as opposed to the shogun or the feudal system under him; *jōi* meant "repulsion of the barbarians," that is, opposition to interchange with the foreigners. After the advent in 1853 of Commodore Perry's "Black Ships," the country was divided between those who advocated interchange with the Western nations and those who violently opposed it. When the Shogunate finally yielded to Perry's pressure and decided to conclude a treaty with the United States without the formal sanction of the Emperor, the incident served to strengthen the hands of those who were conspiring for the overthrow of the Shogunate. *Sonnō Jōi* was the slogan used by the leaders of the revolution to rally the loyal people around the Emperor for the overthrowing of the feudal regime of the shogun, although, as later developments showed, those leaders who advocated *jōi* were not fundamentally opposed to the opening of diplomatic relations with foreign countries. *Jōi* was in reality a mere pretext.

As a matter of fact, the leaders of the Meiji Restoration were at heart not against, but for, Japan's entry into friendly relationship with the foreign nations. Perry's "Black Ships" had visually and incontestably demonstrated to them the superiority of Western nations in matters of transportation, communication, and warfare with the use of firearms. Interestingly enough, some of the young men who took prominent parts in the revolution of Meiji, using the slogan *Sonnō Jōi,* had secretly learned the languages of and had acquired knowledge about the advanced Western nations. Some had studied Dutch, for, even during the period of Japan's rigid isolationism, the Dutch people, as a single exception, had been allowed to continue relations with the Japanese. Some young men of Japan had been studying modern medicine and other sciences of the West through the medium of the Dutch language in Nagasaki, the port open only to the Dutch.

This was precisely why the new government under Emperor Meiji, almost immediately after the fall of the Shogunate, launched a bold policy of opening up the country for full intercourse with the Western nations, as if it had completely forgotten the slogan *Sonnō Jōi,* used vociferously until a few years before.

The Emperor's Charter Oath

The character of the new government under Emperor Meiji and the broad policies which the Japanese nation was to follow were clearly enunciated in the historic Charter Oath of the Emperor, proclaimed in 1868 on his ascension to the throne.

The oath consisted of five articles, hence the name *Gokajo no Goseimon,* (Five-Article Oath):

(1) Assemblies widely convoked shall be held and all important decisions shall be made on the basis of public discussion.

(2) The welfare of the entire nation shall be promoted by the combined efforts of the governing and the governed classes.

(3) All subjects civil and military, as well as other people, shall do their best and never grow weary in the accomplishing of their legitimate purposes.

(4) All absurd usages of the past shall be abandoned; justice and righteousness shall regulate all actions.

(5) Knowledge shall be sought all over the world, and thus shall the foundation of the Imperial polity be strengthened.

The important fact about the Charter Oath was not that it contained high-sounding phrases, but that the objectives set forth in the five articles were actually carried out. They were not like the proverbial New Year's resolutions that are never kept. The government and the people worked closely together for the fulfillment of the lofty objectives set by the Charter Oath.

However, this does not mean that there were no exceptions. As later developments show, in order to consolidate the gains of the revolution, the leaders of the Meiji government had to take measures which seemed a renunciation of some of the solemn promises of the Charter Oath. This will be explained in due course.

The Program of Fukoku Kyohei

In an effort to unite the aspirations and endeavors of the people under the new regime, the clever leaders of the Meiji government introduced two slogans which proved most effective. These two were *Bunmei Kaika* and *Fukoku Kyohei.*

If the earlier slogan *Sonnō Jōi* proved a powerful weapon for the overthrow of the Shogunate, the two new ones introduced after the revolution were certainly as effective as the former in achieving the ends sought by the new regime.

Bunmei Kaika means "Civilization and Development." The two words conveyed the sense that Japan needed a rapid opening up, incidentally implying that Japan must reach the stage of enlightenment of the Western nations.

Fukoku Kyohei, which means "Wealthy Country and Strong Army," calls for more comment and explanation than the other, since the emphasis laid on this slogan had its beneficial as well as harmful effects on Japan for many decades. Indeed, these were not slogans so much as they were programs of action. It was these programs which molded the shape of things when Japan had acquired sufficient strength as a modern power.

Whence came the idea of a wealthy nation with strong army? Why emphasize wealth and armament? To answer this question, we must recall how the Shogunate had adopted its rigid policy of isolationism two or three centuries earlier.

The government under the shogun issued in 1672 that severe ordinance prohibiting intercourse with foreigners, an action which resulted in the isolation of Japan from the world for nearly two centuries. That action was taken primarily because of the fear of aggression by the Western powers. The rulers of Japan were frightened by the actions all over the world of the Western nations. But in that period there were still peoples in Africa and Asia who were free and unhampered by the Western nations. By and large, the land and the wealth of the Asian and African countries still belonged to the native inhabitants. However, when Japan gave up the policy of isolation and re-entered the scene of world intercommunication in the latter half of the nineteenth century, a vast change had taken place in the world. For it was the period in which the nations of Western Europe spread their power to the ends of the earth, a period of discoveries of new continents and of subjugation of the natives inhabiting those territories—in short, a period of world conquest and colonization by the Western powers.

In that period, relatively brief in world history, the vast continent of Africa was sliced into chunks of colonies. The natives were being hunted like wild beasts and sold into slavery. India, the home of Brahminism and Buddhism, with its fabled wealth of the nabobs, had been conquered and lay prostrate at the feet of the Western invaders. China, with its ancient civilization 5,000 years old and its people representing a fifth of the world population, was being dismembered by the same Western nations. Did Japan want to share the fate of the "backward races" of Africa and Asia? No; Japan's answer was *Fukoku Kyohei*.

Obstacles against the New Regime

The goals of the new government that implemented the above-mentioned slogans were achieved with remarkable success. A major factor in the relative ease with which such success was achieved was the homogeneity and intelligence of the Japanese people.

Nevertheless, we must not overlook the series of difficulties that did arise in the early years of the Meiji government, which had to be overcome in uniting the nation under the new regime. At least three obstacles lay in the way of the unification without which the new government could not last long. They were: (1) the large number of able and ambitious men of samurai descent who had failed to find suitable jobs in the new government, (2) the conflict within the government among the groups with conflicting views and divergent interests, (3) the radical movement for civil rights and liberties led by ambitious men who challenged the authoritarian policies of the new government.

Of these three difficulties, the first took the form of insurrections that broke out during the first ten or twelve years after 1868. Fortunately these uprisings were limited to local provinces and were quickly suppressed. The only one that threatened to grow into a civil war of menacing magnitude was led by Saigo Takamori in 1878, but even this was successfully subdued before the rebels were able to control the whole island of Kyushu.

The second difficulty, which arose from the disunity within

the new regime, was eliminated by the withdrawal of the dissatisfied minority group in 1881 without further serious conflict.

The third and last of the difficulties was perhaps the most subtle and baffling because of its ideological content. However, this particular obstacle had also diminished greatly by the late 1880s. Nevertheless, because of its close bearing on the labor policies which evolved in the subsequent period, this ideological conflict requires further discussion.

IMPACT OF LIBERALISM, SOCIALISM, AND PROTESTANT CHRISTIANITY

The Movement for Civil Rights and Liberties

The leadership in the revolution to overthrow the Tokugawa Shogunate was taken mostly by the young men of the relatively lower strata of the samurai class. Incidentally, these leaders belonged to one or another of the four major feudal clans of Satsuma, Choshu, Tosa, and Hizen. There were men of a few other clans who had taken part in the movement in the early period, but they dropped away without contributing much. Among the leaders in the four major clans, those coming from Satsuma and Choshu predominated. Inevitably, the result was that, with but few exceptions, the more important positions in the new government were held by the former clansmen of Satsuma or Choshu. This has to be borne in mind from the outset in order to understand the intricate political and social problems in Japan in the Meiji era.

In an effort to maintain their supremacy in carrying out the policies of the new government, the men in positions of high responsibility took rigorous measures to concentrate power for themselves. Centralization of power by the officials of the government involved the suppression of liberal ideas and the restriction of civil liberties movements. Incidentally, those liberal ideas of Western origin were being championed by progressive elements that included the men who had failed to get good jobs in the government despite the parts they had played in the overthrow of the feudal regime. They were the men disgruntled under the new regime and opposed to the high-handed authoritarian policies practiced by the government. As explained above, the men in positions of power and responsibility were for a considerable time limited to those coming from Satsuma and Choshu. And it was they who, consciously or unconsciously, were adopting policies of autocratic absolutism contrary to the initial policy enunciated in the Charter Oath of the Emperor. Absolutism as a governmental policy would have been more consonant with the old feudal regime that had been politically overthrown and ideologically discarded. But the new men of power in the government found it necessary to consolidate their position by adopting an absolutist policy vis-à-vis the liberal forces that were rising among the common people.

There were ample justifications for the adoption of autocratic policies by the government in the early Meiji era. Japan was a late arrival among the nations in a world of increasing capitalistic rivalries. Any responsible government in Japan, awake to the world situation, had to take measures that would be most effective in ensuring a rapid rise of Japan. Until Japan, by facing the difficulties of national rivalries and capitalistic competition, had risen to the position of a world power the nation would have to bear sacrifices. Thus, the government, finding plausible excuses in these arguments, was tending more and more toward suppression rather than encouragement of liberal ideas.

It was in opposition to this tendency that a strong movement, advocating the establishment of civil rights for the people, arose in the early 1880s. The movement championed liberalism against the autocratic rule of the Satsuma and Choshu clans. The leadership for this movement was supplied by the Tosa clan, notably in the person of Itagaki Taisuke (1837–1919), who became the leader of the Jiyū Tō (Liberal Party).

The real character of the liberalism personified by Itagaki needs to be more closely examined.

The Liberalism of Jiyū Tō

Itagaki Taisuke was a samurai of the Tosa clan who, on account of his work in the revolution to overthrow the Shogunate, won the honored position of a *sangi*[5] in the Meiji government. However, as one of those who urged war on Korea, he was defeated and withdrew from the government in protest against the autocratic rule of the men of Satsuma and Choshu. In 1874, Itagaki formed a political group advocating the establishment of a house of representatives elected by popular vote. This group soon became the center of the civil rights movements and at the same time the main opposition to the illiberal government. Rallying the liberal forces among the people, Itagaki in 1881 founded the Liberal Party (Jiyū Tō), of which he became the president. Itagaki was a forceful speaker and his name remains associated in history with the famous words he uttered when he was on the point of being stabbed by an assassin in 1882: "You may kill Itagaki, but not liberty!" Had Itagaki been killed by the assassin at that time, he would have been remembered as a hero and martyr for the cause of liberalism. But he lived on, and in later life re-entered the government, to occupy important Cabinet positions and join hands with Okuma Shigenobu. He dissolved the Liberal Party which he himself had founded, and formed with Okuma Kensei Kai. When he died at the age of 82, he had been raised to the peerage with the title of a Count; he was no longer the popular liberal leader he had once been.

The life of Itagaki incidentally reveals the real character and the extent of liberalism of Jiyū Tō. The party rose as a reaction to the autocratic rule of the Satsuma and Choshu clans, which had monopolized political power. The liberalism of Jiyū Tō was susceptible to change, and it did change when it gained power. Obviously, Japan in the early Meiji period had not reached the proper stage of political development for a more sound and stable liberalism to grow. This in turn meant that the liberal reaction against the government ceased to be an obstacle when the Liberal Party changed its character as a result of the political compromise which its leader Itagaki willingly made with the government.[6]

Influx of Western Ideas

The Charter Oath of the Emperor was a solemn pledge to seek knowledge all over the world, and the slogan *Bunmei Kaika* was an encouragement to adopt the civilization of the Western countries. It is no wonder, then, that the new era in the early period of Meiji witnessed the influx of a bewildering variety of ideas that prevailed in the West. The liberal movement, the agitations for civil rights and liberties referred to in the preceding section, was but one of the effects of the Western ideas that flooded Japan after the Restoration. The movement led by Itagaki ceased to be either a menace or an obstacle to the government under the new regime, but there were still endless ideas of Western origin that the government had to contend with. Since these ideas exerted a strong influence on the ruling class, as well as on the people at large, for decades after the Restoration, our study of the labor problems in Japan, must trace at least the main streams of the political and social philosophies that came into this country from the West.

There was, on the one hand, a school of political thought of Germanic origin which helped the Meiji government establish the doctrine of the sovereign right of the emperor.

Far from "alien" to the proper Japanese philosophy of past ages, the idea of a sovereign emperor might well be considered as indigenous to Japanese thought. But, in adopting the system of a constitutional and monarchical government, the people at the helm of the Meiji government considered it necessary and wise to provide a buttress of Western political philosophy. And there was little difficulty in finding scholars who would fervently champion the cause of the sovereign right of the emperor. Kato Hiroyuki and Tsuda Shindo were among the outstanding scholars of this school.

Kato Hiroyuki (1836–1916) was a samurai before the Restoration, who learned as a youth the Dutch language, and later the German language while studying military science under Sakuma Zozan. Under the Meiji government, Kato was first Minister of Education, then Minister of Foreign Affairs, and later president of the government school, which subsequently became the Imperial University of Tokyo. Early in his academic life, Kato advocated basic human rights and egalitarian philosophy, but he turned into a zealous protagonist of the autocratic rule of the emperor after he engaged in controversies with Itagaki. In defending the absolutist government under the sovereign emperor, Kato had no scruples in attacking Christianity and in denying the civil rights of the people. In expanding the emperor-centered, nationalistic philosophy, Kato, Tsuda, and other scholars of this school obviously drew their inspiration from philosophers in Germany and Austria, the two countries which were at the time at the very height of their power.

On the other hand, as already explained, there were radical ideas diametrically opposed to the absolutism of the emperor, ideas with roots in the philosophies that thrived primarily in England and France. Those ideas were taken up with enthusiasm in the early years of Meiji by the brilliant young men of samurai descent who had risen to overthrow Tokugawa's feudal regime. After the success of the Restoration, the same radical ideas found rabid protagonists among the malcontents who had either failed to find an opportunity to employ their talents in the new regime or were dissatisfied with the developments of the absolutist government. The radical social ideas of the West had a peculiar appeal to the youths of the early Meiji period, faced as they were with conditions of political and economic injustice and disillusionment with the new regime.

As early as 1871, only three years after the Restoration, the ideas of Jean Jacques Rousseau found their way to Japan through the work of Takahashi Tatsuro, in a book entitled *Jiyū Shin Ron* (New Essay on Liberty). Five years later, in 1876, a partial translation of Rousseau's *Social Contract* was published by Hattori Toku, and Montesquieu's *Principles of Laws* was also introduced. The works that had inspired the French Revolution came to Japan a hundred years later, to consummate the work of the revolution in these islands of the Far East.

Special mention must be made in this connection of two other works that had a tremendous influence in propagating the ideas of civil rights and the ideals of democracy: *Gakumon no Susume* (The Encouragement of Education) and *Tsuzoku Minken Ron* (A Popular Essay on Civil Rights). Both were by Fukuzawa Yukichi (1834–1901), a man who did more than any other individual to further the cause of civil rights and democracy in Japan.

Like many other pioneers of Meiji, Fukuzawa Yukichi was a samurai of a low rank in the Nakatsu clan in Kyushu. He had secretly learned Dutch and other European languages before the Restoration, and through those media had learned about conditions in the advanced countries in Europe.

Born the son of a samurai who, under the stoic discipline of the feudal ethics, had learned to despise earthly wealth, Fukuzawa was converted early in his life to the utilitarian philosophy of John Stuart Mill. In 1863, Fukuzawa founded Keio Gijuku, the first private university in Japan, which produced hosts of the financiers, economists, and leading businessmen who contributed greatly to the building of New Japan.

Socialism in the Early Meiji Period

In the early period of Meiji, when Western civilization literally flooded Japan, it was only natural that a great variety of extreme ideas were admitted indiscriminately. Beside the moderate liberalism of British origin, among the extreme ideas that came to Japan were anarchism, syndicalism, and socialism, of Russian, French, and German origin, respectively. Teachings by the Western missionaries of Christianity also spread rapidly, which was a striking fact, considering the severe ban on Christian teachings and the cruel punishments inflicted on anyone professing Christianity under the Tokugawas during the previous two centuries.

On account of the peculiar charm which these Western ideas seemed to hold for the youths of the early years of Meiji, their impact in a study of social or labor problems in this country cannot be ignored.

In dealing with the subject of socialism in the early Meiji period, it should be recalled that the Meiji Restoration of 1868, strictly speaking, antedated the industrial revolution of Japan by at least two decades. It was not until after the victory of Japan over China in the Sino-Japanese War of 1894–1895 that her industrial revolution commenced. This means that as was noted earlier, the "social revolution" that the Meiji Restoration entailed was not a social revolution in exactly the same sense as is understood in most countries of Western Europe.

In the 1860s in Japan, there was as yet no bourgeoisie born of an industrial revolution, no accumulation of wealth by the capitalists, no discontent of the downtrodden, class-conscious proletariat. Japan shortly after the Restoration provided no fertile ground for Marxism to strike root and spread. The socialism that appealed to the intellectual elements among the people in this period was Utopian rather than Marxian.

One name stands out prominently in the early history of social movements in Japan, that of Nakae Chomin (1847–1901). He was a samurai of the Kochi clan in Shikoku. While studying in France in 1871, Nakae was deeply moved by the ideas that had inspired the French Revolution. On his return to Japan, he taught a number of high-spirited youths at the private school which he himself had founded in Kochi. Many of the young men taught by him became leaders of socialist or anarchist movements in later years. A vigorous speaker and writer, Nakae influenced public opinion by spreading the ideas of civil rights, both as a journalist and later as a member of the House of Representatives. He first worked closely with the Liberal Party, but withdrew from it in protest when he saw the moral degradation of the party. It was Nakae who completed the translation of Rousseau's *Social Con-*

tract into Japanese. No other Western thinker had such influence on the Japanese people of the early Meiji era as did Rousseau, and Nakae was the apostle of Rousseau in Japan.

Sakai Yuzaburo was one of Nakae's ablest disciples, who went, as did his master, to France to study; he contributed stimulating articles containing much socialist thought to the monthly journal *Kokumin no Tomo* (The People's Friend). This was during the second and third decades (1878–1897) of Meiji. Few Japanese men did as much as Sakai in effectively propagating knowledge about the socialist movement in Europe. Sakai attended the Congress of the Second International held in Brussels in 1891—probably the first Japanese to attend an international socialist convention.

Kokumin no Tomo, the journal to which Sakai contributed, deserves more than a passing mention for the significant service it rendered in introducing advanced Western thought into Japan. The founder and editor of the journal was Tokutomi Iichiro, better known by his pen name, "Soho."

Tokutomi, born in 1863, died in 1957 at the age of 94. Like Kato Hiroyuki, Tokutomi in his youth was an ardent advocate of people's rights and of socialistic thought; as he grew older, he turned into a champion of nationalism. He graduated from Doshisha in Kyoto, the first Christian college in Japan, where he came under the powerful influence of Protestant Christianity and imbibed much of the advanced social thought of the West.

When he was 24, he began to publish *Kokumin no Tomo* in Tokyo. The publishing house of this journal was Min-yu Sha, of which he was the founder. The first number of this journal, issued in February, 1887, contained a translation of an article by Henry George on socialism and another article on the Nihilist Party in Russia by Sakai. Every number that followed contained no less stimulating articles, dealing with such things as the socialist parties in Europe, and the congresses of the Second International. Tokutomi himself used to write trenchant articles for *Kokumin no Tomo,* for the spread of the socialist ideals. His article entitled "Impoverished People are Crowding in the Metropolis" described the increasingly serious privation and misery among the people. Another of his articles, entitled "The Voice of the Workingmen," was an appeal to the workingmen to form their own unions, which would give them aid in time of need. Further, he urged the unions of workingmen to be prepared for collective work stoppage in case of emergency. In effect, Tokutomi was urging the workers to strike in an emergency.

To the people who knew Tokutomi only in his later years, as a man giving all his support to the government of the day, the brave leadership of his early years in propagating the ideas of socialism or of trade-unionism must have seemed incredible.

It was under Tokutomi's direction that Min-yu Sha, in 1893, started publication of a monograph series entitled *Heimin Sosho* (Common People's Series). The first issue of the series was entitled "Contemporary Socialism," and it had a tremendous effect on the thinking of the youths of the day. Nishikawa Kojiro, who later took part in organizing the first Socialist Party in Japan and became one of the earliest leaders of the socialist movement in Japan, writes that he learned about socialism through this book. *Kokumin no Tomo* and *Heimin Sosho* were two channels through which advanced Western ideas were spread.

There was still another channel through which radical Western ideas were introduced. It was *Rikugo Zasshi,* a monthly published by the intellectuals belonging to the Unitarian Church in Tokyo. Relatively young but prominent professors of Tokyo Imperial University, Waseda University, and Keio University, among others, who had returned from their studies in Europe or America, were among the active contributors to this magazine, which dealt with religious, philosophical, social, and political problems of the day.

The publications mentioned above show that socialism in Japan in the first few decades of Meiji was a set of naive humanistic ideas and humane sentiments, protesting against the autocratic government, wanting to revolt against exploitation and all forms of social injustice, but without organization and devoid of a practical program of action.

Nor is this difficult to understand when we recall the stage of evolution of the socialist movement in Europe at this time. The First International (International Workingmen's Association), under Marx's leadership, had almost petered out in the first decade of Meiji, and the Second International was not born until after the Sino-Japanese War (1894–1895). It had hardly commenced to exert its influence in Europe until sometime after the turn of the century. Furthermore, the Second International itself was, as it may be recalled, far from a united body with a united ideology or program. After all, socialism in Japan during the Meiji period was not much more than a reflection of the current socialism in the Western world.[7]

Impact of Protestant Christianity

In tracing the early influence of Christianity on the social awakening of Japan, it is necessary to recall how this religion was dealt with by the shogun's government before the Restoration.

It was in 1606, only two years after Iyeyasu was appointed shogun by Emperor Goyozei, that the Shogunate decided to take drastic measures to prohibit the teaching of Christianity. The main Christian temple in Kyoto was burned down by the government's order in that year. The ban on Christianity was made more strict in the following years of 1613, 1614, and 1616; more Christian churches were destroyed and the adherents killed or burned at the stake. The insurrection of the Christians, which broke out at Shimabara in Kyushu in November, 1637, revealed that the severe penalties inflicted in order to root out Christian teaching had had but little deterrent effect on its spread. The Shogunate thought it had to resort to even more severe measures to combat the "pernicious" Western teaching, and the persecution of Christians under the Shogunate was consequently of the most cruel nature.

The ban on Christianity was formally lifted in 1873, when the new regime under the Emperor recognized religious freedom for the people. However, it must be admitted that for a considerable period of time there was a stigma attached to the religion, and it had been the object of ruthless suppression. Under repeated edicts, all known Christians had been killed or banished. Edict boards had been posted all over Japan. Suspects had been forced to trample upon a small board bearing an engraved cross. Those refusing to yield had faced death by crucifixion, by burning at the stake, and by burial alive. Therefore, even after the ban against it and the stigma attached to it were formally lifted, tremendous courage was required to confess faith in Christianity.

It was not only the stigma applied to Christianity by the unintelligent citizenry that had to be overcome. The obstacles lay far deeper. The new state of Japan after Meiji was evolving a new philosophy of state in which the emperor, the lineal descendant of the sun-goddess, was assuming the supreme authority. All Japanese citizens, or subjects, to be more precise, must be loyal to that emperor and the code of ethics of the Meiji period, which stressed *chu* (loyalty to the emperor) and *ko* (filial piety) as the two pivots of cardinal importance. Christianity taught something which seemed to be, or was often interpreted as, incompatible with that teaching, for Christianity is a faith in an Almighty Creator, a Father of all mankind, a God of justice and love. Kato Hiroyuki took the lead at one time in arguing that Christianity was incompatible with the national character of Japan.[8]

Clearly, then, it took tremendous courage to identify oneself with the Christian faith, whether Catholic or Protestant, in the early Meiji period. And it is significant that there were a number of brave young men in Japan in the early period who dared confess their faith in Christianity and took leading parts in movements for social reform or for trade-union organization.

An outstanding figure among the Christian leaders at the dawn of the Meiji era was Niishima Jo (1843–1890). Born of an old samurai family at Annaka under the feudal clan of Maebashi, the young Jo was sent to a government institute that today would correspond to the Naval Officers' Training College. There an incident transpired which altered the course of his life completely. Someone lent him a Chinese translation of the Bible, which he secretly read with intense curiosity and interest. Was there in it the lure of a forbidden fruit? In any case, he made the desperate decision to go to the United States for further study of this amazing teaching.

Andover Theological Seminary and Amherst College afforded him the opportunity for study; he became a convinced Christian with a determination to Christianize his compatriots back home. By this time, the ban on Christianity had been lifted in Japan, and a government envoy was proceeding to Washington. The young man who had fled the country at the risk of his life was invited to accompany the government mission to Europe as well. Niishima returned to Japan the year after the ban on the Christian religion was formally removed. In the following year, he founded Doshisha in Kyoto, the first Christian college in Japan. When it started in 1875, eight students were enrolled. Today it has a total enrollment of more than 20,000.

The significant fact in this situation is that the first lectures on socialism in Japan were delivered at Doshisha College by an American professor, Dwight M. Learned, who was invited by

Niishima to teach at the new Christian college in 1875. The manuscripts of his lectures are kept today in the library of Doshisha.

There is no doubt that this devout Christian teacher was there to spread the gospel of Christ and not socialism. It is all the more interesting that among the students following his lectures were men like Abe Isoo, Ukita Kazutami, Yoshino Sakuzo, and others who, as university professors, ministers, and journalists, later played an active part in spreading advanced ideas in Japan. Further, as will be seen later in detail, another significant thing is that a goodly number of the men who became forerunners in the trade-union movement, or pioneers in socialist propaganda work, were young Christians who had either returned from the United States or had been graduated from Doshisha.

The Oriental Socialist Party and the Ricksha Men's Party

As the result of the years of agitation throughout Japan, at long last, the Imperial Decree ordering the establishment of a National Diet was issued in 1881. Immediately, in May, 1882, the first political organization styling itself "socialist" was formed. It was organized under the name of Tōyō Shakai Tō (Oriental Socialist Party) at Shimabara in Kyushu, a spot made historic by the Christian rebellion of 1637–1638, which the shogun's government had great difficulty in subduing.

In spite of its official title, the newly formed party was less socialist than anarchistic in both its professed objectives and its organization. The party chose to have neither a president nor a head office. The anarchistic character of the party was clear from its statement that "the government should ultimately be abolished because it is the offspring of evils. The day that the government is abolished will be the day the world of true civilization at which we aim is attained."

The Constitution of the party stated in Article 1: "Morality shall be the standard of words and actions of this party"; in Article 2, "Equality shall be the principle of this party"; and in Article 3, "The greatest happiness for the people in general shall be the aim of this party." Obviously it was naive philosophical anarchism which motivated the organization. The program of the party stated its intention to extend the movement to China and to Korea; hence the official name, Oriental Socialist Party.

The party was founded by a man named Tarui Tokichi, but

one of the more prominent leaders of the movement was Oi Kentaro (1843–1922), who had imbibed the radical ideas of the French Revolution after studying the political conditions of Europe through the medium of the Dutch language in Nagasaki. Oi had lofty impractical ideals. Before the party launched any practical program of action, the government, which had grown increasingly autocratic and repressive, began to intervene; before the government ordered its dissolution the party, in October, 1883, decided to dissolve.

In the year that the Oriental Socialist Party went out of existence, a movement arose that is of special academic interest. It was called "Shakai To," meaning "Ricksha Men's Party," though pronounced the same as the word which means "Socialist Party." Ostensibly, at least, the aim of the party was to save the ricksha men from the imminent danger of unemployment by opposing the introduction of horse-drawn trolley cars.

The movement of Shakai To was led by Miura Kamekichi, a politically minded boss among the ricksha men, and Okumiya Kenshi, a young liberal fighter under Itagaki. Several thousand ricksha men of Tokyo were drawn into the movement and staged demonstrations in the streets of Tokyo to oppose the introduction of the new means of transportation which menaced their livelihood. The agitation had the backing of such liberal leaders as Oi Kentaro, who had founded the Oriental Socialist Party, and seemed for a while to win sympathetic support of more influential people. In its spirit, however, the agitation was much like that of the "Luddites" in the late eighteenth and early nineteenth century in England,[9] a futile attempt to oppose progress, destined to be of only short duration. The movement in England lasted for more than ten years. The Japanese version of the Luddites' agitation did not last two months.

After the failure of both the Oriental Socialist Party and of the Ricksha Men's Party, Oi Kentaro went ahead to organize still another party in August 1892. This was called "Tōyō Jiyū Tō" (the Oriental Liberal Party). Oi was perhaps the most active fighter under Itagaki, fighting ceaselessly for civil rights and liberties, though he left Itagaki when he saw the decadence of Itagaki's Jiyū Tō. The new Oriental Liberal Party was not any more successful than either of the other two, but the interest in this last attempt lies in the fact that the new organization showed more genuine interest in practical programs of social reform.

The Oriental Liberal Party made its platform "the protection of the workingman." Implementing its policy to promote the interests of the workingman, the party set up under its aegis two organs: Nippon Rodo Kyokai (the Japan Labor Institute) and Futsu Senkyo Kisei Domeikai (the League for Promoting Universal Suffrage). Oi was the president of the former and chairman of the latter.

Though an idealist and a dreamer, Oi was interested in practical work. Many of the practical things he undertook in order to promote the interest of the workingman deserve comment. For instance, when the army was contemplating a system of having soldiers make shoes for the troops, he immediately set out to organize the shoemakers, in order to protect them from unemployment. He led a parade of more than a hundred cobblers who marched to the House of Representatives with a petition to discontinue the plan of having the soldiers manufacture shoes. He had plans also for organizing carpenters and farmers. None of these plans bore fruit, but his program and activities left deep impressions and influenced the young men of following generations.

THE INDUSTRIAL REVOLUTION IN JAPAN

Character of the Industrial Revolution in Japan

The phenomenon known as the Industrial Revolution that unfolded first in England in the later decades of the eighteenth century entailed the adoption of new machinery and artificial power, the use of a vastly greater amount of capital than in the past, and the collection of scattered laborers into huge growing industrial establishments. The Industrial Revolution that occurred in Japan a century later was not different in those respects from what had occurred in England. However, important differences between the two lay in the initiation, or motivation, of the revolution. These differences must be borne in mind, particularly by Western people, in order to understand the Japan of today.

The Industrial Revolution in England, which commenced with Hargreaves' spinning jenny, spread with a series of further inventions—Arkwright's roller spinning system, Crompton's mule, Cartwright's power loom, Watt's steam engine, and so on. England's revolution developed by a series of unexpected inventions— a result of fortuitous events, as it were. There was no consciousness on the part of the people of the vast change which would eventually come about as a result of the adoption of the new machinery.

On the other hand, the Industrial Revolution in Japan might be said to have resulted from definite policies deliberately worked out in the wake of the Meiji Restoration. In the case of Japan, the motivation was largely the desire for national industrial advancement, whereas, in England, the motive for adoption of new machinery was almost exclusively individualistic.

As already mentioned, the slogan *Bunmei Kaika* implied a determination upon a program to Westernize Japan. At the same time, there was another slogan adopted by the government: *Shokusan Kōgyo,* which meant "Industrial Expansion and Business Development." In implementing the primary policy of *Fukoku Kyohei,* "Wealthy Country and Strong Army," rapid industrialization was something inevitable, even without this new slogan. In any case, one logical and inevitable consequence of all this was what we now call the Industrial Revolution of Japan.

The revolutionary change in Japanese industry developed in three or four stages covering a period of approximately four decades. The first stage came in the pre-Meiji period, before the downfall of the Shogunate, when the feudal lords and finally the shogun's own government began to adopt Western methods of manufacture, though only on limited scales. The second stage started with the Restoration when the Meiji government began to implement the slogans *Fukoku Kyohei* and *Shokusan Kōgyo.* The new regime of Meiji politically professed liberalism in the Charter Oath, but economically it could not afford to indulge in laissez-faireism, considering the extremely depressed state of the national economy. With the urgent need to hasten industrial development, there was little justification for nonintervention. Consequently, the second stage, which commenced with the Restoration, was characterized by state initiation and state management of the basic industries. This lasted for about fourteen years, during which time the government owned and ran the model factories in all possible industries, including munitions manufacture, shipbuilding, railways, coal and other mines, silk, wool, and cotton textiles, and paper and glass manufacture.

The third stage of transition, which also lasted for about thirteen years, was reached when the government, seeing the maturity of growth of private enterprise, began to turn over those industries to private firms or individuals. This stage was characterized by state supervision, control, protection, and subsidies, and lasted until the outbreak of the war with China (1894–1895). The war ended in complete victory, resulting in the Shimonoseki Treaty whereby Japan received an indemnity of 200 million taels and the cession of Formosa and the Pescadores off the coast of South China. Japan was forced by the joint intervention of Russia, Germany, and France to renounce the Liaotung Peninsula, which the same treaty had ceded to Japan, but received, instead, a further indemnity of 30 million taels.

The victory over China not only enhanced Japan's prestige, but brought opportunities for commercial and economic expansion. The fourth stage, which was ushered in by the Sino-Japanese War and lasted till the Russo-Japanese War of 1904–1905, was a period of remarkable industrial expansion, during which the Industrial Revolution may be said to have been completed, although industrial expansion was not arrested during the following ten-year period that ended with World War I.

Defense Industry Before Meiji

The Industrial Revolution in Japan largely developed, as we explained above, under state policy. But, as a matter of fact, the necessity for Japan to adopt mechanized Western industry had long been keenly realized by the more foresighted of the feudal lords, or daimyo. Indeed, some of them had dared to erect factories on the Western model on their feudal estates before the Restoration. Significantly, the first such mills were mostly for defense or military purposes.

It was the lords of the major feudal clans in the island of Kyushu, such as Satsuma and Saga, who had had the closest contacts with the Western nations, that went ahead to erect on their estates the first foundries to manufacture Western firearms. In 1842 (13th year of Tempo) a plant to manufacture firearms after the Dutch model was set up in Saga, although this was by no means the first of its kind in Japan. As early as 1836, the Mito clan had cast cannons; they continued to manufacture cannon balls and gunpowder and built a reverberatory furnace in 1855. The bells in the Buddhist temples began to be recast into cannons in that year, the purpose being "to keep these islands of the gods from being defiled by the Western barbarians."[10] It was the visitation of the "Black Ships" under Perry in 1853 that had alarmed Tokugawa Nariaki, the feudal lord of Mito, and had prompted him to take drastic action, to build the furnace and recast the bells of the Buddhist temples throughout his clan into cannon.

However, the first reverberatory furnace built in Japan antedated that of Mito's furnace by five years, having been erected in 1850 by the lord of Saga in Kyushu. And in the following year, 1851, the lord of Satsuma, Shimazu Nariyoshi, set up in Kagoshima a plant for manufacturing cannons, rifles, swords, and gunpowder. It was this plant that was expanded in 1867, and turned later into the military foundry of the Meiji government. The Choshu clan, not far behind the others, also erected a foundry in 1854, and in the following year a shipyard to build warships.

Nor was the central government of the shogun slow to plan for armed defense. In 1853, in the year of Perry's advent, Egawa Tarozaemon began setting up a good-sized reverberatory kiln in the Izu Peninsula, under the shogun's orders. Cannon balls were manufactured by the Shogunate, which commenced also to build steamships in 1854. The Shogunate in 1864 moved the Izu furnace to Takinogawa, on the outskirts of Yedo, in order to have this facility for the manufacture of arms nearer to the seat of the feudal government.

The foregoing brief account of the endeavors of the Shogunate and of the various feudal lords in the pre-Meiji period will suffice to suggest the nature and degree of mechanized industries that were tried in the initial stage. In all their efforts, the feudal lords had to contend with lack of experience, of technical knowhow, and of capital. Yet, their budding industries were considered so indispensable that the new government of Meiji decided to take most of them over to expand and manage them. The Tokyo arsenal was one outstanding instance. It was originally the Sekiguchi Ordnance Factory under the Shogunate and was taken over by the Meiji government in 1868, the first year of Meiji. The Osaka Arsenal was another instance; it was taken over in 1871 from the Shogunate and moved from Nagasaki. Formerly called the Shogun's Iron Foundry of Nagasaki, the entire operation and equipment were transferred from Nagasaki to Osaka. The shipbuilding yard at Yokosuka was still another example. It was first built by the Shogunate in 1864 and ceded to the Meiji government in 1868. The shipyard at Kagoshima was similarly taken over by the Meiji government.

While it would not be wholly accurate to say that the Industrial Revolution in Japan started with these munitions plants or with the defense industry, we must not overlook the fact that the adoption of the more efficient Western machines by the feudal lords and by the Shogunate for munitions manufacture undoubtedly supplied the impetus for the rapid Westernization of Japan in the Meiji era.

Textile Industry in the Early Period

Needless to say, the industrialization policy of the Meiji government was not confined to defense or to any other particular industry. The need for Japan to adopt the more advanced machines of the West in all industries was undisputed.

By singular coincidence, the Industrial Revolution in almost all countries, as in England, has started with the textile industry. Japan was no exception to this general rule, although the defense industries referred to above did seem to take the lead, having begun before the downfall of the feudal government.

As early as 1863, five years before the Meiji, Shimazu Nariyoshi, the lord of Satsuma, erected a cotton-spinning mill at Isomura near Kagoshima. This was the first power-driven cotton-spinning factory in Japan. Then in 1870, the lord of Maebashi set up a cotton yarn mill at Maebashi city not far from Tokyo. Even today, Maebashi is known for its excellent quality products, thanks to its early start. Four years later, in 1874, Marquis Asano built in Tokyo a modern paper-manufacturing mill, while the municipal authority of Kyoto in the same year built a cotton-weaving factory. These were some of the early successful attempts in Japan to adopt the mechanized industries of the West. It should be noted that here again it was the far-sighted and more enterprising feudal lords, acting as a rule on the advice of the keen and intelligent samurai under them, who succeeded in the first trials of Western machine production.

Incidentally, we might note that, although there were these cases of success, far more numerous were the cases of failure. When the feudal government was superseded by the Meiji government, the privileged class of samurai numbered approximately two million men. They had been receiving, as the retainers of the feudal lords, stipends in rice in various amounts for their livelihood. With the collapse of the feudal government and the abolition of the centuries-old class system, the samurai lost their privileges. A very few who had participated in the struggles of the Restoration secured positions of responsibility under the new regime, but the vast majority received nothing except pensions, which, however, were inadequate to support them for any length of time. They sought opportunities in business, farming, or the rather limited lines of occupation which had not been frowned upon by the proud samurai. But, engaging in unaccustomed trades or commercial enterprises, they were bound to fail miserably, hence the proverb which spread at the time, *Shizoku no shōhō,* or "Samurai in business," which came to mean "bound to fail."

Despite this proverbial failure of the samurai, however, Japan was fortunate to have, in the critical period of transition from the absolute and degenerating feudal system to the untried and hazardous new regime, the elite in the daimyo and samurai class, men of foresight and vision, who could and did take leadership in the building of New Japan.

State Management of Industries

Besides the manufacture of arms and textiles that had already started in the pre-Meiji period, in order to promote a well-planned program of industrialization a central organization was created in 1871 by the new government. It was called Kōbu Shō, or Ministry of Industries, and its function was, in a word, to implement the policy implied in the slogan *Shokusan Kōgyo;* under its jurisdiction came mining, railways, telegraphy, civil engineering, shipbuilding, iron manufacture, and so on.

This Ministry of Industries continued for fifteen years, until 1886, when it was abolished and its functions transferred to the ministries of Communications, Agriculture and Commerce, Education, and so on. Contrary to the expectations of the government, the new ministry brought more losses than gains; from a strictly financial point of view it was a failure. However, judged from a broader viewpoint, the Ministry served to supply the necessary stimulus for the development of the modern industries in Japan. The work of this Ministry is summarized below.[11]

Following the Restoration, the government bent its efforts toward the encouragement and protection of the mining industry. The Mines Bureau, which later became a part of the Ministry of Industries, was set up in July, 1868; the plan was for the Bureau to buy up the output of all privately owned mines. This plan was later modified somewhat, so that private persons were allowed to excavate for mines and to buy or sell the mined products; the idea remained unchanged, however, that all products of private mines should be bought by the government in order to enrich the entire economy, with a view to stimulating the development of the mining industry. The government was interested in the development of mining, and it provided guidance and installed heavy machinery wherever needed. In 1872, the government issued a "Notification for Mines," according to which "land surface would belong to the owner of the land but the right to mine any minerals found therein would belong only to the government." It stated further that "any mining performed by the people is also the business of the government." This, it would seem, implied a policy of state management of mining.

The above-mentioned idea of state management was made explicit by the Japan Mining Law of July, 1873, which stated that "any [mineral] discovered in Japan will all be the possession of the Japanese government and only the government shall have the right to extract and use it."

It was under these circumstances that the government management of mining began in order to help develop the mining industry. The government took as its model the more advanced countries of Europe and America, and invited as advisers, or consulting experts, seven or eight mining engineers, geologists, professors, and mining workers from England, France, Germany, and the United States. At the same time, the government undertook to manage directly a dozen or so mines, giving unstinted technical and financial help.[12] It is recorded that as many as eleven major coal, gold, silver, and other mines of Japan, were placed under state management during the twelve years after 1868. All these mines (with one exception, the operation of which was discontinued in the meantime) were handed over to private enterprise during the years 1879–1897, for reasons to be explained later.

The railway industry was another important industry that the government undertook to introduce and manage for itself; it has done so with commendable success from the outset. It is of historical interest that among the presents brought by Commodore Perry in 1853 to the "Tycoon" of Japan,[13] with the aim of inducing Japan to enter the modern world, was a miniature steam locomotive engine. After Japan yielded to the inducement and entered into trade relations with the West, requests for permission to build railways in Japan were addressed to the Japanese government by England, France, and the United States, among others, but the government did not grant any of those requests. In 1869, however, on the advice of Horatio Nelson Ray, an Englishman residing in China as the Chief Commissioner of Customs, the Japanese government negotiated a loan amounting to 930,000 pounds sterling from England. With this loan, work on a railway between Yokohama and Tokyo, a distance of eighteen miles, was begun in 1870 and completed in 1872. Another line connecting Kyoto and Osaka was begun under a similar scheme in 1870 and completed in 1878; still another line between Osaka and Kobe was finished in 1875.

The records show that all railway lines constructed were state enterprises until 1887, when, for the first time, a private company was permitted to start a private railway. It was in 1885 that the Regulation for Sale of Government Factories, enacted in 1880, came into force. The effects of the example set by the railways and of this legislation for the sale of state factories will be traced in the next section.

Decline of Handicraft

During the long period of feudalism under the Tokugawas, the national economy was a closed, self-contained, autarchical economy in which agriculture predominated. This meant that the manufacture, not only of such necessities as soy sauce, salt, tea, sugar, *sake* (rice wine), and tobacco, but of such items as clothing materials, *tatami* (mats), and building materials of various kinds, was undertaken mainly by the peasants, as subsidiary work. This was to meet the actual needs of the common people. For the manufacture of the special artistic commodities and luxury items that only the feudal lords and other aristocratic or privileged classes would require, there were artisans and draftsmen engaged in their respective handicrafts. They manufactured swords, bows, arrows, saddles, and so on, for the samurai; lacquer goods; high quality porcelain and China wares; art objects made of ivory, coral, crystal, or agate stones; gold inlay work; cloisonné vases; and so on, which are appreciated even today for their high artistic attainment.

Handicraft was, as the name suggests, workmanship by hand with little use of machinery. About the only machinery existing in the feudal period was the water mill, used for flour milling, oil extraction, rice refining, and the like. In the manufacture of clothing materials, hand reeling and hand weaving were practiced widely, and the quantity produced, compared with that today, was negligible.

The introduction of Western machine production inevitably entailed the decline of handicraft and cottage industry. Defense industries manufacturing firearms put swordsmiths out of work. Power-driven textile mills drove out hand reeling and weaving. By the outbreak of the Sino-Japanese War, power spinning had already displaced all hand spinning. Although reeling by power machines spread more slowly, it overtook hand reeling during the Sino-Japanese War and handled 85 per cent of all reeling during World War I. Spread of power weaving was even slower, especially as regards the weaving of cloth for domestic consumption, since in the domestic market designs and taste did not change frequently and power-driven machinery was technically less well suited for the manufacture of piece goods and designs. Phenomenal expansion took place only with the plain textiles which lent themselves to mass production.

In mechanical and engineering industries, the introduction of Western techniques brought marvelous effects. One industry in which really revolutionary progress was made early was shipbuilding. The Meiji government recognized the importance for Japan of developing maritime transportation, and issued as early as 1870 a notification urging the change of all privately owned shipping from Japanese-style boats to modern Western-type ships. A drastic measure, issued in 1875, to prohibit the construction of Japanese-style ships of 500 *koku* (1 *koku* = 2.4 bushels) or more had a decisive effect in the mechanization of the shipping industry, though it involved the temporary unemployment of the Japanese-style ship carpenters.

The Westernized engineering industry grew rather slowly in the beginning because of the superior quality of the imported machinery and also the limited market in the country, although a model factory was set up by the Ministry of Industries in 1879 for the encouragement of this industry. The protection afforded by the revision of custom duties on imported machines and the expansion of electrical and transportation industries in Japan after the Russo-Japanese War helped the development of the engineering industry. This industry expanded rapidly during World War I, when imports from Europe and America dropped sharply and the price of imported machinery soared.

Another area in which hand craftsmanship was displaced by Western machinery was paper manufacture. Though the old style Japanese paper is still preferred for certain artistic uses, tremendous demand for Western-style paper has grown so that the old-fashioned hand process has given way to the mechanical.

On the other hand, an industry entirely new to Japan, and one which enjoyed enormous growth in the early Meiji period, was the manufacture of matches. One sad characteristic of match manufacturing in Japan, especially in the early stages, was the employment of women and children, and the use of white phosphorus, which is injurious to health. It was a typical sweat-shop industry which spread rapidly; because of it Japan came to be severely criticized in international markets, particularly in the countries to whom Japan was an undesirable competitor.[14]

Match manufacturing was the first important chemical industry adopted by Japan early in the Meiji era. But, because of its nature, the chemical industry as a whole spread rather slowly. The manufacture of chemical fertilizers was attempted first in 1887, but its real development commenced only after World War I. Manufacture of medical drugs began early in Japan, but mechanical production of chemical drugs is of rather recent origin. Chemicals for industrial use are of even more recent origin. The Osaka Alcali Products Co., set up in 1880, was the first attempt in this line, but it was not until after World War I that this industry made any real advance in Japan, and then only as the result of the stoppage of imports from Europe.

Largely because of the scarcity of mineral resources, the metal industries were among the most retarded in Japan. The war with China brought home the need for Japan to develop her own equipment for metal manufacturing. The much-needed impetus was supplied by the founding of the Yawata Iron Works in 1900. The protection afforded by the government helped greatly the advance of metal—particularly iron—manufacture. Among metal industries, the copper industry might be considered an exception, since Japan has been blessed with relatively rich copper resources. However, until World War I, despite the increased demands for copper wire for electrical and other uses, Japan, because of her lack of technical knowledge, exported copper ores but imported processed copper materials. The exigencies of World War I gave a powerful stimulus to this industry and altered the situation. Still another important industry for which Japan happens to be favored with rich resources is the cement industry. With abundant limestone almost unlimited production of cement is possible. Soon after the Russo-Japanese War, enough cement was produced to meet the domestic needs. Cement has been and still is one of the more important items of export.

Expansion of Industries: Growth in Capital Investment[15]

As mentioned above, the adoption of mechanical industries means as a rule the displacement of handicraft and the decline of cottage industry. The story told in the preceding section of the spread of modern factories is one of rapid economic progress, but inevitably it involved difficult human or labor problems. Those problems will be treated in detail in the following sections. For the time being, in order to complete the brief description of the Industrial Revolution in Japan, we will first glance at the spread of the modern factories and the capital invested in the firms that established those factories in the first decades of Meiji. As early as April, 1868, the first year of Meiji, the government, by establishing the Shōhō-Shi (Commercial Bureau), took measures to introduce and promote modern company organization. Yet the industries requiring high technical knowledge and elaborate preparation could not be established immediately. Although railways, for instance, were keenly desired, they were within the category of industries that could not be started at once. The light industries, such as textiles, requiring little technical knowledge and relatively small capital outlay, spread first. Agriculture should have been among the first industries to be tackled, but such was not the case, and it never came to occupy any important position, owing both to the very limited land area available for its expansion, and to the propensity of the government to favor industrial and commercial expansion even at the expense of agriculture. Because of the acute shortage of capital for all industry during the early years following the Restoration, banking was first and trading next among the industries in which the heaviest investments were made in the early decades. The following table will show that strides were being made before the outbreak of the Sino-Japanese War in manufacturing and commercial undertakings, as well as in banking, as has already been mentioned.

TABLE 6
CAPITAL OF LIMITED COMPANIES BEFORE THE
SINO-JAPANESE WAR

Companies engaged in	End of 1877 (¥1,000)	End of 1887 (¥1,000)	End of 1893 (¥1,000)
Agriculture	—	1,053	2,542
Trading	454	35,904	57,616
Manufacturing	—	14,725	68,259
Railways	—	12,080	57,945
Banking	24,981	75,375	111,635
Total	25,435	139,137	297,997

The figures above reveal a number of interesting and important facts regarding the development of industry. Among others, they reveal that in the twenty-six years before Japan was thrown into the dangerous war with China, effort was being directed mainly towards the building up of enterprises of fundamental importance to the Japan of the period—banking, railways, and other transport industries and manufactures. Of particularly strategic importance in a war on the continent was the completion of the trunk line of the railways. These industrial developments paved the way for Japan's economic growth and for her actions in succeeding decades.

It should be recalled that during the Meiji era Japan fought three wars within one generation, at ten-year intervals, fortunately gaining a significant victory in each war. Victory in the Sino-Japanese War (1894–1895), with an indemnity amounting to approximately ¥400 million, brought Japan an unprecedented boom. Foreign capital amounting to approximately ¥100 million was introduced at the same time, adding to the prosperity. One might say that it was as a result of this accumulation of capital that the gold currency system was established in 1897. Thereafter, industrial capital multiplied year by year at a brisk speed, despite the brief depressions of 1897–1901. After the Sino-Japanese War, the annual capital issue continued to increase by amounts between ¥50 million and ¥100 million. By 1903, the year before Japan's entry into another perilous war, the total amount of invested capital rose to ¥887 million, a 282.3 per cent increase over the ¥232 million invested in 1893.

The Russo-Japanese War (1904–1905), with a victory that the world did not expect, gave Japan further prestige and more opportunities for industrial expansion, as statistics show. A new stage of expansion in manufacturing, transportation, and other industries was ushered in, and continued for the ten-year period up to 1913. As is the case with any country that has fought a war, Japan found the war with Russia a heavy strain in every way, and there occurred the usual depression, which reached its depth in 1907. In spite of this, however, year by year there was an increase in capital investment, varying from ¥150 million to ¥200 million, and reaching a total of ¥1,983 million in 1913, the year before the outbreak of World War I.

Regarding the nature of industrial development in the ten-year period between the war with Russia and World War I, a few significant facts need to be pointed out.

Of the total ¥1,983 million invested in 1913, about 47 per cent, or ¥931 million, was invested in banking and trade, by far the greater part in banking. This had also been the case during the previous decades. However, statistics do show that there was a gradual decline in the relative importance of investment in banking as compared with the two previous decades. Before the Sino-Japanese War, investment in banking accounted for 40.7 per cent of the total. Before the Russo-Japanese War, it was 41.1 per cent, but it fell to 33.2 per cent before World War I. The decline was more pronounced in regard to transportation, as follows: 1839—20.1 per cent; 1903—29.6 per cent; 1913—10.6 per cent. This drop in the last decade before World War I is explained by the nationalization of railways, which involved the purchase by the state of some seventeen private railways during this period. On the other hand, we see that manufacturing and mining made strides during this period, the capital invested in manufacturing having increased from ¥147 million (16.5 per cent) in 1903 to ¥657 million (33.1 per cent) in 1913, and in mining from ¥24 million (2.7 per cent) in 1903 to ¥158 million (7.9 per cent) in 1913. The manufacturing industries in which most notable progress was made were machinery, shipbuilding, chemical, electrical, and gas. Especially remarkable was the advance of electrical manufacturing, with an investment of ¥199 million, accounting for 10 per cent of the total capital investment of the year, and surpassing both mining (7.9 per cent) and textiles (7.0 per cent).

The last stage of Japan's phenomenal economic growth, which completed her Industrial Revolution, commenced with

World War I. Japan enjoyed unprecedented economic prosperity during and after World War I, because, for one thing, the European nations that had hitherto dominated the world market were prevented from satisfying the needs of that market. Nominally, Japan in that war was on the side of the Allied Powers, but her part in the actual fighting was a minor one, whereas it was Japan that was called upon to satisfy the needs of the markets on the seacoasts of Asia and Africa that had been perforce neglected by the European nations. The war ended in 1918, but because of the damages sustained by their industry and transportation facilities, the nations of Europe were not able to tend to their overseas markets for some years after the war. In the meantime, Japan's manufactures for export and her shipping facilities developed by leaps and bounds. Ironically, the catastrophe of World War I, the tragic scenes of which unfolded mostly in Europe, afforded Japan what some European writers called "a golden opportunity" for expansion in industry and trade.

As a consequence of such opportunities for expansion, in the years during and after the war, capital investment increased greatly. As usual, after the war there was a period of depression, beginning in 1920. It grew to serious dimensions, but despite the panic and setback, investment kept increasing at a rate ranging from ¥100 million to ¥150 million per annum. Thus, total investment, which was ¥1,983 million in 1913, rose to ¥9,312 million in 1921.

Table 7, giving the total amounts of paid-up capital for all limited companies, shows the extent and the directions of most industrial growth after the three wars.

THE RISE OF TRADE-UNIONISM

Effects of the Industrial Revolution

The description that G. D. H. Cole gives in his memorable work on the Industrial Revolution in England in the eighteenth and early nineteenth centuries[16] applies with striking analogies—despite some basic differences, a few of which have been pointed out—to the Industrial Revolution which took place in Japan a century later.

The term "Industrial Revolution" signifies, not a single event, but a great process of economic and industrial change—a process which, in the case of England, evolved without any plan or

TABLE 7
MOVEMENT OF CAPITAL INVESTED IN VARIOUS INDUSTRIES (1893–1921) (¥1,000)

	1893		1903		1913		1921	
	Capital	%	Capital	%	Capital	%	Capital	%
Agriculture and Fishing	2,014	0.9	3,197	0.3	27,651	1.4	134,390	1.4
Trade and Banking	110,585	47.7	451,680	50.9	931,216	47.0	4,089,214	43.9
Trade (foreign)	601	0.3	4,573	0.5	15,621	0.7	227,865	2.5
Banking	94,513	40.7	364,706	41.1	615,659	31.1	1,692,650	18.2
Manufacturing Industries	40,132	17.3	146,756	16.5	656,567	33.1	3,551,210	38.1
Textiles	22,582	9.7	55,660	6.3	138,546	7.0	830,603	9.0
Raw Silk	5,685	2.4	6,424	0.7	5,461	0.2	102,927	1.1
Cotton Spinning	12,841	5.5	39,677	4.5	87,566	4.4	355,354	3.8
Weaving	3,787	1.6	7,447	0.8	32,861	1.6	290,620	3.1
Engineering	2,578	1.1	14,580	1.6	61,132	3.1	676,154	7.3
Shipbuilding	1,194	0.5	10,530	1.2	28,440	1.4	127,880	1.4
Chemicals	7,779	3.4	24,959	2.8	94,114	4.7	569,128	6.1
Paper	2,741	1.2	8,730	0.9	24,469	1.2	121,392	1.3
Artificial Fertilizer	131	0.1	1,850	0.2	16,365	0.8	74,543	0.8
Food and Drink	2,865	1.2	29,629	3.3	65,904	3.3	326,438	3.5
Breweries	1,877	0.8	11,380	1.3	38,963	2.0	165,844	1.8
Sugar	562	0.2	2,710	0.3	14,770	0.7	63,252	0.7
Electric Enterprises	2,033	0.9	12,152	1.4	199,009	10.0	788,264	8.5
Gas	—	—	5,545	0.6	64,783	3.3	78,823	0.8
Mining and Oil	11,632	5.0	23,590	2.7	157,737	7.9	710,773	7.6
Coal	5,103	2.2	4,498	0.5	39,247	2.0	204,999	2.2
Mineral Oil	481	0.2	7,610	0.9	31,522	1.6	86,209	0.9
Transport	67,603	29.1	262,383	29.6	210,061	10.6	826,485	8.9
Railways	52,342	22.6	220,225	24.9	132,982	6.5	310,254	3.2
Shipping	13,588	5.9	39,225	4.4	70,214	3.5	435,673	4.7
Total	231,966	100.0	887,606	100.0	1,983,232	100.0	9,312,072	100.0

SOURCE: S. Uyehara, *The Industry and Trade of Japan*, p. 32. Statistics originally taken from *Nihon Teikoku Tokei Nenhan* (Statistical Year Book of the Japanese Empire).

forethought, transforming the country from a predominantly agrarian one into the "workshop of the world." The process in Japan evolved first under a plan or a series of plans that transformed Japan into a workshop for a considerable portion of the world. As in England, it tore up or threatened to tear up the roots of old social relationships and institutions that were the foundations of national life, disrupting the tranquil life of the villages and creating the baffling problems of the new factory towns. In England, as Cole says, "it compelled Parliament to reform itself and raised the middle classes to political power as well as to affluence." In Japan, it compelled the government to adopt social policies to mitigate the suffering of the victims of the revolutionary changes. But it was an absolutist, and not a liberal, government that was in power. Whether the Industrial Revolution in Japan raised the middle classes to political power or to affluence is a matter of dispute. Most likely a candid observer would say it did not.

Last but not least, according to Cole, the Industrial Revolution in England "created the modern wage-earning class—the proletariat which, nominally free, can live only by selling its labour for a wage." Moreover, it gave the working class a class consciousness. As Cole says: "Only with that Revolution did the wage earners become conscious of themselves as a class and begin to make common cause over an area wider than that of a single occupation or industry." Can the same thing be said in the case of Japan? The answer is no. The transformation from an agrarian to an industrial economy was swift in England and the proletarianization of the working class went on rapidly, whereas in Japan there were old institutions and practices that survived the radical reforms of the Meiji Restoration and prevented so rapid an emergence of the class-conscious proletariat as in England.

The first and most important cause of the comparative slowness of the workers of Japan in acquiring class consciousness as an industrial proletariat despite the rapid rate of industrialization was the survival of time-honored feudal ethics. Honesty, industry, frugality, self-denial, gentle obedience—these were cardinal virtues which the common people had been taught under feudalism. The idea of "basic human rights" was alien to the feudal ethics of Japan.

The second cause had to do with the age-long practice of mutual aid and dependence within the "family," in the larger sense of a clan embracing all blood relations. This was particularly true of the peasant class. In times of economic crisis, the family comes to the rescue and almost automatically absorbs the unemployed worker, who would have been literally helpless in a Western country with a strong tradition of individualism. The best "social security" was afforded, and indeed still is, by the family in Japan.

Prior to the abolition of the system of *i-ye* (rural homes) by the revision of the civil code after World War II, the institution of primogeniture was in force in Japan. In practice this meant that, owing to the extremely limited cultivable area, all boys other than the eldest, who was the heir, had to go out into the towns in search of jobs. It was they who contributed to the swelling of the urban population. On the other hand, in case of a depression involving the closing of workshops and mass unemployment, it was their *i-ye*, their rural homes, that took them back into their folds. This was done without compulsion; the institution was regarded as a noble custom or duty which no decent man would refuse to abide by. No doubt it is a beautiful custom, but the fact is that it has served to turn the rural agricultural homes into a reservoir of cheap labor, a reservoir for the absorption of unemployed workers and available for the benefit of the capitalistic scheme of industry.

The third cause is to be found in a peculiar economic policy that the government has until recently pursued steadily. We said earlier that the government tended to favor industrial developments even at the expense of agriculture. What that policy involved must be explained in some detail.

At the outset, the Meiji government carried out a bold land reform in order to ensure government revenue from the land tax. That was both a necessary and a wise step to take at that time. However, in carrying out the reform, the men who had advised it apparently had not foreseen the evils in maintaining the old tenancy system. Instead of abolishing this iniquitous system, the scheme was to secure the revenue thereby. The scheme not only preserved the evils but even led to the gradual downfall of the proprietor farmers and to the increase of tenant farming. The landlords received the profits of the tenant farming. Those profits, however, did not enrich or strengthen the farmers, for instead of investing the profits in agricultural enterprises, the landlords purchased more land for tenant farming or invested in commercial or industrial enterprises. This was an age of mercantilism fostered by the government. The government did not discourage the landlords' investment of profits in commercial enterprises, hence the statement earlier regarding "industrialization at the expense of agriculture."

One intended result of these practices was rapid industrialization. An unintended result was the impoverishment of the farming population, which consisted increasingly of tenant farmers and semi-proprietor–tenant farmers. The prevalence of the tenant system and the survival of the old farming system that turned the rural agricultural regions into reservoirs of cheap labor, as explained above, were the conditions that gave rise to many of the labor problems characteristic of Japan.

Germination of Seeds of Discontent

A study of labor problems in various countries of the world reveals that there are generally four stages in the evolution of labor problems. The first stage is that in which the problems are primarily of a humanitarian or sentimental nature; in the second they have grown into problems of a socio-economic nature; in the third they have become predominantly political; and in the fourth they are primarily ideological.

In the first stage, which dates from the distant past down to very recent times, the problems center mainly on the individual worker. This is the stage in which the question is, in German, *Arbeiter-frage*, that is, the problem concerning the working man or woman. In this initial or primitive stage, the worker generally is indigent, ignorant, and weak. He is apt to be maltreated or exploited. The solution at this stage is found in the charity or benevolence of the enlightened employer. In other words, the problem being of a sentimental nature, the solution could be found in humanitarian acts.

In the second stage, the nature of the problem has changed. The problem no longer centers on the weak and pitiable individual worker, but concentrates principally on the collectivity of workers who are awakened to class consciousness. The worker may still be largely uneducated, inexperienced, and poor, but he belongs to a union which is gaining strength and he will assert his basic rights. When this stage has been reached, the traditional approaches of pity, benevolence, and time-honored paternalism will no longer afford an adequate answer, no matter how genuine or noble the employer's motivation may be. The failure of the government or of the employer at this stage to grasp the import of such evolutionary changes will turn an industrial enterprise into a veritable hotbed of labor problems. Let us readily admit that such was the Japanese experience during the early decades of Meiji, when the policies of industrialization were first being steadily pursued.

As has been noted, the Industrial Revolution in Japan was a planned course and not a fortuitous happening; there were, however, developments of a serious nature which had not been planned or foreseen. The sudden growth of a capitalistic economy brought in its train a series of social evils, against which the government failed to take effective measures, and which led inevitably to the germination of the seeds of unrest and protest among the working class.

Briefly, the industrial expansion of the early Meiji period was lopsided, or asymmetrical. On the one hand, there were the munitions industries, such as arms manufacture and shipbuilding, which were either government enterprises or heavily subsidized private industries. Iron and steel, coal and metal mining, and transport by both land and sea were industries falling under this general classification.[17] They were mainly heavy industries. On the other hand, there was a rapid expansion of the textile and other light industries, including the home industries and the industries for the manufacture of so-called "miscellaneous articles" for export. In the industries in this category, employment relations were along traditional lines, mostly maintained under the old feudalistic concept of the family system. Long hours of work, low wages, wide employment of women and children, lack of proper safety equipment, unsanitary working and living conditions, among other problems, began to characterize the industries of this country, in large plants as well as in medium-sized or small industries. The prevalence of inferior working conditions in Japan later led to criticism from foreign countries that were suffering from Japanese competition in the world market. The conditions were ripening for appropriate legislative action, on the one hand, and for the growth of union organizations, on the other.

Impact of the Sino-Japanese War

Every war that Japan had to fight after the Restoration, except perhaps Saigo's Rebellion in 1878, which was a civil war, had a tremendous effect on the national life. Of all those international wars, the Sino-Japanese War was the first major war, and its impact was startling, particularly in industrial relations.

To what extent that war was a "capitalistic war" in the sense of having been planned by and promoted in the interest of capitalists is of slight interest to us here. But it is of interest to note that the capitalists did help maneuver the war to a successful conclusion, a service for which the Mitsuis and Iwasakis were raised to the peerage. Such captains of industry as Hiranuma Senzo and Okura Kihachiro were also decorated and/or raised to the peerage. They learned, through the experience of the war, the advantages of close dealings with the men of power in the government. One morning they awoke to find that they were themselves men of power, though not in the government. Indeed, it was more advantageous not to be in the government, but to control it from outside. The story of the *Zaibatsu*, or financial oligarchy, has its first chapter in the Sino-Japanese War.

Inevitably, as in any country engaged in a successful war, Japan in the Sino-Japanese War had unscrupulous men speculating in business and profiting heavily from munitions industries under contract with the government. The material gains on the part of those speculators were unfortunately accompanied by suffering and resentment on the part of the masses of workers, on account of the program of arms expansion, higher taxes, mounting prices, and general inflation. The program of arms expansion received a spur when Japan was forced, under pressure from Russia, France, and Germany, to surrender her rights on Liaotung Peninsula, rights acquired under the Treaty of Shimonoseki. The extent of economic development during the war can be seen in the increases in state revenue, in the numbers of commercial firms and banks, and in the amounts of investment. (See Tables 8 and 9.)

Table 9, which shows a rapid expansion of state revenue, shows also a rapid increase in the per capita burden of the nation. This is only an indirect indication of the hardship inflicted on the people in this period; the response of the workers was shown in the spread of strikes.

Prior to the Sino-Japanese War, spontaneous work stoppages in protest against maltreatment of workers were not unknown. Called *domei hiko* (concerted work stoppage), the practice had gradually spread in Japanese factories since the early years of

TABLE 8

INDICES OF ECONOMIC GROWTH THROUGH THE SINO-
JAPANESE WAR (1893–1895)

	1893	1895	Increase
Joint Stock Companies	1,135	1,471	336
Capital (¥)	108,190,719	189,383,092	81,192,363
Capital paid up (¥)	66,189,073	106,520,721	40,331,648
Banks	135	1,197	1,062
Capital (¥)	62,916,100	211,432,042	148,515,942
Private Railways	28	40	12
Capital (¥)	73,123,000	121,138,000	48,015,000

TABLE 9

INCREASE OF STATE REVENUE AND PER CAPITA BURDEN
AFTER THE SINO-JAPANESE WAR (1895–1897)

	1895	1896	1897
State revenue (¥)	90,000,000	100,000,000	239,000,000
Per capita burden (¥)	2.18	4.67	5.67

Meiji. After the English word "strike" was introduced widely by
Takano Fusataro and other leaders of Shokko Giyu Kai (the
Workers' Volunteer Society), this practice came to be better
known by the English word, as were many other useful things
introduced from the West. However, it was only after the Sino-
Japanese War, during the recession in 1897 and 1898, that strikes
became a more or less established institution in industrial relations in Japan.

To mention some of the more notable cases of protest that
occurred in 1898: work stoppages broke out among the locomotive
engineers of the Nippon Railways, the operators of silk filatures in
Tomioka and Shirakawa, the cigarette makers in Okayama and
Saga, and the printing workers in Fukagawa, Tokyo. As will be
shown later, some of these strikes were carried out under careful
plans and competent leadership.

Thus, the effects of the Sino-Japanese War were the emergence of a bourgeoisie and financial oligarchy conscious of its
power, on the one hand, and, on the other, wage earners rising in
protest against the conditions in which they are placed.

Beginnings of Modern Trade-Unions

Although no effective action was taken at once, the government was not slow to recognize the need for legislative action to remedy the lot of the maltreated workers. The records show that the first move to enact a protective law was taken in 1881. However, the project did not materialize until the first Factory Law was promulgated in 1911.

More prompt and effective than the government's plan for a remedy were the spontaneous protests of the workers. The protests, some of which assumed serious proportions, first arose in the 1870s, but they were sporadic, unorganized, unsystematic, and hence of only short duration. There were mob uprisings, often accompanied by violence, that led to police intervention. On the ground that they disturbed the public peace, the participants in strikes were in some instances penalized, the charge being that they had violated the business right of the entrepreneur. There were prefectural police decrees forbidding strike action. Sometimes the guild organizations of employers issued rules laying down sanctions against strikes, with the permission of the prefectural governor.

The employers' practice of blacklisting labor agitators seems to have commenced in this period, although the first recorded case of blacklisting is not found until 1898, after the strike of printers at the Fukagawa Printing Company in Tokyo. In the absence of any legal protection in the matter, a strike, regardless of its legitimacy, would as a rule result in the discharge of a certain number of the men leading it. Until legislative action was taken in 1945 to mitigate the severity of such reprisals, a worker, by merely attempting to organize a union, ran the risk of dismissal.

It was in answer to a situation such as this that the first modern workers' unions were born in Japan in 1897. It is an interesting historical fact that the first action toward organizing Japanese workers was taken not in Japan but in San Francisco.

Somewhere around 1890, a dozen Japanese met at the YMCA in San Francisco and formed Shokko Giyu Kai (the Workers' Volunteer Society). Leadership in this movement was taken by Takano Fusataro, Sawada Hannosuke, and Jo Tsunetaro. An idealist intellectual, Takano Fusataro (1868–1904) was born in Nagasaki and graduated from the Commercial College in Yokohama, and on his return to Japan became a journalist with the

Advertiser; he had come into personal contact with Samuel Gompers and had been influenced by the noted American labor leader. By 1896, all three had returned to Japan and, meeting with Katayama Sen and others in Tokyo, they formally launched Shokko Giyu Kai in April, 1897.

The first thing this pioneer body of modern trade-unionism in Japan did was to issue a manifesto, which they circularized widely in factories. The document was entitled *Shokko Shokun ni Tsugu* (Address to Worker-Comrades), and its importance to Japanese trade-unionism is comparable to the importance of the Communist Manifesto of Marx and Engels to international socialism, though the tone of the Japanese document was more sober and restrained. Because it left its imprint on the thought and behavior of Japanese trade-unions, some of the more striking passages of this historic document deserve attention. The first paragraph of the document reads:

In the coming year, 1899, Japan will be opened wide for foreigners to reside where they like.[18] Foreign capitalists will crowd into Japan in order to amass profits by exploiting cheap wages and skilled laborers. They are not merely different from us in customs and habits, but are noted for cruel treatment of workers. It is they who will be your employers within less than three years. Unless you are prepared early, you may not only suffer from the same evils as the workers in Europe and America, but be subjected, judging from recent developments, to changes in your relations with your own employers of Japanese nationality. Some people argue: "Material profits will prevent human sentiments from entering in; the rich will become richer, the poor poorer. In view of the injustice inflicted on the workers and the misery they are in, the only remedy for them is a revolution and equalization of wealth." This is folly. If a revolution could effect all reforms, that would be fine indeed, but things are not as simple as that. . . . Inequality of wealth is inevitable as long as some are born wise and some unwise. Equalization of wealth can be talked about but not realized. We call upon you to firmly reject revolutionary ideas and sternly refuse to take radical action. We unhesitatingly advise you to leave to the proponents of wealth-equalization the foolishness of seeking for yards without succeeding in taking a foot. . . .

As regards the form of organization that the workers' unions should take, the document goes on to explain:

1. When there are 7 or more workers of the same trade in a county or town, they should organize a local trade-union. 2. Various local trade-unions in a county or town should organize a local federation. 3. Local federations throughout the nation should organize a national federa-

tion. 4. National federations should be united in a Great Japanese Federation.

In the above brief excerpts, the vast difference can be noted between this new movement and the movement started earlier by Oi Kentaro and his followers. The earlier movement was politically inclined, whereas this movement launched by Takano and others who had returned from America was nonpolitical and of the craft-union type, interested more genuinely in trade-union action. It advocated moderate, gradual reform instead of radical or revolutionary tactics. As noted earlier, Takano had contacts with the American Federation of Labor and its leader, Samuel Gompers, who was opposed to socialism and used to deprecate political action of trade-unions. Perhaps it is fair to say that the stress laid at the outset on a nonpolitical, moderate, and gradualist program for Japanese trade-unions, under the influence of the American trade-union movement at that time, had a wholesome and steadying effect on the workers' movement.

Katayama Sen and His Work

Prior to 1897, there were local unions of workers who were mostly artisans or craftsmen. They had agreements among themselves to maintain certain standards of craftsmanship, to respect and refrain from trespassing upon the clientele of one another, to regulate in certain cases the prices of the products, and so on. These were mainly the remnants of the craft guilds of the Tokugawa era, and membership was confined largely to the masters and not to the workers employed by them. Within each organization, the relationship between the master and the workmen was the relation of *oyakata* (literally, parent side) and *kobun* (literally, child part), more patriarchal in nature than democratic. In fact, there was very little democracy in those organizations. For these reasons, we may dispense with any further reference to these pre-modern unions.

The first trade-unions of the modern type were brought into being under the aegis of Rōdō Kumiai Kisei Kai (the Society for Promotion of Trade-Unions), established in the summer of 1897 by the men who had organized Shokko Giyu Kai, with the support of broad-minded business men, progressive scholars, and liberal politicians. Chief among the men who co-operated closely with Takano and played a leading part in promoting this Kisei Kai was Katayama Sen (1859–1933).

Because of the very prominent place he occupied in the promotion of both socialism and the trade-union movement in the early period, Katayama Sen deserves more than passing mention.

Born into a poor peasant family in Okayama, he had little means for study abroad, although he had vision and the ambition to do so. At the age of 25, Katayama managed to go to the United States for study. Earning his way by menial work of all kinds, he briefly attended Maryville College in Tennessee, Grinnell College in Iowa, and Yale Divinity School at New Haven, Connecticut. To observe social and industrial conditions, Katayama made extensive trips on foot, since he could not afford travel by train. His travels extended even to England, though only for a brief stay. When he returned to Japan in 1893 at the age of 34, Katayama was a zealous Christian socialist, eager and ready to start reform work.

The first task which Katayama undertook on his return to Japan was social work among the poor. Within a year after his return, he established in Kanda, Tokyo, Kingsley Hall, the first social settlement in Japan. Next he set out to establish, in co-operation with Takano and others, Rōdō Kumiai Kisei Kai, mentioned above.

The main objective of Kisei Kai was to promote the organization of trade-unions, but it did many other things, such as promoting protective labor legislation and spreading information concerning co-operative unions. For these purposes, Kisei Kai sponsored in Tokyo and in other large centers mass meetings, street demonstrations, and so on, which were suppressed one after another by the police. The organization published journals for the purpose of worker education. When the government's draft of the Factory Act was made public, Kisei Kai issued bold comments on it and also submitted memoranda to the government, recommending improvements on defective points in the proposed draft. Kisei Kai ventured to oppose the government when the latter pressed the enactment of the Public Peace Police Law, which aimed at the suppression of trade-union activities. It warned the government that such repressive measures would only result in aggravating the problems of labor.

These acts of Kisei Kai were found useful and effective in many ways, but of all its activities, the most successful was the help it gave in establishing new trade-unions.

The Ironworkers' Union was the first to be set up, in

December, 1898. On the day of its inauguration ceremony, 1,080 ironworkers employed in the army arsenal, railways, and elsewhere already belonged to this trade-union. Its growth was spectacular in that within two years, by autumn of 1900, the union had no fewer than 42 branch locals with a combined membership of 54,000, with headquarters in Tokyo. However, its growth was short-lived; the chief cause of its failure, was the lack of experience on the part of its leaders, as well as the lack of interest of the rank and file.

The Printers' Union, organized in Tokyo in 1898, was the next important union, with a membership of over 2,000. The first printers' union, started in Fukagawa, Tokyo, was soon disbanded; it was followed by a second, also dissolved in no time, and superseded in turn by a third. As in countries of Europe and America, the printers were literate and susceptible to ideological influences. For this reason, they organized before others did, often into radical organizations. The union of printers in Tokyo was a moderate union at the outset, but, under the influence of the rapidly spreading socialist thought, grew to be more radical. Its first president was Shimada Saburo, a famous liberal politician, and honorary members included such prominent scholars as Kato Hiroyuki and Kuwata Kumazo; they were mere names, however, and took no responsibility. The chief reason for its dissolution was that it depended more on the names of the leaders than on the members' own strength.

Beside these unions, there were the Tokyo Ship Carpenters' Union, the Cooks' Union, and others, none of which lasted very long. The only other union of this early period which aroused much public attention was the Locomotive Engineers' Union, Kyosei Kai, although this did not last long either.

This Locomotive Engineers' Union[19] was organized in 1898 by the locomotive engine drivers of the Nippon Railway Company, under the leadership of Katayama Sen. The union won its notoriety through a spectacular strike that amazed authorities. Early in February, 1898, a manifesto was circulated among the locomotive engineers of the Nippon Railway Company, calling upon them to organize "a union of minds" and to address demands for the improvement of working conditions to the president, vice president, and other high officials of the company. "Being a union of minds," the manifesto said, "it will have no president, no secretary, no fear either of spies or of turncoats." Upon discovering the plan, the company at once dismissed a dozen of the chief organizers of the proposed union and assumed that all was over. The company was completely dismayed, however, upon finding out that the men were communicating with one another by the use of secret telegraphic codes, and were all set to paralyze the entire railway system north of Tokyo as far as Aomori for two days, April 24 and 25, with the participation of more than 400 locomotive engineers. The company, appreciating the gravity of the situation, yielded to the demands of the union and reinstated the men who had been discharged. This was a complete victory for the workers. Thereupon, Nippon Tetsudo Kyosei Kai came officially and openly into being. We should note here that the name "Kyosei" had an elevated moral meaning, signifying rectification or reformation of character. In the selection of such a name for the trade-union, we may detect the influence of Katayama Sen, who was an ardent Christian reformer in those days, though later in life he became a Communist and ended his life in Moscow. The U.S.S.R. honored this veteran socialist leader with a state funeral when he died in 1933 at the age of 74.

Rōdō Kyōkai and Theories on Labor Relations

While Kisei Kai was actively engaged in promoting trade-unions of the craft union type in and around the Tokyo area in the east of Japan, another organization was formed in 1899 in the western area around Osaka, led by Oi Kentaro and Yanai Yoshino-shin, under the name of Dai Nippon Rōdō Kyōkai (Great Japan Labor Institute). In a way, this was a revival of Rōdō Kyōkai, which Oi first organized in 1892 as part of the political agitation he had started. However, there was a feature in this new organization that was distinctive and different from the former Kyōkai. The new organization had a concrete program of action to improve the lot of the workingmen. The program included the following items: (1) vocational retraining centers to provide penniless workers with access to appropriate jobs; (2) vocational training for ex-convicts; (3) night schools for workers' children; (4) hostels for special classes of workers, such as the textile workers; (5) free baths for the above category of workers; (6) free clinics; (7) special savings banks for workers; (8) special life, sickness, and injury insurance for workers; (9) special fire insurance for workers; (10) placement facility for factory and mining workers, free of charge or at low charges if any; (11)

legislation to provide relief to workers on railways, in mines, in fishing, and so on, in case of accidents; (12) legislation for the control of the recruitment of fishermen in Hokkaido.

The concreteness of the program shows considerable progress in the thinking of the organizers of the movement. Instead of mere sentimental protest against social injustice of the earlier period, they had begun to lay down concrete and workable plans. The program also reveals that the interest of the organizers was not confined to one industry or one class of workers.

In the realm of theory, different schools of thought on labor and labor relations became evident for the first time in this period. Incidentally, these schools of thought had a lasting influence on the thinking of people in following years. At a lecture meeting on July 9, 1899, sponsored by the Printers' Union at the YMCA Hall in Kanda, Tokyo, a debate took place between the three speakers of the evening: Professor Kuwata Kumazo of Tokyo Imperial University, the trade-union leader Katayama Sen, and a publicist, Kanai En, also of Tokyo University. In a speech called "On Reformism," Professor Kuwata said, in part:

... To sum up, we consider that under the economic principles, workers and capitalists ought to harmonize and co-operate with one another for economic progress. It is clear that the socialists who are engaged in labor movement have a mistaken conception of the relationship between capital and labor. They regard the capitalists as good for nothing. They would exterminate the capitalists and turn capital over to state ownership ... but is it really possible to have a country where all capitalists are done away with and all people under heaven are turned into laborers?

Obviously this was the stand of reformism, advocating the harmony of capital and labor. Diametrically opposed to this view was the stand taken by Katayama Sen, who argued:

Surely, harmony between capital and labor is necessary, but that is not feasible under present conditions. What we have today is not harmony. Continuance of present conditions will mean perpetuation of the relation of lord and retainer, nay, the relation of master and slave.... In order to realize true harmony, we must let the workers raise their banners.... Therefore unions are a necessity. So is the strike.

Against this speech of Katayama, which was entitled "Harmony-ism vs. Socialism," Professor Kanai rose and spoke on the "Refutation of Socialism," in the following vein:

I consider that trade-unions should conduct themselves for purely economic objectives. . . . In my thinking it is disadvantageous for them to seek much for political connections. . . . Think what socialism ultimately boils down to. As a Japanese, I can never agree with it. . . . This "ism" is something that cannot be realized without overthrowing the present organization of state.

Clearly Kanai sided with Kuwata, and their harmony-ism seemed to carry the day. Yet, even though it accepted harmony-ism, the printers' union was disliked by the capitalist of the day. Within a short while, the union crumbled under pressure from the employers. It should be noted that there was real progress when the workingmen's movement began to lay out a concrete program and to study their own orientation by listening to the discourse of learned or experienced leaders. But they soon discovered that action in the economic sphere alone was inadequate, and they entered the next stage of development—the political domain.

SPREAD OF SOCIALIST AGITATION, AND GOVERNMENT REPRESSION

Shakai Shugi Kenkyu Kai and the Social Democratic Party

"Socialism and the trade-union movement are twin offspring of the same mother," says Professor Suehiro.[20] This is a remark which will perhaps apply universally, and Japan is no exception; the introduction of socialism to Japan occurred much earlier than that of trade-unionism. The two grew in the same mother soil, as it were, of social maladjustments and discontent among the people. We have noted already how socialist thinking was introduced to Japan in the early years of Meiji by Sakai Yuzaburo (Nakae Chomin's disciple), Tokutomi Iichiro, and others. However, we shall see that it was not until after the Sino-Japanese War that Japan really saw the sudden upsurge of both socialism and of trade-union activities and that the government, alarmed by it, turned quickly to repressive measures.

In October, 1898, at the Unitarian Church in Tokyo, a group of idealists, mostly Christian, devoted to the ideal of social reform, founded Shakai Shugi Kenkyu Kai (the Socialism Study Society). Most of these men had gone abroad to study Christianity, but on their return to Japan, seeing the conditions of social maladjustment, they found they could not remain complacent, satisfied with the mere study of theology. If they were true to the teachings of Jesus, they thought, they must see that his teachings were applied to life on this earth. The ills of society must be set right. The kingdom must be built on this terrestrial world. The core of the newly organized socialist society consisted of young and ardent Christians interested in social reform, such as Murai Chishi and Abe Isoo. At the organization meeting held on November 20, Murai Chishi was elected chairman and Toyosaki Zennosuke secretary. The objective of the society as formulated at this meeting was "to study the principles of socialism and the desirability of applying them to Japan."

The membership of this society included, besides Murai and Abe, such men as Katayama Sen and Kotoku Denjiro, whose names have already been mentioned; Saji Jitsunen, a Unitarian scholar who was previously a Buddhist priest; Kanda Saichiro, managing director of the Unitarian Church; and Kawakami Kiyoshi, who later fled to the United States and became a famous writer and critic on international questions. As this brief account shows, the membership was comprised of men of many different professions and trades. They were believers in education, and conducted the society steadily in a program similar to that of the Fabian Society in England. It was at the monthly meetings of this society that the ideas of Henri de Saint Simon, Joseph Pierre Proudhon, and others were first discussed and propagated in Japan.

This organization lasted more than two years, but the monotony of its very moderate program proved fatal, and the members began to lose interest. The discontent with the stagnancy led to the formation in May, 1901, of Shakai Minshu To (Social Democratic Party), the first political party of socialists in Japan. The founders included Abe Isoo, Katayama Sen, Kawakami Kiyoshi, Kinoshita Naoe, Kotoku Denjiro, and Nishikawa Kojiro. Among these founders were moderate gradualists as well as extreme revolutionaries, but the "statement" they issued as a sort of manifesto of the party was a carefully worded, rather restrained document. It was published in a special issue of *Rodo Sekai* (The Labor World), a periodical edited by Katayama Sen and circulated throughout Japan.

Being the first important document of this nature in Japan, it should be examined closely; however, because of limitation of space, only a small part of this historic statement of the Social Democratic Party, issued on May 20, 1901 can be quoted here.[21]

The House of Peers represents of course only a small number that belongs either to the nobility or to the wealthy class. Representatives, when examined closely, will be found to represent the landlords and capitalists. Therefore it will be no exaggeration to say that our National Diet today is a parliament of the rich. Yet, remember that the large majority of the nation consists of laborers who work either on the farms as tenant-farmers or at factories as operatives. Why is it that those workers cannot send their own representatives to the Diet? Is it because they are ignorant and illiterate? No! Is it because they are morally inferior to the rich? No!

The Social Democratic Party has been for the welfare of the majority of the nation. But, we are not so narrow as to defend the poor only and antagonize the rich. We shall plan for the strength and wealth of our state, but not be so egoistic as to do it at the expense of other countries. Forthrightly stated, our aspiration is to take into consideration world conditions and the trend of economy, and to win victory for pacifism by breaking down the barrier between the rich and the poor through the principles of socialism and democracy. Therefore, the ideals of our party will be attained along the following objectives:

1. World brotherhood to be realized regardless of racial or political differences.
2. Total abolition of armament for world peace.
3. Total abolition of class differences.
4. Public ownership of all land and capital necessary for production.
5. Public ownership of all means of transportation such as railways, ships, canals, bridges, and so on.
6. Equitable distribution of wealth.
7. Equal access to political power for all people.
8. Equal access to education for all people and entire education at the expense of the state.

It was admitted that immediate attainment of the ideals enumerated above would be difficult. The party had therefore laid down for more immediate action a program consisting of twenty-eight items, including notably the following: (1) municipal ownership of monopoly enterprises; (2) compulsory education through elementary school (8 years) at public cost; (3) establishment of a Labor Bureau to administer all matters pertaining to labor; (4) eight-hour day, and Sunday rest for all workers; (5) general suffrage; (6) abolition of capital punishment; (7) abolition of the House of Peers; and (8) repeal of the Public Peace Police Act.[22]

What was the reaction of the government to all this? Today, little more than half a century after this happened, one would say there was nothing particularly striking or radical in either the statement or the program of the party. But, Japan was different fifty years ago. Records show that the government was alarmed when spies discovered the plan of organization of the Social Democratic Party. The Home Minister, the Director-General of the Metropolitan Police Board, and other top officials of the government conferred and decided on the immediate suppression of the party.

The organizers of the party had sensed, even before the report on the formation of the new party was filed with the police, what the reaction of the government would be, and had taken steps to ensure wide circulation all over Japan of their statement. No sooner was the report on the formation of the party filed with the police than a dissolution order was issued by the government. But the statement had already been printed in such leading newspapers as *Mainichi, Hochi, Yorozu, Shin Boso,* and *Tokai;* the sale and circulation of the papers were forbidden and the publishers of the papers were fined.

From this account, it would seem that all the Social Democratic Party did was to issue a statement and to disappear immediately after. But the repercussions were far from slight or momentary, as later developments revealed.

The Public Peace Police Act, 1900

In order to understand the spirit and behavior of Japan in the early decades of Meiji, we have to recall the position of Prussia— and later, Germany—a rising power in that period in the Western world. Ito Hirobumi (later Prince Ito), who was ordered by the Emperor to prepare the draft of the Constitution, chose to go to Prussia and stay there as long as possible while preparing the draft. In the sphere of social policy, too, Japanese statesmen were led naturally to revere the Bismarckian *Sozial-politik* type of legislation. When the government of Meiji was first confronted with the opposition of groups of men disgruntled with the new regime, and later with the spread of socialist thought that seemed a menace to the absolutist regime of the Japanese Empire, one example of effective legislation that the astute statesmen in the government bureaucracy could think of to follow was the legislation that Bismarck had applied in 1878 to suppress socialism. The German Chancellor had proclaimed in the Reichstag a policy "to help the development of workers' organizations for the maintenance or improvement of working conditions." But thereafter, the law of 1878, originally intended to prohibit public assembly, street demonstrations, pamphleteering, and other socialist activities, was used for effectively restricting the activities of any militant trade-unions.

In July, 1890, the Japanese government had enacted a law entitled *Shukai Oyobi Kessha Hō* (Law on Assemblies and Associations), the real object of which was simply to regulate assemblies and associations. Considering more stringent legislation necessary, the government in 1900 went ahead to replace this ten-year-old law with a new law, which had the definite aim of restraining the associations of workers. The government's objective in submitting to the Diet the bill for the new legislation is made clear in a statement made by Secretary of the Home Office Arimatsu in the House of Representatives at its session in February, 1900. He said: "It is quite likely that the associations of workers will become rampant in the future. How can peace and order be maintained in such an event, if dissolution cannot be ordered until after their assemblies are held?"

Commenting on this bill of the government in 1900, a writer who has made a close study of the absolutism of the Meiji government says: "The former [the law of 1890] was aimed at suppressing parliamentary opposition—the party urging revision of the absolutism, consisting of the landlords and bourgeoisie—whereas the latter [the new law of 1900] was aimed at suppressing the proletariat. This meant that the absolutist government and the bourgeoisie had now discovered a true common enemy."[23]

It was not until March, 1900, that the Japanese government succeeded in having the Diet enact and promulgate the Public Peace Police Act,[24] a law that had baneful effects on social and labor movements in Japan for nearly a quarter of a century.

Previous to this national legislation, there had been a government decree, in the nature of an administrative police regulation, issued in 1874.[25] It authorized the police to take necessary measures "to prevent calamity among the people" and to maintain public peace. Another decree, issued in September, 1884, authorized police officers to deal with petty police offenses by summary procedure without having to resort to court action.[26] However, these decrees were considered inadequate to deal with the rise of serious political, social, and labor problems.

As explained above, the primary objective of the Public Peace

Police Act was to restrain the political activities of those opposed to the new regime; the restriction of trade-union activities was secondary. Before the enactment of the legislation, there were as yet fewer cases of trade-union activity than of the above-mentioned political actions. It was after the promulgation of the law that more cases arose of the activities of trade-unions and socialist groups. Obviously, that did not detract in the slightest, in the estimation of the government, from the value of the legislation.

The Public Peace Police Act required, first, the filing with the police of a report on the formation of a political association; there was a fine for failure to do so (Article 1). Political assembly had to be reported at least three hours in advance (Article 2). Public meetings not necessary for maintenance of peace and order had to be reported (Article 3). Outdoor mass meetings and actions had to be reported twelve hours in advance, subject to a fine for offenses (Article 4). A policeman might, if necessary for peace and order, restrict, prohibit, or dissolve an outdoor assembly or mass action or crowds of people (Article 8). If an indoor assembly, he could, for similar cause, dissolve it. Those who refused to obey the order of restriction, prohibition, or dissolution could be fined or sentenced to minor imprisonment (Article 23). When necessary for peace and order, the Home Minister could prohibit an association (Articles 8-11). Offenders against this order were liable to imprisonment of not more than six months (Article 23). A police officer in uniform could visit or request a seat at the assembly and ask questions. Refusal to comply with the request or to reply was punishable by fine (Articles 11, 25). All secret associations were prohibited, offenders being liable to imprisonment of six to twelve months (Articles 14, 28).

The provision that proved to be one of the most obnoxious obstacles to social or labor movements was the article whereby the police officer, on his own authority, could prohibit display, distribution, reading or singing or giving vocal or other expressions to literature, a document, or a song which in his judgment was liable to disturb peace and order (Article 18). However, even worse than this were Articles 17 and 30, which ran as follows:

Article 17: No one shall commit violence or threaten others or publicly slander others for the purposes of the following paragraphs, or seduce or incite others for the purpose of paragraph 2 below:

(1) In order to let others join, or to prevent others from joining an

organization which aims at collective action concerning conditions of work or remuneration.

(2) In order to let the employer discharge the workers, or to let him reject an application for work or to let a worker stop his work, or to let him refuse an offer of employment with the view to organizing a lockout or a strike.

(3) In order to compel the other party to agree to the conditions of remuneration.

No one shall commit violence or threaten the other party or slander him publicly in order to compel the other party to certain conditions of rental of land for the purpose of farming. . . .

Article 30: Those who violate Article 17 shall be liable to a heavy imprisonment of 1 to 6 months and in addition a fine of from 3 to 30 yen. The same shall apply to those who commit violence on, threaten, or publicly slander persons who have not joined the employer in a lockout or the workers in a strike.

Government Repression and Its Repercussions

The Public Peace Police Act was not by any means the only legislative action taken by the government to cope with the spread of socialist movements. In the same year, three months after the enactment of the Police Act, another law was promulgated to enable the administration to take immediate action to suppress any act which it considered dangerous. The law was called *Gyōsei Shikkō Hō* (Administrative Action Act);[27] Article 1, Paragraph 1 authorized the police officer to impose restraint at once "when he sees the necessity of preventing a person from committing violence or fighting or an act which is liable to disturb public peace."

Even without either of the above-mentioned laws, it was not impossible for the government to deal with most offenses by using the existing provisions of the Civil Code and the police regulations already mentioned, but later developments showed that these laws were useful, and were used, for restricting the spread of the social movements.

When we recall the generally antirevolutionary, idealistic, and moderate character of both the trade-union movement and the socialist party, the repressive attitude taken by the government does seem to us today somewhat inordinate. Therefore, it is of interest to see what were the final effects of the drastic attitude taken by the government.

The immediate effects and the ultimate results were not the

same. The more immediate effect of the legislation and its application was the decline of organized trade-unions. But that did not mean any decrease in interest on the part of the workers in trade-unions. For, as a matter of fact, the workers of Japan were only beginning to awaken to their new status. There was little "class consciousness" which needed to be stifled or killed. Most writers on the subject seem to agree that the effect indeed was the reverse.[28] The highhanded acts of the police authorities served to stimulate the interest of the workers in trade-unionism instead of weakening it. This in turn meant that the ultimate effect of repression of the movement, particularly of the left wing, was to drive the movement underground and to turn it into radicalism.

The Social Democratic Party, the first socialist party in Japan (except the Oriental Socialist Party, which was less socialist than anarchist) was, as has been pointed out, antirevolutionary and restrained in character, all its founders (with the exception of Kotoku Denjiro) being Christians. But it was dissolved by the government on the day of its formation. No sooner was the party dissolved than its founders formed another party under a different name and in a different form, and duly filed a report on the new party with the police. The police, however, in turn lost no time in suppressing it. The new party was ordered to dissolve at once. The organizers had no choice but to abandon the idea of a political party for a while.

The socialists' next step was to establish Shakai Shugi Kyokai (The Institute of Socialism), which on the face of it was not a political party. Actual leadership in this Institute was taken by Katayama Sen and Nishikawa Kojiro, while Abe Isoo, Kinoshita Naoe, and Kotoku Denjiro gave their active co-operation to the new body. Here again, all these men, with the sole exception of Kotoku, were Protestant Christians. Kotoku was the only non-Christian, and was an avowed materialist.

As already noted, Katayama and his comrades were succeeding in organizing a number of workers' unions. They could not confine their movement only to trade-union action. The organ of the Institute, edited by Katayama, had been entitled *Rodo Sekai* (The Labor World). They now proceeded to alter the title of the organ and called it *Shakai Shugi* (Socialism). Instead of the principle of harmony between capital and labor, it began to promote "class war." At this point, the movement entered a new phase. The men engaged in it became more aware of the risks involved in their movement, which made them more determined than ever to carry on and to fight for the cause.

Strangely enough, as with Christian evangelism, the persecution or awareness of it tended to make the leaders of the movement more heroic and ready to sacrifice themselves. Katayama, Nishikawa, and others began to travel far down to Kyushu to address meetings of workingmen, and the gospel which these Christians now carried was that of socialism.

Besides the repressive measures of the government, a great event occurred that was to try the vigor and depth of the faith of these men: the outbreak of the Russo-Japanese War. But that is for another chapter; a discussion of Heimin Sha (the Commoners' Society), which made its appearance before the war, comes first.

Heimin Sha and Its Antiwar Stand

The fact that the Meiji Restoration, despite its deep significance, was not a "civil revolution" in the Anglo-Saxon or French sense has been pointed out. It will be recalled that the government of Meiji, after abolishing the old feudal hierarchy of daimyo and samurai, still retained, or created, rather, a feudalistic, hierarchical social order made up of *kazoku* (the nobility consisting of princes, marquises, counts, viscounts, and barons), *shizoku* (the old samurai class, without any of the privileges of the feudal period), and *heimin* (the common people). The *heimin* were largely equivalent to the plebeians of Rome, without any of the class privileges that the nobility enjoyed. Progressive thinkers in Japan were opposed to the new system of social inequality. The socialists naturally attached importance to the nonprivileged, plebeian class of *heimin*.

In November, 1903, Heimin Sha (the Commoners' Society) was founded by Kotoku Denjiro and Sakai Toshihiko. These young socialists, who had been employed by the newspaper *Yorozu*, had had heated and bitter debates with the president of the paper, Kuroiwa Shuroku, on the question of war and peace. Kuroiwa held a position which approved of Japan's entry into war with Russia "in defense" against Russia's aggression, whereas the socialists disapproved of the war from the point of view of the proletariat. On the same paper was Uchimura Kanzo (1861–1930), who was opposed to the war from the standpoint of pure Christian pacifism. Kotoku, Sakai, and Uchimura sent in their resignations to the paper jointly and launched in October, 1903, a new weekly called *Heimin*, published by Heimin Sha.

The founding of Heimin Sha and the publication of the paper *Heimin* created a sensation in the country, especially because it took a brave stand against the war. While the news of the outbreak of the war in January, 1904, and of victory of the Japanese troops in each successive battle were causing excitement among the people, it took unusual courage to proclaim an antiwar stand; *Heimin* dared to take that stand. Naturally, that aroused the anger of the government and of the patriotic people. The writers were arrested and imprisoned, the paper was seized, the printing installation was confiscated. The weekly paper that had aroused so much sensation came to an end in October, 1905, having lived for barely two years, at a time of unprecedented national crisis.

The ultimate effect of the severe repression will be found in developments following the Russo-Japanese War, which will be discussed in the following section.

AGRARIAN PROBLEMS

Origin of the Agrarian Problems

Because rice happens to be, as it always has been, the staple food of the Japanese people, while the land space for its cultivation is very limited, and because of the frequency of droughts, hurricanes, floods, and other natural disasters affecting crops year after year, the people of Japan were "predestined," as it were, to suffer from the agrarian problems. Agrarian problems in Japan center on two essential items: farm land and its chief product, rice. One of the drastic reforms carried out by General MacArthur was land reform, which greatly eased the situation. In recent times, Japan has been favored by continued bumper crops of rice year after year, with the domestic production fairly meeting the domestic consumption need. Moreover, the people of this country have been increasingly demonstrating readiness to change their age-old habit of eating rice by eating more wheat. In the light of these changes, one might be tempted to conclude that the old agrarian problems no longer exist in Japan. However, it is not certain whether so complacent a conclusion is warranted as yet.

In Japan's history, from early periods, we find records of "peasant uprisings." They were the direct result of the agrarian problems of those days.

In 1429, under the reign of Ashikaga Yoshinori in the
province of Harima, not far from Kyoto, the then capital city,
there occurred a peasant uprising that was among the first of a
series that broke out in the following years throughout Japan. The
causes of these uprisings were numerous, but invariably there was
the question of a poor crop of rice resulting from some natural
calamity. Money economy was not widespread in the country until
the eighteenth or nineteenth century. In the meantime, rice was
used as a medium of economic or social evaluation. A given
number of *koku* (1 *koku* equals 2.4 bushels) of rice would be
collected as tax by the lord. The retainers in his household would
be given so many bales of rice instead of receiving salaries in
currency. Later, as is well known, under the Tokugawa Shogunate,
the number of *koku* of rice produced in the fief of each daimyo, or
feudal lord, was rigidly determined by the Shogunate, and those
amounts virtually fixed the ranking of the lords in the hierarchy of
the feudal government.

The landlords were notorious in their exaction of the
amounts of rice to be submitted by the tenants, as land tenancy in
rice farming became more and more common. The landlords were
as a rule unmindful of the damages caused by droughts and floods
to the crops of rice. They were always ready to raise the rent, but
seldom prepared to reduce it. It was disputes over the amounts of
rice to be submitted that led first to joint actions of the tenants
against the landlord. It was not long before these joint actions of
the tenants assumed a political and ideological color—the resentful poor against the arrogant rich.

In the beginning, the uprisings of the peasants were sporadic,
instinctive, and unorganized riots. Gradually, the peasants learned
by experience the wisdom of organization and planning. What was
riotous mob action at first soon turned into planned action under
thoughtful leadership.

The government as well as the landlords in the feudal society,
as might well be expected, sought peace in the *status quo*. The
feudal government, even before the Tokugawas assumed power,
forbade the sale of land from one hand to another. Had those
orders been consistently observed, concentration of power in the
landowners might have been averted, but of course they were not.
Economic forces are more relentless and long-lasting than the
decrees of a government. The increasing economic powers of the
landowning class were contributing to two fateful effects: one, the

cooling off of the feeling of affinity between tenant and landlord; the other, the decline of the feudal system itself. The feudal society was a rigidly stratified structure, with a hierarchical order commencing at the top with the shogun exercising powers in place of the emperor, and going down in the following order: daimyo (feudal lords), samurai (retainers), farmers, artisans, and merchants, with undefined coolies at the bottom level. The rise to power of the rich landowners and merchants was undermining this feudal hierarchy.

Tenancy Disputes in the Pre-Meiji Period

The period in which the first recorded momentous peasant uprising took place, namely the Ashikaga Period (A.D. 1333–1573), has been referred to by an American historian[29] as the "Ashikaga Anarchy," not for alliteration's sake, as he explained, but because it was indeed a period of misrule, lawlessness, and general disorder. It is historically significant that it was during this period that the first recorded peasant uprisings broke out. The uprising of the discontented elements in society, organized in bands, had the effect of inducing the government to issue moratoriums on loans, mortgages, and pawned articles. These moratorium orders, called *tokusei rei*, became more and more common. During 1443 and 1474, there were as many as thirteen such orders or edicts. Literally, *tokusei* meant "virtuous government." In one way it was certainly an indication of genuine "virtue" on the part of the government, but in another way it was a disclosure of the weakness of the government, which inevitably led to further uprisings. The government soon met with the difficulty of suppressing the robber gangs, roaming warriors, and armed monks of the new Buddhist sects that arose in those years, who would go around the country "plundering, destroying, or burning down storehouses of the wealthy or pawn shops, temples, and shrines."[30] Hugh Borton, who has made a special study of the subject, goes on to say: "Thirty-six such disputes have been recorded between 1426 and 1526, mostly centering around Kyoto, and four appeared during the next seventy-five years, bringing us to the Tokugawa Period, at which time they definitely took the shape of 'peasant uprisings.'"

In the present study, there is no need for a detailed narration of the uprisings during the Tokugawa Shogunate (1603–1867). Our treatment here will be confined to matters which serve to provide the background against which the problems of labor relations in modern Japan have grown.

It is interesting, in the first place, to see the statistics of the uprisings, because the increase in the number of the disputes is considered symptomatic of the decline of the power and authority of the Shogunate. During the first hundred years of the Tokugawa Shogunate (1603–1703), there were 157 cases, distributed fairly evenly throughout the century; but in the next fifty years (1703–1753), 176 cases were recorded, showing an increase of more than 100 per cent, with 51 of these uprisings occurring between 1743 and 1753. In the last 150 years of this period, there were on an average over 6 uprisings per year. Inevitably, there was in these events political as well as economic significance. This becomes clearer when we look into the nature of the demands presented by the peasants and the manner in which the mobs of demonstrators conducted themselves.

For example, in 1783, in the fief of Matsue on the south-western coast of Japan, in an uprising in protest against the raising of taxes accompanied by other malpractices of the land-lords, several thousand men beat on doors with split bamboo sticks, calling out with loud voices demanding that the people come out and join them. The men broke down the walls of a rich landlord's property, pulled down the outbuildings, walked into the rooms of the house with muddy feet, and broke open the godown and distributed some 533 bales of rice stored there. The rioters were demanding relief from the high taxes. To the demands of the enraged peasants was attached a comment which read: "If you do not listen to our appeal, all the farmers in the district will rise up and attack the castle. This is important!" They demanded that: (1) they be freed from an increase in taxes; (2) they be allowed five years in which to pay back any borrowed money; (3) they be allowed a loan of 10 *koku* on every 100 for food to be paid in five years; (4) the abuses of the villages be redressed and help be given the starving; (5) the sale and manufacture of *sake* (Japanese rice wine) should cease; (6) they be lent money for the purchase of livestock; (7) there be restrictions on payment of *yomai* (rice paid in lieu of wages).[31]

In order to prevent the uprisings, the first step taken by the feudal government was to pass severe laws for the punishment of offenders. The government also saw the need of helping farmers who were incapable or less efficient than others and who had difficulty in making payment of taxes in rice. That was why, as early as in 1721, all farmers were ordered to form five-man groups (*gonin gumi*) and take joint responsibility for aiding one another. They were obliged to pledge not to form mobs. In 1741, the death penalty was fixed for leaders of mobs formed for presenting appeals. The chief of a village in which an uprising broke out would be banished. The chief of the five-man group would be banished and his fields confiscated. Moreover, an increase in taxation, instead of the decrease demanded, would result. After the 1770s the uprisings became more frequent and more menacing; heavier penalties were enacted for the leaders. Neighboring daimyo were allowed to join together to suppress an uprising. Finally, in 1839, the law expressly allowed the use of guns or swords "to tranquilize" the farmers.

However, experience in all countries has shown that it is not the severity of punishment, and certainly not the use of guns or swords, that restrains discontented people for any length of time. In the Tokugawa period, another method was resorted to on more than one occasion: the official of the domain would take sole responsibility for the disorder. He would come before the mobs, confess that he was guilty of negligence of his proper duties, counsel the demonstrators to withdraw and present their demands to their lord. Then, to demonstrate the veracity of his confession, he would commit suicide. However, this was an extreme method which could not be resorted to frequently, and, after all, it was no real remedy for the basic problems. These problems, which had contributed to the decline of the feudal government, were left as a legacy for the new regime of Meiji to tackle.

Agrarian Policy of the Meiji Government

It must be admitted that the Meiji government did not have an "agrarian policy" carefully formulated for the protection of the people dependent on agriculture, at least not carefully formulated in comparison with the high degree of attention paid and protection given by the government to industry and commerce. Mercantilism was stressed at the expense of agriculture. The slogan *Shokusan Kōgyo*, mentioned earlier, meant encouragement of mechanization in industry and modernization of business, but it did not include agriculture.

For this reason, the heading of this section, "Agrarian Policy of the Meiji Government," might be criticized as misleading. It is really the absence of such a policy that is to be related here.

Strange as it may seem, when the Shogunate was overthrown and the age-old feudal hierarchy abolished, the planners of the new regime did not introduce either the concept or the system of equal citizenship. Though the shogun, the daimyo, and the samurai and their privileges were abolished, three new classes, as mentioned before, were created: the *kazoku* (the nobility), the *shizoku* (the gentry), and the *heimin* (the commoners).

The *kazoku,* or nobility, was a class comprised primarily of those who had been, or were descended from, feudal lords. Also, the men who had rendered meritorious services to the state in war, government administration, diplomatic service, industry, or commerce were raised to peerage from time to time. But there was another category of people who were given such titles as baron and viscount mainly because of their large land holdings. In the House of Peers, these people had seats with the title of "High-Taxpaying Members." These individuals at the time of the Restoration of Meiji in 1868 owned about a third of the cultivable land in Japan. From the early years of Meiji, radical thinkers looked at these High-Taxpaying Peers as "parasitic" members of society. The seeds of discontent were sowed when the Meiji government deliberately decided to protect these "parasitic" elements by adopting the system described above. And the discontent was not allayed, but aggravated, when the land tax system was revised in 1874.

Hitherto, that is throughout the feudal period, the tax was payable in crops, the size of the crop cultivated on each piece of land being officially assessed. The farmer had to turn in each year as land tax a proportion of the crop which the land in question was officially supposed to yield. The revision required payment in cash instead of in kind. To effect this change, each piece of land was evaluated by the size of the crop it was supposed to yield; and three per cent of that evaluated amount was to be paid, in cash, to the government as the tax for that land.

Fixing of the land value by the government according to crop size and requiring the farmers to pay three per cent of the crop value as land tax had the advantage of enabling the government to predict the exact government revenue for each year. There was a distinct advantage in this for the government, but it obviously entailed much hardship for the farmers, for whom the annual yield of their land was not a constant or predictable factor. Moreover, in the early years of Meiji, money economy had not spread widely, and farmers, as compared with the merchants and industrial entrepreneurs had but little access to cash. The result was that the land tax revision gave rise to more unrest or resentment against the government than one might have anticipated.

Rise of Tenants' Unions and Spread of Tenancy Disputes

Bad crops because of floods, droughts, insects, poor market conditions, and so on, were among the chief causes of agricultural tenancy disputes, which spread and increased from year to year after 1875. It was in 1875 that the first recorded important dispute on agricultural tenancy broke out at Yoki Mura in Gifu Prefecture. The name of this village needs to be remembered, not simply because the first important dispute case in the Meiji period occurred there, but because the first tenants' union was formed there. This will be discussed later.

After the one at Yoki Mura in 1875, disputes of no less dimension or gravity in outlook occurred in 1894, 1902, 1904, 1905, in an increasing number of prefectures. Demand for reduction of the tenancy rate was almost always the central point in dispute. The tenants, disgruntled with the high tenancy rate and in desperation, would refuse to till the land for over a year, obliging the landlord to till it for himself. Neglect of land in protest against high tenancy conditions often proved effective, as was the strike of the mill workers. The landlord would have to give in and the dispute would end in the reduction of the tenancy rate.

In fairness to the landlords, it must be recalled that the government was placing a hardship on them in the form of increased taxes so as to cope with the sudden expansion of government expenditures. The landlords were automatically shifting the burden onto the shoulders of the tenants.

The rural exodus in eighteenth-century England, described by Oliver Goldsmith in his *Deserted Village,* was taking place in the Japan of the late nineteenth and early twentieth century. As Goldsmith wrote:

> And trembling, shrinking from the spoiler's hand,
> Far, far away, thy children leave the land.

Ill fares the land, to hast'ning ills a prey,
Where wealth accumulates, and men decay.[32]

There was the rise of a *petite bourgeoisie,* or small owners of capital, who saw more profit in the running of textile and other mills by the use of power-driven machinery. Capital poured into towns or industrial centers; investments grew rapidly in industrial and commercial enterprises, and agriculture was relegated to the rear. All this inevitably meant desertion and impoverishment of the agricultural villages and their inhabitants. Such results could be traced in the increase of tenancy disputes in the agricultural villages, since the tenant farmers, who constituted either a majority, or, in any case, a plurality, were struggling to lighten the burden of higher living costs and the higher taxes imposed on them.

The increase of disputes was distressing enough to the authorities, but a phenomenon that was to harass the authorities even more was the rise of agricultural tenants' unions.

At the outset, the tenants' unions were genuinely conciliatory in nature; they were honestly seeking to establish amicable relations between the tenants and their landlords, to promote mutual aid among the tenants, to prevent any harmful competition among the tenancy lands, and to improve agricultural methods. However, the basic character of the tenants' unions was destined in due course to undergo a change as the result of gradual awakening of class consciousness among the tenants. It can be argued that the so-called "awakening of class consciousness" among the farm tenants was not natural, but artificial and even superficial, in that it did not come about as an indigenous or spontaneous growth, but as a result of the influences from abroad, and that it was incited by a relatively small number of intellectual or more or less professional agitators. Numbers of instances could be cited to substantiate such arguments. Nevertheless, one cannot deny the wide extent to which the change came about in the character of the farm tenants' unions, so that, even if the transition did not come about as "spontaneously" as some people would like to believe, it soon reached a stage when the change could hardly be called with any justice "superficial."

The movement of the tenants' unions in the new stage after the above-mentioned transition began to assume a more belligerent and intransigent character. They would "object absolutely" to any tenancy rate increase. They would demand, in the years of poor crops, as much as 50 per cent reduction of the tenancy rate, if not total exemption. They would even place obstructions against the farming of the owner farmers in order to strengthen the position of the tenant farmers.

After Emperor Meiji passed away and the new era of Taisho (1912–1926) was introduced, the numbers of the farm tenants' unions, as well as of their members, increased from year to year. Such growth of unionism among the tenants meant, of course, an increase in the prestige and strength of the unions, but it did not mean any decrease in the number or intensity of the farm tenancy disputes. In fact, it was just the contrary. The number of tenancy disputes in the prefectures where they were most frequent in the twelve years between 1917 and 1928 are given below:

TABLE 10
SPREAD OF TENANCY DISPUTES
(1917–1928)

Prefecture	Dispute cases
Hyogo	2,553
Osaka	2,090
Gifu	1,033
Aichi	1,017
Fukuoka	858
Niigata	641
Nara	558
Miye	542
Kyoto	511
Okayama	453

The relationship between unionism and disputes is reflected in Table 11, giving statistics of farm-tenancy disputes and tenant farmers' unions during the years of ascendency of unionism.

What accounts for such tremendous growth of unions and spread of tenancy disputes? There are causes that might well be called "intrinsic," which are analyzed in the following section. However, there is one thing that cannot be minimized or ignored as a vital cause: the impact of the war, and, more particularly, the revolutionary war that swept over Europe during and after World War I.

A very pertinent illustration of this point is found in the fact

TABLE 11

GROWTH OF TENANT FARMERS'
UNIONS AND SPREAD OF TENANCY
DISPUTES (1918–1928)

Year	Tenancy Disputes	Tenants' Unions
1918	256	88
1919	326	84
1920	408	91
1921	1,680	373
1922	1,578	525
1923	1,917	633
1924	1,532	596
1925	2,206	587
1926	2,752	625
1927	2,052	509
1928	1,744	—

SOURCE: Kyocho Kai, *Saikin no Shakai Undo,*
p. 386.

that the highest numbers of tenant farmers' unions formed and of
tenancy disputes reported were in the prefectures of Hyogo and
Osaka, neither of which is a typically agricultural or farming
prefecture. If anything, they are typical industrial prefectures;
Hyogo has the biggest shipbuilding yards at Kobe, while Osaka,
known as the "Manchester of the Far East," is unquestionably the
industrial center of Japan.

During World War I, the European nations that had hitherto
dominated the mercantile marine industry of the world were
absorbed in war, and Japan rose to fill the gaps left by them.
Shipbuilding, which had thrived in Kobe on only a small scale
before the war, was expanded by the daring organization of the
Harima Shipyards as the Suzuki Company bought up the small
ones and turned them into a single giant shipbuilding yard. This
involved the absorption of most male workers, skilled and un-
skilled, from the adjacent farming villages. Those who were taken
into industrial employment were earning wages which to the
former farm workers were almost fabulous, and an inevitable
consequence of this situation was that the agricultural workers
agitated for better conditions in their farming work. Osaka was one
of the industrial centers where the first trade-unions of industrial
workers sprang up. The leaders and potential leaders in the
farming areas were growing conscious of the disparity between

the industrial and agricultural workers. In those years, there were not many "agricultural workers" in the sense of wage-earning workers in farming work. The consciousness of the disparity between industry and farm work in such a situation was more acute among the tenant farmers. In any case, what should be noted here is that there was the growth of an acute sense of social injustice in those years. And it is interesting to note that toward the end of 1920, a large number of leaflets were circulated in the farming villages adjacent to Osaka, containing the statement: "The relationship between the landlord and the tenant farmers is identical to that between the capitalist and the workers. Therefore, the tenant farmers should organize their unions and fight!"

Strikes broke out in the series in the Osaka-Kobe region. In particular, the strike at Kawasaki Dockyards in Kobe was unprecedented in its scale. These strikes were referred to later as "the alarm bells that awoke the sleeping peasants." Indeed, it was after these strikes of the industrial workers that the disputes of the tenant farmers grew more frequent.

Causes of the Tenancy Disputes

The impact of the war was a most formidable cause, but it was an external cause. There were half a dozen causes which were internal or intrinsic, and among them, perhaps the basic one is the smallness of the cultivable area and the large number of tenant farmers—too little land for too many people.

Too little land for too many people. Table 12, giving the farm land acreage as against the number of agricultural households engaged in cultivation in 1927, shows that more than a third of the agricultural families were cultivating less than 1.23 acres. Nearly 80 per cent were tilling farms of less than 2.5 acres. Only 1.27 per cent were cultivating farms of 12.25 acres or more. These figures will suffice to explain the relative poverty of the farmers of Japan as compared with the farmers in the United States. In the United States, it is known that a farmer will be generally regarded as more or less "well off"; in Japan, the reverse is true. A farmer or a peasant (*hyaku sho*) is described often as *mizu-nomi*, "water-drinking," the implication being that all the peasant has is water and that he must live on water.

The households shown in this table include both proprietor farmers—those cultivating their own farms—and tenant farmers —those cultivating land belonging to someone else. In addition,

TABLE 12
ACREAGE OF FARM LAND CULTIVATED PER
FAMILY AND THE NUMBER OF HOUSEHOLDS
FARMING THEM (1927)

Acreage of land cultivated	Households cultivating	%
Less than 1.23	1,944,533	34.96
1.23–2.45	1,895,837	34.09
2.45–4.90	1,195,332	21.49
4.90–7.35	321,741	5.79
7.35–12.25	133,661	2.40
Over 12.25	70,541	1.27
Total	5,561,645	100.00

there were proprietor-tenant farmers, who were cultivating small tracts which they themselves owned but were also cultivating farms belonging to someone else. In terms of percentages, in 1927, the proportion of the three categories of farmers was as follows:

proprietor farmers	31.2%
tenant farmers	26.9
proprietor-tenant farmers	41.9
Total	100.0%

The proportion shown here changed in time. First, because of the lifting of the ban on the sale of farm land, the proprietor farmers began selling their land in order to get out of financial difficulties, and were becoming proprietor-tenant farmers. The result was that in the period from 1910 to 1927 there was a slight increase of proprietor-tenant farmers.

Excessive Tenancy Rates. The second of the major causes of the disputes was the excessively high tenancy rates. Those rates did undergo some revisions under the pressure of the disputes, but not to any appreciable extent. For example, in 1885, government inquiries showed that the percentage of the share of the crop claimed by the landlord was as high as 58 per cent. In the period 1908–1911, this maximum dropped to 54.7 per cent. Whether these rates were "high" or "low" cannot be determined without taking into consideration a number of factors. Details cannot be given here, but careful studies show that, when comparison is made of the tenancy rates and the frequency of disputes in various prefectures, the highest frequency appeared in those prefectures where tenancy rates were highest.

Defect in the Tenancy System. One serious cause admitted by scholars and experts is the fundamental defect in the tenancy system itself: the absence of an authoritative or stable standard for determining tenancy rate was a major cause of the grievances.

Frequency of Natural Disasters. Unfortunately, Japan is and always has been prey to such natural disasters as typhoons, droughts, floods, cold waves, hailstorms, insects, volcanic eruptions, tidal waves, and so on, which seriously affect crops in the regions visited by such disasters. From centuries of experience some landlords learned to provide for such disasters, but only in rare instances. Statistics of the Meiji and Taisho periods show that from 30 per cent to as high as 78 per cent of the disputes arose from conditions resulting from natural causes.

Various Economic Causes. In addition to the causes already mentioned, there is always present as the underlying cause the fact of the economic hardship under which the farming population has been struggling. It has been estimated that the farmers of Japan were frequently "short" up to 40 per cent in their yearly income. That perennial shortage had to be met somehow or other. The price fluctuation of agricultural products added to the instability and anxiety of the farmers. Their dependence for decades on only two products, rice and raw silk, also proved a factor which contributed to the unhealthy condition of agriculture, and was a cause of the disputes and turbulent atmosphere in the agricultural villages throughout Japan.

Remedies for Tenancy Difficulties

Attempts to remedy the situation were made, of course, from time to time, with some good results locally or for short periods of time, but not with any widespread or lasting effect.

One of the remedies tried was the "land company," first begun in 1922. The company undertook two things: (1) to collect rentals on behalf of the landowners, and (2) to help develop the land for better crops.

Joint management of farms was experimented on in various ways. One was joint management among landlords only, another was among tenants only, and still another was joint management by landlords and tenants.

One new proposal that attracted much attention was of German origin. First suggested in 1890 by a German agricultural adviser, it was in the nature of insurance against crop failures caused by natural disasters beyond man's control, such as heavy rain and flood, drought, storms, and so on. The proposal was incorporated in the Commercial Code, but repealed when the new Code was enacted in 1899. There were proposals also to insure against the effects of tenancy disputes, but they never bore fruit. Among the arguments opposing the proposal of crop insurance was that such a scheme would "tend to promote laziness among the farmers" and that "the government could not afford excessive burdens" of that sort.

Perhaps the most noteworthy of the proposed remedies was to carry out a fundamental inquiry into prevailing conditions, and to work out a standard formula for fixing tenancy rates. Such an inquiry was carried out in Nakahara Mura in Miye Prefecture by the village branch of the Japan Peasants' Union; the following formula was worked out as the standard for the share of crops between landlord and tenants:

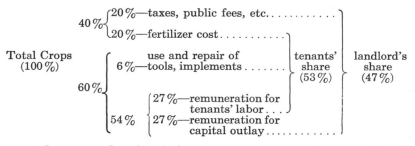

The proposal outlined above was accepted in Nakahara Mura, and revision of tenancy rates was carried out in every section of the village, the land being divided first into twelve grades for fixing the amount of the total crops for each section. It is interesting to note that as a result of the revision of the tenancy rates in application of this formula, there was a reduction of from ˙o 30 per cent from the previous rates.

To complete the picture of the agrarian problem, it is ˙ary to trace the development of peasants' unions. This will ˙e in the following chapter, in connection with the discus- ˙he expansion of the trade-union movement.

CHAPTER III

From the Russo-Japanese War to World War I (1914–1918)

AFTERMATH OF THE RUSSO-JAPANESE WAR

Political Effects of the War

The victory of Japan over Russia in the war that was fought in 1904–1905 was of historic significance in that it was the first time in several centuries that a nation outside of Europe had defeated a European power. Until this war, every war fought by a European nation with a non-European nation had been won by the European nation, and it had meant the further subjugation of the non-European peoples of the world by the European. As a matter of fact, world history prior to the Russo-Japanese War for a period of two or three hundred years was a history of world conquest by a relatively small number of Western or European powers.

Incidentally, it was also a war between a Caucasian, or white, people, and a Mongolian, or yellow, people.[1] For the first time in the memory of many people, a nonwhite nation rose to fight and beat a giant empire of white people. The fall of Port Arthur, the collapse of the Russian forces at Mukden, and the spectacular defeat of the Baltic fleet in the naval battle of Tsushima were unexpected and unbelievable events.

In effect, the Russo-Japanese War ended the chapter in world history of world conquest and colonization by the European powers. At least the victory of Japan in that war marked the beginning of the end, if not the end, of Western colonialism. Inevitably, Japan's victory raised her status in the world community of nations.

More than any other single incident, this war against the mighty Russian Empire served to unite Japan. It is true that there was a small number of socialists and religious people who dared to take an antiwar stand. That has to be recorded for later reference, but apart from these minor exceptions, the experience of the war contributed to the unification of the Japanese people in their dealings with foreign nations.

The unity which the necessities of war imposed on the people, to put it bluntly, was unquestionably an asset for the country and a felicitous matter as far as it went, but there was also the growth of a by-product that could not be averted. It was the rise and spread of nationalism, which was to become a most forceful element in the life of the nation in the following years. As time went on, nationalism in this country assumed, as it did in many other countries, the character and characteristics of an ideology, eventually wielding its influence to lead the island empire into fateful adventures.

One of the unmistakable evidences of the recognition of this small island empire by the Western powers was the extension, in 1905, for a further ten years of the Anglo-Japanese Alliance. As a matter of fact, when Great Britain, abandoning her vaunted policy of "splendid isolation," had concluded the Alliance in 1902, before the outbreak of the Russo-Japanese War, it was the first time in modern world history that a Caucasian nation or empire had sought to form a military pact with a non-European and non-Caucasian nation.

Political events of more recent years, particularly the developments following world wars I and II, would convince a careful observer that the indirect effects of Japan's victory over Russia on the other peoples of Asia and of Africa were even more meaningful and consequential than were the immediate effects on the Japanese people themselves. The success of the Japanese in the war seemed to herald the dawn of a new era of independence and freedom, and an equal share in the responsibility of shaping the future destinies of the nations.

Economic Effects of the War

If the political effects of the war were profound, the economic effects were even more so.

Although Japan had received an indemnity of 200 million taels after the Sino-Japanese War, she failed to receive a single ruble from Russia. This great disappointment to the Japanese people led to riots in the streets of Tokyo, but the acquisition of the southern half of Saghalien and of control over Korea and southern Manchuria, with its railway of high economic and strategic importance, were undeniable gains which gave new life to Japanese economy.

The second stage of the industrial revolution was reached as the result of the war, with an increase in the number of factories. There was an expansion of the iron and steel industry, coal and metal mining, the electrical industry, and so on. A sudden increase in textile manufacturing was noted and this was accompanied by a sudden expansion in exports.

It was after the Russo-Japanese War that Japan embarked upon an aggressive colonial expansionist policy with the full knowledge or recognition of the powers that had read the terms of the Peace of Portsmouth, concluded under the good offices of President Theodore Roosevelt of the United States. For colonial expansion into South Manchuria and later to China proper, full use was made of the rights or powers ceded by Russia. Japan had men to manage the South Manchuria Railways to her best political and economic advantage.

There was an expansion in shipbuilding and in the shipping of Japanese-made goods to world markets, which had been monopolized hitherto by the West European nations. It will be seen that expansion along these lines continued in the following years, through World War I, until it began to alarm the Western world: it would not be wrong to consider that the start in this direction was made in the Russo-Japanese War.

Industrial or manufacturing expansion was, as a matter of course, accompanied by an increase in factories and industrial workers. New modes appeared in goods, clothing, and in living conditions as a whole, all of which inevitably entailed a rise in the cost of living. However, the higher cost of living was not accompanied by a corresponding rise in wages or earnings.

There was no decrease in the production of rice, the staple food. In fact, more rice was produced, but there was a constant decrease in the number of farm workers and the price of rice rose constantly. This meant hardship for the industrial workers. As is usually the case in any country at war, the wages of workers had been practically frozen, while the prices of commodities were rising because of shortages.

This is merely an outline of the main economic effects, which are readily recognized as problems requiring adjustment. How these problems were adjusted by legislation, by the actions of public bodies, and by employers and workers in their negotiations during the interwar period, constitutes the content of the present chapter.

Social or Ideological Effects of the War

If the economic effects of the war were perplexing, the ideological effects were even more baffling because of their elusive and imponderable character.

When we look back on the ten-year interwar period after World War I and compare it with the ten-year period after the Russo-Japanese War, we find that the ideological impact of World War I on the nation was like that of a colossal tidal wave. Nonetheless, it must be admitted that the uprisings of tenant farmers and industrial workers that spread over Japan after the Russo-Japanese War were alarming to the authorities. In most cases, the disputes were over wages or the proportion of their crops that tenants had to surrender to their landlords. In this sense they were "economic" disputes and not "political" in the generally accepted sense of the term, but a close examination would reveal a definite shift in the thinking or attitude of the workers in presenting their grievances. They were no longer interested in merely receiving higher wages or surrendering a lesser share of the crops to the landlords. New social ideals lay behind the demands of the workers. This is precisely why the expression "social or ideological effects" was chosen here. The impact of the war had effects on the thinking of the whole industrial society. This subject will be treated more concretely in the sections that follow.

Period of Futile Agitations[2]

Emperor Meiji, the illustrious sovereign ruler of Japan for forty-five years, died in 1912. The Meiji era was one of remarkable development and expansion of the Japanese Empire, but, from the point of view of labor policy, it was a period of blind search for orientation, on the part of the government, the employers, and the workers. And, at least for the workers, up to the last year of the Meiji era, it was a period of futile agitation. The following table shows how the unrest among the workers expressed itself in the outbreak of disputes.

TABLE 13

LABOR DISPUTES IN THE CLOSING PERIOD OF THE MEIJI
ERA (1897–1911)

Year	Cases	Number of Partici- pants	Partici- pants Per Case	Remarks
1897[a]	32	3,517	103	Rodo Kumiai Kisei Kai founded
1898	43	6,293	146	
1899	15	4,284	285	
1900	11	2,316	211	Public Peace Police Act issued
1901	18	1,948	101	
1902	8	1,849	231	
1903	9	1,359	152	
1904	6	879	146	Russo-Japanese War began
1905	19	5,013	263	Russo-Japanese War ended
1906	13	2,037	156	
1907	57	9,855	173	
1908	13	822	63	
1909	11	310	28	
1910	10	2,934	293	
1911	22	2,100	95	

[a] Figure for July–December, 1897.
SOURCE: Kyocho Kai, *Saikin no Shakai Undo*, p. 322

The early years covered in this table were years of an
economic depression that had lasted for some years. Takano
Fusataro and Katayama Sen, mentioned earlier, were active
leaders of workers' movements during those years, rejecting
revolutionary tactics and working ceaselessly with the tenets of
reformism. They were successful in the support they gave to the
ironworkers' union, but when they intervened on behalf of some
eight men discharged by the Nippon Railways Company, collected
contributions from the railway workers' union and formed a
united front of the workers, the company retaliated with the
discharge of twenty-eight men who had taken active leadership in
the united front. This experience proved, if anything, the ineffi-
cacy of the organized workers' movement in this period of
immaturity of unionism. That was in 1899.

The year 1900 saw the promulgation of the Public Peace
Police Act, which, as already explained, had a devastating effect
on the nascent trade-union movement. Writers on the history of
trade-unionism in Japan refer to the period of a decade or so after
1900 as *Chinsen Ki* (the Period of Submersion). As no normal
trade-union activity was possible, the workers thereafter resorted
to direct-action tactics which involved violence, a course which

seemed natural when the door to quiet and orderly negotiation through collective bargaining was closed.

During this period of submersion of trade-unionism, labor disputes were apt to take the form of riots, with the wrecking or burning of properties of the companies. From 1899 to 1900 onward, the number of participants in disputes kept diminishing, but there was an increase in destruction. The peak of violence was reached in 1909 when the number of cases of dispute, total number of participants, and the number involved per case were the highest ever recorded. The first of the outbursts occurred in February, 1909, at Ashio Copper Mine, where 1,200 miners demanded higher wages and better treatment. When the demands were rejected, the men cut off electricity, smashed electric lamps, threw bombs, and burned the company housing. Finally, they seized the company's stores, whereupon three infantry companies were dispatched from Takasaki Regiment Headquarters to suppress violence.

Among the disputes accompanied by violence in the latter part of the Meiji period, one that left a deep impression was the strike of the city tramways of Tokyo. The tramways, which had been a private undertaking until the end of 1911, were bought up by the city, which meant the dissolution of the company. In effecting the dissolution, allowances were given to the entire staff. The lower staff men discovered that the allowances given to higher staff men were far higher than those given out to the lower staff. This discovery ignited the dispute; it took the form of a strike, which began on the last day of 1911 and ran into the following New Year's Day. Depriving the citizens of their transportation on New Year's Day naturally aroused the anger of the population. In order to appease the men, the chiefs of the transportation and the lighting sections distributed all they had received and the dispute came to an end on January 5. Thus, the dispute was finally settled, but the intervention of the authorities was severe: forty-seven men were arrested at work and imprisoned. Of particular significance is the fact that this was the first tramway strike in the history of Japan.

With this brief account of the labor disputes, the review of the turbulent scenes of industrial relations in the Meiji era comes to an end. The national economy of Japan kept growing in the years after the Sino-Japanese War. The rapid pace of industrialization was further accelerated during and after the Russo-

Japanese War. Rise of trade-unionism was but a natural consequence, but obviously the authorities were not sufficiently awake to the need for trade-unions. They were not aware of the constructive functions that could be performed by workers' unions. The passage of the Public Peace Police Act in this period was symptomatic. As long as the government pursued repressive policies against normal trade-unions, working-class movements were but futile agitations.

Trials and Errors and More Errors

The workers' trade-union movement in the early stage was not devoid of intellectual leadership. Takano Fusataro, Jo Tsunetaro, and Katayama Sen were able and dedicated men. Katayama, particularly, was a Christian socialist with a practical idealism, but nonetheless the union movement in the latter period of Meiji and in the early years of Taisho continued to stumble about. They were continuing, apparently, to struggle with trial and error, without a clearly defined program of action. They were destined to do so till they succeeded in organizing national unions or federations.

When the Meiji era closed with the death of Emperor Meiji, and the new Taisho era commenced, voices were raised here and there seeking for a *Taishō Ishin*. People remembered how the great *Meiji Ishin* (Meiji Innovations) had stimulated the people and had brought new life to the nation. They wanted their country to undergo another *Ishin*. This spirit was shared by fairly large numbers of people and was reflected in the labor movement. In 1912, the first important trade-union, Yuai Kai (Friendly Love Society) was formed. Much space could be given to the work of this new union. Here mention will simply be made of the success which this new union had in helping the phonograph workers at Kawasaki, although this was exceptional, since business conditions had become unfavorable with the outbreak of World War I. Factories had to be closed down and workers discharged in the dislocation of industry brought about by the war. Many disputes arose as the workers tried to maintain the *status quo*, i.e., the conditions they had won previously. The war necessitated partial or total curtailment of production in textile mills, which occasioned mass dismissals of workers. The strikes in the first and second years of the war (1914–1915) ended mostly in defeat for the workers.

During the fall of the second year of the war (1915) the situation altered. Business began not only to pick up but to thrive in certain lines. It was then that the period of the *nouveau riche* began. New factories were established, and new unions were set up; new waves of strikes set in also, reaching an all-time high in 1919. A comparison of the following table of disputes for 1916–1918 with the previous one for 1897–1911 shows the phenomenal rise in the strike propensity of Japanese workers. The figures of dispute cases and participants in 1918 were seven times those in 1916.

TABLE 14

LABOR DISPUTES IN THE EARLY YEARS OF TAISHO (1916–1918)

Year	Cases	Number of Participants	Participants per case	Remarks
1916	108	8,413	78	3rd year of war
1917	398	57,309	144	4th year of war
1918	417	66,457	159	5th year of war

SOURCE: Kyocho Kai, *Saikin no Shakai Undo*, p. 323

There is statistical information available on the demands of the workers in these disputes which shows that almost 80 per cent of these disputes arose from the workers' demands for higher wages. Many of the strikes in 1916 ended with unfavorable results. There were more cases of compromise on the part of the workers. The comment of the Kyocho Kai report on this point is that the increase of compromise cases, slight as it was, might be taken as a sign of some progress on the part of the workers, as compared with a few years earlier. But, it continues to say, the unions in those years could hardly be said to have outgrown the stage of infancy, since most of the disputes lasted only one to three days. To put this in today's terms, the unions of those days were undergoing a stage of trial and error, perhaps with more error, owing to a lack of trained leadership.

Incidentally, we might note that the largest portions of the participants in the disputes in those years (1916–1918) were engineering and metal workers, followed by the stevedores and mining workers. Further, these were the industries or branches of industries that expanded most briskly under the stimulation of the war.

The story of this period of futile agitations is not complete without the mention of two incidents of an inglorious nature, recorded as the doings of the "socialists." One is the so-called "Red Flag Incident" and the other the "Great Treason Case" (*Dai Gyaku Jiken*). In narrating these incidents as the actions of the socialists, it is necessary to recall once more the stage of development of socialism and the socialist movement in Europe and America in those years. The socialists of the world were united in the Second International. This international movement had in its membership all shades and degrees of radicalism. Some were moderate reformists of the gradualist school; others were radical revolutionaries, advocating violent overthrow of existing bourgeois governments. The split between the moderate and the radical had not taken place, and would not until 1919, when Comintern (the Third International, 1919–1943) came into being. The young socialists in Japan were therefore exposed to the influences of socialist thought of many different colors.

The so-called "Red Flag Incident" was so "incidental" that the whole affair could be dismissed today as ludicrous.

On June 22, 1908, a public assembly was held at the public hall, Kinki Kan, in Kanda, Tokyo, to welcome the release from jail of Yamaguchi Gizo. The meeting adjourned without any incident. When the crowds streamed out of the hall to the street, several young men spread out two good-sized red banners, one of which had in big letters the words *Musei fu Shugi* (Anarchism) and the other the words *Musei fu Kyosan* (Anarchism-Communism). Police, in their attempt to wrest these banners from the youths, were drawn into a scuffle when the latter resisted. It was not the scuffling that surprised the public so much, but the punishments inflicted on the leading socialists arrested on this occasion. Yamakawa Hitoshi, Arahata Katsuzo, Osugi Sakae, Sakai Toshihiko, and others, ten in all, were sentenced to terms of imprisonment varying from one to two years. After this incident there were so many arrests and court trials that the socialist movement in Japan came to a standstill, as it were, for a considerable period.

The so-called "Great Treason Case" was not such a childish affair; it was more startling. There are varying accounts of this case, and it is still in dispute. The following is from Kyocho Kai's classic work:

In the summer of 1910, Kotoku Denjiro and 25 other people were arrested. This was the so-called Great Treason Case that startled the world. According to this statement of Mr. Koyama Matsukichi, currently Attorney General, then chief prosecutor responsible for the case, the case called "Kotoku Shusui [Denjiro]'s 'Great Treason'" started with a roundup on May 25, 1910, by the Matsumoto Police Office of Nagano prefecture. An operative by the name of Miyashita Takichi, employed at Meika Lumber Mill in the Obayashi Police District in Nagano prefecture, was discovered to be manufacturing and keeping bombs. Investigation revealed that he had a plot to throw a bomb at the Emperor's carriage at the Emperor's Review of the military maneuvers in the fall of that year. As the result of the trials of the Court, Kotoku Denjiro, Kanno Sugako [and others whose names are omitted here] were sentenced to death penalty. Sakamoto Seima [and eleven others] were sentenced to life imprisonment and two other men were sentenced to from 8 to 10 years of prison.

After this case, the control of the socialist movement became extremely severe, with the result that the socialist movement seemed completely crushed and gone from Japanese society.[3]

BIRTH OF YUAI KAI AND OTHER UNIONS

Yuai Kai and Suzuki Bunji, Its Founder

With the birth on August 1, 1912, of Yuai Kai, the history of the working-class movement in Japan entered a new stage.

Suzuki Bunji (1885–1946), founder and for many years president of this trade-union organization, who was referred to in the Japanese press occasionally as "Wa-sei Gompers" (Japan-made Gompers), was a pious Christian and deserved his nickname, which had been given him as a term of endearment or appreciation for his great pioneering work. Yuai Kai soon changed its name to Sodomei (or, more properly, Dai Nippon Rodo Kumiai Sodomei Yuai Kai), and it underwent vicissitudes of fortune, as did the Confédération Générale du Travail in France, the Deutscher Gewerkschafts Bund in Germany, and the American Federation of Labor in the United States. However, like those great national federations of trade-unions, the organization he founded remains to this day the mainstay of trade-union organizations, at least in a moral sense, even though, like the CGT in France, Sodomei currently happens not to be the biggest national federation in membership.

Because of the significant role played by Yuai Kai in the formation of the unions in Japan, due space will be given to the description of its birth and growth.

Suzuki Bunji graduated from the Literature Department of the then Tokyo Imperial University in 1910. For a short while he was employed by the Asahi Newspaper, but very soon he entered the Unitarian Church in Tokyo, as secretary to Dr. Clay Macauley, the Unitarian minister. Not much is recorded of the work of this Unitarian missionary, but he is credited with helping Suzuki in starting an evening lecture course in the church building for the workmen in the neighborhood. Meetings were held only one evening per month, but there was apparently sufficient interest manifested by those who attended the lecture meetings to warrant organizing these workers into a permanent body. The call for *Taishō Ishin* may have given Suzuki further stimulus for taking the step. At any rate, Suzuki started Yuai Kai, with a membership of fourteen men, comprising such humble workingmen as *tatami* makers and water sprinklers on the streets of Tokyo. One thing that characterized Yuai Kai at its start and gave it stability, strength, and even prestige, was the circumspection with which Suzuki conducted his organizing work.

Yuai Kai means, literally, "Friendly Love Society," a name suggested by the Friendly Society in England. Suzuki secured the support of such eminent scholars and prominent civic leaders as Kuwata Kumazo and Ogawa Shigejiro as advisers, and Horie Kiichi, Takano Iwasaburo, Takeda Yoshisaburo, Uchigasaki Saku-saburo, and Minami Ryo as councilors.

From the outset, Suzuki aimed at a moderate and stable organization. This aim is spelled out in the three articles of the platform of Yuai Kai. For this reason, the new organization was free from any socialist color. This was a precaution well worth taking in this period when socialism was suspected and hated by the government authorities and in respectable society, as communism is today in the Western nations.

The Platform of the Yuai Kai read as follows:

1. We will harmonize with one another and endeavor to attain the objective of mutual aid through unity and co-operation.
2. We will abide by the ideals of the public and endeavor to develop intelligent opinion, cultivate virtue, and make progress in technical arts.
3. We will depend on the power of co-operation and endeavor to improve our status through sound means.

One might read this and say that this sounded more like the pledge of a Sunday School club. No mention of the working-class interest, no suggestion of class consciousness, no indication of a struggle to achieve emancipation of the wage-earning masses.

Suzuki was an idealist and a Christian, but was not unaware of the urgent necessity for workers to rise in a body to attain the lofty aims urged by other belligerent leaders. He knew that his chosen course of action was the sure way.

The first local belonging to Yuai Kai was formed on the premises of Yuai Kai in the building of the Unitarian Church. It is significant that Yuai Kai remained in the same building for years, virtually occupying it after the church moved away until the whole building was destroyed by fire in the great earthquake of 1923. Moreover, when the headquarters of the organization was rebuilt after the earthquake, it was rebuilt on the same site. Incidentally, Sohyo occupies the building on that historical site. Perhaps it is proper to note this fact and for the Japanese trade-unions to give due recognition to the Unitarian Church for its bequest of the valuable estate.

In the following year, locals were set up in Kawasaki City, in eastern Tokyo, in Oyama City, in Hokkaido, and a year after it started, the membership of Yuai Kai reached 326. At headquarters were a savings department, legal advice, medical care, athletics and recreation, publication, and other offices. These new undertakings attracted the attention and interest of the workers.

The outbreak of the war caused temporary hardship for the small firms and the workers generally on account of the economic dislocation necessitated by the war. We have mentioned already the success achieved by Suzuki and Yuai Kai in intervening in some of the strikes. As a matter of fact, the war afforded unique opportunities for the expansion of Yuai Kai. Organizers were dispatched all over Japan and even to Manchuria where, as a result, locals were set up. But an opportunity which had never before come to a labor leader was presented when the war in Europe became a world war involving both Japan and the United States. Suzuki, in his capacity as president of Yuai Kai, was sent on a goodwill mission, accompanied by his faithful lieutenant, Yoshimatsu, to attend the Convention of the AF of L and the Conference of the California State Federation. This was in May, 1916. In September of the same year, on account of a growing complexity in the Japan–United States relationship, Suzuki was dispatched a second time to the United States, at which time he attended also the Convention of the International Seamen's Union, as well as the conference of the AF of L and the California State Federation.

During those visits Suzuki made the acquaintance of America's labor leaders, including Samuel Gompers himself. Gompers took special interest in this young, chubby labor leader of Japan, then 29 years of age, and apparently he was generous with his time, giving helpful guidance to the eager pupil from across the sea in matters of organization, financing, and administration of trade-unions. It was there that Suzuki saw and learned some of the techniques in working of modern craft unions. On his return from those two trips, Suzuki did much to reorganize and solidify his union. Departments of general affairs, accounts, publication and education, and so on, were set up at the headquarters in May, 1916. A women's department was added later. Good accounting was one of the strong points of the "business unionism" of the AF of L. Whether Gompers said so in so many words to Suzuki is not certain, but it is a good thing that his businesslike lieutenant, Yoshimatsu, accompanied Suzuki on the first trip and met Gompers and his staff. As compared with other unions, Yuai Kai had an unquestionably sound financial organization. Incidentally, Kotoku Denjiro, who met William Haywood and other leaders of the IWW, turned into a syndicalist revolutionary and was finally executed for his alleged leadership in the Great Treason. It is instructive to note how the workers' movements abroad influenced the movements in Japan.

Growth of Rival Unions

As we have already noted, both socialism and trade-unionism were Western institutions brought from overseas, not plants indigenous to the soil of Japan. This explains the dominant part played in this country by scholars and intellectuals who could read or had access to foreign-language materials, and also by those who had had the chance to go abroad. Because of this, the growth of trade-unions in Japan was different from that in the United States or England where craft unionism and, later, industrial unionism grew as natural consequences of the changing processes of industrialization. The ideas and practices of socialism and trade-unionism, which, in the West, grew gradually in response to the changing phases of mechanization or of industrialization, were brought into Japan pell-mell, particularly during the period under review.

To continue with the development of Yuai Kai, Suzuki, its founder, was an idealist of the Christian faith, whereas Kotoku, who also went to America, was an athiest and met Debs and Haywood instead of Samuel Gompers. On his return to Japan, Suzuki reorganized Yuai Kai after the AF of L model, while Kotoku busied himself in spreading or trying to spread the thought and action of revolutionary syndicalism or anarchism. Kotoku wrote in 1897, while still a young man of 30, a striking book entitled *Imperialism, the Spectre of the Twentieth Century,* also a forerunner in presenting Marxian socialism in Japan. We have already mentioned the punishment inflicted on him for translating in 1900, jointly with Sakai Toshihiko, the *Communist Manifesto.* His last work was written in prison in 1911, and published posthumously—after he was executed. It was entitled *An Essay to Blot Out Christ.* It is an irony of history that he himself was hung and blotted out, as it were.

On the other hand, Suzuki, an earnest and devoted reformer, continued his work of what might be called conservative unionism. He left one book entitled *Twenty Years of Labor Movement.* It gives a faithful account of the work of union organization that he pursued steadily and without fanfare—although in the early years of Yuai Kai or of Sodomei, he knew how to make the trade-union assemblies attractive to the rank and file with brass bands, union songs, and colorful union banners. In the early years of the ascendancy of the workers' movement, in the period of romanticism, this no doubt was even necessary.

From the first year of Taisho (1912) until the outbreak of the war in Europe there was nothing remarkable except for the rise to prominence of Yuai Kai. But, as the ravages of the war in Europe spread to other parts of the world, Japan was among those to feel the effects. Rising prices and living costs, spread of unrest among the working class, and the stimuli of the revolutionary outbreaks in Europe were bound to have their effect on the working-class movement in Japan. The first important tangible outcome of this situation was the printers' union called Shinyu Kai.

Shinyu Kai owes its origin to O-yu Kai (literally, European Letter Friends Society), first organized in 1907 by Japanese setters of type for European-language publications. The outbreak of the war in Europe meant a sudden drop in the number of subscribers to English and foreign-language papers, resulting in the discontinuation of publication of most of them. This naturally had a fatal effect on O-yu Kai. After remaining moribund for some time, the semidefunct union was revived by shock at the action of a number of printing firms in discharging the elderly printing workers who had long served them; the pretext for this action was the enforcement of the Factory Act of June 1, 1916. The members of the dying organization began the work of resuscitating it. The revived organization took a new name, Shin-yu Kai (Faithful Friends Society), and held its organizing assembly in April, 1917. Having learned from the wisdom of Yuai Kai, the platform adopted by the new organization was extremely simple and moderate, though it soon came under the influence of Osugi Sakae, the anarchist leader, and began to challenge the moderate program of Yuai Kai with its violent anarchist program. The organization published a monthly journal called *Shin-yu*.

The platform of Shin-yu Kai read as follows: "(1) Let us study techniques and raise our status. (2) Let us extend our welfare and raise our status. (3) Let us cultivate our character and raise our status."

Another organization, with a tendency different from either of the above two, was born in Osaka in May, 1916. Organizers of this body included almost exclusively such workers of the brawn as Domae Magosaburo, Sakamoto Kozaburo, Yokota Chiyokichi, Nishio Suyehiro, Hirai Eizo, and Tsutsumi Hyozo. The organization was named Shokko Kumiai Kisei Doshi Kai (Society for Formation of Factory Operatives). The platform of this new body, modeled after that of Yuai Kai, was also discreetly worded and read as follows: "(1) We factory operatives intend to form sound trade-unions to raise our status. (2) We desire to organize ideal factory operatives' unions and to solve labor problems in order to lay the basis for a wealthy nation with strong arms. (3) We factory operatives intend to cultivate the spirit of self-government, develop common sense, and improve our technical ability." The organization published the organ entitled *Kojo Seikatsu* (Factory Life). We might note that in its platform is an expression of national, rather than class, consciousness.

The membership of this new body spread in the major mills of Osaka, such as Kubota Iron Works, Sumitomo Steel Works, Osaka Electric Light Company, Osaka Arsenal, Osaka Iron Works, and Ujikawa Iron Works. Its membership kept increasing, but after a year it broke up because of internal difficulties. The significance of this short-lived union lay in that it had as its organizers men who were destined to play leading roles in the workers' movements in later years—Domae, Sakamoto, and

Nishio. It also attempted to settle disputes by mediation, and to provide stability of the worker's livelihood by organizing consumers' co-operatives. The organizers were ambitious, but whether their ambitions were warranted by the equipment of the organization was questionable.

Immaturity of the Working-Class Movement

If keenness or acuteness of class feeling or class consciousness means either progress or maturity of the workers concerned, then during the period from the Russo-Japanese War to World War I the workers of Japan were still immature. This was true, not only of farm workers, but equally of most industrial workers.

The influx of liberal and radical ideas from Western Europe and Russia greatly influenced the workers' movements in Japan after World War I. The comparatively few workers' trade-unions that were formed before World War I were in most cases weak, and without proper financial organization. The organizers, because of their lack of experience, had no confidence in themselves. There was a pernicious habit among the workers of "pulling the leg" of those leaders who had become famous or prominent. There was also jealousy among the leaders, with the result that one could seldom remain long in a position of responsibility. Rivalry of this sort resulted in depriving the movement of experienced and dependable leaders.

Among the agricultural workers, the difficulty was even more deeply rooted than in the case of the factory workers, because of the attachment of the poor tenants to the land they were cultivating. Most of their demands were presented to the landlord as supplications or entreaties. But, as it says in the Proverbs, "The poor useth entreaties; but the rich answereth roughly" (Prov. 28:23), and this was as true in Japan as it was in Judea. For ages past, the demands of the tenants had been for the most part addressed individually, seldom collectively. The tenants might unite on certain occasions, but they would disband immediately once their demands were granted.

The first tenants' union after the Meiji Restoration was organized in 1875 in the village of Yoki Mura, in Gifu Prefecture. The object of the union was to prevent internecine competition among the tenants. In the following year, the union formed in Shiwoe Mura in Kochi Prefecture was to guard permanency of the tenants' right to farm. The unions started during 1887–1893 in other villages in Gifu Prefecture had the dual objectives of preventing the raising of tenancy rates and of stopping competition among the tenants. The one formed in Kyoto Prefecture in 1888 aimed at improvements in agriculture, while the one organized in Nagasaki proclaimed that its purpose was to promote the common interests of landlord and tenant. In 1896, the union formed in Shimane Prefecture was to promote savings. This rough view of the objectives of the tenants' unions in the early period reveals that there was very little intention or inclination to engage in a collective struggle; instead, they were more interested in mutual aid, agricultural improvements, harmony between landlord and tenant, and prevention of competition among the peasants.

It will be recalled that the agricultural villages were the reservoir of manpower for the industrial expansion of Japan. The task falling on the shoulders of the leaders of the working-class movement was not an easy one, in view of the "immaturity" of the masses of workers.

DEVELOPMENT OF LABOR LAWS

Early Attempts to Protect Mining Labor

Labor laws in Japan today can be roughly divided into four classes: (1) laws for the protection of the workers from the ravages of industrialism, (2) laws to safeguard the workers' rights of organization, (3) laws concerning social security, and (4) laws for the administration of labor laws.

As in many other countries, the laws for the protection of labor developed first. Laws to guarantee the workers' rights to organize and to bargain collectively developed later; and then came the social security laws, though some phases of the social security laws are found in rudimentary form in the early laws for labor protection. The last-mentioned class of laws, for labor administration, usually accompany, as it did in Japan, the development of other labor laws.

First attempts for protection of labor in Japan were made in the early years of Meiji, particularly in the mining industry. In the fifth year of Meiji (1872), long before the Diet was established as the national legislature, the government issued the so-called *Kozan*

Kokoroe (Instructions on Mining). It was made clear therein that all minerals were owned by the state; individuals could engage in mining only by renting the land from the state. In the following year (1873), the Japanese Mining Law was promulgated, reaffirming state ownership of all mines, and restricting the mining right of individual mining agents to only fifteen years. This law remained in force for twenty years. As far as this law was concerned, the state was interested in affirming the state's right and not particularly that of the mining worker. A departure from this was made only in 1890 in *Kogyo Jorei* (Mining Regulations), by providing five articles concerning mines police and nine articles on protection of the mining workers, known as *Kōfu Hogo Kitei.* The protection stipulated in the regulations was of a primitive nature, rather inadequate as far as helping the workers was concerned. Revision of the defective regulations was urged for a long time; at last, in 1902, when the Mining Bill was presented by the government, it finally succeeded in passing both Houses. That was the Mining Act, finally promulgated in the spring of 1905.

Under this act the mineowner was obliged to make up regulations for employment of mining workers and secure approval of the authorities on these rules. The employers' liability to compensate the worker for illness or injury sustained in the course of performance of work, that is, workmen's compensation, was set forth clearly. This was the first ruling of this sort in Japan. Problems involved in workmen's compensation will be discussed in more detail later.

First Factory Legislation

The story of how the first factory law came to be enacted in this country is not only interesting but is morally instructive as well, since it shows how patience, persistence, and over thirty years of faithful work bore fruit.

In 1881, when the Department of Agriculture and Commerce was first set up—being responsible, among its many other functions, for the protection of workers—it started to investigate their needs to see how to go about the task of worker protection. After two years of study, the work of drafting the law began in 1883, and the draft of Factory Operatives' Regulations, consisting of forty-six articles, was completed in 1887. (There was another draft of Factory Apprentices' Regulations, consisting of thirty-one articles, but this was subsequently discarded.) These regulations were modeled after the *Gewerbe Ordnung* of Germany and of Austria and were quite advanced for Japan of that day. Four years later, in 1891, the government submitted this draft to the Chamber of Commerce, and in 1895 asked the prefectural governors for their opinion as to the opportuneness of enacting such a law. There were strong views that, because of the immaturity of the industries in Japan, enforcement of such a law would have a disastrous effect on the young and growing industries. Apparently, the government itself was inclined to the same opinion; that was perhaps one of the reasons the government made no haste about enacting the legislation.

In 1897, the newly created Industries Bureau in the Department of Agriculture and Commerce was charged with the work of preparing a new draft of the Factory Law. The draft was completed a year later and then submitted for opinions to local chambers of commerce. The latter suggested numerous revisions and at the same time urged the necessity of making a thorough on-the-spot investigation of factories and of factory operatives. In consequence of this recommendation, a Temporary Investigation Commission was set up, which in 1902 drafted an outline of the Factory Bill. A questionnaire concerning the proposed Factory Bill was prepared by this Commission and submitted to various quarters. On the basis of the Factory Bill of 1902, the government finally took the step in 1909 to complete the Government Bill, now consisting of twenty-three articles, for submission to the Diet.

In fairness to the government, which could be criticized for acting slowly in promoting this legislation, it should be said that the men responsible for drafting the law were keenly conscious of the need for the law to be observed faithfully once it was promulgated. It was necessary to be sure that there was readiness on the part of the employers to abide by the provisions laid down. Before submitting the bill to the Diet for action, the government in October, 1909, circulated widely among the people concerned with industries and commerce a carefully written pamphlet entitled "Explanation of the Factory Bill." The government invited comments in order to secure understanding and support of men in responsible quarters. Among those who replied, the Central Hygiene Institute, interested in industrial hygiene, proposed that nightwork for young persons under sixteen and for women be prohibited within five years after the institution of the law. The Ministry of the Interior, which was now the government department responsible for labor administration in place of the Ministry of Agriculture and Commerce, acting on this suggestion, revised the provision of the Bill concerning nightwork of young persons and women, to make the prohibition enforceable ten years after the law came into effect. What the Hygiene Institute had intended to stress was obviously that nightwork should be prohibited not later than five years after promulgation of the law. The idea of a grace period of five years encouraged the government to stretch it to ten years. Here "the medicine proved more effective than the prescription intended."

Incidentally, in 1907, an organization of university professors and scholars interested especially in labor protection called the Shakai Seisaku Gakkai (Academy of Social Policies) was formed. The discussions that arose in the Academy inevitably had their repercussions on the thinking of the Diet members, newspaper writers, and civic-minded people. When the bill was presented in 1910, the Diet was a scene of interminable uproar and turmoil, its debates centering mostly on the question of nightwork. Apparently, in the opinion of those who opposed the proposed law, the idea of prohibiting nightwork for women and young persons in factories was "premature" for Japan. Japan's industrial growth was so dependent on the day- and night-work of those workers that the country could not afford to prohibit it—even ten years after promulgation of the law.

The government, however, would not give in. It had to withdraw the bill in February, 1911, but, determined to overcome the opposition, undertook to investigate the practical effects of nightwork in the spinning industry, and appointed a seventeen-man commission, with Shibusawa Eiichi as chairman, to inquire into the feasibility of abolition of nightwork. Shibusawa Eiichi, by the way, is remembered and revered universally as the man who perhaps did most to establish capitalism in Japan. For that reason a short description of the man and his work might be appropriate.

Shibusawa was born into a rich farmer family near Edo (now Tokyo) in Saitama Prefecture in 1840. Unlike most other men of samurai rank, who contributed to the overthrow of the Shogunate and the establishment of modern Japan, when the question arose of the opening of Japan to foreign trade, he was opposed to the whole idea. He fought for the maintenance of the Shogunate and of its isolationist policy. He even took part in a plot to burn out the foreign settlement in Yokohama, which, fortunately, was not carried out. He was raised to the rank of samurai, and the year before the Meiji Restoration (1868), accompanying the younger brother of Tokugawa Yoshinobu, the last shogun, he went to France to study conditions in that country. Brief as was his stay in France, Shibusawa learned a lot. On his return, he borrowed from the government half a million yen in paper money and established the first stock company in Japan. Employed in the Finance Ministry, he first headed the Taxation Bureau. He was raised to a position of high responsibility in the Finance Ministry; however, disagreeing with the growing military strength and opposed to the heavy state expenditure for arms, Shibusawa tendered his resignation. Thus he ceased to be a government official, but few people have done as much as he to lay the foundations for Japan's growth as a modern capitalist state. He was responsible for the foundation of the First National Bank, the Oji Paper Mill, the Osaka Spinning Company, the manufacture of fertilizers, the spread of the use of gas, and so on. At least 500 companies in major industrial, financial, and other enterprises owe their origin to the industry, ingenuity, and inspiration of Shibusawa. Later in life, his interests spread to the areas of education, social work, and international understanding. He was responsible for the founding of the Government University of Commerce (now Hitotsubashi University), and the Old People's Asylum. Shibusawa took an interest in Suzuki Bunji, the young labor leader who founded Yuai Kai. It is probable that Suzuki received financial aid from Shibusawa for his two trips to the United States in 1914. In his later years, Shibusawa was raised to the peerage for his meritorious services to the state, and was "Viscount" Shibusawa when he died in 1931.

As mentioned above, it was Shibusawa who was appointed chairman of the commission to deal with the baffling question of the prohibition of nightwork for women and young persons in the textile mills. The original proposal was to prohibit the nightwork after ten years. Shibusawa was not against it, but the revised bill called for it to be prohibited after fifteen years. The bill, so revised in accordance with the recommendations of Shibusawa's commission, was presented to the Diet on February 2, 1911. It passed the two Houses without any opposition or amendment. On March 28, 1911, all legislative formalities were completed, and after thirty years of travail, the first Factory Act of Japan was born.

Content and Problems of the First Factory Act

While this is not the place to enter into matters of historical detail that are of purely academic interest, nevertheless, there are matters of importance which must be raised in any case.

Scope of application.   The Factory Act of 1911 was to apply to workplaces normally employing fifteen or more operatives, as well as to workplaces where the nature of work was either dangerous or injurious to health. This would limit the application of the law to only a small percentage of factories and workers. The question arises as to why it could not be applied more widely, if not to all workplaces.

Workers affected.   Not only would the above-mentioned provision delimit the scope of application, but it effectively deprived adult male workers of any protection. This becomes clear when the coverage of the Act is examined. Why should male workers be deprived of the benefit of legal protection?

Coverage of the Act.   One of the principal items covered by this Act was the maximum working hours for persons under the age of fifteen and of women, which were limited to twelve hours per day. Another important item was nightwork for persons under fifteen and women. Night was defined as the hours between 10 P.M. and 4 A.M. (subject to the proviso that these hours could be shifted to 11 P.M. and 5 A.M. with special permission). As a matter of fact, in addition to the grace period of fifteen years on the enforcement of these provisions, there were so many exceptions that the result was that the prohibition of nightwork was not being enforced at all in Japan. How this was changed as the result of the ILO Convention of 1919 as it applied to Japan will be explained later.

There was no provision for weekly rest for any worker, except that women and workers under sixteen were to be given "at least two days of rest per month." Only if they were working two shifts, night and day, were they to be given at least four days of rest per month. Here again there was a grace period on enforcement: in the case of factories, enforcement was to start in 1929; in case of mines, in 1933. In other words, until those dates there was no weekly rest at all, even for women and those under sixteen.

As already stated, there was a provision for workmen's compensation inserted in this law, which was certainly a definite improvement, although there had existed in Japan the old tradition of paternalism. Under that tradition, in the absence of any legal compulsion, the worker would receive from his or her employer certain special allowances in case of death, illness, or injury sustained in the course of his or her work. With the sudden increase in the numbers of employed personnel, accompanied by a proportionate increase in accidents and illnesses, the need for definite legal provision for workmen's compensation was generally recognized. The subject of workmen's compensation will be discussed in detail later.

Another interesting feature of this new law was the provision for a factory inspection system. No law serves its purpose unless it is observed, and observance of the law presupposes an efficient system of factory inspection. As for the Factory Act of 1911, it must be admitted that, although the idea was excellent, the adequacy of the inspection left much to be desired. For one thing, there were never enough inspectors to go around.

Furthermore, preparations for its enforcement took time. The outbreak of World War I prevented the government from putting it into immediate operation. It was only in August, 1916, that the Imperial Ordinance for the Administration of the Factory Act was promulgated; the Act finally came into force on September 1, 1916, in the midst of a war in which Japan was involved. Perhaps, however, the Japanese government deserves commendation for its courage in bringing the Act into force, rather than criticism for the deficiencies in this new and important legislation.

CHAPTER IV

From World War I
to World War II (1939–1945)

ADVENT OF THE ILO AND ITS IMPACT ON JAPAN

Part Played by Labor in Creating the ILO

The significant part played by labor in creating the ILO is an interesting and even exciting story when told in full in its proper setting. This, however, is no place to attempt it. Authoritative accounts are found in the volumes issued by the Carnegie Foundation for International Peace as well as in the works of independent scholars, some of which have already become classics in the field.[1] We must confine our remarks here to matters which have a bearing on Japan either directly or indirectly.

The ILO today is an independent international organization working closely with, but not under, the United Nations. It is known as one of the so-called "specialized agencies" of the United Nations, but it is not a part of that political world organization. When the ILO was created it was different; it was created by the Treaty of Versailles as a definite part of the League of Nations. It is true that the First General Conference of the International Labor Organization was held in November, 1919, at Washington, D.C., whereas the League of Nations did not come into existence legally till January 10, 1920. This was simply because a sufficient number of ratifications of the Treaty of Versailles had not been registered in November, 1919, when the ILO's first conference, scheduled long before, met. In fact, the *de jure* birth of the League of Nations was merely a matter of formality. Its *de facto* birth, as it were, had not been questioned by any authority, so that it did not matter that the League of Nations had not come officially into existence when the ILO held its first important General Conference. The ILO has existed since 1919, functioning steadily with authority and with increasing prestige. How labor helped create this organization and the part played by labor in founding this world organ to defend and promote workers' rights will be discussed next.

In summary fashion, the contributions made by three major sources will be recalled: the First and Second Internationals, the International Association for Labor Legislation, and the workers' movements in Great Britain, France, and the United States.

First to be recalled is the historic meeting held in 1866 at Geneva, Switzerland, by the International Workingmen's Association (the First International), at which resolutions were adopted demanding the limitation of hours of work, the prohibition of employment of young persons nine to thirteen years old, prohibition of nightwork for women, the prohibition of work processes injurious to health, and, particularly, demanding that governments adopt laws for protection of labor on an international basis.

This association, known more popularly as the "First International," was called together by Karl Marx and others who were largely men with extremely radical or revolutionary ideas. Because of the ideological conflict between Marx and Michael Bakunin, and a lack of businesslike organization, it died out without accomplishing much beyond the pronouncement of lofty and often impractical thoughts, but the resolutions adopted at the Geneva meeting furnished what proved to be the standards of labor legislation and of the aims of organized labor for the leaders of the labor movement and for the more progressive governments in the following decades. It has to be admitted that the ILO benefited much, although not directly, from the inspiration which these resolutions supplied. Needless to say, both the First and Second Internationals had discussions and adopted resolutions on labor legislation that were later brought to the attention of the various governments.

In connection with the activity of the International Association for Labor Legislation, the international conference held in Brussels in 1897 must be recalled. This was a sequel to a rather spectacular conference called in Berlin by Kaiser Wilhelm II, and in which Chancellor Bismarck played a role. The representatives of fourteen countries of Europe participated in the conference and passed a series of resolutions, expressing desires for proper protection of labor. The Brussels conference of 1897 was a follow-up, so to speak, of the Berlin conference. One action of historic significance taken at Brussels was the decision to establish the International Association for Labor Legislation. This association was formally established in 1900 at a meeting held in Paris, a meeting attended by representatives not only from Europe but from Australia, Mexico, and the United States. It is this association that, among its various other activities, adopted in 1905 at Bern a resolution concerning the prohibition of the use of yellow phosphorus in the manufacture of matches and another on the prohibition of nightwork for women. In the following year, 1906, a conference of diplomatic representatives met to sign international conventions with binding power, one on the prohibition of yellow phosphorus matches and the other on nightwork for women. The procedure devised by this Association of adopting international labor conventions was later taken over by the ILO. From this incident, one might say that the International Association for Labor Legislation was the "prototype" for the ILO.

To complete the record, it might be added here that in 1913 another conference was held at Bern by the International Association for Labor Legislation, which adopted two resolutions, one on the prohibition of nightwork for young persons and the other on the limitation of working hours for women and young persons to ten hours per day. The thought was to turn these resolutions into international conventions with binding power at a diplomatic meeting in the following year (1914) as had been done with other resolutions at the meeting in 1906. Because of the outbreak of war, the diplomatic meeting did not take place. The work of this Association, however, was later brought to fruition by the ILO, which adopted international conventions dealing with these two subjects.

Precisely speaking, the work of the First and Second Internationals and the work done by the International Association for Labor Legislation, might be called, in either case, "work *for* labor" rather than "work *by* labor," since it was mostly, though not exclusively, the work of the intellectuals, some of whom had never been manual workers. With the exception of a few outstanding leaders, particularly in the earlier years, the workers themselves were inarticulate. But we now come to the third group, the working-class movements. A great many workers' movements were involved; only the more outstanding ones will be cited here.

During World War I, the part played by labor or laborers was bigger and more significant than in any previous war. The governments recognized it; the workers were conscious of it, too. Numerically, it is estimated that of the 30,000,000 men who participated in the war, a large majority belonged to the working class. It will be recalled that for centuries wars had been fought only by professional warriors or mercenaries. The awareness on the part of the workers of the sacrifices borne by them in the war was indeed an important factor in the evolution of events during and after World War I.

The first important incident recorded in this connection is the AF of L Convention held in Philadelphia in 1914. The Convention adopted a resolution which read in part:

> ...in view of the general Peace Congress which will no doubt be held at the close of the war, for the purpose of adjusting claims and differences, [the AF of L] holds itself in readiness and authorizes the Executive Council to call a meeting of representatives of organized labor of the different nations to meet at the same time and place to the end that suggestions may be made and such action taken as shall be helpful in restoring fraternal relations, protecting the interests of the toilers and thereby assisting in laying foundations for a more lasting peace.

The text of this resolution was sent to the headquarters of the International Federation of Trade Unions at Amsterdam, to the national centers of trade-unions in many countries, and to the president of the United States.

The next labor action to be noted was the International Labor Conference held at Leeds, England, as the result of the Paris meeting of the labor delegates from Britain, France, Italy, and Belgium. The resolution adopted at the Leeds conference contained in the preamble the following significant declaration:

> The conference declares that the peace treaty which will terminate the present war and will give to the nations political and economic independence should also insure to the working class of all countries a minimum of guarantees of a moral as well as of a material kind concerning the right of coalition, emigration, social insurance, hours of labor, hygiene, and protection of labor, in order to secure them against the attacks of international capitalistic competition.

In the voluminous body of the resolution was a suggestion that an international commission be established for the purpose of supervising the application of the laws of labor protection. The resolution also suggested the establishment of an International Labor Office for co-ordination and consolidation of various studies and inquiries.

Switzerland, because of her neutrality, was a more favorable location for international conferences during the war than was any belligerent nation. In October, 1917, under the auspices of the Swiss Labor Union, an international labor conference was held at Bern. Delegates came from Germany, Austria, Hungary, Bohemia, Bulgaria, Denmark, Norway, Sweden, the Netherlands, and Switzerland. Delegates from France and Britain were prevented from attending by the difficulty of obtaining passports. One significant result of this conference was a demand addressed to the governments of the belligerent nations that formal recognition be given in the forthcoming Peace Treaty to the International Association of Labor Legislation, in order to promote labor legislation and to ensure its enforcement.

The position taken by the AF of L at its annual convention at Buffalo in November, 1917, was a much bolder one than that of three years earlier. In a resolution adopted unanimously, the convention demanded two significant things: (1) the insertion in the Peace Treaty of provisions prohibiting the international trade in goods manufactured by workers under sixteen, the enforcing of the eight-hour day, and the prohibiting of forced labor, and (2) participation of the workers of each country in the Peace Conference. It is interesting to note that the British Labor Party also asked on several occasions that labor delegates should participate in the forthcoming Peace Conference.

As the outcome of these and other demands, the Paris Peace Conference at its Second Plenary Sitting, on January 25, 1919, decided to appoint a special commission to deal with questions of labor. By virtue of a resolution finally adopted after many modifications, the Commission for International Labor Legislation was created. The resolution ran as follows:

That a Commission, composed of two representatives apiece from the five Great Powers, and five representatives to be elected by the other Powers represented at the Peace Conference, be appointed to inquire into the conditions of employment from the international aspect, and to consider the international means necessary to secure common action on matters affecting conditions of employment and to recommend the form of a permanent agency to continue such inquiry in cooperation with and under the direction of the League of Nations.

It was the work of this commission which finally gave birth to the International Labor Organization. The work of the commission will be discussed further in the following pages.

Japan's Part in World War I and After

It does not require much study to see that World War I, in spite of its name, was essentially a European war, a war in which the major powers of Europe fought a life-and-death struggle caused by a series of cumulative maladjustments in international relations arising almost wholly among the people of Europe. Japan did enter the war early after its outbreak in Europe, and while her part was not an unimportant one, neither was it a decisive one. The sinking of the *Lusitania* and other desperate German actions finally drew the United States into the turmoil and turned it into a world war, but there was great reluctance on the part of America to become involved in a fracas among the old nations in faraway Europe. What then was the occasion for Japan's participation in this war?

It will be recalled that after the Sino-Japanese War, by the conclusion of the Shimonoseki Treaty, China ceded to Japan the Liaotung Peninsula along with the Island of Formosa and the Pescadores group of islands. Shortly after, Germany, Russia, and France interfered, declaring "that any holding of Manchurian territory by Japan would constitute a menace to Asia." Japan, after the strain of war, was not in a condition to resist the intervention of those powers. She relinquished Liaotung, accepting a small money indemnity in lieu of the land; but she was surprised to see within a short period of time that all three powers were leasing land from China at points of strategic importance. That was how Germany acquired a bridgehead at Kiaochow Bay. Germany also gained control of the Marshall Islands in the South Pacific. Whether those islands were of any economic value, on account of their products, is questionable, but their potential as a base for a far-flung action in the Pacific could not be contested. To safeguard her interests in those islands and in the Far East, Germany always maintained a fleet in the area, the size of which varied from time to time. But the size of the fleet was of secondary importance; Germany's main interest lay in maintaining footholds in this hemisphere. A late arrival in the arena of colonial expansion, Germany was being watched by other nations, and one must admit that her concern about her possessions in the Pacific was only legitimate.

Be that as it may, Britain and other powers in Europe which had been watching with anxiety the rise of the German Empire as a formidable naval power were keenly apprehensive about the possible ravages that might be caused by the German fleet among their territories and possessions scattered about the wide Pacific. Meanwhile they had their hands full in Europe, for the attack of the German forces was swift and terrible, both on land and at sea. They wished to ensure the safety of their possessions in the Pacific without diminishing their defenses in Europe. Britain turned to Japan. Japan rose to the challenge, took possession of the islands and also, of course, of Kiaochow Bay. Neither France nor Great Britain had to worry any more about the security of their colonies and possessions in the Pacific basin after the Japanese Navy swept away the German forces in this hemisphere. This was an achievement.

As for the sacrifices made or damages sustained by Japan in achieving this, statistical inquiries reveal an amazing—an ironical —fact.

During World War I, a total of 65,000,000 men were mobilized; 8,500,000 men were killed or died and an additional 21,000,000 men were wounded. Of this total, the twelve major powers mobilized a total of 42,188,810 men. The contingent that Japan contributed to this total was 800,000, while the United States, which did not enter the war until 1917, sent 4,355,000, and France, which stood through the four years of war, had 8,410,000 men. There were 300 Japanese lives lost. This was not a small sacrifice, but it will be recalled that the United States had 126,000 men killed and France 1,363,600. As for the wounded, Japan sustained 907 casualties as against 234,300 for the United States and 4,266,000 for France.

Statistically, one might say that the losses suffered by Japan were relatively small compared to the enormous sacrifices borne by the major belligerent nations in Europe, or the United States. Nevertheless, one must recognize the crucial fact that, had it not been for the prompt and effective action taken by Japan at the early stage, no one knows what course the war might have taken.

Fortunately the importance of Japan's action was recognized by the Allied Powers. When the Peace Conference met in Paris, Japan was accorded a role of no mean importance as one of the Principal Allied and Associated Powers, along with the United States, the British Empire, France, and Italy. How ably Japan played that role at the peace negotiations at Paris is an interesting story, but here we must confine our attention to the part played by Japan in matters relating to labor.

As already mentioned, the Paris Peace Conference appointed a special commission to deal with labor questions; called the "Commission for International Labor Legislation," it consisted of the following members:

United States: Mr. Samuel Gompers, President of the AF of L; The Hon. A. N. Hurley,[2] President of the American Shipping Board.

The British Empire: The Rt. Hon. G. N. Barnes, M.P., Member of the War Cabinet; Sir Malcolm Delevigne, Assistant Under-Secretary of State, Home Office.[3]

France: M. Colliard, Minister of Labor; M. Loucheur, Minister of Industrial Reconstruction.[4]

Italy: Baron Mayor des Planches, Commissioner-General for Emigration; Signor Cabrini, Deputy Vice-President of the Supreme Labor Council.

Japan: Mr. Otchiai Kentaro, Japanese Minister to Rome; Dr. Oka Minoru, former Director of Commercial and Industrial Affairs, Ministry of Agriculture and Commerce.

Belgium: M. Emil Vandervelde, Minister of Justice and of State; M. Ernst Mahaim, Professor at Liege University, Secretary of Belgian Section, International Association for Labor Legislation.

Cuba: Senor de Bustamente, Professor at Havana University.

Poland: Count Zoltowski, Member of the Polish National Committee.

Czechoslovakia: Mr. Benes, Minister for Foreign Affairs.

After the League of Nations was set up, in accordance with the provisions of the covenant of the League of Nations, Japan was accorded one of the five permanent seats on the Council. That position was held by Japan until she withdrew from the League in 1933. Though the aggressive maneuvers of the Japanese army in Manchuria led to the fateful incident of a war, as far as the representatives of Japan on the Council of the League of Nations were concerned, they performed their duties with integrity, dignity, and judgment, so that on many occasions they were called upon to mediate in much-entangled disputes. The nations of Europe had long-standing disputes involving complex economic, ethnic, and cultural questions which required unbiased judgment of persons without any previous alignments. Japan's part in some cases was of conspicuous importance.

How Suzuki Bunji Was Involved

The advent of the ILO had far-reaching effects on Japan: in the development of trade-unions, in the formation of public policies regarding labor, and in the evolution of labor laws. It might be said that in these respects there were few parallel cases among the member states of the ILO.

Suzuki Bunji's involvement in this makes a fascinating story. As already mentioned, Suzuki made two trips to the United States in the first year of the war. In those early years, only a few people could afford to travel abroad. Only government officials of high responsibility, wealthy and influential businessmen, and prominent scholars and publicists traveled to foreign countries; as a result, some glory was inevitably attached to foreign travel. Suzuki's trips were no exception. Moreover, in his case the trips were made in a new capacity—as a representative of organized labor. This is a point to be noted.

When the Japanese representatives to the Peace Conference arrived in Paris, headed by Prince Saionji and accompanied by Count Makino, Baron Chinda, and other venerable personages, they were surprised to learn that labor leaders were to participate in the work of the Conference. President Woodrow Wilson came, accompanied by Samuel Gompers, president of the AF of L. The British delegation included G. N. Barnes, M.P., who was a labor leader before the war, and a member of the war cabinet. Other delegations also included names of former labor leaders. When the question arose as to who, among those of the Japanese delegation, was to represent labor, the elder statesmen and other venerable representatives of Japan seemed completely taken by surprise; they asked the younger staff members whether Japan had any trade-unions and, if so, who would be the union leader who might be called to Paris to fill the role. A cabled inquiry went from Paris to the Foreign Office in Tokyo; officials there remembered the name of a young man who had traveled twice to the United States representing Yuai Kai. That was how Suzuki was sent to Paris.[5]

Suzuki went to Paris with great expectations, "prepared to promote the cause of the toiling masses," as he said. In Paris he was told to wait till he was called by the delegates; he waited in his hotel room patiently every day, but he was never called, and the Peace Conference came to a close. Apparently, the representatives of Japan at the Peace Conference were not interested in matters of labor protection. Nor, presumably, were they sufficiently informed on labor matters to make use of the young labor leader either for the good of the working class or for the advantage of the Japanese Empire.

Whatever the explanation of the total negligence of Suzuki by the representatives of the Japanese government at the Paris Peace Conference, Suzuki returned to Japan with full knowledge of the meaning of the ILO. He knew that in the Peace Treaty there was a chapter devoted to labor, which created a new organization, the ILO, a tripartite international organization. He knew that the first official conference of the ILO was to be held at Washington in October–November, 1919, and that all countries signatory to the Peace Treaty (including Japan) would be represented. And, above all, he knew that under the Peace Treaty each country must send three kinds of representatives—two representing the government, one representing employers, and one representing workers. The workers' representative must be chosen in agreement with the most representative workers' organizations in the country. In the case of Japan, Yuai Kai was precisely the organization that was qualified. Who should go to Washington to attend the first session of the International Labor Conference as the workers' delegate? Obviously Suzuki Bunji himself.

This was the reasoning Suzuki followed, quite correctly, with full and precise knowledge of the provisions dealing with labor (Part XIII) of the Treaty of Peace. On his way back from Paris, he passed through the United States, where he met Samuel Gompers and expressed the hope of meeting him at the forthcoming conference of the ILO in Washington. Back in Japan, he went around the country reporting at public gatherings on the meaning of the creation of the ILO—a dream dreamed by many leaders of the working-class movement for decades in the outside world, and by himself (since his visit to Paris) for the future of Japanese workers.

The Shock of the Washington Conference of 1919

The dream that Suzuki had for Japanese workers, after having been to the Paris Peace Conference, was that they should send a delegate of their own choosing to the world's tribune of labor, the International Labor Conference. It had to be a bona fide labor delegate, "chosen in agreement with the industrial organizations, if such organizations exist, that are most representative of employers or workpeople (as the case may be) in their respective countries" (Article 389 of the Labor Section of the Peace Treaty). Had the provision of the Peace Treaty cited here been strictly adhered to by the Japanese government, the outcome would have been the appointment of Suzuki Bunji as the workers' delegate from Japan at the first session of the International Labor Conference, since he was the president of Yuai Kai, and Yuai Kai was undoubtedly the "most representative" of the industrial organizations of workpeople of the day. However, the government did not choose to adhere strictly to the course laid down by the treaty, and the person finally chosen as the workers' delegate from Japan was not Suzuki, president of Yuai Kai, but another person, a highly paid chief engineer of the Kawasaki Dockyards by the name of Masumoto Uhei. Suzuki's dream was shattered.

Ironically, as we look back on that incident of more than forty years ago, we see that of all the actions taken by the government on labor, nothing so aroused the anger of the organized workers as this did. It served to stimulate their thinking and to unite and strengthen their union organization, contrary to the expectation and intention of the government. The government was not necessarily hostile to Yuai Kai, which at that time was a remarkably tame, moderate organization. But the government, as its representatives in Washington explained when the credentials of Masumoto Uhei were questioned by the credentials committee, as well as at the plenary session of the conference, did not consider it just or judicious to consult only the workers organized in trade-unions, who were still few in number and were in that sense not wholly representative of the total body of workers in the country. For that reason the government adopted a method of selection called *fuku-senkyo ho* (dual-election system). Workers organized in trade-unions were given an opportunity to express their opinion, but not exclusively, since on another occasion the government sought the advice of men who were considered experts in matters relating to industrial relations.

This procedure for the selection of the workers' delegate, which the leaders of organized workers criticized as a violation of the requirement of the Peace Treaty, was followed by the government, on the grounds that "the organized unions in Japan did not include more than 30,000 out of about 4,000,000 workers, and could not therefore be regarded as sufficiently representative of the workers of Japan."[6]

Furious protests arose in Tokyo, Osaka, and several other industrial centers against the action of the government, and unusual demonstrations were staged. For example, on the day that Masumoto Uhei was scheduled to embark on a steamer sailing to America from Yokohama, the demonstrators marched in a procession waving black flags and singing funeral songs. When it was discovered that the demonstrators were planning to duck Masumoto in the sea, he hid himself and embarked after dark.

Letters of protest were addressed by the workers' leaders in Japan to the president of the conference. Suzuki wrote to Samuel Gompers, appealing for help, pointing out that the man chosen by the government was but a dummy. These protests gave rise to a situation that was embarrassing to the government delegates as well as to the workers' delegate of Japan, not only at the meetings of the credentials committee, but in the plenary conference. At the plenary sittings of the conference, the Japanese delegates and the Belgian delegates had been sitting facing one another across a long table. Masumoto had introduced himself as the workers' delegate from Japan to Corneille Mertens, famous Belgian workers' delegate, and they had been greeting each other in a friendly way. But one morning Mertens arose and made an urgent motion to the effect that the workers' delegations at the conference noted the *absence of a properly chosen workers' delegate from Japan* and requested the conference to urge the Japanese government to allow free exercise of trade-union rights.

What a blow this was to the entire Japanese delegation can be understood fully when the implications and effects of such a motion are understood.

The motion was presented by Mertens, a widely recognized leader of the "Amsterdam International," i.e., the International Federation of Trade Unions, which had a predominant position at the Washington Conference because of its affiliations with the most powerful trade-union federations in each country. The wording of the motion presented by Mertens could be interpreted to mean that the workers' delegates at the conference representing the unions belonging to the Amsterdam International could vote against the admission of Masumoto, the "dummy" workers' delegate, since his credentials had been questioned.[7] According to the provisions of the Peace Treaty (Article 389), the conference might refuse admission of a delegate not appointed in accordance with the requirements of the Treaty (i.e., in agreement with the most representative of the industrial organizations of workers). Under the provisions of Article 390, if a country failed to appoint a workers' delegate, the other nongovernmental delegate (i.e., the employers' delegate) would "be allowed to sit and speak at the conference, but not to vote." Application of these provisions to the Japanese delegation would mean that in the event that the credentials of Masumoto were put to scrutiny at the conference and that he failed to obtain the two-thirds majority of favorable votes, not only would Masumoto be disqualified, but the employers' delegate, Muto Sanji, powerful president of the Kanegafuchi Spinning Company, would also be deprived of the right to vote. That would be a humiliation to the government of Japan as well as to the delegates concerned. This was indeed a shock.

Impact of the ILO on the Labor Movement in Japan

The shock was particularly staggering to Masumoto, since the motion was made by Mertens, with whom he had been frequently engaged in friendly conversation. Why was this motion, this overt move to question the credentials of the Japanese workers' delegate, raised by Mertens and not by Samuel Gompers himself, who, as the government delegates knew through the news from Tokyo, had been appealed to by Suzuki? The true circumstances were revealed afterwards. Gompers was willing to act in response to Suzuki, but the prospects of United States participation in the League of Nations (and in the work of the ILO which was part of the League of Nations under the Treaty of Versailles) was dubious, since the attitude of the U.S. Senate towards the question of ratification of the Peace Treaty was growing increasingly hostile. Hence, Gompers preferred to have someone other than himself take the responsibility. He attended the early part of the conference, but after participating in the discussion of the Hours Convention in a plenary sitting on November 5, he did not attend any further meetings. The choice of Mertens apparently was rather accidental. The task could have been assigned to any workers' delegate. The writer happens to know, however, that this choice—that is, of Mertens of Belgium to take the first official action to ensure the adoption by Japan of a more proper course in appointing a duly elected trade-union representative to the ILO—was most significant, since it served to arouse Mertens' interest in Japan and in the workers' leaders of Japan. He became later one of Suzuki's most trusted friends outside of Japan.

The effect of the shock of Mertens' motion was immediate, even dramatic, in the case of Masumoto. Masumoto was a man of broad understanding with a university education. He had written a booklet on labor problems, giving evidence of his sympathy with the working class. Though he commanded a high salary as chief engineer at Kawasaki Dockyards, he had earned public recognition as a person who might prove to be a fairly good spokesman for Japanese workers, and that was how he was chosen. But, should the conference disqualify him as the workers' delegate of Japan, it would ruin him. He would lose his standing in Japanese society. He must impress the conference with his strong sympathy with the downtrodden workers in Japan before the conference proceeded to vote on his credentials.

Thus, Masumoto, on November 27, delivered at the plenary sitting a speech that was startling to the government delegates and other patriotic Japanese people, who had expected him to behave in the restrained manner of a Japanese. At the Washington Conference, in front of each delegation was a small flag indicating the country that the delegation represented. In front of the Japanese delegation was a small flag of the Rising Sun. Masumoto asked the chair for permission to address the conference, and, when recognized, rose and, pointing to the flag of Japan, said:

Mr. President, ladies and gentlemen. Please look at this flag and imagine what the little island empire of Japan is. Believe me, this flag represents several million workers unjustly treated by autocracy, the enemy of social justice. Our principal aim at this assembly is to protect social justice, which is the spirit animating this labor conference. . . .

Ladies and gentlemen, can you imagine that under the cover of this flag there exists a police law aimed at interfering with workers' trade-unions? The Japanese autocrats pretend that this law is to maintain public peace and not to meddle with workers' unions. But that explanation gives to the law the role of a sword in the sheath, since it is an arm freely used whenever an opportunity arises for it.

You do not know what these Japanese autocrats might do. You are now going to place in their hands this dangerous arm of special treatment in industry. The helpless workers in Japanese industry are largely women, who number some 7,000,000. The majority of them are employed in textile mills. Perhaps you cannot believe that their life in the mills is a kind of slavery. It is no exaggeration to say that from a social viewpoint those factories are enjoying the extra-territoriality right which existed in Japan once upon a time. Justice has no access to these factories.

You know, ladies and gentlemen, that you can get rid of such a terrible state of things only by exposing it to light and wresting those privileges from the autocrats. This light is the spirit that animates this Conference, the aim of which is social justice and true democracy. I believe in your good judgment and leave the matter to your decision.[8]

How effective this speech of Masumoto's was in influencing the deliberations of the credentials committee or the final voting of the plenary conference cannot be assessed. In any case, the credentials committee, which consisted of Sir Malcolm Delevigne (government) as chairman, Jules Carlier as employers' representative, and Jan Oudegeest as workers' representative, as a tripartite committee, after careful examination of the situation obtaining in Japan, came to a unanimous conclusion that "no action was required in regard to the Japanese delegate." But, Mr. Audegeest, the workers' member of the committee, placed on record his view that "in the future, the labor delegate should be chosen in agreement with the trade-unions of Japan."[9]

The plenary conference, acting on the recommendation of the credentials committee, took no further action to scrutinize the qualifications of Masumoto, much to the relief of the government delegates of Japan and of Masumoto, himself, but also much to the disappointment of the leaders of the working-class movement in Japan.

Before closing this section of the story, it should be noted that Harold B. Butler, who was the secretary-general of the Washington Conference and who later became the director of the ILO, in connection with the incidents of the credentials of the Japanese workers' delegate and of the delegates of several countries put to scrutiny at the conference, had the following to say:

Thus, the Washington Conference began to form the jurisprudence of the organization in regard to the criteria which should be applied in nominating delegates under Article 389 of the Treaty, which has undoubtedly helped to render the Conference more representative, both of employers and workers, than it otherwise would have been, and thus substantially to strengthen the confidence which both have come to repose in it.

Impact of the ILO on the Government's Policy

The impact of the ILO on Japan has been far-reaching. In the preceding section, the impact of the ILO on Japan's labor movement only at the initial stage has been discussed. In this section will be discussed mainly how the government came to alter its basic labor policy under the impact of the ILO at this early stage.

The disappointment of the leading men in Japan, who were anxious to see the government adopt a more enlightened policy regarding trade-unions in the selection of the workers' delegate to the ILO Conference, was shared by quite a number of the men in the working-class movement. They were watching with keen concern to see how the Washington Conference would treat the "dummy" workers' delegate of Japan. When they learned that the conference decided to accept the credentials of Masumoto, being satisfied with the explanation offered by the government, they were furious, but fortunately they did not turn hostile to the ILO on this score. They concluded simply that the ILO was in need of more sufficient information on conditions in Japan. What happened in this connection at sessions of ILO conferences for several years afterward is instructive. The Japanese workers' representatives kept protesting against the method of selecting the workers' delegate, adopted by the government from year to year, till they were able to bring pressure to bear on the government and compel it to alter the policy.

The Second Session of the ILO Conference, held at Genoa, Italy, in 1920, was an exception in the sense that no question was raised concerning the qualification of the workers' delegate from Japan. It was a maritime conference, dealing with questions of the treatment of maritime and dock workers. Japan has had for years a tradition of close joint consultation and co-operation between shipowners and seamen. Consequently, the workers' delegate selected by the government to attend the Genoa Conference was the president of the Seamen's Union, and the method of selection followed by the government was in conformity with the requirement of the Peace Treaty. There was therefore no protest of any sort against the credentials of the workers' delegate at the 1920 Genoa Conference.

A serious and embarrassing situation arose at the 1921 Conference, which was an "agricultural conference," in that one of the main items on its agenda was on agricultural labor, whereas the 1919 Conference was an "industrial conference," and the 1920 Conference was a "maritime conference." The embarrassment was on the question of selection of the workers' delegate.

Did this conference, in dealing with agricultural labor, properly cover questions relating to tenant farmers? This was a question seriously debated from the outset, for, in those years, Japan had strong tenant farmers' unions and their questions had grown acute, whereas there were but few "agricultural workers" in the strict sense and no union of agricultural workers as such. Leaders of tenant farmers' movements were vociferous in claiming their right to be represented at the conference, but the government, after careful study, took the position that tenant farmers were entrepreneurs, not agricultural workers in the technical sense, and should therefore be excluded from the consideration of the workers' delegate at this conference. On this assumption, the government went ahead and appointed Matsumoto Keiichi, a quiet and dedicated person who had had education in agriculture, though he was actually engaged in social work as director of an orphanage.

The selection made by the government was interpreted by the critics as a wily trick on the part of the government to dodge the difficult questions of tenancy farming, on which the government had been accused of having no policy. A quiet man had obviously been chosen, since he would raise no question to embarrass the government at the conference. However, such an assumption proved false, for, when the conference opened, the quiet delegate rose and delivered a short but an amazing speech in Japanese. Matsumoto said that because he did not know enough English he was asking his adviser, Dr. Nasu Shiroshi, to speak for him. Nasu rose and declared in impeccable English that Matsumoto had come to Geneva fully realizing that the procedure followed by the Japanese government in appointing him was in violation of the Treaty. He had come, accepting the appointment, in order to lay bare the case before the world's tribune of labor. Nasu spoke further to the effect that Japan was contravening the requirement of Article 389 of the Peace Treaty when the government ignored the existence of a workers' organization that was already widely recognized as the most representative of the workers' organizations. If the conference overlooked an infringement of this sort, similar irregularities might occur in the future. The reason for raising the protest was not merely to promote the interests of Japanese workers, but to uphold the principles enunciated by the Treaty. Nasu concluded by stating that he believed the conference would endeavor to induce the government of Japan to reflect upon its attitude toward the working-class movement.

This was in effect a self-denial of the qualifications of the workers' delegate. How dismayed the government delegates of Japan were on hearing this speech can easily be imagined.

The credentials committee was strict but judicious. The chairman of the committee, in reporting on its findings pointed out to the conference the nonexistence in Japan of either a genuine farm workers' union or of a central national federation covering general workers, and the reasons the government felt compelled to take the steps it did on its own authority. The committee wished the situation would come to a point at which the Japanese government could conform entirely with the requirement of the Treaty. Leon Jouhaux, the workers' member on the committee, agreed to the addressing of a diplomatically framed recommendation to the Japanese government that it conform to the provisions of Article 389. In view of the controversy that arose as to the precise meaning of Article 389, the conference unanimously voted to request the Governing Body of the ILO to address a question to the Permanent Court of International Justice on the interpretation of Article 389.

Change in Method of Selecting Workers' Delegates

The incident at the 1921 conference was not the end, but rather the beginning, of the embarrassment of the Japanese government at the ILO Conference. Similar incidents were to occur at the Geneva conferences before a change in the government's policy toward trade-unionism took place.

The ILO Conference of 1922 had on its agenda two items: one on the procedures or rules of the Governing Body and of the conference and one on the collection of information relating to immigration and migration—apparently questions of no vital or immediate importance to labor, particularly since earlier sessions had dealt with more immediate questions of industrial, maritime, and agricultural labor. Nonetheless, in Japan there was considerable interest shown by the workers on the question of the workers' delegate.

As Japan had as yet no Ministry of Labor, the Foreign Office took the responsibility of selecting the workers' delegate. When the Foreign Office sent out circulars calling for caucuses to select the workers' delegate, Sodomei (formerly Yuai Kai) and several other workers' organizations announced their abstention, declaring that participation in any such procedure regarding the ILO was meaningless. After the caucuses were formed and final elections had begun, furious protests were again raised, and the authorities had difficulty in subduing the turmoil. The man finally chosen was Tazawa Yoshiharu, a famous leader of the youth movement. It was not a question of Tazawa personally; the difficulty lay in the procedure adopted by the government, which did not attach primary importance to trade-unions in the selection of the workers' delegate. Tazawa did not deny his own qualification as his predecessor had done, but he admitted the unsatisfactory situation obtaining in Japan. This time a protest was lodged at the conference by an outsider, Tanahashi Kotora, an active leader in Sodomei, who had come all the way from Japan to stage a protest in Geneva. Though an outsider—that is, though he did not belong to the delegation—Tanahashi was successful in maneuvering his protest in the lobby and around the conference. As a matter of fact, the credentials committee took note of the protest presented by Tanahashi on behalf of the organized workers of Japan to the extent that its substance was incorporated in the final report of the credentials committee. The committee did not recommend invalidation of Tazawa's credentials, but it tactfully indicated that there was urgent need for the Japanese government to recognize the full rights of the organized workers in the selection of the workers' delegate. The committee recognized the difficulty the Japanese government was experiencing in the present stage of development of Japanese trade-unions. It understood why the government felt the necessity of adopting the selection procedure it did. The committee could not conclude that the Japanese government had failed to abide by the provisions of Article 389. In the final part of the report, the committee stated emphatically that it believed that in future the Japanese government would not hesitate to adopt methods that would promote a free development of trade-unions or to appoint the workers' delegate in complete compliance with the requirement of the Peace Treaty.

The next ILO Conference, in 1923, was the last one at which the Japanese delegates were subjected to this embarrassing experience. The agenda of this conference comprised the general principles of factory inspection. The government, following its established tradition, as it were, adopted an elaborate procedure for the selection of the workers' delegate.

The Cabinet of Ministers decided on the procedure at one of its regular meetings in July. Factories, mines, and transportation enterprises employing 1,000 or more workers, as well as trade-unions with 1,000 or more members, were invited to elect candidates. The following list shows the number of votes assigned to each, on the basis of one vote per thousand members.

Sodomei 16	Chubu Workers' Federation 1
Engineering Workers Federation	Kojo Kai 1
(Kikai Rodo Kumiai Rengo Kai) 2	Nagoya Kojo Kai 1
Shibaura Electric Workers' Union	Rōdō Kumiai Dōshi Kai 2
(Shibaura Rodo Kumiai 2	Rōdō Kumiai Domei Kai 1
Yuzen Fabric Dyeing Workers 1	Jun Kojo Kai 1

The method proposed by the government was not agreeable to the organized workers. Sodomei addressed a protest to Albert Thomas, director of the ILO, pointing out that the principle of the Treaty of recognizing the organized workers was being violated. Meetings were held in Tokyo and Kobe to denounce the ILO itself for its failure to safeguard the basic principle of the ILO.

As the result of the election under the system described above, Uno Riyemon, a man active in labor education, was appointed as the workers' delegate. When Uno arrived in Geneva, he followed the example set by his predecessors of denying his own qualification as a bona fide workers' delegate from Japan. This act of the official workers' delegate (which Uno was) was supported by Hisatome Kozo, an eminent leader in Sodomei, who had come to Geneva to lodge a protest on behalf of the organized workers of Japan. By this time the conference had become "accustomed" to these protests, so the incident did not create the dramatic effect it had at earlier sessions; but as far as the authorities of the ILO or of the conference were concerned, the recurrence of such incidents could hardly be endured indefinitely. The report of the credentials committee handling the case did not propose rejection of the Japanese workers' delegate, but in stern and unmistakable terms said that if the workers' delegate chosen by the Japanese government came to Geneva the next year under the same conditions as heretofore, the credentials committee, though elected afresh each year and its membership therefore different, would be obliged to recommend rejection of the delegate. Since 1919, when the qualification of Japan's workers' delegate was first questioned, five years had now elapsed. The protests on the grounds of violation of the treaty provision had, instead of diminishing, mounted year by year, and it seemed that the indulgent attitude of the conference toward the Japanese government was damaging the prestige of the ILO among the workers of Japan. The time for change had come.

Fortunately, at the 1923 ILO Conference, the government of Japan was represented by Dr. Adatci[10] Mineichiro, Japanese Ambassador to Belgium, an eminent lawyer, who later became a judge of the Permanent Court of International Justice, and Mayeda Tamon, formerly Vice-Mayor of Tokyo, a man widely revered for his integrity. These two men submitted to the Prime Minister of Japan, after the conference, a forthright representation which had a most decisive effect on the labor policy of the government. The document explained that a sentiment had developed at the International Labor Conference that Japan could not afford to ignore. It was time the government of Japan abandoned its long-standing wariness toward organized labor. The government was urged to adopt a method whereby the selection of the workers' delegate to the next conference would be made by agreement with the workers' organizations, as required by the Treaty of Peace— the only method that would remove all grievances and causes of remonstrance by the workers, and would maintain the honor and prestige of Japan at the international assembly. The motives of these men were lofty; the reasons put forward were indisputable, the effect compelling.

Consequently, in the following year, 1924, the method adopted by the government for selecting the workers' delegate was in complete conformity with the provisions of Article 389, and the man appointed by the government was Suzuki Bunji, president of Sodomei, the most representative of the workers' organizations in Japan. The same legal method was continued in the following years, and thereafter the question of the qualification of the workers' delegate never again arose at ILO conferences.

On the surface, what was involved was the method of selecting the workers' delegate, but the implications of this change were deeper. In adopting the method of permitting only organized workers to select the workers' delegate, the government was granting the right exclusively to workers organized in trade-unions. The effect of this change in the government's policy towards organized labor was tremendous.

So far we have traced the effects of the advent of the ILO on the labor movement and on the government's attitude toward organized labor. The impact of the ILO was seen in the important fields of labor administration and labor legislation as well. Space will be devoted to that matter in later sections.

METAMORPHOSIS OF YUAI KAI AND GENERAL WORKERS' MOVEMENT: MORE INFLUENCES OF THE ILO

Metamorphosis of Yuai Kai

As mentioned earlier, when Yuai Kai was started in 1912, its founder, Suzuki Bunji, was most circumspect, and the organization itself was characterized by moderation. Because of the severe policy of repression that the government was pursuing in those days, because Japan was fast turning into a police state, both wisdom and necessity dictated that Yuai Kai appear as a tame and harmless body. But it was not long before Yuai Kai began to assume a different form and attitude.

"Shy, like an innocent lass, at the start; fast, like a run-away rabbit, at the end"—this old Chinese expression aptly describes the changes that were taking place in the behavior as well as the thinking of Yuai Kai during the last year of the war and for several years thereafter. These changes were bound to exert an influence on the hundreds of new workers' organizations that during this period were sprouting "like mushrooms after rain." The word "metamorphosis," a biological term, appropriately describes Yuai Kai of this period, denoting, as it does, "a marked change in the form or structure of a living body, resulting from development; specifically the alterations which an animal undergoes after its exclusion from the egg and which alter extensively the general form and life of the individual."

The main change, in a word, was the hardening of Yuai Kai, which meant the abandonment of the old principle of harmony between capital and labor, and the adoption of the class-struggle principle in its stead. A series of factors brought about this change, the chief one being the growing discontent among the younger leaders of Yuai Kai with the "lukewarmness" of Suzuki. There was a growing desire among the young and aggressive men to turn Yuai Kai into a powerful fighting body. Their desire came to a head when Tanahashi Kotora, mentioned earlier, and Aso Hisashi, both young idealists recently graduated from the Tokyo Imperial University, joined Yuai Kai. This was in 1919, the year that the ILO was scheduled to hold the first session of the International Labor Conference.

At the annual convention of Yuai Kai, held August 31 to September 2, three decisions were made that were to have important consequences:

1. To change the "locals" and have them belong to the new craft or industrial unions that were in the early process of formation. Yuai Kai itself was, strictly speaking, a "local" in the wide sense. By the proposed change, the Yuai Kai would become a national center for the craft and industrial unions in the country.

2. To prefix to the simple name of Yuai Kai, the grandiose title: Dai Nippon Rodo Sodomei (Great Japan Trade-Union Federation). The leaders were beginning to feel the need of clarifying the identity of this body as a Japanese federation, anticipating the time when the Japanese workers would play their part in the international community of workers.

3. To discontinue the autocracy of the president and to adopt a system of parliamentary deliberation among the councilors.

The declaration that the convention adopted, being something novel in Japan, attracted public interest. It read in part:

Workingmen are people with personalities. They are not to be bought and sold with the wages of the labor market. They must win the freedom of unionization . . . therefore, we producers declare now as follows: We are not machines. In order to ensure the development of individual character and a society of human beings, we demand an organization of society in which the producers can attain perfect culture, stability of livelihood and the right to control our environment.

The convention adopted further the following twenty items as the aims of this organization: (1) the contention that labor is not an article of commerce; (2) freedom of trade-unionism; (3) abolition of child labor; (4) establishment of a minimum wage; (5) equal pay for equal work of male and female workers; (6) Sunday holiday (weekly rest); (7) eight-hour day and forty-eight hour week; (8) prohibition of nightwork; (9) appointment of women inspectors of labor; (10) institution of workmen's insurance; (11) promulgation of a labor arbitration law; (12) prevention of unemployment; (13) equal treatment for national and foreign workers; (14) public management and improvement of workers' housing; (15) establishment of a workmen's compensation system; (16) improvement of home work; (17) abolition of indentured labor; (18) institution of general suffrage; (19) amendment of the Public Peace Police Act; and (20) democratization of the educational system.

In the limited space of this study, all the proclamations and demands of the workers' unions cannot be discussed. These demands of Yuai Kai are cited to show the general mood of the workers. Yuai Kai was being transformed from a tame organization, content with the idea of *ro-shi kyocho* (harmonization of capital and labor), into a belligerent organization.

The failure of the government to send a bona fide workers' delegate to the International Labor Conference and the dispatch, instead, of a "dummy" to Washington served to drive Yuai Kai from the right to the left. Though Suzuki himself was not in that desperate mood, the younger leaders who, recently graduated from the university, had joined the ranks were vociferous in denouncing the government, and the ILO too, when they learned that Masumoto was accepted at Washington as the official delegate representing the workers of Japan.

The danger was foreseen at this time that the discontent among the workers might sweep the unions and that flamboyant syndicalist thought might take over the trade-union movement altogether. It was at this juncture that Tanahashi Kotora, general secretary of the Tokyo Federation of Sodomei, published a trenchant and forceful article in *Rodo* (Labor), the organ of Sodomei, in January, 1921. It was entitled "Return to Trade-Union."

The article was a sharp criticism of what he thought was a shallow and naive concept of the syndicalists, who were teaching "direct action." "Does direct action mean squabbling with the policemen and being held in detention overnight?" he asked. "Does it mean marching on boulevards singing revolutionary songs? With a direct action of that sort can you upset a single capitalist's automobile, not to mention start a revolution? It is not mere craziness to rely on such feeble direct action and abandon the important trade-union of workers—the organization of workers?"

The article recalled how the organized workers of Britain threatened a general strike when the British government was about to give aid to Poland in a Russo-Polish war, and how the British government gave up the idea of aiding Poland. In order for the unions to be effective in their direct action, the unions must be strongly organized. That is the first prerequisite. The article concluded by saying: "The capitalists and the potentates fear much more the quiet hundred men solidly organized than they do a single courageous worker scuffling with the policemen. Working-men, return to trade-unions, your kingdom is there." Naturally, the article was applauded by the sober trade-unionists, but was scoffed at by such syndicalist leaders as Osugi.

As will be shown later, there were factors other than anarchosyndicalism that contributed to the metamorphosis of Yuai Kai.

Rise of Syndicalism and the First May Day in Japan

In order to grasp the full significance of the rise of syndicalism in Japan in this period, one has to know the political and economic background. The kind of syndicalism that reached its peak around 1920 was better known elsewhere as "anarchosyndicalism," and its leader was Osugi Sakae.

Japan in World War I was on the "right side," as it is popularly called, that is, on the side of the Allies, who won the war. The economic depression that follows any war did not reach its full force until 1920. Hara Takashi, the powerful leader of Seiyu Kai, the conservative party, became premier in 1920. This meant a crushing defeat for the more liberal Kensei Kai and Kokumin To. Hara was a man who would and did oppose general suffrage "because it undermines the stability of class system and menaces the modern social organization." With Hara in the saddle as premier, the government was formulating plans to tide over the depression that had set in. There was not much room for the development of sound and free trade-unionism. The "direct action" which syndicalism advocated had more appeal to the workers under these conditions, and it is in this connection that the name of Osugi will be remembered.

Osugi Sakae was born in 1885, in Kagawa Prefecture, to the family of an army officer. He was sent to a military cadet school, since his father wanted him to become an army officer like himself, but the boy disliked it and withdrew. Of his own volition, he enrolled in the French department of the Foreign Language School, and here learned about French syndicalism, which stirred the blood of this high-spirited youth. He formed a close friendship with Kotoku, the anarchist, and joined the editorial board of *Heimin Shimbun*, referred to earlier. Because of his unrestrained radicalism, Osugi was imprisoned repeatedly. In 1914, jointly with Arahata Katsuzo, he began to issue *Kindai Shiso* (Modern Ideas). After the Bolshevik Revolution, Osugi became the leader of anarchosyndicalist thought in the controversies that spread in Japan. In 1922, Osugi succeeded in slipping out of Japan in order to attend the international anarchist congress in Berlin. With a good command of French, Osugi participated in the May Day demonstration in Paris, but was arrested while addressing the crowds and was deported to Japan. On September 16, 1923, during the historic earthquake, Osugi was assassinated along with his wife and their adopted child, by a captain of the gendarmerie. Thus his life ended, but through his writings Osugi has left a lasting influence that cannot be effaced by his assassination.

In this connection should be mentioned the first May Day demonstration staged in Japan, in 1920.[11] It was the Second International, founded in 1889, that started the May Day demonstrations by workers' movements throughout the world. The first May Day demonstration in Japan celebrated the birth of Rōdō Kumiai Domei Kai (the Trade-Union Alliance), comprising the following nine unions:

1. Yuai Kai.
2. Shinyu Kai.
3. Seishin Kai, a union of newspaper workers of 15 newspaper firms in Tokyo.
4. Kōjin Kai, a union of operatives at Tsukiji Naval Arsenal, organized in 1919, with about 1,000 members, whose objective was "not to be spoiled by the new ideas of the day but to study how to raise efficiency and to contribute to a healthy growth of workers."
5. Nippon Kotsu Rodo Kumiai (Japan Transit Workers' Union), founded in 1919 by the tramway drivers and conductors of Tokyo City tramways. The platform of this union was more or less typical of the new unions formed in this period. It said: (1) "We will proclaim the dignity of workers' livelihood through the power of organization and by moderate and upright means.

... We will arouse the spirit of mutual aid and practical brotherly love."

6. Han-ro Kai, organized in January 1920, and drawing its membership from workers at Tokyo Arsenal, Tokyo Gas and Electricity Co., National Railway Department workshops, etc. It mentioned as aims of the union such concrete measures as the setting up of official minimum wages, workers' insurance, an old-age annuity system, profit sharing, and so on.

7. Kei Mei Kai, an organization of primary schoolteachers, organized in February, 1920. At this initial stage, it was more an educational society than a trade-union in the strict sense, because it aimed at "introducing a new civilization, having as members serious-minded men engaged in educational activities."

8. Daishin Kai, an organization of printers engaged at the big publishing house, Hakubun Kan, in Tokyo.

9. Koyu Kai, an organization of factory operatives at the Tokyo Arsenal and in privately managed workshops.

Amusingly enough, the first May Day in the labor history of Japan was not held on May 1, but on May 2, a Sunday. Yuai Kai and some fourteen or fifteen other unions assembled at Ueno Park, with a total attendance of more than 1,000 workers. This figure seems small today, when May Day demonstrations are participated in by half a million members in Tokyo, Osaka, and elsewhere, but it was an alarmingly large number in 1920. It was principally a lecture meeting. Before breaking up, a resolution was adopted, demanding the repeal of Article 17 of the Public Peace Police Act, the prevention of unemployment, and the enactment of a minimum-wage law.

Because very few people in Japan knew what May Day was, prior to this memorable celebration, a small pamphlet written by Shimonaka Keigaku, president of Heibon Sha Publishing Company, was distributed widely in the city. To the police authorities of those days, anything smacking of socialism was tantamount to treason. Shimonaka was fined 200 yen, a considerable sum in those days.

May Day of 1920, compared with those that followed, was a quiet and uneventful affair. By the following year, 1921, it had become a turbulent affair, owing to the newly begun conflict between bolshevism and anarchism. Since there was still some respect for Suzuki Bunji, no one attacked Suzuki squarely, but there were voices demanding "Suzuki's courageous retirement to the rear." Demonstrations were staged in 1921 in Tokyo, Osaka, Kobe, Yokohama, and at Ashio Copper Mines. The Tokyo gathering demanded immediate adoption of an eight-hour day, establishment of a minimum wage, and reform of the military conscription system; the Osaka gathering went even further, demanding the repeal of Article 17 of the Police Act, the right of collective bargaining, an eight-hour day and a minimum-wage system, and the workers' right to control industries.

Conflict between Syndicalism and Bolshevism

For some years after World War I, Japan was an arena of controversy between two conflicting ideologies: anarchosyndicalism, on the one hand, and Marxism, on the other. Although this is now history, the controversy that raged among the leaders of social or labor movements needs to be traced briefly, since it left a deep imprint on the thinking as well as the behavior of the leaders of the working-class movement in the following decades. As a matter of fact, Japan's leaders were rehearsing the heated debates between Marx and Bakunin and their followers at the meetings of the First International more than half a century before.

The ideology of democracy had begun to spread in Japan at the start of World War I as a result of the fact that Japan in that war had happened to side with the Allies. One might say that this was a fortuitous but meaningful happening. Then the success of the Bolshevik Revolution in Russia had a tremendous effect in Japan, giving rise to extreme movements in various quarters, because it gave hope to the workers who had been advocating revolutionary changes in society. The war had accelerated the pace of industrial expansion, which necessitated a sudden increase in the number of workers. Capitalists were prospering, but, with the rising prices of commodities and the shrinkage of real wages, the gap between the rich and the poor was growing more pronounced. In other words, the hostility of the workers against the capitalist war profiteers was growing more acute; and the disputes were spreading beyond the control of the government. The "rice riots" which broke out in 1918 were a manifestation of the unstable social situation. Those riots will be described later in more detail.

In these circumstances, the revival of the socialist and trade-union movements, which seemed to have petered out before the outbreak of the war, was only natural. The advent of the ILO, in particular, supplied the most powerful urge to trade-unionism—by virtually denying to the representative of bona fide trade-unions the opportunity to go to ILO conferences on the grounds of the smallness of their membership it served not to retard their growth but rather to drive them in the direction of radicalism. This was precisely the opposite of what the government had intended. It had not meant primarily to weaken the sound trade-unions, but that was the result.

One factor which added impetus to the radical movement was the postwar depression that set in during March, 1920, until which time the industries of Japan had been enjoying the ephemeral war boom. Panic hastened the closing down of numerous enterprises that had thrived on war needs. Small enterprises with slim capital outlay began collapsing, and unemployment spread all over the country. The workers were now obliged to take only defensive or negative tactics—opposition to the lowering of wages and to what was worse, the dismissal of workers en masse. The government in this situation was more prone to support the employers than the workers, and this led to waves of strikes or disputes, not for higher wages and better treatment, but against the curtailment of staffs and the reorganization of enterprises, both of which necessarily involved the wholesale discharge of workers.

In addition to economic factors, there were political factors that aggravated the critical situation. There was a surge of popular interest in general suffrage during the years 1919–1920, but Premier Hara, in February, 1920, dissolved the House of Representatives—an action that brought an end to the hope of general suffrage, at least for some years to come. Hara Takashi was the statesman who had once declared that general suffrage would undermine the solidity of the Japanese society, based as it was on class distinctions. One might therefore accuse the government of having driven the workers' unions to give up hope in parliamentarism and to prefer the direct-action tactics which the syndicalists advocated.

The effect of the spread of syndicalist ideology could be seen in the sudden outbreak of labor disputes in 1920 and 1921. The statistics on strikes during those years were startling to the government authorities.

It may be recalled that in those years Japan had a number of high-spirited Christian leaders with an interest in the welfare of the downtrodden workers. These leaders, whose names have not yet been introduced here, were continuing their activities, but their influence seemed temporarily to wane in the face of the flare-up ignited by the outbreak of the Bolshevik Revolution in Russia. To the workers inflamed by the bolshevik thought, the humanist approach of the Christian socialists seemed pusillanimous and futile, and in this atmosphere voices began to be raised against such leaders as Suzuki. Suzuki, who previously was politely asked "courageously to retire" (*yūtai suru*), was now condemned as "a degenerate leader to whom a union is more important than revolution." "Let us bury these degenerate leaders!" was the cry now. Aso Hisashi, a courageous leader who had traveled to the Ashio Copper Mine to settle a dispute in the interest of the workers, was now attacked for having brought the riot to an end. The strike that broke out at Kawasaki Dockyards in Kobe involved 35,000 men. In order to deter the infuriated demonstrators, the policemen, who wore sabres in those days, entered the scene with their swords unsheathed, and one workman who was taking a prominent part in the demonstration was killed. The strikers then resorted to the desperate tactic of seizing the whole plant, and the strike lasted a month. Such was the tenor of the strikes that spread over the country, instigated and led by the anarchosyndicalists. The leaders were believers in heroism, and they behaved like the heroes they aspired to be.

No less radical, but of a different sort from these anarchists and syndicalists, were the leaders who regarded themselves as "bolshevists." They considered themselves orthodox Marxists, believing in centralization of power and action controlled from above, or rather, from the center. Gradually, as the bolsheviks in Russia consolidated their gains and began to publicize their program widely, the men who styled themselves bolshevists in Japan began to assume leadership in the workers' movement with more confidence and authority than before. One important landmark at this stage in the development of the socialist movement in Japan was the short but significant article written by Yamakawa Hitoshi, in the socialist monthly *Zen-Ei* (*Avant-garde*) for July, 1922, entitled: "Change of Direction for the Proletarian Movement." In this article, which has become a document of historic interest, Yamanaka urged: "In all battlefronts against the control and power of capitalism, in dealing with every single problem affecting the actual livelihood of the proletarian masses, we must turn from the attitude of mere negation to positive struggle. This, indeed, is the change of direction the proletarian movement must adopt on all fronts."

This was the "shot in the arm" that the workers' movement needed at this time. Hitherto in the hands of a relatively small number of the elite, it now turned into a genuine movement of the masses. Few documents in the history of the working-class movement in Japan had so tremendous an effect as did this article of Yamakawa's. The point of view stressed in this document is widely known as "Yamakawaism" in Japan.

The publication of Yamakawa's view at a time when the controversy between syndicalism and Marxism was at its height had a steadying effect on the whole. It dealt, in any case, a blow to the flamboyant syndicalist movement, which had no definite and clear-cut program. The controversy between Marxism and syndicalism reached its climax in September, 1922, when the trade-unions of differing tendencies tried to form a national federation of Japanese trade-unions. The Marxists took a stand for an organization with a strong national center, whereas the anarchosyndicalists insisted on a loose national federation. There seemed to be no possible compromise between the two factions. The conflict came to an end with the government's order for dissolution of the federation. However, the final blow to anarchosyndicalism in Japan came with the murder of Osugi Sakae, the anarchist leader, in 1923. The tragic end of its powerful leader meant the end of the anarchosyndicalist movement in Japan.

First Split of Sodomei

From the description given so far, it will be understood that the leaders of the working-class movement who were known in Japan as "Bolshevists" were the Marxists, who later came to be known as the Communists. When the influence of the anarchosyndicalist faction declined after the death of Osugi and several others,[12] quite naturally the locus of power shifted to the Bolshevists, who were steadily gaining ground in Sodomei. One could already detect it at the annual convention of Sodomei in October, 1922, where a new platform was adopted, which contained the declaration that capital and labor were absolutely incompatible with each other and that the working class must engage in an out-and-out struggle with the capitalist class. The seven items of its new platform included the enforcement of an eight-hour day, the establishment of a minimum wage, the repeal of the Public Peace Police Act, and the recognition of Soviet Russia. Who could believe that this was the Sodomei which Suzuki Bunji had started hardly ten years before?

The government was contemplating in this period three laws of direct concern to workers: a law for control of radical social movements, a law on trade-unionism, and a law for mediation of tenancy disputes. Sodomei took the lead in launching a nation-wide struggle against "The Three Vicious Bills" (*San Dai-aku Hoan*).

We learn from the history of the labor movement in Japan, as well as in other countries, that a vicious circle is created when either the government sets out to suppress the workers or the workers launch a violent program. In the years after 1923, just such a vicious circle existed in Japan. The government, which had noticed the spread of the revolutionary movement, descended on the Communists at dawn on June 5, 1923, and more than fifty Communists were arrested. That action is recorded in history as "The First Communist Round-up" (*Dai-Ichiji Kyosan-tō Jiken*). This was before the earthquake, which occurred in September, 1923. The arrest and murder of the syndicalists came later.

In order to avoid any misunderstanding, it should be said that it was not the government that murdered the radical leaders. These deaths were the deeds of ill-advised, overzealous policemen who acted on their own responsibility and on the conviction that Japan must rid herself of these "pernicious" radicals. Moreover, the government did not fail to appease the workers at the same time that it was carrying out repressive policies against subversive elements. In September, 1923, the government announced its intention to adopt a system of general election; this announcement had repercussions. The elder and more mature leaders of Sodomei were favorably impressed; they thought they saw some ray of hope concerning the government's future policy. But this optimism of the top leaders was not shared by the younger leaders, who had been much influenced by Yamakawa Hitoshi. They were urging the spread of the battle among the masses, calling this a "realistic policy." The gap between the two groups was not closed at the 1924 convention of Sodomei. A hodge-podge resolution, satisfactory to nobody, was adopted, and the gap only widened between the right and left wings. Any careful observer could have seen that a fateful schism in the organization was bound to come.

Friction continued within Sodomei between the right and the left wings, and the two clashed violently in the struggle for control of the organization; the clash led to a split, first in Kantō Domei, or Eastern Federation of the Sodomei, in October, 1924. The right-wing unions remained in the Federation while the left-wing unions quit and formed Kantō Chihō Hyogi Kai (the Eastern Regional Council), embracing the unions of printing workers, watch and clock manufacturers, ironworkers, and others, mainly in the Tokyo and Yokohama areas.

It should be noted here that the advent of the ILO was an important factor in the split. We have seen how the embarrassment of the government delegates at the ILO conferences in Washington and Geneva was repeated year after year, and how, finally, the delegates to the 1923 Conference advised the government to alter radically its policy on the selection of the workers' delegate. The government took that advice and altered its policy; thereafter the workers' delegate to the ILO Conference was "chosen in agreement with the most representative of the workers' organizations." This was, of course, a crucial turn of events, which the top leaders in Sodomei, who knew best about the opportunities the ILO offered to the working classes of all countries, could not fail to recognize. To them the ILO was the road for the working-class movement of Japan to take, rather than the road of revolution that the Bolshevists were advocating. Moreover, it was at this time that the government enacted the law for general suffrage. The right-wing leaders were feeling, as Suzuki once expressed it, as if "spring zephyrs and spring streams were coming all at once." They were now willing to follow the course outlined by the government. What did this mean? The government of the day was apparently copying the wisdom of Bismarck, whose social policy, it may be recalled, was known as "a policy of honey and the whip." The "honey" of the Japanese government's policy consisted of the promise of the general suffrage law and the decision to send to the ILO conferences delegates of the workers' own choosing. The "whip" consisted of the round-ups of the Communist leaders and the new Bill on the Maintenance of Public Peace (*Chian Iji Ho-an*). As explained later in detail, the chief aim of the proposed law was to suppress subversive movements advocating the change of the political character of the empire and denying the system of private property. The right wing supported the government in these measures. It was willing to give up its negative attitude toward the Bill on the Maintenance of Public Peace, regarding it as a "necessity for the development of sound trade-unionism" in Japan. It rejected the proposed denunciation of the bill and even helped the government secure its passage. On the other hand, the left wing was violently opposed to the bill. A split under these conditions was inevitable.

The annual convention of 1925 was held in March. The right wing, which had the majority of votes, decided on the dissolution of Kantō Chihō Kyogi Kai. It also voted for the expulsion of all left-wing leaders. This decision by the right wing was the signal for the left and right wings to part company. After riotous wrangling, all left-wingers present walked out, declaring it "an honor" to be expelled. Immediately they organized Nippon Rodo Kumiai Hyogi Kai (The Japan Council of Trade-Unions). That is how the historic event—the first split of Sodomei—came about.

Thereafter Sodomei represented the main stream of Japanese organized labor, for harmonization in industrial relations and against communism, while Hyogi Kai stood for class struggle and Communist activities.

When the split took place, Sodomei included 35 unions, with a total membership of 13,960. Hyogi Kai had 32 unions, with a total of 12,655. This was a drastic reduction in membership for Sodomei, but it was an inevitable, even a necessary, unfolding of events, originating from the split that had taken place in the Second International in 1919, when the Third International (or Comintern) was formed in Moscow.

The Second Split of Sodomei and After

After the first split of Sodomei in 1925, the story of the working-class movement in Japan was one of interminable and bewildering splits and confusion among the socialist parties and trade-unions. The confusion seemed to be of a nature that could not be settled in peacetime. In any case, it lasted till the outbreak of the action on the part of Japan's military party that has been called, euphemistically, "the Manchurian Incident." The explanation of this action and what it involved will be discussed later.

In connection with the working-class movement three political parties came into being. On the right wing was Shakai

Minshu[13] To (the Social People's Party), on the left Rōdō Nōmin Tō (the Labor Peasants' Party), and in the center Nippon Rodo To (the Japan Labor Party). In the trade-union field, there was Sodomei on the right, Hyogi Kai on the left, and in the center Nippon Rodo Kumiai Domei (Japanese League of Trade-Unions); the latter was formed in December, 1926, when Sodomei underwent a second split, described below.

When the first split occurred, it was obvious that other splits were bound to come. After the split between the extreme left wing and the moderate right wing, there grew up in the center a powerful group of men who disliked both groups, which they considered extreme and un-Japanese. The members of this central group were more conscious of their nationality. They wanted to be distinctly and uncompromisingly Japanese in thought and behavior. They objected to the left wing's apparent subservience to Moscow. They frowned on the right wing's kowtowing to the authorities. They were not interested in the ILO, which, in their minds, was a compromise with the government and with the employers. On this account, too, they discountenanced the right wing (the Sodomei), which seemed to go along with the government in order to gain recognition for going to Geneva.

This was the background for the crisis precipitated by a political action taken by the leading members of the Sodomei. In order to understand this political action, it must be recalled that friction was growing between the men in the main group of Sodomei and those in the so-called Miners' Group (Kozen-ha). The main group was insisting on a thorough purge of the refractory leftist elements (which in the end went to Hyogi Kai), while certain leaders whose chief support came from the mining workers were not quite as ready or willing to treat them so drastically. Incidentally, the two groups were supporting opposing political parties. The former group, which we will call the "Main Group" (Honbu-ha), was objecting to the admission of the left-wing elements into Rōdō Nōmin Tō (Labor Peasants' Party), but they saw that the party was not succeeding in preventing the penetration of the leftists. Thereupon they withdrew their support of Rōdō Nōmin Tō, and, with the support of such influential men as Abe Isoo, Horie Kiichi, and Yoshino Sakuzo, established a new party, called Shakai Minshū To (Socialist People's Party). This led Aso Hisashi, leader of the mining workers' union, and his associates to form another party of their own, powerful enough to cope with Shakai Minshū To. They were able to enlist the support not only of the miners but of unions of all descriptions, both in Kantō and in Kansai. The Main Group, which appreciated the gravity of the situation, decided to expel the Miners' Union, including Aso, the president, and twelve of his top leaders, Kato Kanju, Sekiya Hiroshi, Ishiyama Torakichi, Takahashi Chotaro, Kaji Yoshio, Iwauchi Zensaku, Mochizuki Genji, Hosoya Matsuta, Fujioka Bunroku, Kasajima Suekichi, Aki Shigeru, and Tanahashi Kotora.

This was a drastic and desperate action on the part of the Main Group of Sodomei, considering the fact that it included men who were the veritable "brains" of Sodomei. The news of this action spread rapidly, and it led to the spontaneous withdrawal of several important unions, such as the textile workers' union of the Kanto region, which had been advised to remain despite the fact that the Main Group had included its name among those to be expelled.

The unions that were expelled and those that spontaneously withdrew formed a new organization on December 4, 1926, Nippon Rodo Kumiai Domei (Japanese League of Trade-Unions), which was to occupy henceforth the central position between the Sodomei on the right and Hyogi Kai on the left. This was the second split of Sodomei.

In the period of fourteen or fifteen years between the second split of 1926 and the dissolution of Sodomei in 1940 (the year before the outbreak of the Pacific War), Sodomei underwent three more splits: in 1929, in 1932, and in 1939. On the other hand, Hyogi Kai was forced to dissolve by order of the government in April, 1928, but re-emerged under a different name, Nippon Rodo Kumiai Zenkoku Kyogi Kai (National Council of Japanese Trade-Unions), in December, 1928. However, because it was considered a subversive organization contravening the Public Peace Maintenance Act, the leaders of this organization were subjected to repeated arrests and mass round-ups, with the result that, despite heroic attempts, they were unable to accomplish much.

It might be said by some that the splits in Sodomei were caused mostly by the central group, which was neither right nor left, or, more cynically, which contained both right- and left-wing elements. It vacillated between the two extremes, influenced by the changing political situation. There were elements that advocated a united action with the right-wing unions, who welcomed a merger with the group that broke off from Sodomei after its third split and changed the name of the central group. But for the elements that favored the left-wingers, this was going too far, and consequently a new group was formed with a more leftist or subversive slant. It was because of this tendency that the group was finally suppressed in 1936 by the military government. The story of these splits and mergers is a fascinating one to students of political history, but of relatively little interest to those more concerned with the practical work or the substance of trade-unionism. The story will be told briefly in the following section.

HOW THE ILO AND THE WORLD SITUATION AFFECTED JAPANESE LABOR

Splits of Trade-Unions Resulting from Japan's Politics in the Far East

World political changes have had repercussions on political, economic, industrial, and social conditions in Japan, perhaps much more so than in many other countries. While we cannot go into the reasons for this, it must be borne in mind when examining the trade-union movement in Japan after 1926. In that year Japan was enjoying great economic prosperity, with expanding industry and an ever-widening world market. That was the year, however, which also saw the second split of Sodomei.

We need not seek far for an explanation of these splits of Sodomei. Both came primarily as the result of the rise in Europe of bolshevism, first evidenced in the Russian Revolution of 1917. Under the Comintern, or Third International, an international federation of revolutionary trade-unions known as Profintern was organized in 1921. The split of the leftist elements from Sodomei in 1925 and the founding of Hyogi Kai could, as a matter of fact, be deemed the direct result of the dictates emanating from the Profintern. As for the second split, which occurred in 1926, the cause has been traced back to the animosity of certain labor leaders toward the ILO, which, in their minds, was an organization compromising the workers' trade-union movement with either the government or the employers. There we saw the involvement of the ILO, and we also saw that the national pride of the Japanese played no small part in producing the split. Nevertheless, is it not undeniable that the primary cause of these two early splits was the beckoning of the Profintern? Pursuing this thought, we will now trace very briefly how the third, fourth, and fifth splits of Sodomei came.

In September, 1929, the third split occurred in Sodomei; it came, not as a surprise, but almost as an anticipated incident in the normal course of development. Sodomei had been regarded, since the time it started as Yuai Kai, as the mainstay of trade-unions in Japan and had been unwittingly performing the function of a general training school for trade-union leaders. Men interested in social or labor problems, dedicated men determined to carry out social reform, frequently college graduates with perhaps naive dreams of a better world, of both moderate and radical tendencies—all sought assignments there, with or without pay. That is why a large majority of labor leaders of the Meiji and Taisho eras were men who had served in Sodomei in one capacity or another for varying periods before entering into other lines of social service. Some were impressed with the program of Sodomei; some were disappointed. The latter resorted to actions which often culminated in splits.

By 1929, Japan had enjoyed several years of national economic prosperity. Japan's representatives to international conferences were enjoying the benefits of the prestige that had accrued to Japan. The top leaders of Sodomei who had gone abroad were men of ability and high calibre, regardless of whether or not they had had previous experience in participating in international conferences. There was no doubt that their experience at the ILO conferences added a certain lustre to their reputations. They were conducting themselves with dignity and decorum; incidentally, their travels abroad and intimate acquaintance with leaders in the world movement of workers had widened their views, so that their opinions and their expressions frequently struck others as more internationalist than nationalist. At heart they were true Japanese and perhaps loved Japan more seriously than those who had stayed only in Japan and were able to view matters from a limited angle. This delicate difference, however, is not always properly understood.

It would be a gross mistake to assign the cause of the third split of Sodomei to either jealousy or misunderstanding on the part of the men who took the lead. At any rate, the men who were dissatisfied with the course followed by Sodomei left the parent body in September, 1929, and formed Rodo Kumiai Zenkoku

Domei (the National League of Trade-Unions), and thus came the third split of Sodomei.

The ideas of the leaders of Zenkoku Domei were so close to those of the leaders of Kumiai Domei, the central body which had split away in 1926, that they decided within nine months' time to join forces with them, and a meaningful merger took place in June, 1930, when they organized Zenkoku Rōdō Kumiai Dōmei (National Trade-Union League) replacing the old Nippon Rodo Kumiai Domei (Japanese League of Trade-Unions). This means that the third split of Sodomei led at least to the change of the name and composition of the center group. Thereafter the center group of Japanese trade-unions was represented by Zenkoku Rodo Kumiai Domei, which in appearance was a good-sized body, wielding even more power because of the Japanese spirit that it emphasized. As a matter of fact, it was this body that took the lead in the formation in 1939 of the Japanese equivalent of the German Arbeitsfront, called at first "Sanpo Kurabu" (Club for Patriotic Service), when Hitler invaded Poland and the war began in Europe.

An increasingly critical situation for normal trade-unions arose after 1931 in Japan because of the military action of the Japanese troops, which began in September, 1931. Japan was a signatory of three international treaties: The Covenant of the League of Nations, The Kellogg-Briand (Anti-War) Pact and the Nine-Power Treaty guaranteeing the territorial integrity of China. On no excuse could the military action of Japan in Manchuria be called a war; it was not a war, but an "incident."

Under the pressure of the veritable warfare raging on the continent, so close to Japan, Sodomei underwent another change or split (the fourth), after Sodomei joined with Zenkoku Rodo Kumiai Domei, as well as the Japan Seamen's Union, which had hitherto remained independent. A loose federation, it adopted the name of Nippon Rodo Kurabu (Japan Labor Club), founded in June, 1931. This "club" eventually transformed itself into Nippon Rodo Kumiai Kaigi (Japanese Trade-Union Congress). Despite the grandiose title, this organziation proved powerless and useless in the increasing turmoil of the war. It died a natural death, in the guise of a "spontaneous dissolution," in July, 1940.

It is interesting to note the chain of actions that took place in the turbulent conditions of the trade-union movement at this time.

In the center group were elements that disapproved of uniting with Sodomei. They split away and formed in November, 1931, Nippon Rodo Kurabu Haigeki Domei (League to Combat the Japan Labor Club), joining hands with the Communist union, Nippon Rodo Kumiai So-Hyogi Kai (General Council of Japanese Trade-Unions), which the Communists had organized in April, 1931. This merger of the center group with the Communists resulted in the founding of Nippon Rodo Kumiai Zenkoku Hyogi Kai (National Council of Japanese Trade-Unions) in November, 1934. This body was dissolved by the order of the government in 1937.

Lastly, as regards the Communist trade-unions, as already mentioned briefly, Nippon Rodo Kumiai Hyogi Kai was once dissolved in April, 1928. But it re-emerged when the leftist members of the center group called on it and formed the League to Combat the Japan Labor Club, but no matter what name it adopted, it was placed under strict police control, so that it could not engage in any effective action to embarrass the authorities.

The accompanying chart may be helpful in visualizing how the splits and mergers occurred. The chart has been taken from Numata Inejiro: *Rodo Kumiai Tokuhon.*

Spread of Trade-Unions and of Labor Disputes

We are not unaware of the objection that can arise in some sensitive minds to the title of this section, since this wording could seem to imply that one was the cause of the other. There is no such presumption, although we feel that in Japan, as in many other lands, the spread of trade-unions invariably has been accompanied by the spread of labor disputes. In the present section the growth of trade-unions will be traced and the causes of disputes analyzed in an effort to see the extent to which the unions were involved in the disputes.

We have already seen that in this country the early growth of unions owed their inspiration to a small handful of men that included dedicated Christians and whose first meeting took place at the YMCA in San Francisco. The Shokko Giyu Kai, started in 1897, was Christian-oriented, and when these men began the union organization on their return to Japan, they had in their minds the craft unions modeled on the AF of L pattern. Their association to promote trade-unionism (Rōdō Kumiai Kisei Kai) proclaimed as its objective: "To establish unions that shall

CHART I
GENEALOGY OF TRADE-UNION FEDERATIONS IN JAPAN IN THE PREWAR PERIOD

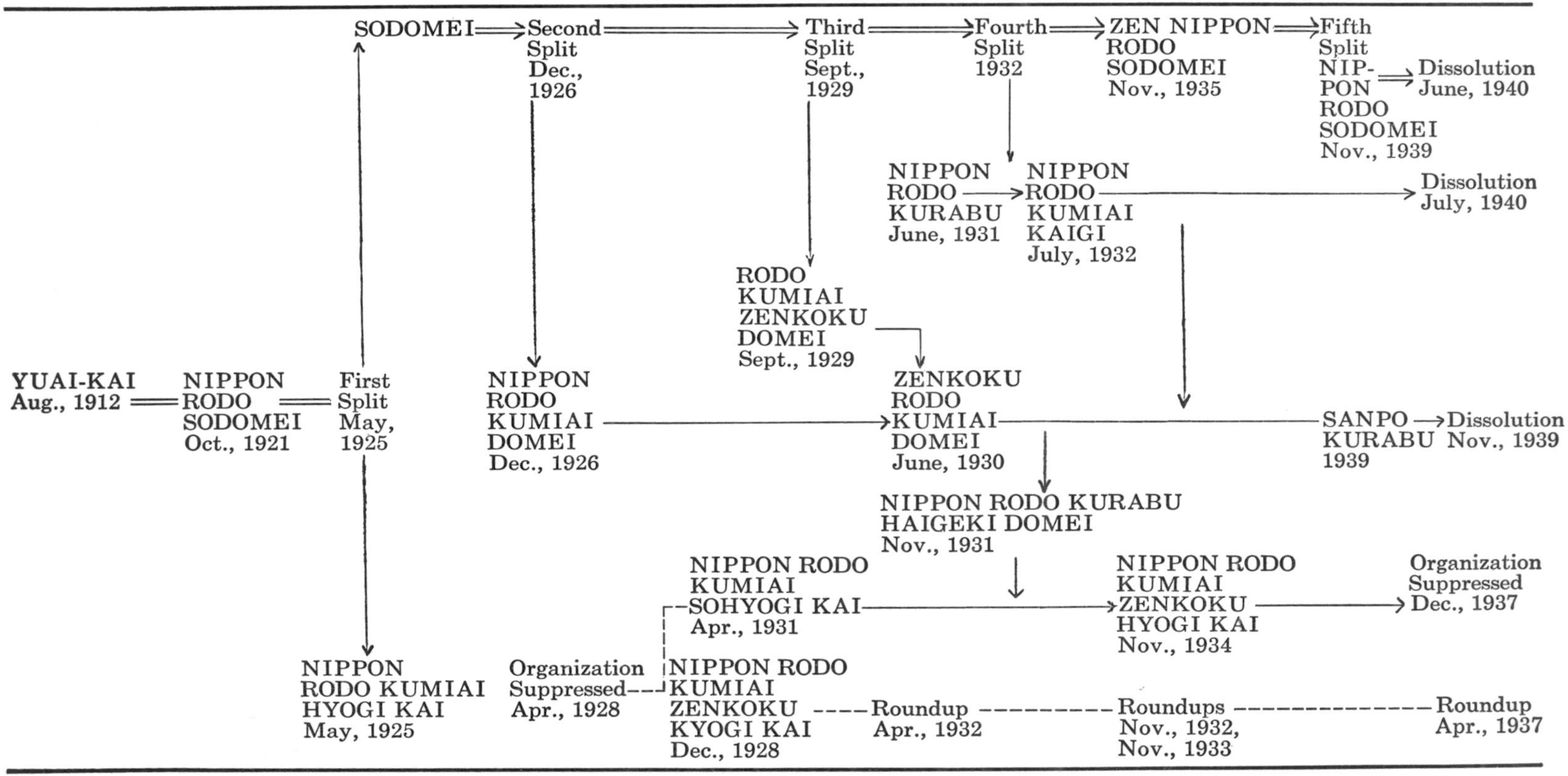

YUAI-KAI
Aug., 1912
═══ NIPPON RODO SODOMEI
Oct., 1921

First Split
May, 1925

SODOMEI ══⟹ Second Split Dec., 1926 ══⟹ Third Split Sept., 1929 ══⟹ Fourth Split 1932 ══⟹ ZEN NIPPON RODO SODOMEI Nov., 1935 ══⟹ Fifth Split NIPPON RODO SODOMEI Nov., 1939 ──⟹ Dissolution June, 1940

NIPPON RODO KUMIAI DOMEI
Dec., 1926

RODO KUMIAI ZENKOKU DOMEI
Sept., 1929

ZENKOKU RODO KUMIAI DOMEI
June, 1930

NIPPON RODO KURABU
June, 1931

NIPPON RODO KUMIAI KAIGI
July, 1932

Dissolution
July, 1940

NIPPON RODO KURABU
1939

SANPO ──⟹ Dissolution Nov., 1939

NIPPON RODO KUMIAI HYOGI KAI
May, 1925

Organization Suppressed
Apr., 1928

NIPPON RODO KUMIAI ZENKOKU KYOGI KAI
Dec., 1928

NIPPON RODO KUMIAI SOHYOGI KAI
Apr., 1931

NIPPON RODO KUMIAI HAIGEKI DOMEI
Nov., 1931

NIPPON RODO KUMIAI ZENKOKU HYOGI KAI
Nov., 1934

Organization Suppressed
Dec., 1937

------ Roundup Apr., 1932 ------ Roundups Nov., 1932, Nov., 1933 ------ Roundup Apr., 1937

source: Numata Inajiro: Rodo Kumiai Tokuhon, p. 47.

enhance the rights of our workers, cultivate refined customs among them, remove obsolete ill practices, and promote intimate relationships among the men in the same trade." They were opposed, as was the AF of L to both revolution and socialism, but were upholding genuine trade-unionism. The programs of the unions of ironworkers, printers, and railway engineers included such items as law education, workers' co-operatives, lecture meetings, the publication of a monthly organ, and so on. One might conclude from this that any strikes launched by these unions were only incidental or of secondary concern. A change came, however, within a very brief period. In 1900, the Public Peace Police Act descended on these unions, and thereafter the trade-union organizers could no longer engage openly in the normal activities of union organization. Their activities became illegal and clandestine.

How should this legislation be interpreted? Table 15 shows that the number of disputes rose from 32 in 1897 to 43 in 1898, while the number of participants nearly doubled—they rose from 3,517 to 6,293. This was alarming enough to the authorities. Maintenance of public order and peace in those days was a matter of grave concern to the government, which had already begun to apprehend the coming of a test of national strength. Military preparations of Russia were spreading through Siberia and Manchuria to Northern Korea. The Russo-Japanese War did not come until four years later, but any astute statesman would have seen the necessity of undergirding the state with legislative and other measures so as to be free from all dangers of riots or uprisings in Japan.

As to whether or not this legislation proved effective, there are contradictory answers, one affirmative, the other negative. Affirmatively it could be pointed out that in the war and its aftermath there were in Japan no rebellious uprisings of the kind that Russia had, thanks to the effective enforcement of this law. The negative answer would be based on the fact that the law ultimately produced effects totally unforeseen. This repressive legislation was one of the factors that gradually turned Japan into a police state and led to the ultimate downfall of the Japanese Empire. Had Japan had a truly liberal law, permitting the growth of a healthy and a sound trade-union movement, the tragedy of the Japanese Empire might have been averted. However, speculations of this sort, interesting as they may be, are out of place. It is

TABLE 15

SPREAD OF TRADE-UNIONS AND LABOR DISPUTES IN JAPAN BEFORE THE END OF WORLD WAR II

	UNIONS		DISPUTES		REMARKS
Year	Number	Membership	Dispute Cases	Participants	
1897			32	3,517	Shokko Giyu Kai is formed
1898			43	6,293	
1899			15	4,284	
1900			11	2,316	Public Peace Police Act
1901			18	1,948	
1902			8	1,849	
1903			9	1,359	
1904			6	879	Russo-Japanese War begins
1905			19	5,013	Russo-Japanese War ends
1906			13	2,037	
1907			57	9,855	
1908			13	822	
1909			11	310	
1910			10	2,937	
1911	32		22	2,100	Factory Act is promulgated
1912	37		49	5,736	Yuai Kai is born
1913	43		47	5,242	
1914	49		50	6,904	World War I begins
1915	53		64	7,852	
1916	66		108	8,418	Factory Act goes into effect
1917	80		389	57,309	
1918	91		417	66,457	World War I ends
1919	162		497	335,225	Washington Conference of ILO
1920	273		282	127,491	
1921	300	103,412	246	170,889	
1922	387	137,381	250	85,909	Social Affairs Bureau is created
1923	432	125,551	290	68,814	Great earthquake
1924	449	175,454	333	94,047	
1925	490	234,000	293	89,387	Repeal of Public Peace Police Act, Art. 17, sec. 38
1926	488	284,739	495	127,267	Labor Dispute Mediation Act
1927	505	309,493	383	103,350	
1928	501	308,900	393	101,893	
1929	630	330,985	576	172,144	Wall street crash
1930	712	354,312	907	191,834	
1931	818	368,975	998	154,528	Manchurian Incident
1932	932	377,635	893	123,313	
1933	942	384,277	610	49,423	Japan withdraws from League of Nations
1934	965	387,964	626	49,536	
1935	993	408,662	590	37,734	
1936	973	420,589	547	30,734	
1937	837	359,290	628	30,900	Chinese Incident
1938	731	375,191	262	123,730	
1939	517	365,804	258	18,341	
1940	49	9,455	226	72,835	
1941	11	895	158	32,160	Pacific War begins
1942	3	111	166	8,562	
1943	3	155	279	9,029	
1944(2)	0	0	216	9,418	
1945	0	0	13	6,627	Pacific War ends

SOURCE: Suchiro Izutaro: *History of Japanese Trade Union Movement*. Figures of labor disputes and their participants after 1933 are confined to the disputes which were accompanied by "dispute acts" such as strikes, lockouts, sabotage, etc.

how the unions themselves behaved after the passage of the Public Peace Police Act that is important.

A significant thing in this connection is that Japanese historians of labor movements refer to the period of ten or twelve years after the passage of the Police Act as *Chinsen Ki*, which means a "Period of Submersion," implying that the activities of trade-unions had to be carried on under water, as it were. If so, how did that affect the frequency and size of labor disputes during the period in question? Statistics indicate that, with the exception of the year 1907, until 1912, when Yuai Kai was organized, the number of disputes never rose above 22 per year. As for the number of participants in the disputes, with the exception 1905–1907, the three years of post-war economic dislocation and special hardship for the wage-earning workers, the number of participants never went beyond the three thousands, whereas in the years before the Police Law came into effect, there were more than three thousand, four thousand, or even six thousand participants in a year. Seeing these figures, one might conclude that this law had served the purpose of suppressing the disputes of the workers.

The Period of Submersion meant the submersion of such normal trade-union activities as collective negotiations, but it did not mean their total cessation. The activities of this period were more violent, often taking the form of destruction of such property as office buildings, warehouses, and company housing. The uprising at Ashio Copper Mine concerned the demand for higher pay and better treatment, but it turned into a riot, with the cutting of electric lines, destruction of the lighting system, throwing of hand bombs, burning of company housing, seizure of the company's warehouses, and so on. Only by the dispatch of troops could the riot be suppressed. Similar violent uprisings happened at Horonai Coal Mine in Hokkaido, Besshi Copper Mine in Shikoku, and elsewhere. In each case troops were dispatched to subdue the riots. It was these spontaneous uprisings that accounted for the exceptionally high figures for dispute cases and participants in 1907.

Mentioned also in an earlier section was the Tokyo tramway strike of 1911, which involved violence on the part of the strikers. The period of violent uprisings continued till the end of the Meiji era in 1912. A new period was ushered in in 1912, when the new Taisho era began and Yuai Kai was formed.

Statistically, during the period from 1910 to 1919, we see a steady annual rise in the number of dispute cases and the number of participants, with only a very slight, almost unnoticeable, setback in the increase of dispute cases in the years 1912 and 1913. Available statistics show that in that ten-year period both the number of trade-unions and the trade-union membership increased steadily. One remarkable thing in this period was that when World War I began in 1914, the repercussions of that war on Japan's economy were more favorable than unfavorable. During the five years of World War I, Japan enjoyed an industrial boom, her exports increased, and the workers received benefits, although on account of higher commodity prices and lower real wages they were experiencing difficulty in adjusting to the new situation. In fact, it was the difficulty of readjustment that gave rise to worker disputes during the war years. From available statistics on the causes of disputes, it is clear that during the ten-year period up to 1919 approximately 80 per cent of the disputes arose from the workers' demand for wage increases.

After 1919, the year of the ILO's first historic conference held at Washington, a new and eventful period began. Table 15 shows that the number of unions rose from 80 in 1917 to 91 in 1918, and thereafter the number of unions kept multiplying till there were 818 in 1931, an average annual increase of 56.5 per cent. Total union membership rose from 103,412 in 1921 to 368,975 in 1931, an average annual increase of 23.2 per cent. How can this remarkable record be explained?

Surely no apology need be made for attributing this phenomenal growth of trade-unions to the ILO. The government of Japan occupied a permanent seat on the Governing Body of this new world organization, since Japan had been designated one of the "eight states of chief industrial importance" in the world. The Treaty of Peace, which contained the Constitution of the ILO (Part XVII, later called the "Charter"), laid down in Article 427 as one of the "General Principles" of the Organization, "the right of association for all lawful purposes by the employed as well as by the employers." Moreover, each member-state of the organization under the Treaty was expected to send to the General Conference of the ILO a delegation consisting of two government delegates, one employers' delegate and one workers' delegate. In the appointment of the workers' delegate, the government had to make their selection in agreement with the most representative of the workers' organizations, if such existed. Holding a position of honor and responsibility as a permanent member of the Governing Body, Japan could not dodge the responsibility of selecting a trade-union representative as Japan's workers' delegate. The government, as already shown, did manifest hesitancy in literally abiding by the stipulations of the treaty in the appointment of the workers' delegate, on account of the inadequate development of trade-unions in the early years of the ILO, but experience showed that the scruples of the government were largely unnecessary, if not totally unwarranted, and brought more embarrassment to Japan than admiration from other nations.

It can hardly be denied that the ILO furnished the most potent impetus for the growth and expansion of trade-unions in Japan. The industrial and economic growth of Japan had reached the stage where, to ensure further healthy and stable industrial order, by the very "logic of industrialism," or the "imperative of industrialization,"[14] a well-organized and responsible trade-union organization was a necessity. The reason the ILO proved so effective in Japan was that by coincidence the ILO appeared at the same time that Japan had reached a comparable stage of industrial development.

If the advent of the ILO had such a tangible or visible effect on the growth of trade-unionism in Japan, what can be said about labor disputes? Did dispute cases increase or diminish in frequency? Did the number of participants multiply or shrink as the result of the steady growth of trade-unions? The reply to this question, interestingly enough, is neither yes nor no. The statistical record will show that the numbers of both cases and participants rose high in the years 1917–1921, reaching a peak in 1919. It is clear that the high figures were due primarily to the economic strain and dislocations of the last busy years of the war and of the tumultuous postwar years. But it is interesting to see that the disputes then decreased in frequency and intensity steadily until 1923. The number of dispute cases rose to over 1,000 in 1926 and over 2,000 in 1930. Also in 1926, the number of participants rose to more than 1,000, but these increases were rather gradual and not disturbing. It may be concluded that neither the growth of trade-unions nor the participation of Japan in the ILO had any appreciable effect on the labor disputes that arose in this period.

In this connection, fortunately, we happen to have government statistics showing the extent of participation of trade-unions in dispute cases. Far from being the cause of disputes, as many hastily assume, the unions, as far as the statistics show, for the most part played a relatively minor role in the disputes during the period covered (1922–1928). Moreover, the statistics show that, at least during the period covered, the largest numbers of disputes involved the unions under Sodomei, generally regarded as the moderate ones, rather than those under Hyogi Kai, known to be extremist or Communist. (See Table 16.)

Detailed statistical information on the workers' demands that gave rise to the labor disputes cannot be given here. We must content ourselves with the summary statement that the largest proportion of the demands were of an economic nature, in most cases requests for wage increases. In general, the conclusion to be drawn is that the immediate causes of labor disputes in this period were economic and internal.

There is no statistical information for the period 1932–1937, during which the Japanese army was engaged in the "Manchurian Incident." Commencing in 1939, the number of trade-unions and the number of members fell drastically to almost nothing in 1944. As for disputes, these dropped rapidly to a few hundred per year toward the end of the war. This was only natural, since the national economy was deteriorating and about to collapse in the last years of the war.

The question of the frequency of labor disputes will be further analyzed later.

The Peasants' Movement

During the turbulent period between World War I and World War II, when Japan was in the birth throes of her democracy, there were two strong movements, apart from the socialist and trade-union movements, that presented at times rather alarming features. One was the movement of the peasants, impoverished and desperate about the iniquitous tenancy and other conditions to which they were exposed. The other was the upheaval, over wide areas, of the traditionally downtrodden and despised caste of people known as the Eta, who were demanding equal treatment. The outbreak of the war stopped these movements. Since the war, thanks to the reforms enforced by the occupation authorities, the very causes of the discontent among these peoples have been largely removed. Consequently, as an English historian writing a "short history" of the British working-class movement would not

TABLE 16
LABOR DISPUTES AND PARTICIPATION OF TRADE-UNIONS (1922–1928)

		1922	1923	1924	1925	1926	1927	1928
	Sodomei							
	Cases	38	63	996	59	71	37	68
	Participants	8,763	10,179	17,671	8,028	6,525	9,024	8,737
	Hyogi-Kai							
	Cases	.....	.....	.....	.....	102	111	55
	Participants	.....	.....	.....	.....	8,255	14,541	4,826
UNIONS INVOLVED	Kumiai Domei							
	Cases	.....	.....	.....	.....	.....	24	19
	Participants	.....	.....	.....	.....	.....	4,688	2,112
	Others							
	Cases	25	42	39	124	180	87	91
	Participants	6,803	8,812	6,295	14,566	23,640	10,174	21,302
	Total							
	Cases	63	105	155	183	353	259	233
	Participants	15,566	18,991	23,966	22,594	38,420	38,506	36,976
Percentage of union involvement in disputes	Cases	25	39	47	62	71	68	59
	Participants	38	52	44	55	57	83	85

omit an account of the Chartist movement,[15] so we must not omit a brief description of these social movements. The space allotted to these two movements is disproportionate to their importance, but it is necessary that the discussion be as brief as possible. Perhaps neither the peasants' nor the Eta movement could be called strictly a "workers' movement," but the two were greatly influenced by the working-class movements.

The original Japanese word for "peasants" is *nō-min*, which means, literally, "farming people." It is important to note here the change in semantics that occurred in the words *Nōmin Undō* or "Peasants' Movement" in this period. We have already traced the rise of the Tenancy Movement (*Kosaku Undō*) and we are now introducing a new terminology which obviously does not mean the same movement. However, the tenants were not simply scattered among the peasants, but in fact formed the major and vital part of the peasants' movement. Various terms have been used, all actually meaning the same thing: *Kosaku Undō* (Tenancy Movement), *Kosaku-nin Undō* (Tenants' Movement), *Kosaku Kumiai Undō* (Tenancy Union Movement), *Nōgyō Rodōsha Undō* (Farm Workers' Movement), *Nōmin Kumiai Undō* (Farming Peoples' Union Movement).

Kosaku Undō (Tenancy Movement) was the name most widely used at first, since it started as a movement of the maltreated tenants against the landlords, but a change had to come about the time that the ILO at its Third General Conference held in 1921 took up the question of the right of agricultural workers to organize. Who were the "agricultural workers"? The workers' delegate for Japan at that conference took the position that the farm tenants were, under the social and economic conditions in Japan, placed in the same predicament as the wage-earning workers, but the government was not ready to support this contention. The tenant, as a matter of fact, was not an employee. He was an independent entrepreneur, strictly speaking. On this basis, the Japanese government went so far as to make reservations on the question of voting for or against the Draft Convention on the right of association of agricultural workers adopted by the ILO Conference of 1921. This incident naturally served to sharpen the issue in Japan.

Moreover, in those days the economic and social conditions among farmers in Japan were anything but satisfactory. Not only the tenant farmers, but all farmers, were in this distressing plight, with the result that the entire peasantry was in a mood to revolt. Union organizers in this situation were finding it difficult to instill class consciousness among the tenant farmers. As already pointed out, the tenant farmers' unions at their start were quite concilia- tory and were more apt to compromise than cling to their original demands. Their attitude toward the land-owning farmer was one of supplication. Once their demands were granted, they were ready to dissolve, and did dissolve quickly in most cases. They were even suspicious, not only of the organizers who came from the cities to start unions, but also of those who rose to organize among themselves. The organizers who had succeeded in negotiation with the landlord had to withdraw speedily from their responsible positions because the other tenants were wary of any powers accruing to the organizers.

These were the characteristics of the peasants' movement in the period prior to 1921–1923. No strong movement could arise as long as these conditions persisted. Several additional forces had to be supplied before the movement could grow in strength. Above all things, education in matters of unionism was necessary to awaken the peasants to their social and economic status. Below is a list of periodicals published during those crucial years to "educate" the peasantry:

Name of Publication	Publisher	Date Started
Land and Freedom	Japan Peasants' Union	February, 1922
The Tenant Farmer	Rural Movement League	April, 1923
The Peasants' Times	Gifu	April, 1923
Agricultural Labor	Okayama Peasants' Union	August, 1924
The Peasants' News- paper	Eastern Federation Japan Peasants' Union	May, 1925
The Okayama Peasants	Okayama Federation Peasants' Union	September, 1925

It will be recalled that the Japanese had attained a rather high degree of literacy early in the Meiji era and that they liked to read, although the level of education of most peasants in the early twenties was not much beyond that of the primary school (four years of elementary and four more years of advanced primary).

Furthermore, in the rural areas, until about the end of World War I, the predominant thinking among the peasantry was that inculcated throughout the nation by the Imperial Rescript on Education in 1890, emphasizing loyalty to the emperor and filial piety. Thus, the platform of the northern Federation of the Japan Peasants' Union had declared: "We uphold the great principle of patriotism and loyalty to our Emperor. . . . We propose to inculcate the spirit of autonomy and mutual help and raise our status by common efforts among ourselves." Obviously, there was a wide gap between this thought of the ordinary peasants and the philosophy which underlay the teachings of class consciousness. Actually, in Mie Prefecture, in which the holy ancestral shrine of the Imperial family is located, the organizers of the peasants' union had to pay each peasant a little sum for attendance, instead of the peasant paying an entrance fee to the meeting!

One important factor that contributed to the closing of the gap was the steady growth in power of the tenants' unions during this period. The increase of tenants' unions from 88 in 1918 to 625 in 1926 was mentioned earlier. This growth was, of course, accompanied by, or was the result of, more maturity in organization, tactics, and philosophy, which would naturally elicit the interest and support of more people. There was, however, a historic event that gave a new character to the peasants' movement—the organization of the Japan Peasants' Union by Kagawa Toyohiko and Sugiyama Motojiro in 1922.

Both Kagawa, mentioned earlier, and Sugiyama were devoted Christian reformers in their early thirties. The story of how Kagawa discovered Sugiyama and made him the leader of the distressed peasantry at this time is told by Kagawa with a colorful touch in his *Shisen wo Koete* (Before the Dawn).

On the night of March 12, 1921, a handful of labor leaders and Christian social workers, including Murashima Kishii, a journalist for the influential newspaper *Osaka Mainichi*, met at a home in the slums of Kobe. The discussion was on the need for organizing the peasants of all Japan for their relief and salvation, and led finally to the convocation on April 9, 1922, at the Kobe YMCA of a national conference, at which delegates from 33 prefectures founded the Japan Peasants' Union (Nippon Nōmin Kumiai).

Sugiyama Motojiro was elected president of the union, and on the board of executives were nine men, including Kagawa. At the time of its foundation, there were locals distributed over eleven prefectures, in each of which a branch of the union was subsequently set up.

The new organization attracted the attention of government authorities, land-owning farmers, and all people interested in the question of the distressing situation of the farmers, primarily because of the effective publicity given in the *Osaka Mainichi* by Murashima. There were also three distinctive features in the new organization. One was that Kagawa and Sugiyama were consciously aiming at the organization of the distressed peasantry. Another was that its leaders consisted of men with experience in organizing industrial workers. A third was that it denounced any resort to violence in the work of emancipating the impoverished peasants. The Christian character of the leaders of the new organization was spelled out:

1. We propose to acquire knowledge, learn techniques, cultivate moral character, enjoy rural life, and bring rural culture to perfection.
2. We propose to enhance the standard of rural life through mutual confidence and cooperation.
3. We peasants propose to attain our common ideals through means that are moderate, sound, reasonable, and legal.

While these planks sound rather like a prayer, vague in content, the organization also adopted the following twenty-one concrete items as aims: (1) socialization of the farming land, (2) establishment of a national peasants' organization, (3) guarantee of minimum age for dayworkers on farms, (4) enactment of a farm tenancy law, (5) enforcement of a law for arbitration in agricultural disputes, (6) general election, (7) amendment of the Public Peace Police Act, (8) stability of life for tenant farmers, (9) completion of supplementary education for peasants, (10) spread of peasants' schools, (11) completion of agricultural cooperatives, (12) establishment of banking facilities for peasants, (13) abolition of indentured agricultural emigrants, (14) improvement of housing for peasants, (15) development of rural hygiene, (16) enforcement of agricultural insurance, (17) enhancement of the status of women in rural areas, (18) development of peasants' folk arts, (19) starting of idealistic agricultural villages, (20) development of science for peasants, and (21) enjoyment of rural life.

At the meeting before the formal adoption of these items a

question was asked as to what was meant by "socialization of farm land." The question embarrassed the man presenting the draft, but Kagawa rose and explained: "Socialization is a term frequently used among the industrial workers. Here socialization will mean the improvement and socialization of the life of the peasants. Therefore you must be patient and wait for a few years." The questioner, apparently, was satisfied with this explanation and resumed his seat without further question!

Was that in any way an indication of the extent to which these aims were supported by the conference? In any case, "Socialization of farm land" was number two among the aims of this organization from year to year, and it is a matter of record that at the second annual conference of the Union, when the same item was adopted, the following explanation was given by the person reporting on the subject: "The expression 'socialization of farm land' does sound somewhat vague. It can mean three things: (1) state ownership of the land—that is, giving up the land and turning it over to state management; (2) ownership of land by the village or by the general public; or (3) ownership of land by the union of those who cultivate it, which will mean ultimately the ownership by the peasants' union."

It was further explained that "state ownership of land is the basic principle for the emancipation of the peasants, but in the present system of capitalistic economic economy, it is only an ideal. However, the Japan Peasants' Union must work ceaselessly with state ownership of land as its final goal."

Due credit must be given to the Japan Peasants' Union for its very practical program for carrying out its aims. In the early years, it had at its headquarters the following department and activities: (1) publications department (organ, pamphlets, leaflets, etc.); (2) research department (disputes, working and living conditions); (3) propaganda department (publications, lecture meetings); (4) peasant school, managed by the Union; (5) cooperatives (obtaining of seeds, pooling of farm implements); (6) planning of ideal villages; (7) free legal advice; (8) encouragement of peasant folk arts; (9) guidance in developing other sources of income; (10) all work for enrichment of rural life.

It should be noted, before bringing the account of this interesting movement to a close, that the Japan Peasants' Union had, at its height, well over 60,000 members belonging to more than a thousand branches, distributed over more than thirty prefectures on the four islands of Hokkaido, Honshu, Shikoku, and Kyushu, as shown below:

Year	Federations	Branches	Membership
1926	24	1,070	67,876
1927	30	1,095	62,020

An account of the political wrangles into which the Union was drawn has been deliberately omitted. One might say that these problems were inevitable. When the union of the peasants grew in strength, the political parties of the industrial workers could not allow it to remain aloof from theirs. The forces within the proletarian political parties that had led finally to the splitting up of Sodomei were relentlessly at work within the movement of the peasants as well.

The Japan Peasants' Union was busy among the proletarian political parties during December, 1924, and poured its energies into these political activities. The leaders were realizing that unless they extended their activities beyond the merely economic ones and joined with the other proletarian forces they would never be able to attain the final aims of the peasants' movement. That was why they participated actively in the formation of Nōmin Rōdō Tō (the Farmer Labor Party), which party formally came into being on December 1, 1925, but only thirty minutes after its formal founding, Minister of the Interior Wakatsuki issued a writ ordering its suppression.

One formal and superficial ground for prohibiting the party was that it admitted as members the trade-unions that had women and minors as members and was thereby violating the Public Peace Police Act, but a more serious ground was the suspicion on the part of the government that the ultimate aim of the party was subversive and that it was thereby violating the Public Peace Maintenance Act. The fact that the representatives of Sodomei had withdrawn from the organizing committee previous to the official formation of the party had no doubt strengthened the suspicions of the government. Be that as it may, the step taken by the Japan Peasants' Union in participating in the formation of a united political front of the proletarian movements could be regarded as "progress" of the movement, but this first step into the politics of the day was a fatal one, and led ultimately to the splitting of the Union. By March, 1926, the first split of the Union had taken place, as a result of the clash between elements that had supported the moderate attitude of Sodomei, which had split away earlier, and those where leftist sympathies lay with Hyogi Kai. This was less than a year after the first split of Sodomei (May, 1925).

During March, 1926, the leftists in the Japan Peasants' Union who had taken an active part in the formation of Nōmin Rōdō Tō (which was immediately suppressed) came into even closer touch with the leftist trade-unions and formed a new party called Rōdō Nōmin Tō (Labor Farmer Party). Thereafter the leadership of the union was divided as to whether to (1) turn to the right, (2) turn to the left, or (3) split. In the meantime, the right-wing leaders who were close to Sodomei proceeded to organize, on December 9, 1926, a new political party, Nippon Rō-Nō Tō (the Japan Farmer-Labor Party), which was neither very moderate nor extreme leftist, but rather neutral in political color; however, by this time the control of the union had fallen into the hands of the extreme leftists, with the result that the twelve men who had organized the new party, including such men as Asanuma Inejiro and Miwa Juso, were all expelled in February, 1927, from the union, on the ground that they were "reactionary elements who ignored the discipline of the union and who obstructed the progress of the union."

After these incidents, the peasants' movement in Japan was involved in the same interminable, ideological controversies as were the trade-unions. This tragic disunity of the peasant and working-class movements came to an end only with the disasters of the Manchurian Incident and the Pacific War.

Suihei Sha or the Levelers' Movement

What precisely was the origin of the class of people in Japan known as Eta?[16] It appears incontestable that the earliest origin of these people must be sought in the slave groups of ancient Japan. At later periods, other groups were assimilated into this caste. The Chinese characters used to designate these people mean literally "filthful" (e-filth, ta-full) and it was in that sense that the term was used in the early days. In ancient Japan, they were mostly butchers, tanners of leather, makers of leather goods, beggars, and vagabonds. Before the introduction of Buddhism, which forebade killing of animals and eating of meat, butchery and the handling of hides and leather were not necessarily condemned or despised vocations. After the spread of Buddhism, trades connected with butchery and the handling of leather came to be held in contempt, although Shintoism, the native religion of Japan, stressing purity and cleanliness and abhorring filth, also seems to have contributed to the general prejudice against these people. They came to be treated as were the *Hi-nin* (literally, "no-man"). The work of executing criminals, burying the dead bodies of vagabonds and travelers of unidentified origin, and other tasks that ordinary people would regard as filthy, were assigned to them.

During the periods of civil strifes among the military families, through the period of the Ashikaga anarchy, lasting from the twelfth to the seventeenth century, the Eta were in a singularly privileged position. There was an increasing need for leather for the manufacture of armor. During the Tokugawa Shogunate (1603–1868) they were, in the rigidly stratified society, classed among the *Sen-min* (despised people) and discriminated against, but economically they were frequently better off than the impoverished common people below whom they were placed. It is believed that during the Tokugawas' rule, there was an increase in the population of the Eta, precisely because of the economic advantages which they alone enjoyed, from engaging in work that was generally despised but which, had it not been for the teachings of Buddhism and Shintoism, would not have been essentially reprehensible.

The Eta and *Hi-nin* were emancipated by law in 1871, but the prejudice cultivated over centuries could not be done away with by a decree or legislation. They were all classed together under law as *Heimin*, or common people, but other people called them *Shin-Heimin* (new common people), and discrimination continued to be practiced widely.

Despite the law, discrimination persisted. This was particularly true in marriages. In the Tokugawa period, an Eta man could marry only an Eta girl. Although Eta girls often are more attractive than others, many a happy marriage came to a sad end, after the Meiji Restoration, on the discovery that one partner or the other was of Eta origin, and the marriage had to be broken by divorce. In public bath houses, which the Japanese people use extensively, in the early Meiji years a man or woman known to be an Eta would be refused admittance. The same often applied to barber shops and restaurants. Ninomiya Shigeaki, who made extensive inquiries, cited cases of discrimination in the army, in teaching professions, in business, and elsewhere. A member of the Diet was publicly insulted because he was an Eta. He subsequently resigned from the post to which he had been elected from a constituency consisting largely of the Eta people. In the 1920s, there were still case after case of suicide resulting from discriminatory treatment or insulting of the Eta. We will not dwell further on these incidents, which are fast disappearing in Japan. The account is given here simply to describe the background against which the *Suihei Sha,* or "Levelers' Movement," rose.

The movement to emancipate the Eta from social prejudices and indignities was started first as a self-directed movement of the Eta, by the Eta, and for the Eta, in place of the benevolent work hitherto carried on by the non-Eta people, to provide economic help to the people of the community. Three young men of the Eta community in Nara, Sakamoto Seiichiro, Nishimitsu Mankichi, and Komai Kisaku founded the movement in January, 1920, as a work of self help among the Eta. The man who should be credited with providing the right orientation for the entire movement was Professor Sano Osamu of Waseda University, who wrote a pamphlet entitled "For the Better Day," which was an elaboration of a more scholarly article he had written in the socialist journal *Kaiho,* "The Principle of Emancipation." Several thousand copies of the pamphlet were printed and distributed widely. It served as a prospectus for the first national convention of the Suihei Sha, held on March 3, 1922, in Kyoto. The gathering was attended by approximately 2,000 people, including delegates from various prefectures. The following Declaration and Resolutions were adopted. Because of their historic interest, we give below the complete texts in translation.[17]

DECLARATION

People of the special communities [*tokushu buraku*] throughout the country, unite!

Our long-suffering brethren! The fact that the reformative undertakings attempted in our behalf by many men and by recourse to various methods during the past half-century have not brought any appreciable results should be taken as due punishment for the violation of the sanctity of humanity by us and others. And when we realize that these sympathetic movements, on the contrary, have degraded many of our brethren, it is inevitable that we should organize a collective movement at this time by which we may emancipate ourselves by our own effort, through self-respect.

Brethren! Our ancestors worshiped freedom and equality and practised these principles; they were the victims of despicable class rule; they were manly martyrs of industry; they were skinned alive in recompense for their work of skinning animals; their warm hearts were ripped out as the price for stabbing the hearts of animals, and they were spat at in ridicule. Yet all through these cursed nights of evil dreams, the glorious human blood has kept on flowing in us. And we who have been born of this blood, have to live in an age when men may turn into gods. The time has come when the oppressed shall throw off the brand mark of martyrdom, and the martyr with the crown of thorns shall receive blessing.

The time has now come when we may be proud of being Eta!

We must never again insult our forefathers or desecrate humanity by our cowardice either in utterance or in action. And we, who know well how cold the world is and how useless charity is, earnestly desire the warmth of the human heart and the light of humanity.

Thus, the Suihei Sha has been established.

Let there be warmth in man's society and light among men!

Third day, third month, eleventh year of Taisho
The National Suihei Sha.

RESOLUTIONS

1. If any intent to insult is manifested against us under such names as Eta or *Tokushu Burahu-min*, either by act or word, we will take thoroughgoing steps to censure the offenders.

2. A monthly periodical called *Suihei* shall be published at the Suihei Sha headquarters to strengthen our ties and co-ordinate our endeavors.

3. We will hear the frank official views of the East and West Hongwanji [Buddhist churches], of which the majority of us are parishioners, concerning our movement and take legitimate steps according to their reply.

It should be noted that many of the Eta parishioners were contributing sizable amounts to their Buddhist churches. The intention behind the last of the Resolutions was to reach an agreement with the churches on the withholding of those contributions for a twenty-year period and their use toward financing the movement of the Suihei Sha.

After the founding of the Suihei Sha in 1922, the movement grew in membership phenomenally from year to year. Minami Umakichi, chairman of the central executive committee, was a man of judgment, integrity, and dedication, and the movement grew in prestige. Each annual convention for the four or five succeeding years registered a substantial increase in membership and in the number of branches. The flag of the movement with the picture of a crown of thorns well indicated the spirit of the movement.

The character as well as the more distinctive activities of this movement can be grasped by a look at the resolutions adopted at the second convention held in Kyoto, March 2–3, 1923. It was attended by approximately 1,500 delegates from various prefectures and about as many sympathetic or interested listeners. Thirty-five resolutions were adopted, including, among others, those endorsing nondiscrimination in schools, nondiscrimination in the army and the navy, direct action until laws were enforced to prevent discrimination, refusal to support Hongwanji, organization of women's and youths' sections in the Suihei Sha, establishment of a circulating library, promotion of producers' and consumers' unions, and the training of the youths for direct action.

One of the activities that aroused the police authorities was the rise in number of direct-action cases of "thoroughgoing steps to censure the offenders," implementing the resolution adopted at the first national convention. The National Department of Justice, Bureau of Penal Affairs, published the statistics of such cases as follows: 1922, 69 cases; 1923, 859 cases; 1924, 1,046 cases; and 1925, 1,024 cases.

Naturally this led to many arrests of officers of the Suihei Sha. The left-wing movements led by the Communists took the opportunity to penetrate into the central body, and in the roundup of the Japan Communist Party in March, 1928, the Suihei Sha suffered considerable damage. Internal dissensions ensued, and a movement arose to restore the Suihei Sha to normalcy. But the account of this movement must end here and attention be turned to more strictly "labor" matters.

Impact of the ILO on Labor Administration in Japan

In matters of labor administration by the government, Japan again happens to be a country where the impact of the ILO was most noticeable and effective. In order to grasp the full significance of the impact of the ILO, it is necessary to examine first how social questions in general, incidentally including labor questions, had been handled by the Japanese government in the past.

In August, 1917, the government set up in the Department of the Interior, a section in the Local Affairs Bureau, called Kyugo Ka (Relief Section), to deal with matters of relief and aid for the indigent and aid for the military personnel, poorhouses, children's

asylums, houses of correction, and so on. In 1919, the name of the
bureau was changed to Shakai Ka (Social Affairs Section). In
August, 1920, the name was changed again to Shakai Kyoku
(Social Affairs Bureau), and, with an increase in personnel, the
Bureau began to assume more importance. However, its functions
were still limited to social questions in the limited sense, covering
only such items as relief and aid to the poor, prevention and relief
of unemployment, protection of children, and so on. In that early
stage of development, labor questions and matters relating to the
ILO were handled by other sections in the Department of the
Interior or agencies outside of the department. For instance, it was
largely the Foreign Office (Department of Foreign Affairs) that
took care of ILO matters, since the ILO was created by the Treaty
of Versailles and all treaties were handled by that office.

Such a division of work was obviously conducive to confusion
and inefficiency. Kyocho Kai, which later will be described at
length, submitted at this time a representation to the government,
urging more co-ordination and unification in the work of government administration. It emphasized the need for creating a proper
government organ through which the various facets of labor
administration might be correlated and brought under centralized
foci. Matters of labor legislation, questions of capital-labor harmonization, of emigration of labor, of social insurance, of collection of labor statistics, and international labor questions—all
pointed to the urgent need for creating a special government
organ. It was felt that national policy should be set up at this time,
and appropriate measures taken to promote industrial progress
and give stability of mind to the people.

The representation was couched in moderate but dignified
and forceful terms. It was signed by the president of Kyocho Kai,
Prince Tokugawa Iyesato, the direct lineal descendant of the
Tokugawa Shogunate, and addressed to the prime minister and to
all other ministers of the Cabinet, dated July 10, 1922. Anyone
following the events would be tempted to give prior credit for
creation of the Shakai Kyoku to Kyocho Kai, although clearly no
representation would have had any effect, had it not been for the
growing external pressure from the ILO. The birth of a new and
powerful government organ for labor administration was but an
answer to the need of the times.

The government saw the need, and on November 1, 1922, an
imperial decree was issued whereby the new agency came into

being, to execute: (1) all the work performed by the Social Affairs Bureau of the Department of the Interior; (2) work concerning labor movements and statistics, hitherto conducted by the Police Bureau; (3) work relating to protection of workers, hitherto in the hands of the Department of Agriculture and Commerce; (4) work on seamen's insurance, previously handled by the Department of Communications; and (5) work on collection of labor statistics, previously performed by the State Census Agency. Other functions assigned to Shakai Kyoku in the following years were (6) the administering of employment agencies, (7) health insurance administration, and (8) work relating to participation in the ILO's program, and so on. Naturally, a number of work items were transferred to new agencies as they were created in the government to deal with those items more properly. For example, the collection of labor statistics was transferred to the newly created Cabinet Statistical Bureau in April, 1925, and the work relating to emigration was transferred in June, 1929, to the Department of Colonization.

During the years prior to the outbreak of the Pacific War, the work of Shakai Kyoku normally included the following items: (1) general matters relating to labor, (2) enforcement of the Factory Act, (3) protection of mining workers, (4) enforcement of the Industrial Workers Minimum Age Act, (5) settlement of labor disputes, (6) social insurance, (7) prevention and relief of unemployment, (8) co-ordination of work relating to the ILO, (9) relief and aid to the indigent, (10) protection of children, (11) relief and aid for military personnel, (12) other matters of social work.

A glance at this brief enumeration of the functions of the newly created government organization is sufficient to convince anyone that, despite its modest title, Social Affairs Bureau, it was to all intents and purposes a labor ministry. The only factor that militated against adoption of the title "Labor Ministry" was that Japan had not yet matured sufficiently to welcome the advent of a labor ministry. She still had to go through the ordeal of World War II before coming of age.

However, the unparalleled importance of this bureau in comparison with seven or eight other bureaus in the same ministry was recognized. (This bureau was called a *gai kyoku* (external bureau); in other words the Social Affairs Bureau was not co-equal with other bureaus, but was of a different dimension and category. Its director-general was of a rank virtually equivalent to that of minister.

Nor did the press fail to recognize the significant role to be played by this new organ. The government was careful to select a man of high calibre to head this new agency. The press made liberal use of headlines in quoting any pronouncements made by the director-general of the Shakai Kyoku during the Diet session. Owing to the liberal and progressive tendency of the programs of social and labor administration laid out by this bureau, its director-general was often referred to in the press as the "pink [not exactly red] director-general." Few ministers in Japan, other than the prime minister, enjoyed such press publicity as did the director-general of the Social Affairs Bureau during the years following its creation. And it must not be overlooked that the interest of the government and the people of Japan in the ILO in those years was at its height.

Without going into detail the organization of the Social Affairs Bureau will be briefly outlined next. Below is a chart describing the structure of labor administration in the central or national government.

CHART II
STRUCTURE OF LABOR ADMINISTRATION IN CENTRAL GOVERNMENT

SOCIAL AFFAIRS BUREAU (Director-General)		
	I. Labor Division (Director)	Labor Conditions Section
		Labor Administration Section — Mediation officers
		Inspection Section — Factory inspectors — Mining inspectors
	II. Insurance Division (Director)	Planning Section
		Comptrolling Section
		Management Section
		Medical Treatment Section
	III. Social Affairs Division (Director)	Protection Section
		Welfare Section
		Vocational Section
	a. General Affairs Section	Personnel
		Documents
	b. Research Work Researchers on Housing, Safety, Hygiene, etc.	

The work of administration is shared, of course, by the local or prefectural governments. Before World War II, Japan proper was divided into forty-seven prefectures. Hokkaido, Tokyo, Osaka, and Kyoto were not called prefectures and they had different names for their governors, simply because of their difference in size from other prefectures; essentially, however, there were no differences in the functions assigned to the forty-seven prefectures. A brief account may be given here of the labor administration work shared by the prefectural governments.

All prefectural governors (with the single exception of the governor of Tokyo, in whose stead the director-general of the Metropolitan Police Board was responsible for this work) were charged with the enforcement of the Factory Act, the Industrial Workers' Minimum Age Act, Labor Disputes Mediation Act, and the Health Insurance Act, and for supervising the administration of general matters of trade-unions, social work, and so on, in the prefectures under their jurisdiction. We should note here that for the enforcement of the Factory Act, Industrial Workers' Minimum Age Act, Labor Disputes Mediation Act, etc., the police department of the prefecture (in Tokyo, the Metropolitan Police Board) was the competent administrative authority. Factory inspectors and labor disputes mediation officers were attached to the police department in each prefecture.

Prefectural governments shared also the work of enforcing the Health Insurance Act, after the Act was brought into force in August, 1926. This Act will be discussed later. Work on a national scale began after Japan ratified the ILO Convention on Unemployment, and the government established an elaborate network of free and public employment exchanges throughout Japan. Division of work for ensuring a completely satisfactory administration of the employment exchange system was much more complicated than in the case of the Health Insurance Act. This will also be discussed in detail later.

The minister of communications was responsible for the protection of seamen. Japan proper was divided into seven districts for the purpose of maritime administration, with local maritime bureaus in Tokyo, Nagoya, Osaka, Hiroshima, Kumamoto, Sendai, and Sapporo.

Lastly, the supervision of mining work was the responsibility of the minister of commerce and industry. Japan was divided into five mining districts, with mining supervision bureaus in Tokyo,

Osaka, Fukuoka, Sendai, and Sapporo. However, the directors of these bureaus were under the supervision of the minister of the interior for enforcement of the laws for the protection of the mining workers. Thus, the functions of labor administration were centralized under the Ministry of the Interior, although shipping, mining, and so on, as industries, were still under different ministries.

Creation of a Permanent Delegation Office in Geneva

The impact of the ILO on Japan affected the reorganization of the work of labor administration in many ways, reaching a climax in the creation of the Social Affairs Bureau, which, as has been pointed out, was to all intents and purposes a ministry of labor, except in name. Also, a rough outline has been provided of how that agency of the central government was organized, both structurally and functionally. Brief reference has been made to the agencies of the local (prefectural) governments, whose work in the field of labor administration was co-ordinated by the Social Affairs Bureau of the Ministry of the Interior. This was all within Japan.

A matter of special international significance was the creation of a Permanent Delegation Office of the Japanese Government in Geneva, Switzerland, at the seat of the League of Nations. It will be remembered that the ILO was created as a part of the League of Nations. Japan was the first state member of the ILO to set up an office of this sort, somewhat similar to an embassy or a legation, accredited to the ILO. A number of other countries saw a great advantage in this action of the Japanese government and followed suit. One might say, without danger of hyperbole, that it added to the prestige of the ILO, which in the earlier years of its development had been in need of more popular support.

The primary thing that prompted the Japanese government to set up such an office in Geneva was, frankly speaking, material necessity. As was mentioned earlier, Japan was selected, when the Governing Body of the ILO was elected in 1919, as one of the "eight states of chief industrial importance," and for that reason the Japanese government was given a permanent seat on the Governing Body. It was foreseen from the outset that the Governing Body would meet frequently, perhaps four times in a year. In the 1920s there was little air travel. Travel by ship from Japan to Switzerland, i.e., from Kobe to Marseilles, took six weeks. Three months a year spent in travel alone would mean that the representative of the Japanese government would be traveling back and forth all the time, hence the need for the Japanese government to set up a permanent office in Geneva. The government was beginning to appreciate the growing importance of labor information. If the government had a man of ambassadorial or ministerial rank stationed at the seat of the ILO, with competent staff and adequate equipment, it would serve the important purpose of keeping the government in Tokyo posted on all crucial matters happening in Europe in the field of labor.

Such was the thinking on the part of the government in creating the office in Geneva. Hara Takashi, the prime minister, was not a "pro-labor" man in the sense of supporting any policy which would be in the special interest of the working class, but he had a shrewd and penetrating mind, and saw great utility in maintaining a special sort of embassy on labor matters in Europe. Consequently a decision was reached by the government, subsequently confirmed by an imperial ordinance, to set up at the seat of the ILO a "permanent office of the Delegate of the Imperial Government to the International Labor Organization." The first person appointed by the government to head the said office and to represent the Japanese government on the Governing Body was Inuzuka Katsutaro, former vice-minister of Agriculture and Commerce. Before the creation of the Social Affairs Bureau, the Ministry of Agriculture and Commerce was chiefly responsible for labor administration. Inuzuka had studied railway administration in Germany before assuming the high post of responsibility in that ministry. Much was expected from this man in his new post at Geneva.

The function of the Delegation Office at Geneva was understood to be threefold: (1) The chief of the office should attend the meetings of the Governing Body of the ILO and deal with important labor matters of interest to the Japanese government; (2) the office should keep the government informed of the progress of labor legislation, labor movements, and so on, in Europe; and (3) it should also supply information on labor in Japan to those who might request it.

The importance attached by the Japanese government to the Delegation Office at Geneva was evident in the care with which it selected the secretaries or attachés to work under the direction of Delegate Inuzuka. Since this occurred before the creation of the centralized Social Affairs Bureau, when labor matters were dealt with by several government agencies, the government took care to select the secretaries from among the competent officers of those government agencies, which included notably the Ministry of the Interior, Ministry of Communications, and Ministry of Agriculture and Commerce.

Circumstances were propitious for making the dispatch of the delegation to Geneva an especially grand affair, as it coincided with the dispatch of the representatives of Japan to the First General Assembly of the League of Nations held at Geneva. A steamship of the N.Y.K. Line, the S.S. *Kumano Maru*, was chartered by the government to carry the delegates, secretaries, and their dependents as far as Marseilles, the port nearest to Geneva. There were big and colorful send-offs at Tokyo Station and at Kobe Wharf, and the press gave ample space to this memorable event.

The Delegation Office at Geneva continued to carry out its functions steadily from 1920 till 1938 when Japan withdrew from the ILO as a consequence of the Manchurian Incident. Inuzuka Katsutaro, as the chief of the Delegation Office, was succeeded by Doke Hitoshi, formerly Director of Agriculture in the Department of Agriculture and Commerce. The men who succeeded in this post were, without exception, men of long experience in government service. It may be said without exaggeration that the Delegation Office rendered services of inestimable value to Japan and to the ILO in promoting progressive labor legislation and sound trade-unionism in Japan. Following are the names and backgrounds of the men who headed the Delegation Office and represented the Japanese government on the Governing Body of the ILO from 1920 to 1938: Inuzuka Katsutaro, Vice Minister of Agriculture and Commerce; Doke Hitoshi, Director of Agriculture; Maeda Tamon, Vice-Mayor of Tokyo; Kasama Akio, Former Minister to Egypt; Yoshisaka Shunzo, Factory Inspector; Kitaoka Juitsu, Factory Inspector.

Though, strictly speaking, it does not belong in this section, the action taken by the Governing Body of the ILO in setting up a branch office in Tokyo to provide every possible facility for supplying information concerning the ILO may be mentioned here. Branch offices were set up by the ILO in London, Paris, Berlin, Rome, Washington, New Delhi, and Tokyo. As the list indicates, the setting up of a branch office in Tokyo was not a matter of reciprocating a courtesy, a gesture in return for the Japanese government's having opened a permanent delegation office in Geneva. It was more substantial than that. The Governing Body of the ILO took this action because it recognized the importance of Japan in the industrial world.

The branch office in Tokyo was housed first in the building of the Kyocho Kai, later in the Hibiya Municipal Building. It maintained a staff of half a dozen secretaries under the director; published a monthly journal in Japanese, as well as numerous pamphlets and leaflets; organized lecture meetings and seminars; and engaged in public relations for the ILO.

Two men served as director of the Tokyo Branch Office from the time the office was established in 1922 until 1938, when Japan was on the verge of entering World War II, and the Branch Office was closed. They were: Asari Junshiro, senior staff member of the ILO, previously factory inspector, who served from 1922 to 1932; and Ayusawa Iwao, senior staff member of the ILO, previously secretary of the Japanese Delegation to the ILO, who served from 1932 to 1939.

Impact of the ILO on Labor Legislation in Japan

We have already seen how potent was the impact of the ILO on the development of trade-unions in Japan. We have also traced the significant and even epoch-making changes made in the system of labor administration under the impetus supplied by the ILO. Turning now to the vast field of labor legislation, we discover that under the direct or indirect influence of the ILO, Japan began to present a "new look," as it were, in labor laws, as compared with the days prior to World War I. It is true that there was a series of labor laws and ordinances enacted in the 1920s and after, without any conventions or recommendations of the ILO directly obliging Japan to take such legislative measures. However, it must be admitted that even in such instances the government was conscious that every possible improvement in labor conditions needed to be made, since Japan was in a position of prestige and responsibility as a permanent member of the Governing Body of the ILO. This fact was constantly on the lips of the men who were urging the necessity for more advanced labor laws. *Noblesse oblige* was the Western adage applicable to Japan at this period, and for this reason it seems permissible and proper to treat the principal labor laws and ordinances of the years after 1920 under the above heading, though we do not ignore the fact that the laws had no distinct origins in the decisions of the ILO. However, before proceeding to treat the various laws, it should be explained how the whole question was handled by the ILO Conference of 1919 at Washington.

The Special Countries Committee at Washington, 1919

Before World War II, the Factory Act and the Mining Act were the two major laws in force in Japan for the protection of workers employed in factories or mines. We have already seen how the two laws first came to be enacted. We saw that the enforcement of the Factory Act was delayed, but was finally put into effect in 1916, five years after the enactment of the law. Japan had had barely three years of experience in administration of this important labor law when the first session of the ILO's General Conference met. The first item on the agenda of that historic conference was to limit the working hours of all workers, male and female, to eight hours per day and forty-eight hours per week, whereas the Factory Act of Japan had limited the working hours of only women and young persons under fifteen. The maximum working hours allowed for these "protected workers" (women and young persons under fifteen) was twelve hours per day, and there was no limitation whatever on working hours for adult male workers. Moreover, even these loose limitations of maximum working hours were to apply to "factories" which, under the Factory Act, were workplaces where fifteen or more workers were normally employed. How could Japan be expected to adopt the new world standard of working hours? The government of Japan was anxious to come up to and abide by the world standard set up by the ILO. The national honor was at stake. On the other hand, Japan had to protect her new industries. Adoption of too advanced regulations might simply crush the sprouting buds. National federations of associations in silk yarn manufacture and cotton spinning and of other employers' bodies put up the strongest objections to any rash action of the government which might result in handicapping their growing enterprises. The government of Japan, in short, was confronted with a dilemma.

Fortunately, difficult situations of this kind were foreseen when the labor section (Part XIII) of the Peace Treaty was being drafted, and in an article of the Treaty the following provision (originating from a remark made by the representative of the

Japanese government, Dr. Oka Minoru, at the Commission on International Labor Legislation[18]) was laid down:

> Article 405: (3) In framing any recommendation or draft convention of general application, the Conference shall have due regard to those countries in which climatic conditions, the imperfect development of industrial organization, or other special circumstances make the industrial conditions substantially different and shall suggest the modifications, if any, which it considers may be required to meet the case of such countries."

The Washington Conference had recourse to this provision of the Treaty. As a matter of fact, there were several important countries, notably Japan and India, that found themselves in a situation in which the provision above would offer the much-needed relief—*modus vivendi*—in their respective predicaments. Accordingly, a special commission was appointed by the Washington Conference—the Committee on Special Countries. The committee selected George N. Barnes of Great Britain as chairman. He conducted the discussions of the committee with such competence and tact that the conclusions finally reached were the result of remarkable concessions on the part of the participants in the controversial debates. On this committee, which Japan regarded as of crucial importance, this government was represented by Dr. Oka Minoru, former Director of Industries; the employers of Japan by Muto Sanji, president of the Kanegafuchi Spinning Company; and the Japanese workers by Muto Shichiro, who was adviser to Masumoto Uhei, and who had intimate personal knowledge of working conditions in textile mills. This impressive list of Japan's representatives shows the degree of importance Japan attached to the deliberations of this committee. Also, there were dozens of young and active reporters of the Japanese press present at the committee sessions. Never before had so much concern been manifested by the Japanese press in an international conference. In fact, this was the first international conference at which vital questions affecting Japan were discussed and where the people could come freely and listen.

Dr. Oka, who had previously attended the Paris Conference and had already made the acquaintance of the leading delegates of other powers, including Chairman Barnes himself, was by then accustomed to Western conference procedures and was therefore adept and at ease. Dr. Oka explained in detail the difficulty the Japanese government was up against even though it desired to conform as far as possible with the proposed world standards on working hours, rest days, and so on. The employers' delegate, Muto Sanji, talked on the disastrous effects any premature laws would have on the young industries in Japan, which were struggling with scanty capital and little experience. He emphasized that Japan simply was not ready to face or to agree to the standards which were perhaps suited to the more advanced industrial powers of the West but not to the newly developing areas of the world. On the other hand, the workers' delegate, Muto Shichiro, a namesake of the employers' delegate, but no relation, martialed arguments from the humanist or humanitarian standpoint, referring to the unhealthy conditions of work prevailing among the textile mills of Japan. The only way out of this entanglement was a compromise of the three points of view represented on the committee.

In passing, we might note here that the title or the name of this committee, the "Special Countries Committee," translated into Japanese, was *Tokushu Koku*. This had an odious connotation to most Japanese in those years, since the village communities of the former outcasts (known generally as Eta), as explained elsewhere, were often called *tokushu buraku* (special communities). This was purely incidental, and at the conference, of course, nobody dreamed of treating either Japan or India as a *tokushu* nation in that invidious sense. Nevertheless, it was an unfortunate incident, a mistake, at which some sensitive people in Japan took offense. We understand that this was one of several reasons why the ILO, after the experiment at the Washington Conference, was never tempted to appoint another "special committee" for any group of nations, whether advanced or underdeveloped.

Be that as it may, the compromise adopted by the committee regarding working hours, rest days, and so on was a happy one for Japan, and it was incorporated in the Convention on hours of work. The part relating to Japan read as follows:

CONVENTION 1. Limiting the hours of work in industrial undertakings to eight in the day and forty-eight in the week

Article 9. In the application of this Convention to Japan the following modifications and conditions shall obtain:
(a) the term "industrial undertaking" includes particularly the undertakings enumerated in paragraph (a) of Article 1; the undertakings enumerated in paragraph (b) of Article 1, provided there are at

least ten workers employed; the undertakings enumerated in paragraph (c) of Article 1, insofar as these undertakings shall be defined as "factories" by the competent authority; the undertakings enumerated in paragraph (d) of Article 1, except transport of passengers or goods by road, handling of goods at docks, quays, wharves, and warehouses, and transport by hand; and regardless of the number of persons employed, such of the undertakings enumerated in paragraph (b) and (c) of Article 1 as may be declared by the competent authority either to be highly dangerous or to involve unhealthy processes;

(b) the actual working hours of persons of fifteen years of age or over in any public or private industrial undertaking, or in any branch thereof, shall not exceed fifty-seven in the week, except that in the raw-silk industry the limit may be sixty hours in the week;

(c) the actual working hours of persons under fifteen years of age in any public or private industrial undertaking or in any branch thereof, and of all services of whatever age engaged in underground work in the mines shall in no case exceed forty-eight in the week;

(d) the limit of hours of work may be modified under the conditions provided for in Articles 2, 3, 4 and 5 of the Convention, but in no case shall the length of such modification bear to the length of the basic week a proportion greater than that which obtains in those Articles;

(e) a weekly rest period of twenty-four consecutive hours shall be allowed to all classes of workers;

(f) the provision in Japanese factory legislation limiting its application to places employing fifteen or more persons shall be amended so that such legislation shall apply to places employing ten or more persons;

(g) the provisions of the above paragraphs of this Article shall be brought into operation not later than 1 July 1922, except that the provisions of Article 4 as modified by paragraph (d) of this Article shall be brought into operation not later than 1 July 1923;

(h) the age of fifteen prescribed in paragraph (c) of this Article shall be raised, not later than 1 July 1925, to sixteen.

LABOR LAWS UNDER THE IMPACT OF THE ILO

Improvements in Protective Labor Laws

A perusal of the ILO conventions of 1919 on hours of work, minimum age in industry, nightwork for women, and so on, will enable anyone to imagine the tremendous effect of these conventions on the protective laws of Japan. We will now examine first the more important changes made in the factory and mining labor laws of Japan. This is the area in which the influence of the ILO was more direct and tangible. For reasons already explained, Japan, like few other countries, has reacted to the stimulus of the

ILO in a uniquely sensitive way, and that is why we give the account here in some detail.

Application of Factory and Mining Labor Laws

In the Factory Law of Japan there was never a definition as such of either a factory (*kōjō*), or a worker (*shokkō*), but there was a common understanding of the terms, according to which a *kōjō* was a "fixed place where workers are employed continuously for a certain period, for the purposes of manufacturing, processing, finishing, or packing, baling, and so on," and a *shokkō* was a "person engaged at a workplace, at work involving the output of the product of the factory, as well as anyone engaged in labor that contributes directly to this work." In the case of mining labor, the Mining Act defines both "mining" and "mining worker"; according to Article 1 of the Mining Act: "mining means prospecting for and extraction of minerals and work connected with it." "Minerals," in their turn, mean twenty-three specific items, including gold, silver, copper, iron, coal, kerosene oil, and so on (Article 2). "Mining workers" are those engaged in mining work. Building stone not being regarded as minerals for the purpose of the Mining Act, quarry work does not come under Mining Law, nor does the work of finding and extracting alluvial minerals come under this, since alluvial deposits are omitted.

A somewhat special approach was made to the matter of protection of workers regarding their working hours, because of the situation described above.

As mentioned already, under the Factory Act of 1911 a factory was not defined as such, but coverage of the Act, the scope of its application, was fixed. The law was to apply to workplaces where fifteen or more workers were normally employed, or where the processes of work were dangerous or injurious to health. The processes deemed to be dangerous or injurious to health were minutely laid down. The Washington Conference took into consideration the practical difficulty for the Japanese government of immediate enforcement of the limitation of working hours for all workers at all workplaces. Under Article 9 of the Convention on Hours of Work, it was decided that the terms of the Convention on the limitation of working hours should apply to workplaces where ten or more workers were normally employed. Japanese industry was developing in those days by leaps and bounds. Consequently, the government proceeded to formulate revisions of the content of the Factory Act of 1911. A bill for revision of the Factory Act was subsequently presented to and passed by the Diet, and the Revised Factory Act was promulgated on March 29, 1923.

Under the Revised Factory Act, the law would henceforth apply to workplaces where ten or more persons were normally employed. Moreover, even if the number of workers employed was less than ten, the law would apply in part if the factory was using power-driven machinery. As regards the mines, they were not exempt from the application of hours' regulation on account of the number of workers employed; however, by a revision made in the mining law, the limitations of the law would apply after 1926 not only to mineral extraction but also to mineral prospecting. (It should be noted here that the Factory Act was enforced in government-owned factories, but, because the powers of factory inspectors did not extend there, the various administrative authorities of the government were responsible for inspection in their respective factories.)

Minimum Age.   Minimum age of admission to gainful occupation was a matter to which the ILO paid great attention from the outset. It was mentioned emphatically in the labor part of the Peace Treaty, and that was the reason it was discussed as one of the major items on the agenda of the Washington Conference. The conference adopted a convention in which Japan had to ask for a special treatment. The change that was required of Japan as the result of the ILO Convention of 1919 is given in brief below.

Under the Factory Act of 1911, twelve years was the minimum age of admission to employment, *in principle*. In practice, *as exceptions*, children between ten and twelve years of age could be employed in "light work," which was defined, and for recourse to which special permission had to be previously obtained from the authorities. In mining work, however, twelve years was the minimum age without exception. The poverty of the parents, who would have difficulty in sustaining the family if children were deprived of the opportunity to earn small sums, has of course been a principal argument advanced in opposing a minimum-age law. In the case of Japan, the shortness of experience in enforcing the minimum-age law was one of the pleas made for a period of grace. The Washington Conference took into consideration the difficulty that the Japanese government would suffer if the universal standard of the international convention (in which sixteen years was the minimum age) were imposed on Japan immediately. The ILO did not wish to compel any nation to enact laws which it could not abide by. The text of the Washington convention on minimum age in industry of 1919, as it related to Japan, is as follows:

CONVENTION 5. Fixing the minimum age for admission of children to industrial employment

Article 5. (1) In connection with the application of this Convention to Japan, the following modifications of Article 2 may be made.

(a) Children over twelve years of age may be admitted into employment if they have finished the course in the elementary school;

(b) As regards children between the ages of twelve and fourteen already employed, transitional regulations may be made.

(2) The provisions in the present Japanese law admitting children under the age of twelve years to certain light and easy employment shall be repealed.

In pursuance of the ILO Convention of 1919 on Minimum Age of Admission to Industrial Employment, the Japanese government proceeded to revise the existing provisions in the Factory Act and other relevant laws or ordinances and promulgated the Industrial Workers' Minimum Age Act, March 29, 1923. The great earthquake of that year wrought damage to and caused dislocation of many industries in the country, but the law was put into force beginning July 1, 1926.

Under this law, fourteen was, in principle, the minimum age of industrial employment. Children who had finished the compulsory primary school education could be employed, as exceptions, by special permission of the authorities. One of the main points of interest in this legislation lay in the fact that, after this initial step, the same rule was soon extended to mining, quarrying, construction, transportation, and other industries.

Protection of Women and Young Persons. "Underdeveloped" as it was in many respects, Japan nonetheless was conscious of the imperative need of protecting the health and well-being of the women who were the actual or future mothers and the young persons who constituted the next generation of the nation. This was precisely why the "protected workers" in the early factory and mining laws were primarily women and young workers; also, why the Japanese government, despite much criticism, acceded to the special provisions of the ILO conventions of 1919 on hours of work and nightwork for young persons. Below is the text of the article of the Washington Convention of 1919 on nightwork for young persons as it applied to Japan:

CONVENTION 6. Concerning the nightwork of young persons
employed in industry

Article 5. In the application of this Convention to Japan until 1 July 1925, Article 2 shall apply only to young persons under fifteen years of age and thereafter it shall apply only to young persons under sixteen years of age.

Obviously the Japanese government, which acceded to this text at the Washington Conference, deemed it wise not to impose a restriction on nightwork for young persons all at once, but to do it by degrees so as to ensure complete observance of the provisions. Thus, under the convention, fifteen would be the minimum age until July 1, 1925, and sixteen years, the international standard, would become enforceable only after that date.

Similarly, under the factory and mining labor laws, the protection regarding working hours, nightwork, and so on, was to apply only to women and young persons under fifteen, but under the revised provisions of 1926 the age was raised to sixteen years. Because there was a grace period of three years, the change was to come into force as of July 1, 1925.

In order to appreciate fully the importance of the legal protection provided for women and young persons in the early period of Japan's industrial expansion, it is necessary to have an idea of the age distribution of women and young persons actually engaged in various industries. Table 17 (page 188), giving the statistical figures for October 1, 1926, in textile mills, was taken originally from *Kojo Kantoku Nenpo* (Annual Report of Factory Inspection), *1927*. While a detailed examination of these figures cannot be entered into here, the rather high proportion of workers under sixteen should be noted. In the case of male workers, only 8 per cent were under sixteen; among female workers, who constituted a large majority (89 per cent) of textile workers, 22 per cent were under sixteen.

Working Hours. One might say that the most difficult change the Washington Conference of 1919 imposed on Japan was the restriction of working hours. The universal standard that the ILO Convention of 1919 set up was eight hours per day and forty-eight hours per week for all workers, male and female alike. As against this, what was the current practice in Japan?

Under the Factory Act of 1911, the maximum working hours, for women and young persons only, was twelve hours per day, and there was an exception even to this. For the manufacture of silk fabrics for export at factories certified by the prefectural governors, as well as for the manufacture of silk yarns by machinery (instead of by hand), extension to thirteen hours per day was allowed until August 31, 1931. By the revision of the law, prompted by the Washington Convention of 1919 and promulgated in June 1926, there was a reduction of one hour, so that the maximum working day was eleven hours, in principle; since the reduction applied to the exceptional cases as well, the maximum working day in these enterprises was twelve instead of thirteen hours. Spinning was still another industry added as an exception. However, if the workers were divided into day and night shifts and were working alternately, this provision was not to be applied. In this connection, it was laid down in the Revised Factory Act of 1926 that after June 30, 1929, in the spinning industry, the system of day and night shifts must be entirely discontinued.

As regards mining work, there was no restriction whatever of working hours for adult male mining workers working on the surface. This was the same as the Factory Act, which had no restriction of working hours for adult male workers. However, by the revision of the Regulations for the Aid of Mining Workers made in September, 1928, the working hours of adult male mining workers for underground work were limited to ten hours per day, enforceable as of September 1, 1930, which allowed a two-year grace period. This was an extraordinary measure for the Japan of that period, justified on the basis that mining work is dangerous and unhealthy, and that the male mining worker who is the head of the family should be allowed the privilege of a limited working day.

In the mines no distinction was made between different kinds of mining. The maximum workday, both surface and underground, was twelve hours. By the revision made in June, 1926, it was reduced to eleven hours. In the work of coal screening, mainly the work of women, the female worker could, with special permission, work twelve hours. A revision was made in the regulation of September, 1928, whereby the working hours were reduced to ten hours per day for both male and female mining

TABLE 17

AGE DISTRIBUTION OF WORKERS IN TEXTILE MILLS (October 1, 1926)

Factories	MALE WORKERS					FEMALE WORKERS					Grand Totals
	Under 14	14–15	15–16	Over 16	Total	Under 14	14–15	15–16	Over 16	Total	
Silk fabric	150	335	589	9,574	10,648	1,921	3,278	4,492	39,017	48,708	59,356
Cotton fabric	164	620	1,138	22,025	23,947	4,751	9,125	13,484	85,668	113,028	136,975
Silk-cotton mixed	10	18	43	867	938	190	291	380	4,130	4,991	5,929
Hemp fabric	9	33	54	2,161	2,257	101	313	407	4,004	4,825	7,082
Cotton-hemp mixed	…	…	…	55	55	25	33	50	214	322	377
Woolen fabric	26	91	179	9,831	10,127	1,896	2,129	2,935	26,389	33,349	43,476
Cotton-wool mixed	…	…	…	41	41	1	2	32	260	295	336
Carpets	…	…	2	110	112	5	1	11	274	291	403
Miscellaneous fabrics	1	17	32	630	680	21	66	89	1,701	1,877	2,557
Total	360	1,114	2,037	45,294	48,805	8,911	15,238	21,880	161,657	207,686	256,491

workers, effective from 1930 on, which allowed a two-year period of grace. Further, employment of women in underground work was to cease as of September, 1933.

Weekly Rest Days. No weekly rest day equivalent to the Sabbath of Jews and Christians existed in Japan. Neither Buddhism nor Shintoism has such a holiday. The Factory Act and the mining laws in force before World War II laid down no compulsory rest days for adult male workers. It was only for women and young workers under sixteen that the employers were required to provide at least two rest days per month. Further, only if the workers were performing their work in two shifts of night and day were the employers obliged to grant them four rest days per month, and their shifts must be changed round every ten days. There were still other excuses provided in the factory and mining laws for withholding the weekly rest day, such as natural disasters or the threat of such. Japan has been known for the frequency of typhoons, floods, droughts, earthquakes, fires, and so on.

We have already noted that the Hours Convention of 1919 had a provision requiring that all workers receive the benefit of a weekly rest day of twenty-four consecutive hours. This requirement was not met by legislation in Japan before World War II, in spite of the serious efforts of the officials in the government to promote the healthful institution of weekly holidays.

Daily Rest Periods. Adult male workers had no legal provision for daily rest periods. Only women and young workers benefited by the provisions in the factory and mining laws granting thirty minutes of rest when a day's work exceeded six hours and one hour of rest for work of over ten hours. In actual practice, however, it is known that, as a rule, adult male workers were given a total of one hour rest per day and two days of rest per month, as were women and young workers. In the mines, moreover, and particularly in underground mining work, it is known that regardless of any legal compunction, the mining workers, male and female, were left free as regards mealtime, rest periods, and so on. The tremendous improvement in working conditions in these respects will become clear in the following sections.

Nightwork. Of all the ills of industrialism that spread throughout Japan, there is little doubt that the one that needed to be dealt with first was nightwork for women and young persons. The magnitude of the problem is evident in the seemingly fruitless efforts of the Japanese government to pass effective laws to limit nightwork.

We have already mentioned the work of the International Association for Labor Legislation, which adopted the first international convention on the subject. The Western world had awakened to the problem early. India was not much advanced in modern industrialism, but her Factories Act of 1911 had prohibited work between 7:00 P.M. and 5:00 A.M. for women and young persons under fiftcen. But Japan had not done so in the years that Japanese export goods were being shipped in increasing quantities to foreign markets, and was inviting severe criticism abroad on this account.

As a matter of fact, the evil effects of nightwork on women in textile factories had drawn the attention of the government before the Sino-Japanese War of 1894–1895. The problem of young girls exhausted by nightwork in the mills, some of whom were even contracting tuberculosis by sharing beds with other girls who were tubercular patients, appeared in newspaper accounts, which the government could not afford to ignore. Owing to the seriousness of the situation, there was incorporated in a draft of regulations concerning employment of workers drawn up in June, 1887, an article that read: "Women and young persons under 14 years of age shall not be employed at night." Although this was deleted in the final text because of the employers' objections, the government would not give up. In the outline of the Factory Bill first drawn up in November, 1902, and in the pamphlet distributed by the government in 1909, the necessity for the discontinuance of women's nightwork was stressed. There was a vigorous protest, which the government took into consideration; the bill presented to the Diet in 1910 provided that nightwork for women would be prohibited by law but that enforcement would not commence until ten years after promulgation of the Act. Again there was such strong objection that the government had to withdraw the bill. From then on the government adopted a more cautious attitude. Wide inquiries were made by the government and a new proposal was formulated for "gradual abolition" of nightwork, to come into effect after a grace period of five years. A commission of investigation concerning production studied and completely disapproved of the government's proposal of gradual abolition. The only way out, the government thought, was prolongation of the grace period, and this time an extension to fifteen years was proposed.

The bill containing the provision for prohibition of nightwork for women, with a grace period of fifteen years, was presented to the Diet in 1911, and this time it was passed, becoming the Factory Act of 1911.

Under the Factory Act of 1911, "nightwork," which meant work between 10:00 P.M. and 4:00 A.M., was prohibited, but if the work was performed in two or more shifts, the nightwork was allowed to continue for fifteen years. Moreover, the fifteen-year grace period was applicable also to all young persons under fourteen and young women under twenty, on three conditions: (1) that the work in question needed to be finished at one stretch; (2) that the work in question needed to be done at night; (3) that the work in question required continuous day-and-night work, but was performed by workers divided into two or more shifts. With the law so ingeniously worded, the employer had no difficulty in engaging women or young persons. In effect, there was actually no prohibition of nightwork in Japan. It will be recalled that the Factory Act of 1911 was not put into force until 1916. The grace period of fifteen years from that date meant that the prohibition of nightwork would commence only in 1931.

The Factory Act of 1911 underwent drastic revisions in 1923. "Nightwork" came to mean work between 10:00 P.M. and 5:00 A.M. Even if performed in two or more shifts, nightwork would be prohibited after only three years' grace. Since the Revised Factory Act came into force in June, 1926, the prohibition of nightwork became effective in June, 1929.

This is not the place to discuss the economic or moral effects of these legislative measures, but it is necessary to recall here that for long years after World War I, textile goods were the principal items of Japan's export and that 75 to 85 per cent, or more, of the workers engaged in textile mills were young women, that the ratio of female to male workers was between 3 to 1 and 6 to 1, and that 80 to 90 per cent of these women, numbering around 200,000, were employed in nightwork. The nightwork of women caused the spread of tuberculosis, not among the factory girls alone, but also in the farming villages from which they came. Nightwork was sapping the vitality of the young women, but at the same time it was the source of national income and of the income of the impoverished farmers. It is easy to understand why employers would strongly object to any hurried discontinuance of the system.

Lastly, it should be noted that after World War I there was a great deal of nightwork for women in the mines. With the expansion of power-driven machine industries there was a perennial shortage of coal, and this necessity was used to justify the practice.

When the Regulations for the Aid of Labor of Mining Workers were enacted in 1916, nightwork for women was prohibited in principle, but, because of the proviso to the effect that this prohibition would not apply if the work was performed by workers divided into day and night shifts—precisely the same as the proviso in the Factory Act—the law was a dead letter. The Regulations underwent a revision in June, 1926, but the question of nightwork was left with a special commission for special studies. The commission produced its report, which resulted in the Revised Regulations of 1928. According to this revision, nightwork for women was prohibited between 10:00 P.M. and 5:00 A.M., but a grace period of five years before enforcement was allowed. There were three exceptions to this prohibition. If the employees were working in two or more shifts, they could work till 11:00 P.M. In coal-sifting work, if the workers were working in alternate shifts, the work could continue till 12:00 P.M. If the sifting was done in three or more shifts the work could go on without a stop for twenty-four hours! Where was the prohibition of nightwork under these conditions? Obviously, the rule was a farce.

It must be noted here that on the part of the mining workers themselves there was much hesitancy or unwillingness to forego the employment of women. Very frequently, in fact as a rule, in coal mining the work at the face was performed by man and wife. A wife was the best companion and helper for the face work, quite apart from the income which it brought. From the standpoint of the employer, too, it was easier and more convenient to employ the wives of the men in their mines: for one thing, the wages for women were, of course, lower, and, also, the teamwork of the family, including the children in many cases, was most efficient and profitable. We can understand why it was difficult for the government to enforce the prohibition of nightwork of women in the mines.

Dangerous or Unsanitary Work.   Early in the history of labor legislation, the Japanese government began to pay special attention to the need for protecting workers from the ill effects of dangerous or unsanitary work. That was the reason there was a provision in the Factory Act of 1911 defining a factory to which the law was to apply as a workplace where fifteen or more persons were normally employed or where the work performed was dangerous or injurious to health. The same consideration was given to mining work, as is shown in the Regulations for the Aid of Labor of Mining Workers (hereafter called "Mining Workers' Regulations"). Definitions of dangerous or unsanitary work were found in Articles 9 and 10 of the Factory Act and Articles 12 and 13 of the Mining Workers' Regulations. In the Factory Act, "dangerous" meant physically dangerous, and "unsanitary" meant chemically dangerous or injurious to health. Women and young persons under fifteen (sixteen, after revision) were prohibited from engaging in either kind of work. More precisely, dangerous work under the Factory Act meant:

1. cleaning, oiling (lubricating), examining, or repairing of machinery during its operation, or of the dangerous parts of the power transmission apparatus;
2. work of fixing or removing belts or ropes on machinery during its operation, or of power transmission apparatus;
3. other dangerous work;
4. work using poison, drastic drugs, or other injurious materials;
5. work using explosive, ignitable, or inflammable materials;
6. work at a place where dust particles are thrown out and scattered about seriously or where noxious gases are emitted;
7. work at other dangerous or unsanitary places.

In the Mining Workers' Regulations, sixteen items were listed as dangerous, in which the employment of women and young persons under fifteen (later sixteen) was prohibited. There were also three items enumerated as injurious to health and in which the employment of young persons under fifteen (later sixteen) was prohibited.

As regards underground work in the mines, all underground work had to be considered dangerous and injurious to health. Under the Mining Workers' Regulations, there were many limitations placed against employment of women and young persons, but owing to the series of exceptions provided in the Regulations, for long years approximately 50,000 women continued to be employed in the coal mines. However, the government was conscious of the evils of women working in the mines; that was why the Regulations were revised. Under the Revised Regulations issued on September 1, 1928, the work of women and young persons under sixteen came to be definitely banned, with a grace period of five years—that is, it became effective as of September 1, 1933.

The prohibiting of employment of workers affected by certain kinds of disease should be noted in this connection. Both the Factory Act and the Mining Workers' Regulations had provisions on this matter. Roughly speaking, the ban was as follows: (1) absolute prohibition in cases of mental illness, leprosy, tuberculosis, erysipelas, measles, recurrent fever, and other acute fevers; (2) employment permissible only after treatment of such contagious diseases as scabies, trachoma, and so on; (3) prohibition in cases where there was danger of aggravation of the disease, such as pleurisy, heart disease, and beri beri.

We might add here that the list of the diseases was expanded later, and that provisions were added in the factory and mining labor laws making physical examination compulsory at the time of employment and periodically thereafter. These points will be treated later in the appropriate sections.

Maternity Protection. Maternity protection is a matter of concern to all those interested in protective labor legislation. The First Session of the General Conference of the ILO in 1919 took up this matter, and a convention was adopted. The convention provided for: (1) protection of the mother in pregnancy, (2) protection of the mother after childbirth, and (3) protection of the baby. Under this convention, a woman worker expecting childbirth could, on a doctor's certification, ask for leave six weeks before childbirth. She could not be required by her employer to work until six weeks after childbirth. During absence from work she was entitled to a subsistence allowance from various sources. She was entitled to free medical care and free midwifery help. When she returned to work she was entitled during working hours to two thirty-minute recesses for feeding the baby. The employer was not allowed to deduct pay for her rest periods before or after childbirth or to serve her with a notice of dismissal to become effective during the same period.

The Factory Act of 1911 did not fail to provide maternity protection, but its provisions were rudimentary compared with those of the Washington Convention of 1919. Consequently, great improvements were made along the lines of the Convention, though not completely, when the Factory Act was revised in 1926. According to the revision, when a woman worker expecting childbirth within four weeks asked for leave her request had to be granted. She had the right, as a matter of principle, to six weeks' leave after childbirth. An exception to this was that if a physician examined the woman four weeks after childbirth and declared that no harm would result, she could then resume work. For the protection of a baby less than a year old, the employer had to grant the mother two thirty-minute recesses for feeding the baby. In the case of women workers in mines, the provision was slightly different since they worked at some distance from the pit head. The employer was not required to grant mothers the time for feeding the babies provided he put up a nursery on the premises of the mine.

Furthermore, in order to enable the mothers to take full advantage of their leave periods, the law provided that women would receive the equivalent of 60 per cent of their daily wages during the four weeks before and the six weeks after childbirth. Allowances in cash were also given at the time of the delivery of the baby.

Special Conditions of Labor in Japan

Under this heading we shall take up several problems which, strictly speaking, were not peculiar to Japan but which either took more acute form in Japan or were treated by the government with more particular concern and for that reason deserve special attention.

Recruitment of labor for factory or mining work.   Known widely as a country of dense population, even of overpopulation, Japan should have no difficulty in meeting her manpower needs. Such is the reaction of a superficial observer who has not looked into the nature of the problem. Nonetheless, the ambitious entrepreneurs experienced considerable difficulty, especially in the years after World War I, in recruiting workers for the factories and mines. There are several reasons for this phenomenon.

A major cause has been mentioned earlier. Because of the war in Europe, the industrial powers in Europe that had been fulfilling the needs of the world market had ceased to perform that function, and Japan's industries were called upon to fill the need. This was particularly true in the textile industry, which required relatively small capital outlays and less technical preparation than some other industries. Thus, in the years after the war there was a tremendous demand for textile goods for export, and that increased production was made possible by an increase in the number of workers engaged in textile industries. The following table tells the story eloquently:

TABLE 18
INCREASE IN TEXTILE WORKERS IN JAPAN (1914–1926)

Year	Workers	Year	Workers
1914	628,958	1921	975,424
1915	713,371	1922	688,422
1916	718,185	1923	687,742
1917	880,923	1924	656,571
1918	949,534	1925	622,993
1919	1,058,605	1926	584,019
1920	958,033		

SOURCE: *Shōkō Tōkei Hyō*, in Kyocho Kai, *Saikin no Shakai Undo*, p. 66.

Because the need arose suddenly, recruitment at the mills or in the town where the mills were operating was not possible. Dependence on word-of-mouth communication was of course totally useless. Newspaper advertisements helped some but never enough. The most effective means of recruitment was the dispatching of troops of recruiting agents to distant villages. Elaborate preparations included the accumulation of presents to be delivered to the prospective workers, mainly young girls in their teens, or money to be handed to the needy parents of the girls. Sizable amounts would be left with the parents as "advance payment" against the girls' wages.

This practice of advance payment had both a bright and a dark side. On the one hand, it provided considerable relief to the poverty-stricken villages, where the shortage of currency was acute. On the other hand, it amounted to "buying up" the young women, to virtual enslavement of the girls for the period of their employment in the mills.

The government was awake to the problems involved, and had taken up the matters of employment, discharge, and employment-service in Article 17 of the Factory Act of 1911. An Imperial Decree was to be issued on this matter, but it never appeared. Thirteen years after promulgation of the Factory Act of 1911, in

1924, an ordinance was issued calling for police measures in controlling the recruitment of workers. At first it was sufficient to report to the authorities simply the amount of money received from the prospective employer. As for the employer, the authorities expected them to exercise self-control and not to engage in abusive practices. Obviously that was expecting too much.

Evils arose from two sources. On the employers' side, there were unscrupulous agents who would sometimes accept commissions from two employers for the employment of the same girls; sometimes they would let a girl sign a second contract after she had signed but not executed a previous contract. Also, there were frequent cases of the parents' accepting invitations to dinner and presents from more than one agent. The problems of double signatures and double contracts was a constant source of irritation and wrangling in the villages. The government was less rigid than it might have been in order to give the girls fuller freedom of choice as to their employment.

Another serious problem grew out of the fact that recruiting agents, as a rule, traveled hundreds of miles to remote prefectures in search of innocent girls as yet unspoiled by life in the city. When the girls recruited were taken to the factories it meant traveling a long distance under the guard of the agents, who were not always men of high moral character. The need to regulate the conduct of these agents was obvious.

These were the reasons the Ordinance for Control of Recruitment of Workers was promulgated in 1924. Under this ordinance, the recruiting agents were required to explain the conditions of employment to the prospective employees before the contracts were signed. A series of measures designed to prevent abuses in recruitment obliged the employer to restore the worker to *status quo ante* if fraudulent practices on the employer's part were discovered.

For many years after World War I, during the period when raw silk was an important export item from Japan, the need for recruiting a great many women was most acute. The need was quite pronounced in silk reeling; in fact, the problems of recruitment were greater in the silk industry than in any other. Table 19 gives a fair idea of the situation that prevailed for a considerable period.

Three things that contributed to the solution of the acute

TABLE 19

RECRUITMENT OF WORKERS IN VARIOUS INDUSTRIES
(1927)

Industries	Workers Recruited	Male	Female	Total	Per-centage
Silk reeling		14,514	222,081	236,595	66.95
Cotton spinning		2,130	66,088	68,218	19.30
Weaving		1,621	19,117	20,738	5.87
Other textile		646	1,656	2,302	0.65
Non-textile		915	1,350	2,265	0.64
	Total	19,826	310,292	330,118	93.41
Metal mines		34	. . . . . .	34	0.01
Coal mines		9,462	71	9,533	2.70
Oil mines		. . . . .	. . . . . .	. . . . . .	. . . .
Other non-metal		224	. . . . . .	224	0.06
Alluvial mines		. . . . .	. . . . . .	. . . . . .	. . . .
	Total	9,720	71	9,791	2.77
Building		11,775	15	11,790	3.34
Others		1,547	126	1,673	0.48
	Grand Totals	42,868	310,504	353,372	100.00

SOURCE: *Rodosha Boshu Nenpo* (Annual Report of Recruitment of Workers, 1927), in Kyocho Kai, *Saikin no Shakai Undo*, p. 55.

problems of recruitment should be noted here: (1) the spread of the system of free public employment exchanges; (2) decline in export of raw silk; and (3) greater employment stability of workers. It will be shown in due course how the system of free employment exchanges eliminated the evils of the expensive and undesirable recruiting system.

Factory Dormitories.   The sudden expansion of the textile industry meant, as mentioned above, the growth of a recruiting system that gave rise to serious problems, including the need for proper housing and boarding facilities for the large number of young women recruited from distant prefectures. This need was met by dormitories attached to the factories. The attention paid by the government to the problems of factory dormitories and the resulting provisions of the Factory Act have already been mentioned. The question of factory dormitories will be discussed at length later; it is sufficient to point out here that each time the Factory Act was revised improvements were made in diet, hygiene, and so on. The following table will show how widespread dormitories were in the period of normal industrial activity before World War II.

TABLE 20
FACTORY DORMITORIES AND INMATES (1926)

Factories		Workers		
Size	*Number*	*Male*	*Female*	*Total*
Less than 10 workers	946	1,092	4,488	5,580
10–50 workers	1,501	4,911	26,322	31,233
50–100 workers	171	1,342	10,298	11,640
100–500 workers	140	2,869	23,147	26,016
More than 500 workers	27	1,777	35,370	37,147
Total	2,785	11,991	99,625	111,616

SOURCE: *Kojo Kantoku Nenpo* (Annual Report on Factory Inspection), in Kyocho Kai, *Saikin no Shakai Undo*, pp. 67–68.

Rules on Wage Payment

Some reference has already been made to the matter of legal protection regarding wage payment. Treatment of this subject here for the period between World War I and World War II will be brief, since there was no substantial change in the principles of law governing wage payment. The whole question will be taken up at more length in connection with the current situation.

The main principle of wage fixing and wage payment in Japan has been that of freedom of contract. This means that the area left for legal protection and intervention is rather limited. Generally, the laws regulated only the time and frequency of payment, method of payment, and, rarely (in Japan, never), the place of payment. The fixing of the amount of wages has been left largely to free bargaining between the parties concerned, and it is only since World War II that the law in Japan has begun to intervene, e.g., by fixing the minimum amount to be paid certain workers.

Under the Factory Act of 1911, and even after many revisions, the legal protection regarding wage payment was confined to the following matters:

(1) *Frequency of wage payment.* Wages must be paid at least once a month, on fixed days, in currency. Payment in kind is disallowed. Although this was the rule laid down in the Factory Act and in the mining laws, in practice there were exceptions. At spinning mills, for instance, where the working girls were housed in dormitories, their rental was considered part of their wages. For

the families of the mining workers living in shacks on the mine premises, mineowners provided rice, the staple food, at low prices. This was also considered part of the wages. These practices were legitimate if the employer reported them in advance as "provisions in the interest of the workers," and obtained permission of the prefectural governor. Concerning frequency of payment, the law required that wages be paid at least once a month, and the more general practice was to pay twice a month, on the fifteenth and thirtieth.

(2) *Recipient of the pay.* At one time wages were often paid not directly to the worker but to a middleman who was supposed to have been designated to receive the money on behalf of the working girls for their convenience. This practice led to all sorts of abuses. The authorities began to pay serious attention to the evils arising from such a practice, and it eventually died out.

(3) *Immediate payment in emergencies.* Article 23 of the Ordinance for Administration of the Factory Act provided that in the event of the death of a worker, his dismissal, his return home, the marriage or funeral of a family member, childbirth, serious injury, or illness the worker (or his wife) would not have to wait until the day fixed for payment but could request immediate payment of wages. A mineowner had to draw up the mine's regulations regarding wage payment and other conditions of work and obtain the approval of the authorities for its enforcement. Also, the Revised Mining Workers' Regulations contained a new provision regarding the check-weigher system. Under previous practice, the check-weigher appointed by the mineowner had sole responsibility for estimating the amount of coal dug out by each worker. Under the revised rule, check-weighing became the work of the company's check-weigher assisted by the miners' representative.

(4) *Ban on punitive reduction of wages.* The employer could, with the permission of the authorities, retain part of the employees' wages as deposits. This amounted to deferred payment and was sometimes beneficial to the worker. However, the employer could not compel the employee to agree in advance that amounts could be deducted from this deposit to cover failure to abide by his employment contract. The employer was required to have the special permission of the authorities to enforce any punitive deduction of wages, and only when he had obtained the permission in advance could he proceed to deduct the amount

fixed for punishment. Moreover, under the law in civil procedure, the workers were protected from seizure by a creditor up to a certain amount. Also under civil law, the workers have the right of pre-emption over their wages. The detailed provisions of these laws are not unimportant, but they cannot be dwelt on further at this point.

Paternalism versus Workmen's Compensation

For seven centuries, until the Restoration of Meiji, the Japanese people were governed under the Shogunate, a typical and elaborate system of feudalism. Not only was feudalism well established as a system of political administration, but it supplied the warp and woof of economic organization during the entire period. Feudalism was seen even in the ethics and moral practices of the people. An institution that has prevailed for so long, governing the peoples' thinking and conduct will not fade out overnight.

Consequently, it is only natural that people of other countries expect paternalism to persist among the employers of Japan. Indeed, it would be entirely misleading to deny the existence of vestiges of paternalism in many forms even today, nearly a century after the abolition of the Shogunate and feudalism. However, in the domain of industrial relations, we will have to admit that the employers of Japan have not acted very differently from employers of other nations having little or no background of feudalism.[19] This much must be said, by way of a preface to the subject of workmen's compensation in Japan.

Under the old feudal ethics, an employer would have felt himself constrained by a sense of *giri*, or social justice, and *ninjo*, or humane sentiment, to do everything possible to relieve an employee from hardships resulting from injury sustained during work, without questioning much where the responsibility lay for the injury. In the hierarchical order of this rigidly stratified society, the employer was the master and the employee was his servant. It was the employer's duty as well as in his own interest to keep his servants hale, sound, and contented with their lot. Therefore there was no occasion for the knotty question of workmen's compensation to arise. But a fundamentally different situation emerged when modern industrialism was introduced into Japan after Meiji. When the civil and penal laws were remodeled and codified early in the Meiji era, the remodeling was carried out, not after the feudal practices, but after new Western concepts. In Japan, as in other modern nations, the liability of the employer in the event of an accident involving an employee was determined by the extent to which the employer was responsible for the accident. It might have been caused either by a willful act of the employer or by a failure on the part of the employer to take proper preventive measures. In either case, the employer would be held liable for the damage resulting from the accident. But, in order to claim damages, the employee had to produce proof. Moreover, if an accident occurred because of either willful conduct or negligence on the part of the employee, he was held liable as well. Occasionally, because of "contributory negligence" on the part of the employee, the employer could be absolved from any obligation. The unsatisfactoriness of this situation in the early Meiji period has already been noted, as well as the manner in which the government dealt with the matter in the Factory Act of 1911. Here the legal provisions found in the early laws will be traced more concretely.

According to Article 72 of the Mining Regulations enacted in 1890, in the event a mining worker sustained an injury through no fault of his own, the employer was obliged to pay for medical treatment and cure. Under these regulations, however, the employer could adjust the extent of his relief measures according to the degree to which the worker contributed to the accident. The regulation was so loose that the employee could be left without any relief in certain cases. This flaw was eliminated in 1905 when the Mining Act was passed. Under Article 80 of this Act, the employer was held liable for injury or death of a mining worker during work "unless it was due to serious fault of his own." In this case it was the employer who was held responsible for producing the proof of a "serious fault" on the part of the worker.

The same principle was applied in the Factory Act of 1911. In the Ordinance for the Administration of the Factory Act, issued in 1916, elaborate rules were laid down concerning relief in accident cases. In the same year, the same rules were laid down concerning relief of mining workers in case of accident. This was an improvement in the protection for both factory and mining workers, but the relief was more apparent than real as long as there was the escape clause saying "unless it was due to a serious fault of his own."

There were representations made by some individuals and

agencies on this subject, notably by Kyocho Kai, advising the government to delete the escape clause. This timely action of Kyocho Kai had its effect. In the Revised Factory Act of 1926, the phrase concerning "contributory negligence" was struck out. However, it must be noted that the employer could still appeal to the prefectural governor if he thought that the employee did actually contribute to the accident in one way or another and that the employer should not be held entirely liable for the damage. In such an event, the prefectural governor would have administrative authorities investigate the matter. Should the investigation establish a serious fault on the part of the employee, the employer need not pay the "allowances for absence from work" or "allowances for lasting injuries" sustained by the victim. However, even in cases where there had been serious fault on the part of the employee, the employer was still under obligation to pay other allowances, including (1) "allowance for medical treatment," (2) "allowance for terminating the aid," (3) "allowance for surviving family" and "allowance for conducting funeral" in the event of the death of an employee resulting from an accident incurred during his employment. Absolution of the employer from obligation to pay the "allowance for lasting injuries" was no small item, since the amounts the employer had to pay for the loss of the use of fingers, eyes, or limbs often constituted a crushing burden on the employer.

Although so far we have mentioned principally the provisions of the Factory Act, it should be noted that almost identical provisions were found in the Mining Workers' Regulations as revised in 1926.

A brief review of the legal provisions shows that before World War II the Japanese workers covered by these laws had, in case of accident sustained in the course of work, the right under public law to claim relief and the right under civil law to claim damage, although the law was carefully drawn up so that compensation could not be duplicated for the same accident.

The expression "accidents incurred in the course of work" has been used here without defining terms. "Accidents" include injuries, diseases, and death. But what injuries or diseases were actually covered by the law? Also what is meant by the "serious fault" of the worker? These are important questions that cannot be left ambiguous. Laws and ordinances have made detailed provisions on these points, but we cannot go into detail here.

DEVELOPMENT OF FREE EMPLOYMENT EXCHANGES

Origin—The Unemployment Problem

Unemployment is an area in which the impact of the ILO was particularly remarkable, although the Japanese government, after its early recognition of the problem could hardly be accused of complete failure to deal with it. After World War I there were two things that made the unemployment problem of the postwar depression period particularly acute: (1) the naval reduction imposed by the Naval Disarmament Conference of Washington in 1921 and the postwar depression period, and (2) the great earthquake of 1923.

As a consequence of the naval tonnage reduction, the Mitsubishi Shipbuilding Yard at Nagasaki, in February, 1922, dismissed no less than 3,732 men because they had to discontinue the construction of two battleships, the *Tosa* and the *Takao*. The company paid, in addition to the regular dismissal allowance required under company rules, a special allowance computed as follows:

Length of service in the company	Allowance computed on the basis of daily wage of each worker
Less than 1 year	Equivalent of 10 days wages
1–2 years	" " 80 " "
2–3 years	" " 100 " "
Over 3 years	" " 120 " "

In addition, the fare home and a small travel allowance was paid.

This was the first mass discharge. In October of the same year, in a second series of dismissals, 1,550 men were discharged. Three more series of dismissals followed, each resulting in the reduction by about one fifth of the total of 21,000 employees.

A similar action was taken by the Asano Shipyards at Tsurumi near Tokyo, when 1,640 men were discharged in April, 1922. At the Muroran Steel Works, 2,500 men were dismissed in four series, followed by the final discharge of 837 men out of 3,072 in the employ of the works in May, 1922. These were carried out with little commotion, thanks to the great care taken regarding discharge allowance, but when the Kawasaki Dockyards in Kobe proceeded to discharge 3,510 men, in July, 1927, it led to a furious protest. The workers had in fact met and demanded that the company make public its balance sheets, and make the best efforts to maintain the *status quo* (i.e., no dismissals), and that the directors of the company make up the losses of the company out of their private fortunes. Obviously, these demands of the workers were unrealistic and unrealizable.

The above are the more notable cases of dismissals. There were others, of course, of lesser dimensions. In the dozen or more arsenals and shipyards owned and operated by the government, there were series of dismissals that involved several thousand men at a time. In simultaneous mass dismissals carried out in May, 1924, the Navy discharged 7,148 men and the Army 11,589. The depressing effect of these drastic measures can be surmised.

A tragic incident that added much to the disaster was the earthquake of September, 1923, in the Tokyo and Yokohama areas. Of 15,000 factories in the Tokyo area, 9,000 were destroyed by fire. Of 135,000 factory operatives, 3,780 men were killed, 31,000 left the city, and approximately 20,000 were without shelter. The number of unemployed workers after the earthquake was estimated at 104,329—78,207 in Tokyo, 26,122 in Yokohama.

After this tragic experience, the authorities decided on an unemployment census. On October 1, 1925, the first important unemployment census was taken in twenty-four important industrial and urban centers of Japan. It should be noted here that the authorities took an early interest in the unemployment of intellectuals, and careful statistics have been compiled on the unemployment of college and technical school graduates.

Ratification of the ILO Conventions

The problem of unemployment has been both chronic and world-wide from the beginning of this century. That was why it was especially mentioned in the Preamble to the labor part of the Peace Treaty (which later became the Charter of the ILO), and also why it was taken up as the second item on the agenda at the First Session of the ILO Conference in 1919. The Conference adopted a Draft Convention which aimed at the establishment of free employment exchanges and eventual abolition of fee-charging or profit-making agencies for employment in industrial work. The following year (1920) at the Second Session of the Conference held at Genoa, Italy, another Draft Convention was adopted, applying the same benefits to seamen.

In Japan, the Convention of 1919 was approved and the law on the subject was enacted in April, 1921. The Employment Exchange Act, embodying the provisions of the Convention, was put into effect in July, 1921. Next, the 1920 Convention was approved and the Seamen's Employment Exchange Act, embodying the provisions of the 1920 Convention, was promulgated in 1922. Ratification of the two Conventions took place subsequently on November 23, 1922.

As the result of enforcement of these laws, a complete network of free public employment exchanges was set up all over Japan. The following chart shows the jurisdiction of the four local bureaus of the exchanges, which were set up in all prefectures as of April, 1927.

CHART III

JURISDICTION OF THE FOUR LOCAL BUREAUS AS OF APRIL, 1927

Local Bureaus	Prefectures Covered
The Tokyo Local Employment Exchange Bureau	Hokkaido, Tokyo, Kanagawa, Gumma, Saitama, Chiba, Ibaraki, Tochigi, Yamanashi, Nagano, Niigata, Miyagi, Fukushima, Iwate, Aomori, Yamagata, Akita.
The Osaka Local Employment Exchange Bureau	Osaka, Kyoto, Hyogo, Nara, Shiga, Tottori, Shimane, Okayama, Hiroshima, Wakayama, Tokushima, Kochi, Kagawa, Ehime
The Nagoya Local Employment Exchange Bureau	Aichi, Shizuoka, Mie, Gifu, Fukui, Ishikawa, Toyama
The Fukuoka Local Employment Exchange Bureau	Yamaguchi, Fukuoka, Nagasaki, Oita, Saga, Kumamoto, Miyagi, Kagoshima, Okinawa.

The action of the ILO provided a strong impetus to the spread of free employment exchanges. Table 21 below shows the speed with which they multiplied.

The pains taken by the government to accommodate the needs of workers seeking particular jobs and the degree of specialization of these exchanges is shown by the following figures: number of exchanges for day laborers, thirty-three; for women workers, thirteen; for juvenile workers, six; for technically skilled workers, one; for Korean laborers, three; and for intellectual workers, eleven.

TABLE 21
SPREAD OF FREE EMPLOYMENT
EXCHANGES

Year	Public Exchanges	Private Exchanges	Total
1919	—	—	48
1921	31	18	49
1922	81	28	109
1923	103	32	135
1924	130	45	175
1925	141	40	181
1926	146	41	187
1927	174	38	212
1928	191	36	227
1929	202	36	238

Privileges under Employment Exchange System

Some of the evils arising from the former profit-making and fee-charging employment agencies in this country were mentioned earlier. Rather than rehearse those abuses, we turn instead to the advantages to workers under the new system, some of which are more or less peculiar to Japan, since they are not all the result of the ILO conventions.

The service was performed gratis, but not for charity or from any paternalistic motive. It might, therefore, be regarded as a proper "right" of the worker. This arose from the Convention.

When an unemployed worker was given employment through the exchange system, he was given a 50 per cent reduction of the railway or boat fare to the place of employment. Seasonal workers and girls for silk filatures were denied this at first but later were given the same privilege. Often, day laborers had no money to pay their fares to the place of work. The exchange was prepared to "advance" this to the worker, according to his need. The exchange was equipped to lend tools to those laborers who needed them. At city exchanges, consultation stations were set up to give counseling services to young workers and help place them where they were best suited.

Special Exchanges for Seamen

The evil practices of seamen's employment exchanges are internationally known, and Japan was no exception. In 1922 there were no less than 270 fee-charging employment agencies in Japan. In order to counteract them, the government was subsidizing the employment agencies of the Japan Seamen's Aid Society, despite the fact that they were fee-charging (though not profit-making). In protest, the Japan Seamen's Union joined hands with the Japan Shipowners' Association, and began—with the co-operation of another organization for promoting seamen's welfare in general, the Kaiyo Toitsu Kyokai—a special employment exchange for seamen.

The role played at this juncture by Narasaki Itaro, president of the Japan Seamen's Union must be noted. At the time of the Ninth Session of the ILO Conference (1926), Narasaki went to Geneva as the workers' delegate from Japan and took this opportunity to appeal to the communications minister of the government for permission to establish a Joint Maritime Commission (Kaiji Kyodo Kai), consisting of the Japan Shipowners' Association, the Mercantile Marine Officers' Association, and the Japan Seamen's Union, as a permanent organ to promote co-operation between shipowners and seamen, to improve the treatment of seamen, to prevent and settle disputes, and so on. Of all these activities, one of the most necessary was the establishment of placement or employment exchanges for seamen. The government granted permission and very soon employment exchanges

TABLE 22

EMPLOYMENT EXCHANGE WORK IN PREWAR JAPAN
(1921–1929)[a]

Year	Workers Wanted	Workers Seeking Work	Workers Placed	Cases Handled	Percentage Placed Col. 3: Col. 2.	Exchanges Involved
1921	338,054	312,783	151,304	227,026	48	100
1922	450,729	453,267	199,962	340,564	44	103
1923	817,427	720,438	312,550	516,503	43	132
1924	1,095,567	979,346	444,382	728,072	45	161
1925	853,950	877,982	283,598	585,972	32	171
1926	729,720	780,610	223,001	462,179	29	183
1927	624,550	794,686	215,608	429,172	27	197
1928	690,275	750,798	215,717	416,873	28	214
1929[b]	243,840	273,019	78,839	150,317	29	238

[a] Work done for day laborers is not included in this table.
[b] Figures for January–April only.
SOURCE: Kyocho Kai, *Saikin no Shakai Undo*, p. 873

were established at ten ports: Kobe, Osaka, Yokohama, Tokyo, Otaru, Tobata, Shimonoseki, Moji, Hakodate, and Nagasaki.

The Joint Maritime Commission carried on its work steadily and with remarkable results, so much so that when Albert Thomas visited Japan in 1929, he was impressed with its achievements and was inspiring in his commendation.

Tables 22 and 23 show the results of the work of employment exchanges for workers on land and at sea.

TABLE 23

EMPLOYMENT EXCHANGE WORK FOR SEA-MEN (April, 1927–March, 1928)

Category	Men Wanted	Seeking Work	Placed
Officers	1,539	4,945	1,408
Seamen	23,203	33,991	22,225

SOURCE: Kyocho Kai, *op. cit.*, p. 874.

DEVELOPMENT OF SOCIAL INSURANCE

Social insurance is another area in which Japan made headway in prewar days and even before the ILO was born, but in which her later progress was helped by the adoption of a Convention of the ILO. To complete the picture of Japan's labor legislation of the prewar period, a brief account of the start made by Japan is given below.

Health Insurance

In the days when labor affairs were handled by various branches of the government, there was sufficient awareness among the authorities of the government of the need for social insurance. Studies were being made in the Department of Agriculture and Commerce, the Department of Communications, and elsewhere. In August, 1920, however, by an Imperial Ordinance, a new section called the Labor Section (Rodo Ka) was created in the Department of Agriculture and Commerce with the special assignment of studying the matter of social insurance with a view to preparing a bill. A draft of the bill was presented to a Labor Insurance Commission in November, 1921. The Commission was created by an Imperial Ordinance, and attached to the Ministry of Agriculture and Commerce. It consisted of some thirty high officials of the government and other "men of knowledge or experience." The draft bill underwent a thorough scrutiny by the Commission, and was submitted to the House of Representatives where it was adopted, but was accompanied by the following desiderata:

1. The government should not fail to make clear, in an Imperial Ordinance, the meaning of "standard wages."
2. The government should secure understanding of the entrepreneurs concerning the order to set up health insurance unions.
3. The government should plan to increase the share of the state treasury in the cost of the insurance, since it did not seem adequate.
4. The scope of the "insured persons" should be gradually expanded, since it was too limited.
5. The insurance scheme should be extended as early as possible to include invalid cases.
6. A system of insurance to cover seamen should be set up at the earliest opportunity.

The Bill, with these desiderata attached, was approved by the Diet *in toto,* and the Health Insurance Act was promulgated on April 22, 1922. When the Social Affairs Bureau was created in the Department of the Interior in November, 1922, it was assigned the administration of social insurance. The earthquake damages of 1923 temporarily prevented the government from carrying out the functions of social insurance. It was not until March, 1926, that the Revised Health Insurance Act and the Health Insurance Special Account Act were promulgated; the Health Insurance Act, as revised, became partially effective on July 1, 1926, and wholly on January 1, 1927.

Sickness insurance in Germany under Bismarck was enacted in 1883; Japan's came more than forty years later. However, the ILO Convention on the subject was adopted in 1927, and at that time Japan was among the handful of countries that already had a national law on the subject.

Since the law was enacted, innumerable revisions have been made in the detailed provisions, but the main outlines have remained the same. The gist of the law and how it functioned are given below.

Scope of the Legislation—Insured Persons.   The Act made

health insurance compulsory for all factory and mining workers covered by the Factory Act and the Mining Workers' Regulations. Provision was made for the extension of the scheme to building, transport, engineering, and some other trades, and also to factories not yet covered by the factory legislation, provided the employer obtained previous consent of more than half of the persons to be insured. Administrative employees receiving salaries of more than 1,200 yen a year, workers of foreign nationality (mostly Korean), and temporary workers were excluded.

Insurance Carriers. The state and health insurance societies were the carriers, set up by order of the minister of the interior or voluntarily with the minister's permission. At an undertaking where not less than 300 but fewer than 500 insurable workers were employed, and the consent of the majority of the workers was obtained, a voluntary society could be set up. Several employers with less than 300 employees each could combine to get a total membership of over 300, and could then obtain the minister's permission to set up a society, provided they had previous consent of the majority of their employees. When 500 or more workers were employed, the setting up of a society was compulsory. A society was composed of the employer and all insured persons of his undertaking, together with such of his former employees as still desired to remain insured. A board of directors and a delegates' committee managed each society, the employers and the workers being equally represented on each body. The functions of the state were to see that all regulations were observed and to pay the state subsidy to cover administrative expenses.

The state acted directly as the insurance carrier for all insurable workers not covered by health insurance societies. The state insurance was carried out by offices on a territorial basis; the health insurance societies were organized on a company or establishment basis. In the government offices there was no representation of the employers and employees. The Insurance Division of the Social Affairs Bureau was the central authority for supervision. Local offices were supervised by prefectural governors.

Risks and Benefits. The risks covered by the health insurance scheme were sickness, injury, maternity, and death.

For sickness or injury the benefit was granted in the form of medical attendance and cash payments. Medical attendance included medical advice and medicines, surgical operations, dental treatment, home nursing, hospital care, and conveyance in an ambulance when necessary. Treatment in a hospital might involve reduced cash payment. Family conditions were investigated in cases involving cash payments.

Medical treatment would begin on the day of occurrence of sickness or injury, and would last a maximum of 180 days for the same illness or injury or for a total of 180 days in the course of a year in respect of several illnesses and injuries. Any case lasting for more than 180 days was considered by the legislators as lying outside the scope of sickness insurance and coming more properly under a scheme of invalid insurance.

There was a cash benefit of 60 per cent of the daily wages of the worker concerned, in addition to the medical attendance, which began to be paid from the first day of the occurrence of sickness or injury if it arose in the course of work. Otherwise, the grant of the benefit would commence on the fourth day.

Combination with Workmen's Compensation. The legislators took care to ensure that the sick or injured worker continued to receive the benefits in case he or she was not completely recovered after the expiration of 180 days maximum. If the sickness or injury had resulted from the employment, the Workmen's Compensation provisions of the Factory Act or of the Mining Workers' Regulations would take care of the rest. In such cases, the employer had to pay an "absence allowance" of 40 per cent of wages and continue the medical treatment until the recovery of the worker, or for a period of three years from the date he was incapacitated. When permanent incapacity had resulted from employment, a lump sum varying from 40 to 540 days' wages had to be paid, based on the seriousness of the injury, which was tabulated. In the event that injury resulted in death, a lump sum equivalent to at least 360 days' wages had to be paid to the survivors.

As regards maternity benefits, the health insurance scheme was worked out to supplement the factory and mining laws. Under the Revised Factory Act in force from 1923 on and the mining regulations of 1926, women expecting childbirth could, if they desired, obtain suspension from work four weeks before confinement, and were guaranteed six weeks compulsory suspension after confinement. During these periods of suspension from work, a maternity benefit amounting to 60 per cent of the woman's wages was granted. In order to prevent abuses of the maternity benefit, the law required that the woman must have been insured for at least 180 days before confinement.

The maternity benefit varied in amount since it was 60 per cent of each woman's wages. In addition to the maternity benefit, however, there was a flat lump-sum payment, or "confinement benefit." It was 20 yen at the time the law went into effect, which covered the actual cost at that time. When there was need for it, the woman could be hospitalized and looked after by a doctor or a midwife. In such instances the amount of the maternity or confinement benefit could be reduced by the institution which took care of the woman.

In the event of the death of the insured worker, there was the "burial benefit" to defray the burial expenses, amounting to thirty days' of the worker's wages, payable to whoever among the surviving relatives or dependents of the deceased worker performed the burial.

Financial resources.   The financial resources of health insurance were three: state subsidy, the employers' contribution, and the workers' contribution.

The state subsidy represented 10 per cent of the expenditure on benefits incurred by each insurance institution, and was designed to cover approximately the total cost of administration.

The contributions of employers and workers were, in principle, equal in amount. The law fixed the lowest and highest basic wages, and the workers' wages were divided into sixteen wage classes for the purpose of calculating the contributions. In the case of a worker actually receiving less than the lowest basic wage, the principle of equal contributions of employers and workers was waived and the employer would pay the legal minimum while the worker's share would be below the minimum. In the case of especially dangerous trades, the employer might be required to pay two thirds of the contribution, while the worker's contribution would never exceed 3 per cent of his wages.

It is interesting to note that as long as a worker was receiving cash benefits of any kind (for sickness, injury, or maternity) no contribution was collected from that worker. The collecting of the contribution was done by a checkoff system, or by automatic deduction by the employer from the wages of the workers.

Health Insurance at Work.   To what extent did this system develop? How many workers were actually covered by this law?

We give below the figures for the five years 1926–1930, during which Japan's industries might be considered to have been in more or less normal or healthy conditions. We should add that, at the end of 1930, the total number of workers in Japanese factories and mines was 2,301,867, according to *Rōdō Jihō* of 1931. This means that over 81 per cent of the factory and mining workers were covered by the health insurance scheme.

TABLE 24

WORKERS COVERED BY HEALTH INSURANCE
SCHEME (1926–1930)

Year	Insured at Health Insurance offices	Insured in Health Insurance societies	Insured in Mutual Aid societies[a]	Total
1926	1,140,865	800,581	160,000[b]	2,101,446
1927	1,115,221	774,023	160,000[b]	2,049,244
1928	1,160,953	772,679	158,333	2,091,965
1929	1,032,380	773,529	165,955	1,971,864
1930	1,079,128	639,019	159,688	1,877,835

[a] In Japan the government is engaged in various important enterprises, and a large number of workers are employed. In the following ten enterprises mutual-aid societies were established, which undertook the insurance with the sanction of the Minister of the Interior: Printing Bureau of the Cabinet, Monopoly Bureau, Mint, military arsenal, naval arsenals, Forestry Bureau, State Iron Foundry, State Railways, Postal, Telephone and Telegraph Services, and Civil Engineering Works.

[b] Mere estimates, which naturally would affect the accuracy of the total figures for the year.

SOURCE: *Rōdō Jihō*, March, 1931

As already explained, the health insurance societies were institutions set up by private bodies with the permission of the minister of the interior. The figures in Table 25 are interesting, since they show the extent of development of social insurance in private enterprises.

Post-Office Insurance

It is not quite appropriate to take up Post-Office Insurance under a section entitled "Development of Social Insurance," since it is not "social" insurance. Employers have no part in it, though the government is the insurance carrier. It is an ordinary insurance, except that ordinary insurance is run on a profit-making

TABLE 25
HEALTH INSURANCE
SOCIETIES (1931)

Textile factories	137
Machine and tool factories	58
Chemical factories	38
Food and drink factories	12
Electricity, gas, smelting	3
Miscellaneous	13
Coal mines	51
Metal industry works	19
Metal refining works	3
Non-metal industry	1
Others	9
Total	344

SOURCE: *Kenkō Hoken Jihō*, January, 1932

basis, whereas the sole objective of Post-Office Insurance was to help the people of small means who could not afford to take out ordinary insurance, which was expensive. The Japanese expression for this is *Kan-yi Seimei Hoken* (Simple Life Insurance). In English it is called "Post-Office Insurance," since the whole business is carried on at post offices throughout Japan.

Ordinary insurance was introduced into Japan in 1881, but, noticing that it was too costly for people of small means, the government investigated the matter and, as a result, the Simple Life Insurance Act was passed early in 1916, and went into operation in October, 1916.

Under this Act anybody between twelve and sixty years of age could take out insurance at the post office without undergoing a physical examination by paying very small premiums, which either could be paid at the post office window or collected by the mail carrier monthly. If one preferred, it could be paid on a yearly basis. If an insured person was incapacitated after having taken out the insurance, he was exempted from payment of premiums thereafter. In case a person failed to pay a premium, he was allowed a two-month period of grace, after which the policy was invalidated, but the same person could renew the contract within a year's time. A policyholder might benefit by loans from the insurance system at very low rates of interest (4.8 per cent). In case of surrender or lapse of a policy, a sum equivalent to from 80 to 98 per cent of the reserve accumulated for the insured person might be refunded, provided that one year had elapsed since the contract had come into force.

In order to prevent persons in too poor a state of health from taking out insurance, the full sums insured were not paid if the person died within two years from the policy's date of issue. Instead, if death occurred within one year, the premiums paid up to the time of death were refunded, and if within two years, one-half the value of the policy was paid.

The system was a success from the start. At the end of 1929 some 14,275,000 policyholders were insured for a total of 1,895,884,000 yen. The insurance combined a system of endowments, or old-age insurance. Of those 14,275,000 policies, 4,129,-000 were life insurance and the rest were old-age insurance.

PREVENTION AND SETTLEMENT OF LABOR DISPUTES

The Crucial Year of 1926

In the world outside Japan, and particularly in Europe, the year 1926 was the memorable year that Germany was admitted into the League of Nations; this removed the tension that had paralyzed the new organ for international peace. The League of Nations henceforth would cease to be a tool of victor nations and would become a body to promote genuine co-operation among all nations. "Never again a war!" was the declaration of both Briand of France and Streseman of Germany at the Assembly of the League of Nations. World peace and economic prosperity now seemed assured.

In Japan, by coincidence, 1926 was the year when several legislative measures of surpassing interest to the working class were taken simultaneously. They were: the Health Insurance Act, brought into force in 1926; enforcement of the Revised Factory Act, which came to be applied on a much wider scale than before; repeal of Public Peace Police Act, Articles 17 and 30, thereby extending the freedom of workers in exercising their trade-union rights, and promulgation of the Labor Disputes Mediation Act. In the preceding sections the contents of the first three have been explained; only the last needs to be examined here.

The Labor Disputes Mediation Act, 1926

According to the statistical table of labor disputes, 1926 was a peak year in both the number of dispute cases and the number of participants. Strong opinions were expressed, both inside the government and outside, that the Public Peace Police Act should be amended, but as to the timeliness of legislation concerning mediation, there was no agreement. Some employers urged that a mediation law should be enacted only after the question of a trade-union law was settled, and that if a mediation law must be enacted, the terms of mediation awarded by the mediation board should be compulsory. Some contended that private enterprises should be excluded from application of the law. Some scholars and newspapers, who had seen the draft of the proposed law, criticized the lack of power of compulsion on the part of the mediators. Trade-unions, on the other hand, were unanimous in approving the repeal of the Public Peace Police Act, Articles 17 and 30, but were opposed to the proposed mediation law.

Content of the Act—Coverage. The law provided for an *ad hoc* committee to be set up at the outbreak of a labor dispute. What constituted a labor dispute was not defined. But it was clear that disputes involving individuals were not covered, nor did a dispute come under the law if it had nothing to do with conditions of work. A dispute did not necessarily have to involve a strike or a lockout, nor were disputes confined to any particular industry. The only distinction made was between disputes involving public utilities and those in industry.

Machinery of mediation. Mediation under this law could be effected only through the mediation board, tripartite in composition, with three men representing the employers, three the workers, and three neutral. It was not a permanent board, but an *ad hoc* committee appointed to deal with a specific dispute.

In the case of public utilities, a mediation board would set to work with or without the request of the parties to a dispute, but in the case of private industries, the request for mediation had to come from both sides. The parties, upon receipt of notice from the authorities, had to select three men to represent them and file the report thereon within three days after receipt of the notice. If either party failed to file the report, the government had to engage the representatives within four days. When the selection process was completed, appointment of the representatives by the prefectural government had to take place.

The board had the power of summons and of inspection of records. The members of the board also had the power to go to the spot where the dispute arose. The board had to complete its work within fifteen days after it took up a dispute and present an award of mediation.

Effect of mediation.   The award of a mediation board was in the nature of a recommendation and had no binding effect, its objective being simply to arouse public sympathy or support. Nor was the board under obligation to publicize the matter if a compromise was reached.

Limitation of dispute action.   A limitation was laid down on the matter of arousing the sentiments of employers or workers regarding the dispute. Only "the employers or workers actually involved in the dispute and officers or staff members of either the employers' or workers' organization" were allowed to engage in dispute activity.

TABLE 26
LABOR DISPUTES SETTLED BY MEDIATION
(1922–1928)

Year	(A) Dispute Cases	(B) Settled by mediation	(C) Percentage B:A
1922	584	77	13
1923	647	117	18
1924	933	157	17
1925	816	120	15
1926	1,260	261	21
1927	1,202	351	29
1928	1,013	250	24

SOURCE: Kyocho Kai, *Saikin no Shakai Undo*, p. 812.

Results achieved.   The Labor Disputes Mediation Act was promulgated on April 7, 1926, and went into effect July 1, 1926. The Labor Section of the Social Affairs Bureau of the Ministry of the Interior was the national center of administration of this Act. A number of officers were appointed on a full-time basis in twenty-one of the more industrialized prefectures in the four islands of Hokkaido, Honshu, Shikoku, and Kyushu, all trained and set for action.

In the course of fifteen years (1927–1942), this law was resorted to in only six cases. It may not be too severe to say that this law was not a success. However, as the table above indicates, a large number, even an increasing number, of disputes were settled by mediation. The other statistics available on the subject show that there was also an increasing interest in mediation on the part of such government officials as mayors of towns and villages, civil servants, and police officers. It may be said that the law served to arouse their interest and activity in this direction.

The Trade-Union Bills

So far, the laws in force for the prevention or settlement of labor disputes have been examined. The only law which remains to be examined is one conspicuous by its absence, i.e., the trade-union law. That Japan had no law guaranteeing the basic rights of a trade-union was anomalous, considering the degree of industrial development she had achieved so far. Following is how the matter stood before Japan entered World War II.

Early Steps of the Government. There were forces at work that kept pushing the government to enact a trade-union law, because the ravages of industrialism were leading to acute restiveness of the workers and to criticism of the government and employers from various quarters. One thing that had a compelling and decisive effect was, of course, the advent of the ILO. Having been assigned a position of honor and responsibility in the ILO as a permanent member of the Governing Body, Japan could no longer afford to dodge the issue. She had too many laws restricting the free exercise of normal trade-union rights. There were too many disputes arising because of those laws. Too many unions were being born. They needed recognition.

As a matter of fact, the government did begin a study of the question in June, 1918, when the Ministry of the Interior established a Commission for Study of Relief Work, and charged it with looking into the question of how to harmonize capital and labor. As a result of that study the commission adopted a resolution in March, 1919, to the effect that "it is best to leave the trade-unions to grow naturally." However, the government was not allowed to maintain for long such a blissful attitude of nonchalance. As far as the ILO was concerned, the very honor or prestige of the Japanese government was at stake. In February, 1920, by Imperial Ordinance, Rinji Sangyo Chōsa Kai (the Temporary Commission for Investigation of Industries) was appointed. One of the main tasks of this commission was to draft a trade-union bill for the government. About the time this commission started its work, newspapers reported that Minister of the Interior Tokonami Takejiro had expressed the opinion that only unions vertically organized within an enterprise should be recognized officially. This report led to an explosion of controversy among the business-men, industrialists, and scholars. The report in the papers was denied by Tokonami, but it rendered a signal service by starting a lively discussion, and it is still regarded as an incident of historic moment. Tokonami explained at a special committee meeting of the Seiyu Kai that the rumor was both warped and misleading. What he had intended to say was that a committee to facilitate exchange of ideas between capital and labor should be set up. Tokonami, in addition to being minister of the interior, was concurrently the governor-general of the railways, and it was at his initiative that the national railways department had had works committees organized in the various shops of the railways. It is possible that he had something of that sort in mind when he made his widely misquoted statement.

Draft bills of the Government Departments.   As was pointed out earlier, before the creation of a proper Department of Labor, labor matters were not handled in a clear-cut fashion, which led to an interesting rivalry between the Ministry of Agriculture and Commerce and the Ministry of the Interior. They both studied the matter seriously, and both published draft bills on trade-unions.

According to the draft of the Ministry of Agriculture and Commerce, made public in January, 1920, trade-unions had to be based on crafts or occupations closely related to one another, they had to be organized territorially on a prefectural basis, they were to be legally constituted and established and were to come into existence by official permission of the authorities, and the govern-ment would have the power to dissolve the union or change its officers. The union would be strictly watched by the authorities, and practically no privileges would be granted. In the explanation attached to the draft there was the statement that "trade-unionism is spreading all over the world, exerting influence on the develop-ment of industry. Should the labor movement turn wrong, it is apt to undermine the foundations of industrial organization and bring about confusion of national ideas. That is the reason it is urgently necessary to have a trade-union order to provide the proper orientation to the labor movement."

In sharp contrast to this draft was the one prepared by the

Ministry of the Interior and published in May, 1920. Here a trade-union was defined as "an organization, or a federation thereof, of fifteen or more workers organized with the objectives of maintaining or improving the conditions of work, promoting mutual aid or culture among the members, or protecting or extending the common interest of the members." There was no limitation on the trade or territory covered by a union. Nor was there a need to obtain permission of the authorities to form a union. All that was necessary was to file a report after formation of a union. Acquisition of legal personality was optional. Freedom of association was guaranteed. The aim of legislation was to bring present and future unions under legal protection.

The publication of these drafts by the two government departments aroused great excitement among the men engaged in trade-union work, especially since they were resentful of the government's attitude in practically ignoring the existing unions. The Kansai Federation of Sodomei in April, 1920, adopted a Resolution demanding, "in view of the turmoil resulting from the failure of the government to recognize the existing unions, that the existing unions be officially recognized and that the capitalists who were obstructing union activities be penalized." After this, there were drafts of trade-union bills published by the employers' organizations, academic societies, various political parties, and other bodies. But, because of the nonrecognition of the existing unions by the government in the selection of the workers' delegate to the ILO Conference, the attitude of most trade-union leaders was turning into the proverbial "sour-grapes" attitude of dislike. Direct action instead of parliamentarianism was the general attitude of the workers of Japan till 1925.

In the meantime, there was a change in the political climate of the world outside of Japan, influenced by the emergence of the Labor Government in England in 1923. In Japan, general suffrage was finally achieved in 1925. It was in this changed political climate that the draft of the Social Affairs Bureau was presented to the meeting of the Councilors of the Bureau. The gist of this draft, which has since become a classic, was as follows:

The trade-union was defined as "an organization, or a federation thereof, of ten or more workers, organized with the objective of maintaining or improving the conditions of work" (Article 1).

No limitation as to trades or territory was made, no official permission was needed for forming a union, and the mere filing of a report on formation of a union was sufficient (Article 2).

Acquisition of a legal personality was optional (Article 4).

The right to join a union was guaranteed (Article 11).

Provisions regarding the effects of collective bargaining were laid down (Article 12).

Provisions regarding the forcible dissolution of a union were deleted.

On the whole, the draft bill prepared by the Social Affairs Bureau was decidedly more progressive than the one prepared by the Ministry of Agriculture and Commerce. It was popular among trade-unions, except those that denied political action of any sort. Other organizations of businessmen and industrialists were engaged in the study of a trade-union bill and published their views on the matter. It was the outbreak of the Manchurian Incident that put an end to practically all discussion relating to trade-union legislation.

THE ILO AND JAPANESE LABOR

The ILO Tokyo Office Established

The tremendous effect on Japan of the Washington Conference of the ILO in 1919 has been described earlier in these pages. "Sensational" is perhaps the best word to describe the situation that developed in Japan during and soon after the conference. How organized labor agitated in the turmoil that resulted has also been traced briefly, and how labor legislation developed steadily under the influence, direct or indirect, of the ILO.

Parenthetically, three incidents that occurred in Japan after the Washington Conference and highlighted the course of fruitful relations between Japan and the ILO will be described here briefly. The first of these was the establishment of a branch office of the ILO in Japan in 1923. The ILO had branch offices already set up in London, Paris, Berlin, Rome, and Washington. The action of the Governing Body in setting up a branch in Tokyo was welcomed by the government and the people of Japan as a tangible expression of the importance the ILO attached to Japan as a nation of high industrial importance.

The action of the Governing Body was both timely and propitious, in that conditions in Japan at this time were fast reaching the point that not only government officials, but also employers and trade-union leaders, could now derive full benefit from the stimuli supplied by the ILO.

One thing that made this action of the ILO doubly propitious was the choice of Asari Junshiro as director of the Tokyo Office. Asari, who was appointed to that important post by Albert Thomas, then director of the Geneva Office, was by training a mining inspector for the Ministry of Agriculture and Commerce. A young man, barely thirty, he did meet some opposition to his appointment to a post of such high responsibility, but he overcame this by his lofty idealism, courage, and devotion to his work. On arrival in Tokyo, after about a year's training at the Geneva office, he was able to secure the advice and friendly backing of leading university professors, influential journalists, prominent members of the Diet, and others in pursuing his work.

Asari organized the office in the building of Kyocho Kai, a private organization set up by liberal-minded business men for the "harmonization of relations between capital and labor." He was fortunate in finding such capable and promising young staff members as Miss Ichikawa Fusae, who later became the leader of the women's suffrage movement in Japan, and a young scholar who later became the president of Kyushu University, Dr. Kikuchi Isao.

Asari died of tuberculosis in 1934, and was widely mourned by all who knew of his devoted work for the ILO.

Albert Thomas' Visit

In 1929, Albert Thomas, the active and indefatigable director of the ILO, came to Japan, accompanied by Edward Phelan, chief of the Diplomatic Division, and several other staff members of the Geneva Office. The primary object of the visit was to promote the cause of the ILO generally by arousing the interest of the government and people of Japan in matters relating to the ILO, through direct personal contact with the government officials and leaders in industry and in workers' movements.

Thomas was received by the Emperor; he also met the prime minister and all other members of the Cabinet, and addressed gatherings of employers and capitalists, university professors and students, social workers and unionists. He visited a large number of factories and workshops, and met and spoke intimately with the working men and women.

A man of tremendous energy, Albert Thomas was able to speak convincingly to people of all ranks about the need to establish a wholesome industrial order based on "social justice." Thomas was a man of eloquence and great personal charm. He left a deep impression on all he met. Indeed, few visitors from abroad were ever received with the degree of spontaneous enthusiasm and appreciation that greeted Albert Thomas.

His visit provided the occasion for the organizing of Rodo Rippo Sokushin Iinkai (the Committee for the Promotion of Labor Legislation), an organization that Sodomei and other national unions of the right wing had been planning for months. The first meeting of the committee was held on December 5, 1929, at Kobe, where Thomas' party landed, and Thomas himself addressed the historic gathering.

Thomas' visit served also to strengthen the Joint Maritime Commission, which the shipowners and seamen of Japan had organized previously, since Thomas had been urging the shipowners and seamen of Europe to take the same course of action as the Japanese had.

More than thirty years have passed since Albert Thomas came to Japan, but even today he is remembered in this country with esteem and affection by those who met him.

The Mission of Fernand Maurette

In 1932, three years after Thomas' visit, another high official of the ILO came to Japan: M. Fernand Maurette, chief of the Scientific Division of the ILO. This visit had a more precise and clearly defined purpose, which was to investigate on the spot the charges of unfair trade practice of which Japan had been accused in international conventions and in trade journals.

It must be recalled in this connection that during World War I the textile manufacturers of Europe were practically forced to abandon their foreign markets. This deficiency during the war years and for several years thereafter was met largely by goods made in Japan. It is said that the worst period of a war is the postwar period. After World War I it took many years for Europe to recover; in the meantime Japan, with the advantage of machinery newer and more efficient than the outmoded mills of Lancashire and Lyon, was advancing into the world markets that the European nations had been forced to neglect or abandon.

In complete disregard of the truth of the situation, Japanese manufacturers were being charged at international conferences with "social dumping." Japan was accused of unfairly underselling other nations with goods manufactured by workers who were being paid very low wages and were required to work under inferior conditions.

M. Maurette visited factory after factory all over Japan. He visited a few mines also. He met the government officers in charge of factory inspection, and trade-union leaders, particularly those working at textile mills. He met employers and journalists, and, not content with written reports, he tried to verify conditions personally.

After nearly a month's study on the spot, he came to the conclusion that the charges of social dumping were unfounded. He had discovered that the machinery in Japan was newer and much more efficient than that used by the nations who were complaining about Japanese competition. The Japanese, he found, were often more industrious and hard-working than the workers in some other countries. As for wages, hours, and other conditions, he found that higher real wages were being paid, hours were shorter, and conditions of work were improving from year to year. If "social dumping" meant lowering conditions of work or deliberately keeping them low so that a nation could undersell others, such a practice was not found in Japan. This was M. Maurette's conclusion.

Unquestionably the fair and unbiased report of M. Maurette was effective in refuting the charge of social dumping. Not only that: it served also to enhance the moral authority of the ILO itself.

JAPANESE LABOR IN WARTIME (1931–1945)

The Fourteen Years' War

Depending on the angle from which the whole event is regarded, various names have been given to the war, or, rather, the chain of wars, that began in the 1930s and ended in 1945. In Japan, it began in 1931 as the "Manchurian Incident," which dragged on and degenerated into the "China Incident" in 1937, and ended in the "War for Greater East Asia" or the "Pacific War" (1941–1945). Leaving aside political and ethical considerations, it is unrealistic to call it "World War II." World War II officially broke out in September, 1939, with Hitler's invasion of Poland.

But *de facto* war had started back in 1931. In studying labor relations and the interests of the working class, one must be realistic. The Japanese might call it the "Fourteen Years' War," since for them it lasted that long.

By a series of tragic incidents, which cannot be dwelt upon here, political power in Japan had fallen into the hands of a desperate military group in 1931. A carefully planned military action of the Japanese army commenced on September 18, 1931. At lightning speed, Japanese troops swept over the whole territory of Manchuria, and, in 1932, the puppet state of Manchu-Kuo was established. The League of Nations was taken by surprise and proved powerless in the face of this overt action by Japan. (Japan withdrew from the League of Nations in 1933.[20]) The Japanese invasion spread like a flood over China proper, and the China Incident broke out in 1937. Then, like a tidal wave, it advanced farther south and, in 1941, submerged French Indo-China. The United States protested, and Japan responded with the surprise attack on Pearl Harbor. The Pacific War, which began then, came to an end with Japan's final surrender on August 15, 1945. For Japan, it had been a long war, the longest she had ever fought— fourteen years.

In this war, Japan took the wrong policy vis-à-vis the labor movement, just as Germany did in both world wars. In the case of Germany, that policy finally proved fatal. In Japan's case, it was not quite fatal, but nearly so. Both Axis powers at the outset of the war adopted a policy of weakening or suppressing the genuine trade-union movement, instead of strengthening it and securing, as the Allied Powers did in the two wars, the full co-operation of organized labor in the prosecution of the war. In Germany, in World War I, Kaiser Wilhelm II's policy of suppressing labor led to the downfall of the empire. Hitler did not learn from this, nor did Japan for that matter, as will be seen in the following pages.

Japan withdrew from the League of Nations in 1933 and from the ILO in 1938. The latter step, incidentally, involved the breaking away from all other forms of international co-operation. Japan was pursuing policies like those of the two other Axis powers, Germany and Italy—which meant that democratic institutions were being step by step suppressed. Strangely, at the general elections in 1936 and 1937 the parties of the working class registered a remarkable advance, but this was a passing phenomenon. In 1938 the General Mobilization Law was promulgated, which was the signal for preparation for a headlong plunge into total war.

Labor's Lot in the War Period and the Birth of Sanpo

For a brief period after the "success" of the Manchurian Incident, when, because of its apparent impotence in dealing with the new state of Manchu-Kuo, the League of Nations had become a laughingstock among cynical critics throughout the world, Japan's war industries were enjoying illusory gains and the workmen employed by them were living in a fool's paradise. Unemployment was disappearing. Wages were on the increase; industries were expanding. A drop in the exchange rate of yen as a result of the inflation occasioned by the sudden expansion of the munitions industries meant an increase in exports. The result was that trade-unions gained strength through increased membership. In fact, Japanese trade-unions reached the highest peak of the prewar period in 1936, with a total of 420,589 members.

As a result of the favorable economic situation, the number of dispute cases decreased from the outbreak of the Manchurian Incident up to 1935; also, there were fewer strikes and the number of participants in disputes decreased from year to year, as Table 27 shows.

However, the illusions of the fool's paradise could not last much longer. The China Incident became a contest in which every move Japan's war leaders made only dragged the Mikado's loyal troops farther into a muddy river from which there was no return. Munitions works were kept busy, employment increased, nominal wages kept rising, but peace industries were all condemned and shrinking. Sickness and accident cases multiplied. Deterioration of working conditions led to an increase in labor disputes. To cope with this situation, the government, which was under military control, only tightened economic controls. In Japan, as in any country at war, it was the working class that bore the heaviest burden of sacrifice. Under wartime control the workers had lost the freedom to choose their occupations. Prices were rising at the same time that wages were under strict control. The inevitable consequences were lower efficiency, more disputes, and widespread unrest.

In this situation it was only natural for the workers to show signs of resistance. It has been noted that trade-union membership in prewar Japan reached its peak in 1936. The leaders of the

TABLE 27

WARTIME TRADE-UNION STRENGTH AND LABOR DIS-
PUTES (1931–1944)

Year	Dispute[a] Cases	Strikes[b] and other stoppage	Partici- pants	Unions	Member- ship
1931	2,456	993	64,536	818	368,975
1932	2,217	893	54,783	932	377,625
1933	1,897	610	45,423	942	384,277
1934	1,915	626	49,536	965	387,964
1935	1,872	590	37,734	993	408,662
1936	1,975	547	30,900	973	420,589
1937	2,126	628	123,730	837	359,290
1938	1,050	262	18,341	731	375,191
1939	1,120	258	72,835	517	365,804
1940	718	226	32,160	49	9,455
1941	330	158	8,562	11	895
1942	259	166	9,029	3	111
1943	417	279	9,418	3	155
1944	236	216	6,627	0	0

[a] Disputes including those which did not end in strike, sabotage, etc.
[b] Only those disputes which ended in strikes or other work stoppages.
SOURCE: Suehiro, *Nihon Rōdō Kumiai Undō Shi*, p. 73

organized movement, increasingly aware of the approaching
totalitarian control, joined forces in 1934, and the left-wing body
called Rōdō Kumiai Sō-Hyōgi Kai (the General Council of Trade-
Unions), which had professed to remain a legal or law-abiding
leftist federation, combined with Nippon Rōdō Kurabu Haigeki
Dōmei (the League to Combat the Japan Labor Club) and
formed Nippon Rodo Kumiai Zenkoku Hyogi Kai (the National
Council of Japanese Trade-Unions), but this action proved futile
under the military dictatorship of the day. It was ordered dissolved
in 1937, as was mentioned earlier in connection with the splits in
the main stream of the growth of trade-unions. As for Sodomei
itself, the tragic end of that mainstay of Japanese trade-unions
must be recorded here.

The rightist elements in Sodomei, always few in number but
ever present, had left it earlier. The top leaders, known as the
Kanbu-Ha began reluctantly to show signs of supporting the war
effort at about the time of the outbreak of the Manchurian
Incident. They tried to maintain the precarious life of the
organization by combining, as a compromise, with the more

nationally minded "central" group, Zenkoku Rōdō Kumiai Dōmei (the National Federation of Trade-Unions), but this was no more effective than a plaster as a cure for a fatal malady. When the order to form the Sanpo, the patriotic national organization of labor, was handed down, the office of Sodomei crumbled. In 1940 Sodomei ceased to exist, ending a life that began with Yuai Kai 28 years earlier, in 1912.

Sanpo is the abbreviation of the longer Japanese title Sangyo Hokoku Kai (Industrial Patriotic Society). It was designed to ensure the co-operation of management and labor in all plants throughout the nation for the effective prosecution of war. People are apt to equate it with the Arbeitsfront in Nazi Germany, but this is inaccurate, since, although the basic ideas of Sanpo and Arbeitsfront are largely identical, the movement in Japan started at the suggestion of local police officers who had been engaged in labor relations control work. The sporadic trials of the local police impressed the central authority, especially since Kyocho Kai assumed sponsorship in turning this into a national organization in response to the National General Mobilization Law in March, 1938. In August of that year an official memorandum issued jointly by the vice-ministers of Welfare and of the Interior suggested to the prefectural governors that they promote the organization of the Sanpo. Another joint communication of the two vice-ministers directed the governors to establish the Sanpo in their respective prefectures; it also directed that each governor become the president of his prefectural organization.

How did organized labor react to this? As already intimated, the pressure was too great. Reluctantly but steadily it succumbed. In Sodomei, the central group, led by Matsuoka Komakichi and Nishio Suehiro, tried in vain to maintain as far as possible the identity and autonomy of organized labor by co-operating with the war effort of the military government; the more nationally minded group, led by such men as Kono Mitsu, urged that organized labor should dissolve completely and become an integral part of the patriotic national organization. The latter position had the approval of the government, which, at the Diet Session in February, 1940, explained that it "wished the trade-unions to dissolve in the developmental sense," and that "its policy was to spread the Sanpo movement so as to remove the need for the trade-union movement."

The philosophy on which the Sanpo was predicated was that

of the old traditional family system. *Jigyo Ikka* ("Enterprise Family") was its slogan. The head of the enterprise or of management was the father of the family and all the employees represented his children. All were to work together in harmony for higher productivity and ultimate victory in the war. In the years around 1940–1941, the movement seemed to thrive, with more than 19,060 organizations throughout Japan with a total membership exceeding three million supporting it. It apparently succeeded in reducing membership in trade-unions, but it did not succeed in reducing the number of labor disputes, shown in Table 27.

Labor Legislation of the War Period

Ordinarily one does not—indeed, one must not—expect a normal development of labor laws in any country at war. It is a delightful surprise, therefore, to find in Japan some instances of progress in labor legislation during this period, though in no case could it be considered substantial progress.

Generally speaking, labor laws of a liberal nature were at a standstill during the fourteen war years. The attempt to enact a trade-union law came to an end in 1931. The laws designed primarily to "protect" labor, such as the Factory Act and the Mining Workers' Regulations, underwent major improvements for the last time in 1929. The legal benefits of workmen's compensation, hitherto confined to factory and mining workers, were extended in 1931 to such outdoor workers as those engaged in construction and transportation works. Another remarkable development was the *Shōten Hō* (Commercial Shops Act), enacted in 1938, which placed workers in commercial shops under the protection of law. This was not strictly a "war necessity" but it was done nonetheless.

In 1938 a new department of the government called the Welfare Ministry was created. The government was awakening to the necessity of safeguarding the health and well-being of the nation and of establishing for that purpose a new ministry. One might say that in this instance war necessity was a major motivation. As a matter of fact, innumerable modifications were made in the rules regulating conditions of work as *senji tokurei* (wartime exceptions). There was, for instance, a rule made in 1938 to limit working hours to twelve hours per day. This measure was enforced to prevent the exhaustion of manpower. In other words, it was war necessity rather than liberal or humanistic ideas which prompted the government to take this measure. The idea of protection of labor was only incidental or secondary—prosecution of the war was the paramount need.

However, of all areas of labor legislation, the one in which Japan seems to have done most in this period is that of social insurance. We have already mentioned the Health Insurance of 1926, which underwent important revision in this period to expand the coverage and increase the benefits. In 1938, a law on a wider scale called National Health Insurance Act (*Kokumin Kenkō Hoken Hō*) was enacted; this was followed by the Seamen's Insurance Act (*Sen-in Hoken Hō*) in 1939, and by the Workers' Annuity Insurance Act (*Rōdōsha Nenkin Hoken Hō*) in 1940. It happens that the last two acts were the first Japanese laws providing an annuity system for invalids and aged people. The contents were meager compared with the more ample provisions found in certain other countries, but these were the first steps taken in the right direction.

The need for proper unemployment insurance had long been argued but no action had been taken. In its place a law called the Retirement Reserve and Retirement Allowance Act (*Taishoku Tsumitatekin Oyobi Taishoku Teate Ho*) was enacted in 1936. We have said "in its place," but nobody would venture to suggest that that law was an adequate substitute for an employment insurance law. We must explain that this was absorbed later into the Welfare Annuity Insurance Act (*Kōsei Nenkin Hoken Hō*) of 1944. The content of this law will be explained later.

CHAPTER V

From Surrender (1945) to the Outbreak of the Korean War (1950)

THE MacARTHUR REVOLUTION

War Damages of World War II

The war damages sustained by Japan in World War II were considerable. It was noted earlier that, in terms of men killed and wounded, the losses suffered by Japan in World War I, as compared with the losses sustained by the major Western powers, seemed relatively slight. In World War II, Japan lost 1,506,000 military personnel killed and missing between 1937 and the end of the war. This meant the loss of 1 in 46 of the population of the Japanese home islands. Allied military personnel losses totaled 10,650,000, and the Axis powers' losses amounted to 4,650,000. Japan's losses, as compared with those of the Allied powers and Axis powers, represented 14.1 and 38.7 per cent, respectively.

Under the terms of the Potsdam Declaration, Japan lost all territory other than the four islands of Honshu, Hokkaido, Shikoku, and Kyushu, and the minor islands adjacent to these four; this reduced the area of Japan by 42 per cent. The territories lost to Japan included vital sources of food and raw materials, notably Formosa, Korea, the southern half of Sakhalin, and her territory in Manchuria.

In the defeat that ended fourteen long years of war, the national economy collapsed completely. As a matter of fact, prior to the surrender nearly all productive equipment had been destroyed by continuous bombing during the four years of the Pacific War. All resources had been concentrated during the war years on munitions production, and even necessary repairs to machinery were mostly foregone. Mining equipment had also been left in disrepair. The result was that at the end of the war productivity of factories and mines had fallen to one-sixth of prewar production. In other words, more than 80 per cent of the productive equipment in mining and manufacturing had been destroyed, either by direct bombing or by the disrepair into which it had fallen, with the result that more than four months after surrender, in January, 1946, industrial production (including manufacturing and mining) amounted to only 18.3 per cent of the prewar (1932–1938) average, and industrial activity (mining, manufacturing and utilities) to 32.5 per cent. Rice paddies and upland farms had suffered from the lack of manpower and fertilizers, with the result that agricultural productivity had declined sadly. Lumbering had been pushed recklessly without the least attention to reforestation. River banks, harbors, roads, railways, and other means of transportation had also suffered neglect. The disastrous effect of such neglect on Japanese industry, agriculture, transportation, and life in general can be fully understood only by those acquainted with other aspects of Japan's history, including such natural disasters as hurricanes, floods, and droughts.

Coal production during the last four war years, for instance, averaged 4,500,000 tons. In November, 1945, it had fallen to 550,000 tons. The rice crop in 1945 was about the worst that Japan had experienced at any time during the war. Had there been some reasonable control of food, fuel, and other necessary items during this period, the suffering of the people might have been mitigated slightly. But all food, fuel, and other materials disappeared mysteriously into the black market.

The food shortage was greatly aggravated by the demobilization of military personnel and the repatriation of Japanese who had been residing in the territories that Japan lost in the surrender. There were about 6.5 million Japanese overseas at the time of surrender, and virtually all had to be repatriated and fed in the four islands, whereas the rice that used to be imported from Korea and Formosa ceased to come since those territories were lost to Japan. Even the importation of soya beans, which had been available in great quantities, was now completely stopped, since Manchuria was no longer under Japan's control. Japan, noted for her "over-population," was now faced with an even greater burden.

The Potsdam Declaration and Douglas MacArthur

Italy had succumbed in September, 1943. Germany capitulated in May, 1945. Japan remained as the sole Axis power, fighting a war of attrition with no hope of victory. The United States, released from Europe completely, was assembling ever larger land, air, and sea forces for the final decisive actions in the

Pacific. The British Commonwealth was getting ready to deal more effective blows at the Japanese forces in Southeast Asia and in the South Pacific. The Chinese were preparing, for the first time since their country was invaded, for an offensive movement against the invaders scattered all over their territory. Soviet Russia, still technically honoring her pact with Japan,[1] of whose integrity Japan had not had the least doubt and whose good offices she was seeking for some sort of peace without dishonor, was busily transporting forces across Siberia for deployment in the Far East.

During the month of July, 1945, the heads of the Allied Nations met at Potsdam, outside of Berlin, to discuss ways and means of ending the war in the Pacific. Momentous and fateful decisions were made as the result of the conference. While we must resist the temptation to give a detailed account of those conversations,[2] we give below the full text of the Potsdam Declaration,[3] because it was on Japan's acceptance of this text that the war came to an end; moreover, it is there that our narrative of the development of labor in postwar Japan rightfully begins.

THE POTSDAM DECLARATION

July 26, 1945

(1) We—the President of the United States, the President of the National Government of the Republic of China, and the Prime Minister of Great Britain, representing the hundreds of millions of our countrymen, have conferred and agree that Japan shall be given an opportunity to end this war.

(2) The prodigious land, sea and air forces of the United States, the British Empire and of China, many times reinforced by their armies and air fleets from the west, are poised to strike the final blows upon Japan. This military power is sustained and inspired by the determination of all the Allied Nations to prosecute the war against Japan until she ceases to resist.

(3) The result of the futile and senseless German resistance to the might of the aroused free peoples of the world stands forth in awful clarity as an example to the people of Japan. The might that now converges on Japan is immeasurably greater than that which, when applied to the resisting Nazis, necessarily laid waste to the lands, the industry, and the method of life of the whole German people. The full application of our military power, backed by our resolve, *will* mean the inevitable and complete destruction of the Japanese armed forces and just as inevitably the utter devastation of the Japanese homeland.

(4) The time has come for Japan to decide whether she will

continue to be controlled by those self-willed militaristic advisers whose unintelligent calculations have brought the Empire of Japan to the threshold of annihilation, or whether she will follow the path of reason.

(5) The following are our terms. We will not deviate from them. There are no alternatives. We shall brook no delay.

(6) There must be eliminated for all time the authority and influence of those who have deceived and misled the people of Japan into embarking on world conquest, for we insist that a new order of peace, security and justice will be impossible until irresponsible militarism is driven from the world.

(7) Until such a new order is established *and* until there is convincing proof that Japan's war-making power is destroyed, points in Japanese territory to be designated by the Allies shall be occupied to secure the achievement of the basic objectives we are here setting forth.

(8) The terms of the Cairo Declaration shall be carried out and Japanese sovereignty shall be limited to the islands of Honshu, Hokkaido, Kyushu, Shikoku and such minor islands as we determine.

(9) The Japanese military forces, after being completely disarmed, shall be permitted to return to their homes with the opportunity to lead peaceful and productive lives.

(10) We do not intend that the Japanese shall be enslaved as a race or destroyed as a nation, but stern justice shall be meted out to all war criminals, including those who have visited cruelties upon our prisoners. The Japanese Government shall remove all obstacles to the revival and strengthening of democratic tendencies among the Japanese people. Freedom of speech, of religion, and of thought, as well as respect for the fundamental human rights shall be established.

(11) Japan shall be permitted to maintain such industries as will sustain her economy and permit the exaction of just reparations in kind, but not those industries which would enable her to re-arm for war. To this end, access to, as distinguished from control of, raw materials shall be permitted. Eventual Japanese participation in world trade relations shall be permitted.

(12) The occupying forces of the Allies shall be withdrawn from Japan as soon as these objectives have been accomplished and there has been established in accordance with the freely expressed will of the Japanese people a peacefully inclined and responsible government.

(13) We call upon the government of Japan to proclaim now the unconditional surrender of all Japanese armed forces, and to provide proper and adequate assurances of their good faith in such action. The alternative for Japan is prompt and utter destruction.

On August 14, the Japanese government decided to accede to the terms of the Declaration, which said "We shall brook no delay" and ended with the stern warning: "The alternative for

Japan is prompt and utter destruction." Japan's delay in replying to the Declaration invited the disasters of Hiroshima and Nagasaki. We are aware now that any further delay could have led, literally, to "utter destruction" through the use on a much wider scale of the deadly atomic bomb.

A careful reading of this document reveals one or two striking things that are important to note at the outset. While it is a document of paramount historic importance, couched in sufficiently solemn and even awe-inspiring terms, it was obviously drawn up in a hurry. We say this because quite a careful analysis is required before one discovers, by inference, that the objective of the Potsdam Declaration was not wholly and exclusively punitive or retaliatory. It had a motive or objective of a quite different dimension, namely, to reform Japan and transform her into a democratic nation. In other words, there was a dual purpose in the conditions of this peace—retribution and reform. This, however, was not made at all clear in the document as it was drafted.

Of the thirteen paragraphs of the Declaration, the first five constitute a preamble, as it were, and the last paragraph the conclusion. The remaining seven paragraphs (6–12) lay down the punitive or retributive conditions of surrender, except the latter half of paragraph ten which reads: "The Japanese government shall remove all obstacles to the revival and strengthening of democratic tendencies among the Japanese people. Freedom of speech, of religion, and of thought, as well as respect for the fundamental human rights shall be established."

This passage has nothing in common with the one immediately preceding it, in which the Japanese government was warned of the stern justice to be meted out to all war criminals. Probably the draftsman of this historic document did not realize that the insertion of this second passage made this whole document unique. For the first time in history, the nations that emerged as victors from a devastating war were not content with mere retaliation. Japan was fortunate that the Supreme Commander for the Allied Powers happened to be a man of high calibre who did not fail to see this. When General Douglas MacArthur arrived on the soil of Japan on August 30, 1945, he had not come, at least as far as he was concerned, merely as the representative of the powers that conquered Japan. He was conscious of the dual character of the mission resting on his shoulders. With the assistance of dedicated aides, General MacArthur carried out his mission with dignity, authority, and high competence. Let us now see what sort of a man Douglas MacArthur was.

A full, fair, and unbiased appraisal of MacArthur's role in history would obviously require more attention than can be given here, but as far as his achievements in Japan are concerned, we may go into some detail. The data available are complete and conclusive, and authoritative volumes have already been written.[4] While we hesitate to devote too much attention in this study to any one individual, MacArthur is one man whose personality and work must be assessed in some detail in tracing the development of labor in Japan.

To appreciate Douglas MacArthur fully, one must first know a little of his family background. His father, General Arthur Mac-Arthur, served throughout the American Civil War in the volunteer infantry, in which he advanced through the ranks from lieutenant to colonel. Raised to the rank of colonel at the age of twenty, he was affectionately known as the "Boy Colonel of the West." He had been wounded three times, brevetted four times, and cited for "gallant and meritorious service." The regiment under his command had gained fame in General Philip H. Sheridan's division in the Army of Cumberland. During the Russo-Japanese War (1904–1905), General Arthur MacArthur was detailed as a special observer with the Japanese Army. He observed closely the sanitation and hygiene of the Japanese Army, the discipline and morale of the Japanese troops, and made the intimate acquaintance of General Tamesada Kuroki of the great battle of Mukden, General Maresuke Nogi of the Siege of Port Arthur, and Admiral Heihachiro Togo, the hero of the naval battle of Tsushima. He appreciated Japan's high knightly tradition of *Bushido,* much as a Japanese might honor Puritan backgrounds of America.

Douglas MacArthur was twenty-three when he graduated from the United States Military Academy at West Point, first in his class and senior officer in the corps of cadets. He naturally followed with the keenest interest the developments of war in the Far East and the accounts of his father's observation of the Russo-Japanese War. An unverified legend has it that immediately after the Japanese invasion of Manila, a framed letter from Admiral Togo to General Arthur MacArthur was found hanging on the wall of the chamber that had been Douglas MacArthur's headquarters. Apparently General Douglas MacArthur had treasured this me-

mento of his father's, and chose to hang it on the wall of his room, even on the eve of a great conflict in which he was to cross swords with the warriors of Japan.

General Douglas MacArthur was widely read in history and endowed with a deep historical sense. When he entered Tokyo Bay on board the flagship *Missouri* to sign the Instrument of Surrender, he could not forget that less than a century earlier, in 1853, the same bay had been visited by another American, Commodore Perry. Perry's visit had ushered in an era of enlightenment for Japan. With MacArthur's arrival, another new and eventful era was to begin for Japan, presaging even greater development of this nation. This presumably was the thought in the mind of General MacArthur; hence the legend that, prior to sailing into Tokyo Bay, the General had sent for the star-spangled banner which Commodore Perry had flown in Yedo Bay in 1853 and had ordered it flown from the mainmast of the *Missouri* during the surrender ceremony.[5]

Despite the tragic start at Pearl Harbor, Douglas MacArthur kept his faith in the Japanese people throughout the war, until the last day, a significant fact borne out by innumerable incidents and anecdotes. Entering Japan at Atsugi by plane, he and the men around him were completely unarmed. This is described by the man closest to MacArthur, Major General Courtney Whitney:[6]

MacArthur's unarmed entrance into Japan was later described by Winston Churchill as the most daring and courageous venture of the entire war. It was indeed a daring venture. Our small security force, accompanied by its commander-in-chief and other senior officers, entered this nation in arms and faced over 2,500,000 still uncommitted, fanatical enemy soldiers, sailors, and airmen who had been organized, trained, and armed for a final stand in defense of Japanese soil. None knew better than MacArthur the nature of the gamble. But he had accurately assessed the Japanese character in the light of the formally undertaken surrender commitments. With an intuitive understanding of the Orient gained in a half century of service there, he knew it would pay off.

The plane carrying the General and his staff swung down toward Atsugi. The aides close to MacArthur had misgivings about the antiaircraft guns of the Japanese. "The aircraft guns could not possibly miss at this range," writes Whitney. "I held my breath. But, as usual, he had been right. . . . He knew the basic Japanese character too well to have thus gambled blindly with death. He knew and trusted that national spirit of traditional chivalry called *Bushido.*"

Whitney writes that he found it difficult to resist the impulse to snatch MacArthur's plate away from him at the first meal after landing on the soil of Japan, to make sure that his food had not been poisoned. When MacArthur was informed of these misgivings, he merely laughed and said: "No one can live forever."

One other anecdote sheds light on the character of MacArthur. The troops at his headquarters had been ordered to procure some eggs for the Supreme Commander's breakfast; there was not one to be had in the hotel. A major general and his airborne division were entrusted with the mission, which produced exactly one egg. This was for MacArthur a confirmation of the complete exhaustion of the Japanese food resources. "He promptly issued an order forbidding the consumption by the occupation forces of local food. The order remained in effect throughout the occupation."[7]

United States Policy for Japan

In addition to the Potsdam Declaration, there was a document of surpassing importance which served to determine the character of the great political and economic reforms for Japan that were carried out by MacArthur. Indeed, MacArthur's policies and actions were guided and regulated basically by this document, although his own ideas, aspirations, and character did, of course, play a very big part in the dramatic unfolding of the whole reformation. The official title of this document was "The United States Initial Post-Surrender Policy for Japan." Dated August 29, 1945, the document consisted of a preamble entitled "Purpose of this Document" and four parts, subdivided as follows:

Part I. Ultimate Objectives
Part II. Allied Authority:
    1. Military Occupation
    2. Relationship to Japanese Government
    3. Publicity as to Policies
Part III. Political:
    1. Disarmament and Demilitarization
    2. War Criminals
    3. Encouragement of Desire for Individual Liberties and Democratic Processes
Part IV. Economic:
    1. Economic Demilitarization
    2. Promotion of Democratic Forces

3. Resumption of Peaceful Economic Activity
4. Reparations and Restitution
5. Fiscal, Monetary, and Banking Policies
6. International Trade and Financial Relations
7. Japanese Property Located Abroad
8. Equality of Opportunity for Foreign Enterprises within Japan
9. Imperial Household Property

As its title makes clear, this document was originally a statement of general initial policy only of the United States relating to Japan after surrender, approved by the President of the United States and radioed to General MacArthur, the Supreme Commander for the Allied Powers, and distributed to appropriate U.S. departments and agencies for their guidance. Actually it was the work of a joint body called the State-War-Navy Coordinating Committee (later State-Army-Navy-Air Force Coordinating Committee, or SANACC), but as an authority on the subject has said:

this document . . . proved itself to be a wise and practical statement of objectives. Broad in scope and flexible in detail, it has provided us [the United States] with an over-all program which has proved to be sound in concept and on the whole feasible in execution. Despite rapid changes since the war throughout the Far East and in American understanding of what international realities actually were, this document has remained as valid for the present situation as for that which our policy makers thought they were facing in the summer of 1945. While most other American foreign policies have required serious revision since 1945, this one has stood the test of time and change.[8]

Special interest in this document arises from the fact that the United States turned out to be in practice the predominant, if not the sole, occupier of Japan, with the result that what was initially called the United States Post-Surrender Policy for Japan became the Allied Post-Surrender Policy for Japan. This was reinforced by the fact that the Supreme Commander for the Allied Powers was an outstanding citizen of the United States, and the staff under his command, who were predominantly Americans, displayed unreserved readiness, high competence, and enthusiasm in implementing these policies. It was pointed out that in the Potsdam Declaration the requirement of the democratization of Japan as a condition of surrender appeared rather casual or incidental. Thanks to the policy elaborated in this document, the program of political and economic reformation of Japan based on democratic principles has come to occupy the major attention of the occupation authorities, although the document did stress as one of the ultimate objectives the need "to insure that Japan will not again become a menace to the United States or to the peace and security of the world." It involved the task of disposing of war criminals and insuring demilitarization in the economic sphere as well as the military.

For the purpose of our present study, we must refrain from overstepping the proper bounds of labor's interests, though indirectly the political and economic questions dealt with in this document are vitally related to labor. We give below the part of the text having directly to do with labor:

Part IV. Economic
2. Promotion of Democratic Forces
Encouragement shall be given and favor shown to the development of organizations in labor, industry, and agriculture, organized on a democratic basis. Policies shall be favored which permit a wide distribution of income and of the ownership of the means of production and trade.
Those forms of economic activity, organization and leadership shall be favored that are deemed likely to strengthen the peaceful disposition of the Japanese people, and to make it difficult to command or direct economic activity in support of military ends.
To this end it shall be the policy of the Supreme Commander:
(a) To prohibit the retention in or selection for places of importance in the economic field of individuals who do not direct future Japanese economic effort solely towards peaceful ends; and
(b) to favor a program for the dissolution of the large industrial and banking combinations which have exercised control of a great part of Japan's trade and industry.

The Far Eastern Commission

For the control of Japan after surrender, the Far Eastern Commission (FEC) was set up, as a result of the Foreign Ministers' Conference held in Moscow in December, 1945, as the supreme policy-making organ of the Allied powers. The seat of the Commission was located in Washington, and it held its meetings in the former Japanese Embassy building. The Commission consisted of the representatives of eleven nations—Australia, Canada, France, New Zealand, India, the Netherlands, the Philippines, and the four major powers: the United States, the United Kingdom, China, and the Soviet Union. Its first meeting was held on February 26, 1946, and thereafter weekly meetings were held *in camera,* to discuss the principles and policies necessary for implementing the terms of surrender, to make decisions on the orders to be given to the Supreme Commander, to review any measures taken by him, and the terms of reference agreed on among the participating powers. The chairmanship of the Commission was held always by the United States. The Commission was quite active in the early days, having divided its assignments among seven subcommittees. However, about the time the United States commenced the preliminary work for peace with Japan, in the fall of 1947, the Commission began to lose much of its usefulness and was immobilized.

A number of factors contributed to the immobilization of this body. First, most of the questions of occupation requiring any formal decision making by this body were settled by the winter of 1947. Second, the East-West tension, a totally unforeseen situation, was growing far too cumbersome and was rendering impossible any effective decision by a body constituted as the Far Eastern Commission was. Third, the Supreme Commander for the Allied Powers (SCAP) had developed at his Headquarters (GHQ) an impressive organizational structure consisting of about a dozen special staff sections, each responsible for a different field of civil affairs activity, and comprising, under the Chief of Staff and the Supreme Commander, at least 2,000 well-trained personnel, exclusive of Japanese employees. GHQ under SCAP had developed into so efficient, competent, and effective a machinery of administration that any attempt by a heterogeneous body, such as the Far Eastern Commission, to give guidance or instruction to SCAP from a distance of over seven thousand miles began to appear unrealistic, if not preposterous. SCAP was constantly faced with concrete situations which required prompt action. No doubt some measures taken by SCAP seemed to certain FEC members arbitrary and even lacking in proper respect for the policy-making prerogatives of the Commission, but the actions effectively taken by SCAP with dispatch and resolution, which were *faits accomplis,* met with the approval of most members of the Commission. This meant that the role of FEC was diminishing in importance, so much so that a scholar summed up the situation with these words: "Feeling that effective control has come to rest almost entirely with SCAP and the United States government, some FEC representatives have indicated willingness to let the FEC 'die on the vine' if effective direct relations could be established through the diplomatic channel."[9]

Among the decisions taken by the Far Eastern Commission, there was one, adopted on December 12, 1946, and transmitted to SCAP immediately, that laid down specifically the policy of the Allied Powers on labor movement and labor administration in Japan. The officers in the Labor Division under SCAP translated the entire text into Japanese and sought earnestly to educate the government as well as organized labor in Japan to formulate their plans and to mould their future in accordance with the principles laid down in this document. The document was entitled: "Principles for Japanese Trade Unions." The full text is given below.

PRINCIPLES FOR JAPANESE TRADE UNIONS
Adopted by the Far Eastern Commission, December 12, 1946

1. Japanese workers should be encouraged to form themselves into trade unions for the purpose of preserving and improving conditions of work participating in industrial negotiations to this end, and otherwise assisting the legitimate trade union interests of workers, including organized participation in building up a peaceful and democratic Japan.

2. The right of trade unions and their members to organize for these purposes should be assured and protected by law. The freedom of workers to join trade unions should be provided for by law. All laws and regulations preventing trade unions achieving these objectives should be immediately abrogated. Employers should be forbidden to refuse employment to, or discriminate against, a worker because he is a member of a trade union.

3. Trade unions should have the right of free assembly, speech and the press, and access to broadcasting facilities on a nondiscriminatory basis, provided only that such assembly, speech, or writing does not directly interfere with the interests of the occupation.

4. Trade unions should be encouraged to negotiate with the employers on behalf of their members regarding terms and conditions of employment. The Japanese Government should establish mediation and arbitration machinery for dealing with industrial disputes that cannot be settled by direct and voluntary negotiation between the worker or his representatives and the employer. The mediation and arbitration machinery should operate under conditions assuring the protection of the interests of the workers, and if employers are represented on the machinery, trade unions should be given equal representation.

5. Strikes and other work stoppages should be prohibited only when the occupation authorities consider that such stoppages would directly prejudice the objectives or needs of the occupation.

6. Trade unions should be allowed to take part in political activities and to support political parties.

7. Encouragement should be given to organized participation by trade unions and their officials in the democratization process in Japan

and in measures taken to achieve the objectives of the occupation, such as the elimination of militaristic and monopolistic practices. But such participation should not be encouraged in such a way as to hinder the achievement of the principal obligation and responsibility of the unions and their officials to organize for the protection of union members and union interests.

8. Trade unions should be encouraged to promote adult education and an understanding of democratic processes and of trade union practices and aims among their members. The Japanese Government should as far as possible assist trade union officials in obtaining information on trade union activities in other countries. These objectives should be given due weight when allocations of paper supplies and imports of foreign publications are made.

9. The Japanese should be free to choose the form of organization of their unions, whether on a craft, industry, company, factory or territorial basis. Emphasis should be placed on the importance of a solid local basis for future trade union activity in Japan. However, unions should be allowed to form federations or other groupings, for example in the same area or in related industries or on a nationwide basis.

10. The formation of trade unions should be a process of democratic self-expression and initiative, proceeding from the workers themselves. Employers should not be allowed to take part in the organization or conduct of unions or to finance them.

11. Trade union officials and standing committees should be elected by the workers concerned by secret ballot and democratic methods. It should be the responsibility of the unions to ensure that all officials have been democratically elected at regular stated intervals and that all their activities are democratically conducted.

12. No person who is subject to the purge directive of 4 January 1946, or to subsequent purge directives, should be allowed to hold office in a trade union. All persons who were directly connected in the past in a responsible capacity with the obstruction or repression of trade union organization or activity should be prohibited from employment as union officials, in labor agencies or as mediators, conciliators, or arbitrators. All persons who held office in government-sponsored or controlled trade unions should be subject to screening before being allowed to take office again.

13. Japanese Government and other agencies which were set up or functioned for the purpose of obstructing or in such a way as to obstruct free labor organization and legitimate trade union activities should be abolished or their powers in respect to labor revoked. No police or other government agencies should be employed in spying on workers, breaking strikes, or suppressing legitimate union activities.

14. Any undemocratic workers' organizations or their affiliates, such as the Patriotic Industrial Associations, should be dissolved and not allowed to revive. No new workers' organizations with militaristic, ultra-nationalistic, fascist or other totalitarian aims should be permitted.

15. Persons who have been imprisoned because of activity or "dangerous thoughts" in connection with trade unions and other labor organizations should be released.

16. The balance sheet and table of income and expenditure of each trade union showing also the source of large contributions should be available for public inspection. Safeguards such as annual audit by a professionally competent auditor appointed by the members should be taken to ensure the accuracy of these statements.

A careful perusal of the full text reveals a few things that deserve special comment here. The principles laid down in the documents were elementary principles, in the sense that they were of basic and universal importance. They have been widely quoted in Japan as *Kyokutō Iinkai Jūroku Gensoku* (FEC's Sixteen Principles) and "used" in every sense of the word by the workers' leaders of both wings. Because the trade-union movement in those days was still in its infancy, one might say that the educational aim of this proclamation was its primary objective. However, to anyone following the work of either the occupation authority (SCAP) or the Japanese government in the field of labor administration, the document seemed elementary. Some Japanese officials wondered if the Far Eastern Commission was kept informed of what was being done in Japan, for the Japanese government had already enacted both the Trade Union Law and the Law for Adjustment of Labor Disputes in which these principles, as far as trade-union principles were concerned, were fully complied with. The language and content of the document might have been somewhat different and more effective had there been more co-ordination between FEC and SCAP, but as we have noted already, there had been less and less because of the growing tension between the two ideological blocs. We know that SCAP was more embarrassed than helped, for instance, by Principle No. 6, which stressed the importance of participation of trade-unions in political activities. SCAP had begun to sense increasing Communist influence among the unions of the government workers. The Communist leaders were pleased with this principle and used it to their advantage.

Finally, a few words might be said here about another august body set up by the Allies for the control of Japan, namely the Allied Council for Japan. It consisted of the representatives of the United States, China, the British Commonwealth, and the Soviet Union. It met regularly at SCAP headquarters in Tokyo, under the chairmanship of the United States representative. We have seen how FEC was immobilized by its internal tension. How did this other important body function? The following description given by a prominent American scholar and diplomat suffices to reveal the character of this body, accessory to the Supreme Commander:[10] "The case of the Allied Council for Japan was even sadder. Limited in its duties largely to consultation with and advice to the Supreme Commander, it degenerated almost at once into a debating society, in which the American and Russian members carried on an acrimonious argument in front of the embarrassed British and Chinese representatives. Then it lapsed into a moribund state." This paragraph ended with a quotation from Mr. Macmahon Ball, who was for a year and a half the British member of the Council: "In these circumstances, it was inevitable that the Council should have been on balance a failure, and at times a fiasco."[11]

Needless to say, then, this body had but little to contribute to the administration of labor in Japan.

MacArthur's Own Directive to Shidehara

The occupation of Japan, as is generally known, was in theory an allied occupation, and General MacArthur, as the Supreme Commander for the Allied Powers was legally an international functionary and not solely or merely an American administrator. It was only fortuitous, yet fortunate for Japan, that the occupation was so predominantly American instead of an inter-Allied and divided occupation such as that in Germany.

So far, we have examined the nature and content of the Allied organs under or with which the Supreme Commander had to perform his duties. We come finally to the policies MacArthur worked out for himself in implementing the Potsdam Declaration, as opposed to those formulated by the Allied organs.

It will be recalled that when Japan surrendered, the man appointed as Prime Minister was Prince Naruhiko Higashikuni, a prince of the imperial blood nearest to and senior to the Emperor. He was regarded as the only person in all Japan who could perform the awkward task, without precedent in history, of surrendering to foreigners without incurring the wrath of the nation. When the assigned task was finished, the Prince was replaced by Baron Kijuro Shidehara, Foreign Minister during the "liberal twenties" and long-time opponent of the military clique. Shidehara, who took office on October 9, 1945, prepared his slate of cabinet members and, on October 11, paid a formal visit to Supreme Commander MacArthur with the slate. MacArthur saw it, nodded approvingly, and before parting handed the Baron an envelope. The latter took it to his official residence where, on glancing over it, he realized that it was a memorandum, or more precisely a directive, from the Supreme Commander setting forth the framework of a policy requiring implementation by the government for the democratization of Japan.

The document read, in part, as follows:

In the achievement of the Potsdam Declaration, the traditional social order under which the Japanese people for centuries have been subjugated will be corrected. This will unquestionably involve a liberalization of the Constitution.

The people must be freed from all forms of governmental and secret inquisition into their daily lives which holds their minds in virtual slavery and from all forms of control which seek to suppress freedom of thought, freedom of speech or freedom of religion. Regimentation of the masses under the guise or claims of efficiency, under whatever name of government it may be made, must cease.

In the implementation of these requirements and to accomplish the purposes thereby intended, I expect you to institute the following reforms in the social order of Japan as readily as they can be assimilated:

1. The emancipation of the women of Japan through their enfranchisement. . . .

2. The encouragement of the unionization of Labor . . . that it may be clothed with such dignity as will permit it an initial voice in safeguarding the working man from exploitation and abuse and raising his living standard to a higher level; with the institution of such measures as may be necessary to correct the evils which now exist in child labor practices.

3. The opening of the schools to more liberal education—that the people may shape their future progress. . . .

4. The abolition of systems which through secret inquisition and abuse have held the people in constant fear. . . .

5. The democratization of Japanese economic institutions to the end that monopolistic industrial controls be revised through the development of methods which tend to insure a wide distribution of income and ownership of the means of production and trade.

Baron Shidehara, a statesman of farsighted and mature wisdom who had steadily opposed militant autocracy, realized the surpassing importance of this memorandum, which suggested concrete lines of action that the government under his premiership must follow. This directive issued by General MacArthur— though it was not treated as a directive, as were the hundreds issued thereafter—was of cardinal importance. The Prime Minister immediately convoked the newly appointed ministers to discuss how to comply with the various requirements of the directive. The Japanese government under Premier Shidehara set out at once to formulate concrete programs for the postwar democratization of Japan. Of those programs, the most important features were:

1. Adoption of a new Constitution, whereby the people, not the Emperor, were declared to be the depository of sovereignty; basic human rights were assured to the people; all armaments were to be abolished and the right of belligerency of the nation renounced. It is now established historically that the ideas of abolition of arms, renunciation of the right of belligerency, and dependence on the justice and faith of the peace-loving peoples of the world for the security and existence of the nation were Shidehara's and were incorporated in the Constitution with warm support of General MacArthur.

2. Emancipation of women through enfranchisement, which was effected, enabling a fair number of women to hold seats in both Houses of the Diet as well as in the prefectural assemblies.

3. Nationwide educational reform, not only in the structure of the school systems, but in the very foundations of education.

4. Far-reaching land reform, which was boldly carried out, giving a vast number of former tenant farmers the new status of proprietor farmers.

5. Break-up of the *Zaibatsu* (the powerful plutocracies that had controlled Japan's economy in the prewar period). This was commenced on the presumption that the *Zaibatsu* was closely linked with the military clique and had contributed to the military aggressions of Japan, but the program to break up the *Zaibatsu* was balked halfway when the United States realized that it was necessary not to crush completely the economic strength of Japan, but to retain it for security and peace in the Far East. Antitrust laws were consistently enforced, but the program regarding the *Zaibatsu* underwent modifications.

6. More than 200,000 Japanese—those who were supposed to have been the leaders of Japan in prewar and war periods—were purged and replaced with new men in government administration, business, education, journalism, and in other positions of leadership. This purge applied largely to those who had formerly held public offices, though influential businessmen were barred from

engaging in their former businesses, and teachers from their teaching profession. There were some sweeping purges by category, which paid little attention to individual differences within the particular category, and occasionally resulted in the punishment of individuals who were friendly to America and not in basic sympathy with Japan's aggressive actions. Obvious errors of this sort can be understood only in the light of the strong motivation of SCAP to root out militarism from the soil of Japan.

7. Lastly, a new status was assured to the workers; by national constitution and by statutory laws their rights have been guaranteed to organize trade-unions, to engage in collective bargaining, and to conduct collective action in labor disputes, enabling them to assume power and responsibility in industrial relations. This part of MacArthur's reform program will be dealt with in detail hereafter.

Rōmu Hōsei Shingi Kai and the Three Basic Labor Laws

Under the old "Constitution of the Great Japanese Empire," the Emperor was "sacred and inviolable" and "invested with sovereign power." He gave sanction to laws, issued ordinances, determined the organization of the different branches of the administration and had "the supreme command of the army and navy." There was none above or beside the Emperor. Under the Instrument of Surrender, however, after September 2, 1945, the authority of the Emperor and the Japanese government to rule the state was "subject to the Supreme Commander for the Allied Powers," and, in the vein of the Potsdam Declaration, a directive of the Supreme Commander brooked no delay. Prime Minister Shidehara, well versed in the laws of the nations, was fully aware of the implications of the Instrument of Surrender solemnly adhered to by Japan with the signatures of her representatives given on September 2. His Cabinet set to work at once to formulate concrete plans for complying with the memorandum of October 11. As a matter of fact, this was the chief work of the government under Baron Shidehara and other prime ministers who succeeded him. Attention here will be confined to Point 2 of the memorandum, which had to do with unionization of labor.

Fortunately, Shidehara had selected for the post of welfare minister Ashida Hitoshi, a liberal statesman of high calibre, who later became prime minister. It was the Welfare Ministry which was responsible for labor administration, pending the creation of the Labor Ministry. When the Cabinet discussed the SCAP memorandum and the Prime Minister asked what the Supreme Commander was ultimately seeking by requiring the "encouragement of unionization of labor," Ashida was able to explain to the whole Cabinet that what Japan needed badly in the sphere of industrial relations was precisely that. With the full support of the Prime Minister and the Cabinet, Ashida called upon the most influential industrialists employing a large number of workers, the best-known experienced leaders of the prewar working-class movement, as well as a handful of scholars in the fields of law and economics, and one long connected with the ILO; to use the vernacular of government circles, he selected representative employers and workers and "men of scholarship or experience." These men were appointed by the Prime Minister to what was officially called Rōmu Hōsei Shingi Kai (Labor Legislation Council), which began to function October 27, 1945, under the chairmanship of Baron Okura Kimmochi, a man with liberal views and experience in financial administration. The Council set up by the Cabinet was an impressive body of thirty-four men, comprising members in the following categories: government officials responsible for various branches of labor administration, ten; "learned or experienced" men, seven; representatives of employers' interests, six; representatives of the workers' interests, five; and members of the two houses of the Diet, six.

When the Council finished a general discussion at two plenary meetings, a small committee was appointed to summarize the views expressed at the Council meetings and to submit a draft of a proposed trade-union law. The subcommittee consisted of the following: Ono Rokuichiro, high official in the Ministry of the Interior with long experience in labor administration, chairman; Ayusawa Iwao, former director of the ILO office in Tokyo; Fujibayashi Keizo, professor of Keio University; Matsuoka Komakichi, former president of Sodomei; Nishio Suyehiro, former labor leader in Sodomei; Suehiro Izutaro, professor of Tokyo Imperial University; Takahashi Tsuneya, director of Labor Administration, Ministry of the Interior; and Yasukawa Daigoro, industrialist.

All of the members of the Labor Legislative Council itself cannot be listed here, but it is interesting to find among them the names of men who played vital roles in the history of labor in this country. To name only those who have died, there was Matsuoka Komakichi, president of Sodomei, who later became Speaker of the

House of Representatives; Tokuda Kyuichi, a Communist leader who had recently been released by General MacArthur from jail after eighteen years of prison life and who subsequently became the secretary-general of the Japan Communist Party; and Professor Suehiro Izutaro, an authority on labor law, who later headed a nerve-racking mission as chairman of the Central Labor Relations Commission and performed pioneering work of conciliation, mediation, and arbitration in labor disputes in Japan.

Naming a Communist leader here as one of the figures who played a conspicuous role might strike readers, particularly those in the United States, as bizarre, but it must be remembered that shortly after the war there was a period when the Allies had few misgivings about the Communists. It may be recalled that the Sixteen Principles of FEC specifically instructed that "persons who had been imprisoned because of dangerous thoughts in connection with trade-unions should be released" (Section 15); and General MacArthur had, in fact, released sixteen Communist leaders, including Tokuda, on October 6, 1945, more than a year before the FEC principles were drawn up and communicated to him. As we shall see later, experience did show that the presence of belligerent Communists in a deliberative body gave rise to bitter controversies, which sometimes threatened to wreck the whole machinery, although there were aspects of their participation that might be swallowed as the proverbially "bitter medicine." For instance, while Communist members on the Labor Relations Commission were bitterly critical on most matters, they were always punctual and present at meetings. They studied the subjects under discussion with remarkable thoroughness to substantiate their criticisms, often more thoroughly than other members. Their seriousness of purpose and self-sacrificing dedication were impressive and sobering to other members. We might add that SCAP in the early stages of the occupation did not merely tolerate but welcomed the participation of Communists in such important bodies as the central and local labor relations commissions.

The Council was fortunate in having as chairman Baron Okura, who had the breadth of view and the courage to take responsibility for bold proposals that an ordinary man in politics, as chairman, would have hesitated to accept. These qualities of the chairman became evident as soon as the Commission started its work.

The first and foremost assignment of this Commission was to

hammer out the draft of a trade-union law, the first trade-union law in this country. Before any substantial discussion could begin on the assigned item, however, a stormy scene broke out because of a furious protest raised by the Communist leader, Tokuda, regarding what he considered was "an arbitrary and high-handed" method of the government whereby he was picked to sit in the Commission. In his view, it was in itself a violation of democracy, which he said he could not accept. The storm was allayed only after a member arose and reminded the Council of the tremendous task it had to build a new Japan and hoped that the Council would go forward calmly to accomplish its task "after having been blessed," as he put it, "with this baptism of fire." He was, of course, referring to Tokuda's fiery speech. The same member continued: "We have been called here to perform a historic task—to lay the basis for a new Japan. Let us accomplish a work which is thorough and sound, and produce a law that will be looked back on ten years hence, or fifty years hence, as a document that, by contributing to real democratization of this nation, ushered in a new era in our history."

This was a faltering statement, but it seemed to voice the sentiment that animated the whole of the Council. Even Tokuda expressed his agreement with the speaker afterwards. In spite of eighteen years of prison life, Tokuda had a broad, sunny smile on his ruddy face. He used to bow low to greet people and conducted himself like a civil and even affable individual when he was not fighting.

A detailed account of how the Council worked and finally produced its draft of the Trade Union law cannot be given here, but a few points will be touched on to correct the general impression, still current today, that the law, like some other important ones, was written by certain officials under SCAP in GHQ. Such was not at all the case.

At the plenary sessions of the Council, there was at first a general exchange of views on the subject of a trade-union law. There was general agreement as to the need for a law guaranteeing workers the right to organize and to bargain collectively. Beyond that, however, there were but few concrete suggestions. One member, a prominent labor leader in the prewar period, suggested that the draft of a trade-union law, published by the Social Affairs Bureau of the Ministry of the Interior in 1925, might serve as a model for the Council to consider, but this suggestion was not followed. Another labor leader mentioned the British experience of the Taff Vale case, and another mentioned the importance of providing for the immunity of trade-unions from civil liability in labor disputes, as well as immunization from criminal procedure. The member who had served long with the ILO ventured to argue the necessity of creating a separate, permanent, and democratically structured machinery to administer the trade-union law if the law were to be of real service for the democratization of industrial relations. In order to ensure a free and effective operation of such a machinery, it must be tripartite in its structure, one part representing the employers, another representing the workers, and the third representing the general public, each part elected from among the three respective groups and subsequently confirmed by government appointment.

The suggestion of a tripartite structure was a bold one; the experience of tripartite mediation boards in Japan had not been very encouraging. The long experience of this member at the ILO gave him faith in the working of tripartitism. In the United States, tripartitism seemed to succeed as a wartime measure, and on railroads it seemed to work for some time, but whether it was accepted universally or widely in the United States or anywhere else as a scheme ensuring success in the settlement of labor disputes was not certain. Nevertheless, this member, who had seen the working of tripartitism at the ILO on an international level, insisted that it should be adopted in Japan. Thanks to the adroit handling of the farsighted chairman, this suggestion was taken up with very little discussion. The same member, who obviously contemplated a labor board with semijudicial functions, continued to ask that the board be vested with the right of subpoena, i.e., the power to summon any individual for testimony, and also to require presentation of any books or documents necessary for carrying out its official business. Also, members of the board should be empowered to inspect actual conditions of the factory or workshop. These were powers exercised hitherto only by the courts or government agencies with judicial or police functions. If the proposed tripartite board, consisting of members elected from among the people and who were not government officials, were to exercise those powers, it could be considered a revolutionary departure. Even these proposals, however, were adopted by the drafting committee without serious opposition or comment of any kind.

Professor Suehiro was finally requested after the general discussion to draw up a preliminary draft of a report, embodying the above-mentioned and other ideas expressed in the course of discussion of this Council. On the basis of Professor Suehiro's draft the Labor Legislation Council, at its final plenary discussion, adopted a report containing a draft Trade Union Bill, which was submitted by the Council to the government on November 24, 1945.

Before closing this section of the narrative, it will be helpful to note the relation of this Council to SCAP. At the request of SCAP, the Council kept in close touch with the Labor Division of the Economic and Scientific Section of SCAP, informing the latter of the progress made at each stage in the final draft of the Trade Union Bill. Through this process the entire draft was seen, article by article, by the Labor Division of SCAP, and it was after the text was approved by SCAP that the bill was submitted to the Diet by the government.

In order to avoid repetition, we will omit an account of the drafting of the other two of the "Three Basic Labor Laws"—the Labor Relations Adjustment Act of 1946 and the Labor Standard Act of 1947—in which the Labor Legislation Council followed practically the same procedure.[12]

EXPANSION OF TRADE-UNIONISM

Events Preceding the MacArthur Revolution

Those were eventful days, filled with happenings that were shaking the very foundation of the Japanese Empire. It may help to recapitulate here some of the staggering incidents that preceded the great historical event which we call the MacArthur Revolution.

July 26, 1945: The Potsdam Declaration was communicated to Japan by short wave, suggesting unconditional surrender.

August 6. The first atom bomb in history was dropped on Hiroshima.

August 8. The U.S.S.R. declared war on Japan.

August 9. Another atom bomb fell on Nagasaki.

August 14. Japanese government decided to surrender.

August 15. The Japanese Emperor, for the first time in

Japan's history, addressed the people *viva voce* over the radio, announcing peace.

August 28. First landing of the occupation troops in Japan.

August 30. General MacArthur in his capacity as Supreme Commander of the Allied Powers arrived in Japan.

September 2. Instrument of Surrender was signed in Tokyo Bay.

September 10. General MacArthur announced the Allies' policy for control of Japan.

September 22. The United States gave direction to MacArthur for the breakup of the *Zaibatsu*.

September 25. Labor handbooks in force during the war were banned.

September 30. Sanpo was dissolved.

October 4. SCAP ordered immediate release of political prisoners and abolition of the Thought Police.

October 5. Prince Higashikuni's Cabinet resigned. The Japan Seamen's Union was reorganized. Sixteen Communist leaders, including Tokuda, were released from prison.

October 9. Baron Shidehara was appointed Prime Minister to form a new Cabinet.

October 10. Former leaders of Sodomei met to reorganize a national organization of trade-unions.

October 11. General MacArthur's directive was handed to Premier Shidehara, demanding, among other things, emancipation of women, encouragement of unionization of labor, liberalization of education, abolition of systems that through inquisition held the people in constant fear, democratization of economic institutions, and the more equitable distribution of income.

For the purpose of simplification, one might say that the directive of October 11 to Premier Shidehara marked the formal beginning of SCAP's program for the reformation of Japan. In the unfolding of MacArthur's dramatic reforms, a bewildering series of incidents broke out, some of them a direct outcome of the directive, but others which had no direct relation to it. For this reason we will continue here the recapitulation of the events that ensued during those eventful remaining days of 1945.

October 12. The wartime ordinances that had forcibly recruited students for labor in the prosecution of the war were rescinded.

October 13. The law for control of speech, press, assembly, and organization was repealed.

October 15. The Law for Maintenance of Public Peace (which had made Communism treasonable) was abolished.

October 19. The Japan Communist Party proposed a united front to the organizing committee of the Japan Socialist Party.

October 25. A fifty-day strike of the Yomiuri Newspaper, involving seizure of the plant by the striking workers, began.

October 25. SCAP announced complete stoppage of functions of Japan's diplomatic agencies abroad, ordered cession of all properties of those agencies to the Allied Powers, and recall of all diplomats from overseas.

October 27. The Labor Legislation Council was formally set up and commenced work immediately.

October 30. The War and Navy departments were abolished.

November 2. The Japan Socialist Party was formed.

November 3. The Sodomei was revived.

November 4. The Japan Fishermen's Union was formed. SCAP ordered dissolution of four *Zaibatsu.*

November 8. The first national council meeting of the Japan Communist Party was held.

November 9. The Japan Liberal Party was formed.

November 14. National Conference of government people was held to discuss how to meet the critical food shortage.

November 15. The Pauley Report on Japanese reparations was published.

November 17. The Military Service Act was repealed.

November 21. The Public Peace Police Act was repealed.

November 27. Partial stoppage of national railways was enforced because of coal shortage.

December 1. The All-Japan Teachers' Union was formed.

December 2. SCAP ordered continuance of control of wages and prices.

December 3. Commission to deal with the mounting unemployment problem was created.

December 6. The Pauley Interim Report was published, suggesting that Japan still had sufficient industrial strength left so that further restrictions for complete crushing out of military equipment were feasible.

December 9. SCAP ordered agrarian reform.

December 11. SCAP ordered freezing of capital of eighteen *Zaibatsu* and 330 holding companies.

December 11. The Cabinet decided on dismissal of 65,000 public servants.

December 22. The Trade Union Act was promulgated.

Upheaval of Unionization

The foregoing brief list of the incidents that took place after the landing of the occupation troops shows that the stage was now set for a complete and spectacular revolution. Former restrictions in politics, economics, law, religion, education, and even in thinking seemed completely removed. Particularly impressive was the abolition of the Public Peace Police Act, the Public Peace Maintenance Act, and the other repressive laws, accompanied by the abolition of the police control in any sphere of industrial relations. During the war, the employers had depended much on the Sanpo for keeping the workers under control. When the war ended, most employers fell into a "state of stupor" (*kyodatsu jotai*) and seemed to have entirely lost the power to control the workers.

Under these circumstances, the workers of Japan were completely emancipated. What did this imply?

The Japanese military government had been making reckless use of the Korean workers in the mines. When the war ended with the defeat of Japan, there were inevitable uprisings among the hitherto maltreated Korean mining workers, but the occupation troops responsible for maintenance of order had no difficulty in suppressing these minor incidents. What they could not suppress were the high hopes of the emancipated workers. Some of them were dreaming of a new order under socialism, some under communism. The seamen were the first to organize, or reorganize, their union. Others followed suit, led by the leaders of the old Sodomei. By the end of the year, within a little over three months, more than 500 unions had been formed, with a combined membership of 379,631. Table 28 shows how amazingly rapid was the speed at which the number of unions grew. Starting from scratch when the war ended in August, 1945, union membership rose within a year to more than 3,800,000.

There is nothing surprising in the effective leadership provided by the top leaders of the old Sodomei in organizing new unions in postwar Japan. Their first meeting was held on October

TABLE 28
SPREAD OF UNIONIZATION (October,
1945–July, 1946)[13]

Month	Number of Unions	Member- ship
Oct., 1945	8	4,026
Nov.	74	67,484
Dec.	508	379,631
Jan., 1946	1,516	901,705
Feb.	3,242	1,536,560
Mar.	6,537	2,567,467
Apr.	8,530	3,022,933
May	10,540	3,413,653
June	12,006	3,677,771
July	12,923	3,813,665

15, 1945. They met again on January 17, 1946, agreed on general principles of reorganization, and named some men as temporary officers. As a result of these early actions Sodomei was able to reorganize with due ceremony on August 1, 1946.

The leaders of leftist leaning were not slow in reorganizing, either. They met first on December 5. They met again on January 6 and formed the Kanto Regional Council, with the unions of workers around Kawasaki at their center. The strike at the Yomiuri Newspaper Company, which involved the seizure of the plant by the workers, lasting from October to December, 1945 (a historic strike in that it was the first time that seizure of a whole plant was carried out with remarkable discipline and effectiveness), was staged by these leftist leaders. With the workers of the Yomiuri Newspaper forming the core, a new union of communication workers was founded in February, 1946. Incidentally, this organization furnished the initial impetus for industrial unions as opposed to the craft unionism that had traditionally dominated Sodomei. This new union of industrially organized workers soon became the Nippon Sangyo-Betsu Rodo Kumiai Kaigi (literally, the Japanese Congress of Industrial Organizations, but commonly referred to as Sanbetsu or JCIO).

Spread of Unrest and of Labor Disputes

In the recapitulation of strike incidents in Japan immediately after surrender, reference was made to the shortage of food and fuel. These and other factors contributed to the spread of unrest among the workers. The government was finding inflation beyond its power to control. Shortage of food became increasingly obvious. The workers, who had refrained from engaging in dispute acts for the duration of the war, were now boldly asserting their right to engage in disputes. Generally speaking, during the year 1946 the numbers of dispute cases and of participants in disputes increased from month to month, as shown in the table below:

TABLE 29
INCREASE OF LABOR DISPUTES (January–July, 1946)

	Dispute Cases	Partici- pants	Cases involving dispute acts	Partici- pants
Jan.	74	42,749	52	38,096
Feb.	81	35,153	58	29,482
Mar.	103	83,141	87	81,221
Apr.	109	60,917	93	51,106
May	132	58,978	109	51,903
June	104	33,554	87	27,434
July	111	37,233	98	28,727

Even more important than the statistics is the nature of the demands formulated by the workers involved in the disputes. As one might expect, the principal cause of disputes in the first year after the war was the demand for wage increases. Other major demands included union recognition, right to bargain collectively, shorter working hours, increase in the days of annual paid leave, improvements in working conditions, participation in management, participation in personnel decisions, and objection to certain foremen or men in managerial positions. During this early period after surrender, one thing which characterized industrial relations was the state of stupor on the part of the employers, mentioned earlier, as a result of which most, if not all, of the workers' demands were granted. The workers' movement took advantage of this situation and asked for improvements not only in wages and conditions of work, but in management-labor relations, which helped the progress of democratization of industry.

Seisan Kanri (Production Control)

One of the new things introduced in Japan in this eventful period was a type of dispute act called in Japanese *"seisan kanri"* (production control). It attracted attention because of its novelty, for one thing. In essence it is a form of seizure of the plant by the workers, but one might say that genetically there is a difference between this and an ordinary "sit-down" or "stay-in" strike. In the case of *seisan kanri,* during a strike period the workers take over management and engage in the production and delivery of goods or services for the management. As mentioned earlier, this occurred first at the Yomiuri Newspaper Company, and then at a private railway. The experiment at Yomiuri induced workers in other industries to follow suit, so that it spread to government offices and the municipal office of Tokyo. The government and the employers were dismayed. The government issued warnings against the resort to this form of dispute act, pointing out that it was illegal. The government finally decided to arrest the workers concerned on the charge of violation of private-property rights.

However, the argument in support of this new strike weapon was, in effect: "On account of economic dislocation resulting from the defeat in war, most men in management have lost the will to produce. They do not make the necessary repairs to equipment. What is worse, they restrain production, anticipating higher prices for their products owing to inflation, and they hold back from selling their products. In such a situation, nothing but production control will rescue Japan from a shortage of goods and contribute to the recovery of production."

Professor Suehiro in a way supported this view as a reasonable criticism of the employers' selfish calculations. The government issued a statement on June 13, 1946, declaring that production control was illegal, but in the same statement the government warned the managers that their sabotaging of production would also be dealt with severely. Obviously, the government recognized that the employers were partly responsible for the spread of this illegal practice in disputes, and felt it necessary to give such a warning to the employers, at the same time bringing pressure to bear on the workers to discontinue this particular form of dispute action.

The number of *seisan kanri* cases gradually diminished because of two factors: one was police intervention; the other, which was more fundamental, was the difficulty inherent in the practice. If it called merely for control or supervision of the processes of manufacture or transportation the workers could do it perhaps as efficiently as the employers, but, when it came to financial or commercial management of the plant, the workers lacked knowledge and experience. Where and how should they secure more funds or materials? The workers discovered soon that there were limits beyond which workers' control was of little benefit to them. Following are the cases of *seisan kanri*, listed by month for the year 1946, when they were at their height:

October	1	April	53
December	4	May	56
January	13	June	44
February	20	July	25
March	39	August	13

It should be added here that during this period of labor unrest, which arose from the state of economic dislocation, shortage of food and materials, and general industrial confusion, *seisan kanri* was after all just one manifestation of the vast restiveness of the working class. Whenever a labor dispute was prolonged or grew big, it was apt to become violent. Most workers were not acquainted with the term "collective bargaining" and took it to mean "mass negotiation," since the words "*dantai kōshō*" could be taken to mean either. It was largely because of this misunderstanding that workers crowded into the head office of the company where they were employed and held the president or head of management in virtual captivity for incredibly long hours until they had wrested from him a sealed document granting the workers' demands. Looking back on those incidents, almost twenty years later, one can smile at them, but it must be remembered that the men involved were in dead earnest in their belief that they were engaged in a work the ultimate object of which was to instill democracy in the industrial relations of Japan.

The Role Played by the Government in this Period

From the time of the Restoration of Meiji, the government of Japan had played the active role of guide and philosopher, or, in the case of a war, that of dictator. What was the nature of the role played by the government under the military occupation? We have already seen that, under the terms of the Instrument of Surrender, the authority of the Emperor and the government to rule the state was "subject to the Supreme Commander for the Allied Powers."

Fortunately, the Supreme Commander's occupation was generally considered a "benevolent occupation," but, with all due respect to the occupation forces, it must be admitted that the position in which the Japanese government was placed was an extremely awkward one. It was a government with the facade of responsibility and power, but actually without any real power.

On February 1, 1946, the government issued the so-called "Four Ministers' Pronouncement." The ministers of the Interior, Justice, Commerce, and Industry, and Welfare jointly deprecated the resort to violence, intimidation, or violation of property rights in labor disputes, and stated that any offense along such lines should be severely penalized. This was followed by the communication of the director of the Police Bureau of the Ministry of the Interior "concerning the prevention and control of illegal acts." But how much influence these pronouncements had to restrain the workers was uncertain. The Japanese government further issued on June 13 the "Government Statement Concerning Maintenance of Social Order" in which it was argued that in order to solve the problems confronting Japan it was necessary to stabilize the people's livelihood by increasing production and to maintain social order through observance of democratic methods. It was in this statement that *seisan kanri* was declared illegal and, at the same time, employers were warned against sabotaging production.

The government was helped in its situation by the occupation authority. After the statement of U.S. Secretary of State Dean Acheson criticizing communism, General MacArthur issued a warning against subversive acts in mass movements.

Nevertheless, the role of the Japanese government in this situation remained anomalous because of the relentless progress of inflation and the shortage of food, both of which were harassing the workers. True, the government did not fail to see this predicament early. During December, 1945, the government took advantage of a wartime ordinance and allowed wage increases in private enterprises. Next, the government took steps to pay temporary wage increases to public servants. But those temporary measures were of no real value in the face of the mounting inflation. The government resorted to the Emergency Finance Measure. All Bank of Japan notes currently in use were to become invalid after March 2, 1946. Thereafter, deposits in the banks must be made by March 7. New bank notes of 10 yen and 100 yen were issued. The old notes had to be exchanged for the new before

March 7. Private individuals could receive from the bank the maximum of 100 yen. All the rest had to be deposited and "blocked" in the bank. Thereafter, from the blocked deposit, a maximum of 300 yen per month could be disbursed to the head of a family, and a maximum of 100 yen per individual in a family. As for wages, the maximum payable to an individual per month was 500 yen in cash. The rest could be paid only in notes negotiable with banks for purposes of depositing in a bank.

The rules summarized above were strictly enforced, but this did not ease government finances. The Bank of Japan had to continue to issue more notes. Prices kept rising, and shortages of food and materials led to black-marketing. The 500-yen limit for cash payments became the target of the workers' resentment.

What, or who, was responsible for this plight? We have already seen that Japan had lost 80 per cent of her shipping capacity in the war. Shortage of manpower and of fertilizers during the war had aggravated the painful food shortage. At the same time, six million or more people from abroad were repatriated. Finally, to make the situation even worse, in the last year of war there was a rice-crop failure. This accumulation of unfortunate circumstances culminated in the so-called "Food May Day" on May 1, 1946. Over 250,000 men assembled at the Plaza in front of the Imperial Palace in Tokyo. The demonstrators marched through the main boulevards of Tokyo. It was an impressive sight. The situation was considerably eased by the food generously shipped in from the United States under SCAP orders, though there were complaints about the rationing or distribution of the food.

Did the government have no wage policy under these circumstances? Looking back, one might say that it did not, and, in all honesty, that it could not. The first thing the government tried was the loosening of the tight control it had had during the war. Thereafter, the government and private enterprise from time to time resorted to temporary wage increases and lump-sum grants, but these temporizing measures were found to be not merely ineffective but even harmful in that they tended to prevent the devising of a more thoroughgoing policy. On the advice of SCAP, the government revised the former policy of wage payment under which a worker received, besides the nominal wage, temporary allowances and bonuses of various kinds. They were all converted into a single wage scheme, to be paid regularly. This revision had the merit of simplification of the wage scheme that had been hopelessly complicated before, but it did not make the life of the worker any easier. One might even conclude that all the ineffective steps taken by the government tended to convince the workers that the government had no policy, and contributed to the hastening of the historic showdown of the attempted general strike of public servants.

The Trade Union Act and the Workers' Offensives

In the economic sphere, in matters of inflation, of shortage of food and materials, the government seemed pusillanimous or impotent; however, in the sphere of industrial relations, the government was going ahead bravely, at the behest of SCAP, to enact laws encouraging unionization of labor. The Trade Union Bill, prepared by the Labor Legislation Council, was adopted by the Diet, and the law, promulgated in December, 1945, went into effect as of March 1, 1946. This law guaranteed the rights of organization and of collective bargaining to all wage-earning workers, including public servants, with the exception of policemen, jailers, and firemen. In order to protect the workers in their exercise of the right to engage in labor disputes, the law made it illegal to discharge workers or give them discriminatory treatment for organizing unions or engaging in union activities; it prohibited application of punitive laws for the purpose of restraining proper trade-union actions, and banned any claim of damage arising from proper exercise of trade-union rights.

The effect of such a law on the workers of Japan in this period of utter economic stringency can easily be imagined. It meant, in a word, the rise of an unprecedented labor offensive.

When the text of the Trade Union Law was first published, leaders of the working-class movement realized the great advantage of filing a report with the Local Labor Relations Commission and receiving from the Commission certification of full qualification as a trade-union under the terms of the law. Only when such certification was granted did a union become eligible to participate in the formal procedure provided in the law (e.g., representation on commissions of conciliation and mediation) and to avail itself of the remedies provided in the law (e.g., processing in case of unfair labor practices by the employer). Traditionally, the workers' leaders opposed and objected to any law that smacked of government intervention or control. The provision concerning union certification did seem like government control, but they accepted it, nonetheless. When the Trade Union Law went into effect on March 1, 1946, the machinery for registration and certification of unions was hardly ready, but the existing unions commenced to take steps for registration, and it was reported that by the end of April the number of unions registered had risen to 8,530, with a total membership exceeding 3,000,000. By the end of September, the number of unions had grown to 14,697 and the total membership to more than 4,000,000.

There were two things to be noted in this period of tremendous expansion of unionization. One was the special emphasis laid on centralization of power on a national scale, instead of the disunity and diffusion of strength that had been the bane of prewar trade-unionism in Japan. We have mentioned the efforts of the former leaders of Sodomei to revive it, and have told how the left-wing leaders were assembling forces to establish a national federation of industrial unions. The other move was to unite these two camps into one. This latter movement was quickened by the information, which the workers' leaders received with alarm, that in the proposed law for adjustment of labor relations, the public servants would probably be deprived of the right to strike, and that in public utilities the workers' right to strike would be restricted by a thirty-day "cooling-off" period. However, the proposal of the left-wing unions for a national united front was flatly turned down by Sodomei leaders who had always stood for "sound trade-unionism." The national united front failed to materialize, but there were ample difficulties that the left-wing leaders could take advantage of in inciting or keeping alive a rebellious spirit among the workers. One such difficulty was the need faced by the railways and shipping companies of reducing personnel, which had expanded greatly during the war. The railway workers and seamen were both very strongly unionized, the former with 600,000 members and the latter with 150,000. Neither had belonged to Sodomei or to the leftist industrial workers' federation. In other words, both were independent unions, unaffiliated with any outside organization, and this was precisely the situation that the leftist elements took advantage of. The result was that the disputes of the railway and shipping workers turned out to be Communist-led strikes.

The dispute of the railway workers began when the national railways decided to discharge 75,000 men as part of the program of rationalization of the railways. This decision was communicated to and rejected by the railway workers' union. A nationwide railway tie-up was set for September, but the crisis was averted by compromise reached at the eleventh hour. The dispute of the shipping workers arose, similarly, from the decision of the shipping corporation (Senpaku Un-ei Kai), made with the approval of the government, to discharge 60,000 seamen. This was an unavoidable bit of surgery for Japanese shipping, since Japan had lost in the war some 5,000,000 of the 6,000,000 tons of bottoms she had before the war. Had the planned strike come off, it would have immobilized ships in practically all the major ports of Japan. This crisis was also averted by the intervention of the Central Mariners' Labor Relations Commission.

While the crises in the railway and shipping industries were somehow averted, it did not mean that the basic difficulties which had given rise to these crises were removed or eased. The next major offensive, to which the Japanese writers gave the name Jugatsu Kosei ("October Offensive"), was planned by the organized workers of Japan and launched in October, 1946.

The so-called October Offensive, directed from the start by the left-wing organization Sanbetsu, has historic significance, owing to special features worth noting. First, all unions participating in the dispute demanded not only a wage raise but a uniform or regulated trade agreement approved by Sanbetsu; they demanded further a repeal of the income tax on income earned with labor, and rescission of the limit fixed on wages paid in cash, which was 500 yen, as explained earlier. Second were the high wage figures demanded by the Electrical Workers' Union, later known widely as *Densan Chingin Taikei* (Electrical Workers' Wage Scheme). This was the first time in Japan's labor history that the workers had produced wage demands based not on current needs or usages but on extensive studies of wage theories as well as actual needs. This matter will come in for further discussion later. A third feature was the hurried action taken by the government. The government feared that if the demand of the electrical workers should prevail, it might result only in precipitating the crisis of inflation. But, as a matter of fact, inflation was already progressing so fast that public sentiment seemed to be with the workers.

At this juncture, the government hastened to enforce the Law for Adjustment of Labor Relations, under which the workers in public utility enterprises, such as electricity, were obliged to observe a thirty-day cooling-off period. The government knew that the workers were, on the whole, opposed to this provision, but went ahead and put the law into force. The action taken by the government naturally incurred severe criticism from the workers, but, generally speaking, the main parts of the demands presented by the workers were granted on December 19, when the dispute of the October Offensive was formally settled. The workers succeeded in pressing their demands without resorting to a strike that would have caused considerable inconvenience to the general public.

Professor Suehiro, who was chairman of the Central Labor Relations Commission through this period, commenting on the policy followed by the government in dealing with the labor offensives, had the following to say:

The workers' offensives launched since August have achieved remarkable success. What we should note especially in this situation is that the policy of economic rehabilitation that the government had pursued unwittingly for the interest mainly of the capitalists received a setback through the opposition of the organized workers. The government failed in the reorganization of industries through mass discharge of workers because of the opposition of the seamen and national railway workers. But that was not all. The embankment of the low-wage policy has now been broken through by the Electrical Workers Union. Depending upon the angle from which this is viewed, one could of course say that these incidents contributed to the retarding of economic rehabilitation of the postwar period. However, it was only natural that the government should fail, with the opposition of labor, when it attempted to reorganize industries from a capitalistic standpoint, with practically no proper measures against unemployment, not to speak of unemployment insurance. The government was emphasizing only the point that wage hikes would stimulate inflation, ignoring the fact that the real wages of the workers had already been seriously affected by inflation. In other words, the government was eager to achieve economic rehabilitation at the expense of the workers, and was itself pursuing policies that stimulated inflation. It was only natural that the measures taken by the government to dispose of the labor disputes ended in a failure.[14]

FIASCO OF THE FEBRUARY FIRST GENERAL STRIKE AND AFTER

The Grand Plot which Failed

The Communist-led plot for a spectacular general strike ended in a fiasco. The incident is remembered by the Japanese as *Ni-Ichi S'to* or *Ni-Ichi Zene S'to* (February First General Strike). It was a showdown which did not take place, but which had created so much sensation and uproar that its effect was as devastating as if it had actually happened. It was the culmination of certain policies followed by the working-class movement under Communist leadership. It marked the end of the lenient SCAP policy vis-à-vis the subversive elements. A new chapter began here in the history of labor administration in Japan under occupation. We will first give an account of how the plot progressed.

Of all the unions and federations of unions that sprang up in bewildering succession after the promulgation of the Trade Union Law, the ones with the biggest membership were the National Federation of State Railway Workers (Kokutetsu); All Communication Workers' Union (Zentei), embracing all post, telephone, and telegraph workers; Japan Teachers' Union (Nikkyo-so); and Federation of State and Municipal Employees (Kankō Rō-so), to mention the more outstanding ones. We must not overlook the fact that all these unions were unions of workers in the government enterprises, i.e., railways, communication, education, and government and municipal white-collar services. Each of these federations had a membership of from one third to more than half a million. In the October Offensive of the previous year, the Communist-led Electrical Workers' Union had played the leading role. In the February First General Strike plot, the leadership was taken by Ii Yashiro, the Communist leader previously with the State Railway Workers, but now in a new capacity, as the general secretary of the Joint Struggle Committee, he was conducting the entire campaign against the government during the weeks and months of embittered negotiations.

The start of the negotiations with the government began in November, 1946, when the civil servants' (white-collar) unions in various departments of the government presented their demands for higher wages. This was during the period when the Electrical Workers' dispute was raging. The first to strike then were the railway workers, led by Ii, and the communication workers, led by another Communist leader, Dobashi Kazuyoshi. Dobashi was so humble, genial, and tactful in his deportment that even SCAP's Labor Division officials did not have the least suspicion that he was a leading Communist. In those days, there was in force a provision of the Act for Adjustment of Labor Disputes under which the parties to a dispute in public utilities had to observe a thirty-day cooling-off period.[15] After the expiration of the thirty-day period, legally they were completely free to do as they chose regarding the dispute. The men conducting the negotiations were of course aware of this and presented their formal requests for mediation to the Central Labor Relations Commission in the latter part of November. In the meantime, they approached other unions of government and municipal employees and formed the "All-Government and Municipal Employees United Struggle Committee." On December 3, the committee presented to the prime minister a document containing ten demands. By the end of December, the thirty-day period would have elapsed, and if the prime minister should fail to grant their demands they would all be free to call a strike. That was in fact their plan.

The workers' unions in the government and municipal services were reinforced by the opposition parties which had risen to overthrow the government. The Socialist Party sponsored a meeting of unions of all shades, including Sodomei, Sanbetsu, and Kokutetsu, among others, which was held on November 29 and attended by fifty or more delegates of the major unions. As a result, a mass meeting was held in Tokyo at Hibiya Park on December 17, with the slogan: "Down with the government!" Some friendly officials of SCAP tried to dissuade the workers from going too far into politics, but the workers were more sophisticated now than they ever had been before. Their repartee was: "But how about the Far Eastern Commission's Principle No. 6?" Like children who had memorized their catechism in Sunday School they had faithfully learned the FEC's Sixteen Principles for Japanese Trade-Unions. This was embarrassing to SCAP.

The government was not unaware of the distressing financial conditions of the workers, but it had no resources from which to squeeze the funds necessary for relieving the workers at the year's end. The "year-end bonus" is a big item in the household economy of any wage-earning worker in Japan, and this was one of the ten demands addressed to the Prime Minister on December 3. All that the government could give as a year-end bonus was 1,000 yen per worker, a mere pittance for the workers in their plight as a result of inflation. The workers took this as an insult.

Misfortunes seldom come singly, says a Western proverb. This proved true in Japan as well; in his New Year's greeting to the nation over the radio, Prime Minister Yoshida happend to refer to the actions of the labor leaders with the phrase *futei no yakara,* which would be equivalent to "gang lawlessness" in English. This was a rhetorical expression, which apparently the Prime Minister used with no profound satirical meaning, but it had a devastating effect. It led to the immediate reorganization and strengthening of the Joint Struggle Committee, and the adding of more militant members. A new set of demands was presented on January 11, including one demand calling upon the Prime Minister to apologize publicly for his insulting pronouncement. Eight more unions of public employees joined the forces, making a total of thirteen unions or federations, representing some 2,600,000 members. On January 18, the Struggle Committee announced the calling of a general strike to begin on February 1.

During those days of increasing tension, the Central Labor Relations Commission was busily engaged in the work of mediation in an effort to avert the disaster, but the work of this body, which continued through sleepless nights, proved fruitless. On January 30, SCAP called to General Headquarters the leaders of the Committee; they were counseled gently to refrain from their excesses and told to report back that their Committee had decided to call off the strike. But at 2:30 on January 31, nine and one-half hours before the deadline, there was no such report from the Struggle Committee. It was at this eleventh hour that General MacArthur, "with the greatest reluctance," issued the formal order forbidding the strike.

Because of the historic significance of the document, we give below the full text of the order.

General MacArthur's Order and Its Significance

STATEMENT BY THE SUPREME COMMANDER BANNING THE PROPOSED STRIKE, JANUARY 31, 1947

Under the authority vested in me as Supreme Commander for the Allied Powers, I have informed the labor leaders, whose unions have federated for the purpose of conducting a general strike, that I will not permit the use of so deadly a social weapon in the present impoverished and emaciated condition of Japan, and have accordingly directed them to desist from the furtherance of such action.

It is with the greatest reluctance that I have deemed it necessary to intervene to this extent in the issues now pending. I have done so only to forestall the fatal impact upon an already gravely threatened public welfare. Japanese society today operates under the limitations of war defeat and Allied occupation. Its cities are laid waste, its industries are almost at a standstill, and the great masses of its people are on little more than a starvation diet.

A general strike, crippling transportation and communications, would prevent the movement of food to feed the people and of coal to sustain essential utilities, and would stop such industry as is still functioning. The paralysis which inevitably would result might reduce large masses of the Japanese people to the point of actual starvation, and would produce dreadful consequences upon every Japanese home regardless of social strata or direct interest in the basic issue. Even now, to prevent actual starvation in Japan, the people of the United States are releasing to them quantities of their own scarce food resources.

The persons involved in the threatened general strike are but a small minority of the Japanese people. Yet this minority might well plunge the great masses into a disaster not unlike that produced in the immediate past by the minority which led Japan into the destruction of war. This in turn would impose upon the Allied Powers the unhappy decision of whether to leave the Japanese people to the fate thus recklessly imposed by a minority, or to cover the consequences by pouring into Japan, at the expense of their own meager resources, infinitely greater quantities of food and other supplies to sustain life than otherwise would be required. In the circumstances, I could hardly request the Allied peoples to assume this additional burden.

While I have taken this measure as one of dire emergency, I do not intend otherwise to restrict the freedom of action heretofore given labor in the achievement of legitimate objectives. Nor do I intend in any way to compromise or influence the basic social issues involved. These are matters of evolution which time and circumstance may well orient without disaster as Japan gradually emerges from its present distress.[16]

This intervention of the Supreme Commander was made with reluctance because of his solicitude for the interest of the workers, though an American writer making a special study of the labor situation in Japan, commenting on this statement of General MacArthur, said that ". . . the general tenor of his statement was strongly critical of the unions."[17] The effect of the action deliberately taken by SCAP was immediate. Despite a few hot-heads among the leaders who counseled defiance, the Struggle Committee capitulated forthwith and the strike was called off, much to the relief of the government and of the general public.

One incident in the last stages added to the already dramatic commotion. This was the radio message of the Communist leader, Ii. On account of the provision in the Law for Adjustment of Labor Disputes, all through the negotiations the radio and the newspapers had co-operated to keep the public informed of the progress— or lack of progress—of negotiations. When the dispute came officially to an end with the submission of the workers to SCAP's order, Dr. Suehiro calmly spoke over the radio on behalf of the Central Labor Relations Commission. So did the Finance Minister Ishibashi on behalf of the government. Lastly came Ii. Charged with emotion, trembling, and finally breaking into tears, Ii said the workers "had to comply" with the SCAP's order, but stressed that "the struggle must go on now by other methods, even if it seems like one step forward and two steps backward, till final victory is won for the workers."

Now, some twenty years or more after the incident, when the whole matter can be viewed in the perspective of history, one can understand better why the workers dared to press the matter so far. For many people, the idea of the workers' overthrowing the government through a general strike, no matter how masterfully conducted, would have seemed only rash and puerile, to put it mildly. But it must be recalled that there were circumstances under which some might have indulged in the naive thought that a government that was ineffective and undemocratic, and that lacked the support of the people to the extent that it could not restore order from the chaos of a general strike, could be overthrown. Strike is a social or economic weapon, one of the basic rights of labor guaranteed by the Constitution and by statutory laws, different from resort to violence. Would it have embarrassed the Allied occupation authority if the government, or the form of the government, were changed by the freely expressed will of the people of Japan, through means that were legitimate, legal, and guaranteed by the Constitution? No, indeed: there are, in fact, passages in the U.S. Initial Post-Surrender Policy for Japan that supported such ideas.

Part II. Allied Authority

2. Relationship to Japanese Government

The authority of the Emperor and the Japanese Government will be subject to the Supreme Commander, who will possess all powers necessary to effectuate the surrender terms and to carry out the policies established for the conduct of the occupation and the control of Japan. . . .

The Japanese Government will be permitted under his [SCAP's] instructions, to exercise the normal powers of government in matters of domestic administration. This policy, however, will be subject to the right and duty of the Supreme Commander to require changes in governmental machinery or personnel or to act directly if the Emperor or other Japanese authority does not satisfactorily meet the requirements of the Supreme Commander in effectuating the surrender terms. This policy, moreover, does not commit the Supreme Commander to support the Emperor or any other Japanese governmental authority in opposition to evolutionary changes looking toward the attainment of United States objectives. The policy is to use the existing form of Government in Japan, not to support it. Changes in the form of Government initiated by the Japanese people or government in the direction of modifying its feudal and authoritarian tendencies are to be permitted and favored. In the event that the effectuation of such changes involves the use of force by the Japanese people or government against persons opposed thereto, the Supreme Commander should intervene only where necessary to ensure the security of his forces and the attainment of all other objectives of the occupation.

Another matter relevant to this situation is the question of the position of the Emperor of Japan after surrender. In order to avoid too detailed an account, any mention of this question was omitted in connection with the acceptance by Japan of the Potsdam Declaration, but reference should be made to it here.

One reason for Japan's delay in accepting the Potsdam Declaration was the solicitude on the part of the Japanese government regarding the future form of government or the status of the Emperor. The message, as conveyed on August 10, 1945, by the Swiss chargé d'affaires, of the Japanese government's acceptance of the terms of the Potsdam Declaration contained the statement: ". . . with the understanding that the said declaration does not comprise any demand which prejudices the prerogatives of His Majesty as a sovereign ruler." Had the Allies accepted this statement of the Japanese government, it would not have been an "unconditional surrender." The reply of the Allied authorities dictated by Secretary of War Stimson and wired back through the same Swiss channel to Japan was noncommittal and unequivocal. The relevant passage of the Allies' reply read: "The ultimate form of government of Japan shall, in accordance with the Potsdam Declaration, be established by the freely expressed will of the Japanese people."

Now, in the year and a half between surrender and the proposed general strike, the people of Japan had never been given a chance to freely express their will on the subject. Neither the Far Eastern Commission nor the Allied Council of Japan had formally discussed or decided upon the ultimate form of the Japanese government, and the United States Policy for Japan, as quoted above, had left much leeway for General MacArthur to act as he might see fit "to modify the feudalistic and authoritarian tendencies of the government."

In the meantime, in the early period of the occupation, there were plenty of grounds for the Communists to entertain the naive idea that they might even be looked upon with favor by SCAP. MacArthur released from prison sixteen Communist leaders only a week after his landing in Japan. Participation of those Communists in the work of Labor Relations Commissions was welcomed. SCAP in those days had no misgivings or mistrust of Communists as such. Today it would seem incredible, but Shiga Yoshio, one of the three or four top Communist leaders, sat on the Labor Legislation Council and worked closely with others in drafting the Labor Standard Law. Even toward the violence and intimidation practiced by workers in the early days, SCAP always seemed hesitant to deal harshly with them. After the violence perpetrated on May Day in 1946, SCAP issued the following statement:

I find it necessary to caution the Japanese people that the growing tendency toward mass violence and physical processes of intimidation, under organized leadership, present a grave menace to the future development of Japan. While every possible rational freedom of democratic method has been permitted and will be permitted in the evolution now proceeding in the transformation from a feudalistic and military state to one of democratic process, the physical violence which undisciplined elements are now beginning to practice will not be permitted to continue. They constitute a menace not only to orderly government but to the basic purposes and security of the occupation itself. If minor elements of Japanese society are unable to exercise such self-restraint and self-respect as the situation and conditions require, I shall be forced to take the necessary steps to control and remedy such a deplorable situation. I am sure the great mass of the people condemn such excesses by disorderly minorities, and it is my sincere hope that the sane views of this predominant public opinion will exert sufficient influence to make it unnecessary to intervene.

As indicated above, SCAP saw only "excesses by small minorities" and was most reluctant to intervene. Moderation and reserve seemed to characterize the attitude of SCAP, since but few people were able to conjecture what some Communist leaders were contemplating in the midst of the heated debates with the government authorities during this dispute.[18]

It will be recalled that it was the Soviet forces under Marshal

Zhukov who forced the fall of Berlin, but the U.S.S.R. consented to the divided rule of Berlin and of Germany by the four Allied Powers.

The final fall of Japan was effectuated by the U.S. forces under General MacArthur and the command over Japan remained with MacArthur in his capacity as Supreme Commander for all the Allied Powers, but the rule of Japan was not a divided rule of the four allied powers. Had the general strike broken out with all transportation and communication paralyzed for any length of time, and had the Soviet forces landed in, say, Hokkaido "for restoration and maintenance of order" in that area and stayed on, it would have been difficult for General MacArthur, or anybody else, for that matter, to prevent a divided rule of Japan thereafter, similar to that of Germany.

Land Reform and Its Effects

Before we go further afield in narrating the reforms in labor relations attempted by General MacArthur, our attention should turn to the agrarian problems, which had assumed serious dimensions before the war and in which SCAP tried bold and drastic reforms, with some encouraging results.

By a directive addressed to the Japanese government on December 9, 1945, General MacArthur requested the Japanese government to "take measures to insure that those who till the soil of Japan shall have a more equal opportunity to enjoy the fruits of their labor." This direction was in line with the general spirit of that particular provision in the Potsdam Declaration that required the Japanese government to take measures for the installation of democracy in Japan. More particularly, this was in conformity with the lines in the U.S. Initial Policy for Japan, which stated: "Encouragement shall be given and favor shown to the development of organizations in *labor, industry* and *agriculture*, organized on a democratic basis. Policies shall be favored which permit a wide distribution of income and of the ownership of the means of production and trade."

In response to this directive of SCAP, the Japanese government enacted on October 21, 1946, the Special Measure for the Establishment of Owner Farmers (Land Reform Law) and Agricultural Land Adjustment Law of 1946. An epoch-making land reform was carried out in the framework provided by this legislation. There were two major objectives: transfer of land ownership to farmers who were actually tilling the soil; and improvement of farm-tenancy conditions for those who continued as farm tenants. It should be noted especially that the underlying principle of this law was *private rather than state,* and individual rather than collective, ownership of the land. This basic principle makes the land reform under American guidance different from land reforms carried out in most other countries.

Under this law all the land previously owned by absentee owners had to be sold. Resident landlords might retain 2.5 acres of tenant-cultivated land, except in Hokkaido, where they could retain 10 acres. In order to place the ownership of the maximum amount of land in the hands of as many former tenants as possible, the law also fixed limitations on the size of holdings of owner cultivators. The government did not expropriate the land of the former landowners, but purchased the land at an average price of 3,000 yen per acre for rice land and 1,860 yen per acre for dry or upland fields. Furthermore, in order to encourage land ownership, the government subsidized the sale of land up to 880 yen per acre of paddy fields and 520 yen per acre for uplands. There was a maximum fixed at 7.5 acres per individual seller in Honshu, Shikoku, and Kyushu, and 30 acres in Hokkaido. The government's payment was to be in twenty-four-year annuity bonds, bearing interest at the rate of 3.65 per cent per year. By the same token, a tenant might conclude the purchase in one payment if he chose to, or in several annual installments not exceeding thirty in number, at an annual interest rate of 3.2 per cent.

So much for provisions to encourage owner farming. Another important reform introduced was the reduction in rents and the elimination of rent payments in kind. Rents had to be paid in cash, and the maximum allowed was 25 per cent of the value of the rice crop and 15 per cent of the value of other crops.

Still another thing stressed in the reform was the requirement that tenant-farming agreements, specifying the rent, the period of tenure, and other terms, must in each case be made in writing, not verbally as had been too frequently the case in the past. The principle that the landowner must not take away the land from the tenant was reaffirmed.

What was the result of the reform? The figures in Table 30 are interesting indicators of the results achieved:

TABLE 30
EFFECT OF LAND REFORM ON TENANCY FARMING
(1941–1950)

	Per cent	
	1941	*1950*
Farming families engaged in tenancy farming[19]	68.4	37.4
Tenants (exclusively)	27.4	5.0
Owner farmers	31.1	61.9
Percentage of total farm area under tenancy farming	45.9	9.2

The above figures show unmistakably the successful results achieved by the reforms during the period of occupation. The proportion of the farming families engaged in tenancy farming was reduced in the ten-year period to nearly half of what it was; the families that were purely tenants without owning any land of their own, who had constituted nearly 30 per cent of the total farming families, were reduced to 5 per cent; the owner families who used to be less than a third (31.1 per cent) increased to more than half (61.9 per cent), and, finally, the farm area cultivated solely by tenants, which had represented nearly half of the total (45.9 per cent), was reduced to less than a tenth (9.2 per cent).

In the face of these figures, certainly no one need hesitate to acclaim this as a successful record. However, to be realistic, it must be remembered that Japan's agriculture, indeed, her national economy, is fraught with difficulties peculiar to Japan—difficulties that qualify the success of this record. A few observations on this subject will be made before we return to the discussion of the main questions of labor and industrial relations.

Agriculture is still today the backbone of Japan's economic life. This basic fact is likely to be obscured by the striking advance of Japan's industry, shipping, shipbuilding, electronic engineering, and other technological achievements. The last war seemed to have almost totally wrecked Japan's industrial fabric, and only agriculture survived the devastation of the war. This may account partly for the high proportion of agricultural households that still remain in Japan. As is well known now, Colin Clark, the British economist, divided the industries of a country into the primary, secondary, and tertiary industries, and showed that in the countries of high per capita national income (by which he means the countries of a higher degree of industrialization) the proportion of the people engaged in the primary industries, such as agriculture, fishing, and forestry, tend to be less and less, and those of the secondary, such as construction, manufacture, and mining, and the tertiary industries, such as commerce, communications, and services, tend to grow more. Now Japan is admittedly a country of relatively high industrial development, but what is to be discovered here in the distribution of population among the various industries? Before World War II, as Table 31 shows, the population in the primary industries remained at about 14,000,000. However, there was sudden growth in both the secondary and tertiary industries, with the result that the proportion of the population in the primary industries, which was 54 per cent in 1920, diminished gradually to 49 per cent in 1930, 44 per cent in 1940, and 43 per cent in 1955. The outbreak of war in Korea did disturb the curve slightly, but, generally speaking, one might say that Colin Clark's theory holds as true in Japan as in Western countries. Moreover, we know that Prime Minister Ikeda, in his famous plan to double the national income by 1970, is contemplating a further reduction in the size of the primary industries group. Even then, however, we cannot ignore the implacable problem of too many mouths to be fed in too limited a space. The average size of a farm in Japan is 2.5 acres; in China the average size is 3.0 acres, in Korea 3.6, in the United Kingdom 10, in the United States 47, and in Canada 80 acres.

As shown in Table 33, the acreage under cultivation in Japan is extremely low, whereas the percentage of the population engaged in land cultivation is unduly high as compared with that of many other countries.

An American authority who has studied the problems of occupation with access to all official statistical and other data commented on this situation as follows:

The agrarian reform has come deservedly to be regarded as one of the most successful of the occupation reform programs. The peasant class has been emancipated from exploitation by the landlords, and to the extent permitted by the immutable factor of "too many men on too little land," the economic bases of a peacefully inclined and democratic rural society have been built. Reform, plus the peasants' traditional conservatism and relatively favorable economic conditions in the rural areas since the war appear to have rendered the farming class largely immune to Communist doctrines. Nevertheless, conservative elements, in many cases genuinely believing that reform is not in Japan's best interest, have not surrendered, and can be expected to continue their efforts to bring it down, overtly if feasible, and otherwise by indirection and by playing on the lingering uncertainties of the farmers themselves.[20]

Another important factor that complicates the situation, and the working of which must be watched with care, is the change made by SCAP in the law of succession, or more particularly the right of inheritance, which constitutes the vital part of the right of succession. Under the occupation, incident to the reform in the civil law, the time-honored system of primogeniture has been replaced in principle by the Western systems of dividing the father's estate equally among all offspring of the father, male and female alike. The surviving spouse is specially protected by the law, but apart from that the inheritance will be divided as a matter of practice. It is obvious that the reform aimed at

TABLE 31
STRUCTURAL CHANGES IN INDUSTRIAL POPULATION IN JAPAN (1920–1955) (in thousands)

Year	Primary	Per-cent-age	Sec-ondary	Per-cent-age	Tertiary	Per-cent-age	Total
1920	14,442	54.6	5,576	21.1	6,422	24.3	26,440
1930	14,490	49.5	5,993	20.5	8,788	30.0	29,271
1940	14,192	44.3	8,419	26.3	9,403	29.4	32,014
1950	18,150	51.1	7,913	22.3	9,489	26.7	35,552
1951	16,687	46.1	8,172	22.6	11,357	31.4	36,216
1952	16,890	45.3	8,603	23.1	11,791	31.6	37,284
1953	17,790	45.3	8,950	22.8	12,530	31.9	39,270
1954	17,220	43.5	9,190	23.2	13,160	33.3	39,570
1955	17,680	42.9	9,470	23.0	14,040	34.1	41,190

distributive justice—justice to every individual—but what would be the result if this principle were rigidly observed in the inheritance of every farm, the average size of which, as we noticed, is not more than 2.5 acres? Within a decade or so, the average farm unit would be so small that it would utterly cease to be economical. For this obvious reason, there will probably be a margin automatically fixed beyond which the division will not be

TABLE 32
THE *DENSAN* WAGE STRUCTURE

Standard Wage	Basic Wage	Livelihood-guarantee wage	Covering: Worker himself and family
		Wage for ability	
		Wage for length of service	
	Regional Wage	Regional differential	
		Winter differential	
	Overtime Wage	Overtime allowance	
		Overnight-guard allowance	
Extra-Standard Wage	Special-labor Wage	Special-labor allowance	
		On-duty allowance	
		Special-duty allowance	
	Special-service Wage	Remote-service allowance	
		Special-living-quarters allowance	

mechanically pressed, but this will mean, inevitably, that the farming population will remain a reservoir of cheap labor as hitherto. In Japanese, this is called the problem of *ji-nan bō* and *san-nan bō* (second-born and third-born boy). Because it is uneconomical and meaningless to inherit tiny tracts of farm land, the second-born, the third-born, and other boys often prefer to remain unbound to the land. Some are absorbed in other industries in the urban areas, but others remain in the rural districts and eke out a precarious existence without a fixed occupation.

TABLE 33
INTERNATIONAL COMPARISON OF AREAS UNDER CULTIVATION AND POPULATION ENGAGED IN FARMING

Country	Total area (hectares)	Farm land (hectares)	Percentage b/a	Percentage of farming population against total
Canada	935.0	61.1	6	19.0 (1951)
Denmark	4.2	3.1	74	23.0 (1953)
France	55.1	33.4	60	36.0 (1946)
Great Britain	24.1	19.5	80	5.0 (1951)
Italy	29.3	21.7	74	—— ——
Japan	36.9	6.4	17	42.9 (1954)
U.S.A.	770.0	452.0	58	12.0 (1950)
U.S.S.R.	2,227.0	349.0	15	57.0 (1930)

Surely, this situation was not entirely unforeseen or over-looked by SCAP, but, after all, the occupation was not expected to remain in Japan indefinitely and to solve all Japan's problems. The Japanese authorities have been giving some thought to this and other related problems. Schemes somewhat similar in thinking and in organization to CCC (Civilian Conservation Corps) adopted in the United States under the New Deal have been tried in some prefectures in Japan. The government will have to push these experiments further, also the various schemes worked out under the income-doubling policy.[21]

The Changing Character of the Unions:
the Densan Wage Pattern

The grand plot of the February First General Strike was, in a word, bombastic. Because of that aspect of the spectacular incident, a casual observer may mistakenly assume that the leadership of trade-unions at this time was merely pompous or grandiloquent and completely lacking in careful calculation and planning. That such an assumption is erroneous is obvious from a number of instances that testify to the growing maturity of the leadership in some unions. One instance that would refute such an assumption is the so-called *densan gata,* or *densan* pattern of wage structure which was worked out by the leaders of the Electrical Workers' Union in the course of their dispute in 1946, prior to the general strike plot.

During the October Offensive, in 1946, the Electrical Workers' Union, in their demand for a wage raise, presented in the course of a mediation procedure at the Central Labor Relations Commission a formula they wanted to have adopted in order to insure the payment of adequate wages for electrical workers. The ultimate aim of the formula was to do away with the obsolete, feudalistic wage concept of the past and to establish the wage system on a more equitable and rational basis. In the old system, the wage proper was, as a rule, small in amount. The deficiency arising from the meager wage was made up with a variety of so-called bonuses. The term implied that they were gifts of the employer, as evidence of his benevolence. The worker had no right to claim the gifts. The employer was free to give or not to give a bonus. Even when he decided to give it, the amount was variable according to the financial situation in which the company found itself and, also, according to the mood of the employer at the time he made the decision. The result was that the workers were constantly faced with uncertainty as to their livelihood.

The wage system of the *densan* pattern introduced a new concept of a "basic wage" (*kihon chingin*) that guaranteed the minimum livelihood of the worker himself and of his family, plus increments based on ability and length of his service. The basic wage constituted the bulk of the earnings of a worker. In addition to the basic wage, the worker was entitled to a regional differential in wage. The place where he worked might be in a region where the cost of living was higher than in other regions, or where, on account of severe climatic conditions special additional allowances must be paid by the employer. In the *densan* wage system, the basic wage plus the regional differential wage constituted the "standard wage" (*kijun chingin*).

In addition to the standard wage, the worker was entitled to overtime pay for overtime work, including the special allowance for overnight duty. There were also special allowances for the performance of certain dangerous or disagreeable duties. In some cases, depending on the nature of the work, additional pay would come for being "on duty." Further, there were always additional allowances paid for performance of duties at remote places or where the living was subject to risks of one kind or another. Any additional earnings of a worker under these various special circumstances constituted wages over and above the standard wages, and were called "extra-standard wages" (*kijungai chingin*).

The thinking of the men who worked out the *densan* pattern was that any earning of allowances under the "extra-standard wages" should be strictly extra earnings, in the sense that the worker should be well able to live a life worthy of a human being, without these additional earnings.

The wage structure under the *densan* system is graphically portrayed in Table 32, page 280.

When the representatives of the electrical workers presented the above-given formula to the Mediation Committee of the Central Labor Relations Commission for the first time, all members present at the session were impressed with the novel theoretical analysis of the wages. Employers' representatives offered but little resistance. The proposal of the workers this time was impressive because hitherto they had been asking merely for "more."

The *densan* wage structure contained a number of basic ideas or contentions that, on theoretical grounds, were irrefutable, notably that: (1) wages should be of an amount that would guarantee a minimum livelihood to the worker and his family; (2) wages should rise in proportion to the worker's ability and length of service; (3) wages should rise according to the needs of the locality, the kind of work performed, and the risks or responsibilities involved, and any such increase in wages should be strictly extra income not affecting the standard wage to which the worker is entitled.

In actually computing the amount of the standard wage, and particularly the livelihood-guarantee wage, the electrical workers used the cost-of-living figures derived from the actual cost-of-living inquiries of the government. A method of theoretical computation of cost of living that made use of Engels' coefficient was applied in their search for a system of wage structure guaranteeing a livelihood to each worker. For this reason, in working out the figures, those workers demanded also that the amount of wages should "slide" with the price of commodities.

The triumph of the *densan* wage structure has to be admitted, since it spread widely and rapidly to other industries; it constituted the first step toward establishing a national minimum wage; it took in the principle of ability-pay, which would eventually banish the obsolete practice of payment according to the status or personal relation of the worker to the employer, and paved the way for further democratization of industrial relations in this country.

Two Significant Movements: Mindō and Zen Rōren

The failure of the general-strike plot gave rise to at least two significant movements among the organized workers of Japan: Kumiai Minshuka Undō (the Trade-Union Democratization Movement) and the organization of all trade-unions called Zenkoku Rodo Kumiai Renraku Kyogi Kai (National Council for the Coordination of Trade-Unions), more commonly known by the abbreviated title Zen Rōren. Both of these movements, as mentioned above, were by-products of the failure of the general strike. Since they had considerable influence on the behavior of Japanese trade-unions in the years to follow, a full and forthright account of the circumstances in which these movements arose needs to be given here, especially since the story has never yet been fully told.

"Kumiai Minshuka Undō" is too long a title, even for the Japanese who gave the movement its name; accordingly they shortened it to "Min-dō." The movement arose as a reaction to the leadership of the Communists and other extreme leftists who were beginning to dominate the labor movement. There developed a genuine desire to turn the trade-union movement into a democratic movement. In SCAP General Headquarters there was a small number of well-meaning officials who ventured to take the initiative in giving encouragement and guidance in starting the democratization movement. It spread rapidly in various industries and finally Sangyo Minshuka Dōmei (the League for Industrial Democratization) was formed. Under the careful guidance of the individuals mentioned above, the movement grew into something tremendously powerful and important, as will be seen later.

The other movement, Zen Rōren, was quite different from Mindō, though it arose also as a result of the failure of the general-strike plot. It arose among the leaders of the major federations of labor, including Sodomei and Sanbetsu, democratic socialists and communists, who realized that unless the unions of all tendencies were united they would be powerless. The fiasco of the general strike brought home to them the need for a united front.

One thing which prompted the organization of Zen Rōren was the visit to Japan of a delegation of the new and powerful world organization of labor, the World Federation of Trade Unions (WFTU). At its organization meeting in Paris in October, 1945, there were representatives of sixty-five national trade-union federations in fifty-six countries, with a total membership of 65 million workers. This was the most powerful labor organization in world history, and included the national trade-union federations of the U.S.S.R., 27,124,000 members; Great Britain, 5,600,000; United States (CIO) 6,000,000; Italy, 5,200,000; France, 5,100,000; Latin America, 4,000,000; Czechoslovakia, 1,500,000; Rumania, 1,267,-000; Sweden, 1,087,000; Poland, 1,011,000; Mexico, 1,000,000; Hungary, 888,000; China, 800,000; French Catholic, 750,000; Yugoslavia, 662,000; Australia, 625,000; Cuba, 557,000; and Nigeria, 500,000, to mention only the larger organizations represented at the Paris meeting. A news report appeared to the effect that this newly formed World Federation of Trade Unions was sending a delegation to Japan to stimulate the formation of trade-unions in this country. Now, this was long before the Cold War broke out between the United States and the U.S.S.R., and in the Allied Council for Japan there was general expectation that the delegation of the WFTU would not only be allowed to land in Japan but also to confer with the representatives of organized labor in this country.

To the leaders of organized labor in Japan, this was thrilling news. They felt that the WFTU would give them a unique opportunity for direct contact with the outside world. They thought they might have an opportunity to send their representatives to the congresses of the WFTU held outside of Japan even before Japan regained her independence and the right to participate in international conferences. For these reasons the leaders of the Zen Rōren sought eagerly the opportunity of contact with the delegates of the WFTU. When they found out that one of the members of the delegation of the WFTU was an American Negro by the name of Willard Townsend, the noted founder and president of the Redcaps' Union in the United States, who would arrive by boat in Yokohama as the first member of the delegation to reach Japan, each day, in order not to miss his arrival, they sent to Yokohama a band of men waving huge flags to welcome the colored labor leader.

General MacArthur, when he heard of this, said that he should meet Townsend first and decide whether or not to allow other members of the delegation to come to Japan at all. Consequently, on the day the ship was due in Yokohama, the General sent his own car to the wharf, had the visitor picked up before he could meet anyone, and had him taken to the official residence of the Supreme Commander. MacArthur was impressed with the personality of Townsend and, after dinner with the honored guest, gave his approval to the entry into Japan of the delegation of the WFTU.

Thus the entry of the delegation was approved by the Supreme Commander for the Allied Powers, which incidentally gave strength to the newly organized Zen Rōren. How far this new organization could succeed in its attempt to bring the organized workers of Japan into the fold of the world workers' federation, however, was a different question. As we shall soon see, the WFTU underwent a split in 1949, thereby dividing the world workers' movement into two hostile camps, with the Communist unions under the WFTU, on the one hand, and the democratic unions under the ICFTU (International Confederation of Free Trade Unions), on the other. Since this tragedy befell the world movement so early, one might say that the Zen Rōren, which was born with the mission of bringing the Japanese trade-unions into the main stream of the world movement, was ill-destined from the outset. Its motivation was genuine and legitimate, but, because of the vast changes that occurred in Japan in the course of the Cold War, the lot of the Zen Rōren until its dissolution in August, 1950, turned out to be a sad and inglorious one. Nevertheless, despite its record of nonsuccess, this organization should be given due credit for the first attempt to unite the unions of all ideological shades—left wing, right wing, and neutral.

It has been pointed out that Mindō and Zen Rōren arose as a result of the failure of the general-strike plot. It should be mentioned in passing that in April, 1947, only two months after the February First incident, two important labor laws were promulgated. One was the Labor Standards Act, with the enactment of which Japan had all of the "three basic labor laws" of the postwar period. Because of the surpassing importance of this Act, space will be devoted later to a discussion of it. The second labor law was the Law for Insurance of Workmen's Compensation. It was generally recognized that Workmen's Compensation for factory workers and for workers in construction, mining, and other hazardous occupations would remain a dead issue unless management was protected by social insurance of this sort.

Still another evidence of the slowly growing maturity of the workers was the formation of the Economic Rehabilitation Conference (Keizai Fukkō Kaigi). Both Sodomei and Sanbetsu were willing to compromise and join in. It included major employers' organizations, along with Sodomei and Sanbetsu, sixteen members in all. The conference set to work on February 6, 1947, but was short-lived; it had to dissolve after fourteen months of precarious existence. Here again, credit must be given to the workers' leaders who were disposed to compromise and lend a hand, along with the employers, to the work of economic rehabilitation.

Failure of the Katayama Cabinet and Labor's New Offensive

An experience similar to that of the British workers after World War I befell the Japanese workers after World War II, i.e., the failure of the first Socialist Government under Katayama Tetsu to meet the expectations of the people, much as MacDonald's first Labor Government was a disappointment to the British people who had held great hopes for it. In the first general election after the adoption of the new Constitution, held in April, 1947, the Socialist Party became the first political party on the basis of the number of seats won, though it did not gain an absolute majority at the polls. Katayama Tetsu, a Christian Socialist, in forming his cabinet had to call on two other parties, namely the Democratic Party and the National Co-operative Party. It was a coalition cabinet, and the government that Katayama succeeded in setting up had all the defects and faced all the pitfalls of a coalition government. The working class had high hopes for this cabinet and refrained from any rash action that would embarrass Katayama, but the economic stringency of the country proved to be an insurmountable handicap for this first government in Japan under a Socialist premier. When Katayama's government adopted a system of average wages for various industries, the workers' unions began to attack this as an attempt to impose fixed wages on workers. The Federation of All Government and Municipal Employees was dissatisfied with the new wage basis of 1,800 yen which the government had adopted, and appointed a committee to negotiate with the government. Negotiations began on August 15, with the Federation demanding two things: the establishing of a national minimum-wage system and the granting of a lump-sum aid to help the government and municipal workers cover deficits they had incurred. Negotiations reached an impasse on September 16, when the unions affiliated with the Federation presented pleas to the Central Labor Relations Commission for mediation. The leaders in this action were the union of the National Railway Workers (Kokutetsu) and the All Communication Workers (Zentei), which covered post, telephone, and telegraph workers.

After the experience of failure of the general-strike plot, these workers had become "wise." They remembered that SCAP had intervened and prohibited a strike that had been organized on a national scale. This time, therefore, the strikes were planned not on a national but on a local or regional scale; they took the form, not of organized or centrally planned strikes, but of "wildcat strikes," unorganized and sporadic—at least in form. One demand common to all the workers' unions was for a minimum wage that would insure workers in any locality a daily diet containing 2,400 calories.

The case was handled by the Central Labor Relations Commission. The Commission, after careful examination of the workers' demands, stated in the mediation award that the government should give each worker a lump-sum gift amounting to the equivalent of 2.8 months' salary to help him meet the deficit in his livelihood; the government should also set up a temporary committee to study the revision of the salaries of government and municipal workers. The government, under the Christian Socialist Premier Katayama, accepted the award and arranged to pay before the end of the year to each worker the equivalent of two months' salary. However, the cabinet members, after racking their brains, could not find anywhere the resources to pay the remainder, i.e., the equivalent of eight-tenths of a month's salary to each worker. As a consequence, the government decided to resign in February, 1948. One cannot refrain from commenting on the irony of the situation, when the inability to pay only eight-tenths of a month's salary to the electrical workers led to the downfall of the first government under a Socialist Prime Minister!

Ashida Hitoshi followed Katayama as prime minister. By this time, the salary revision committee suggested by the Central Labor Relations Commission had been set up and had recommended to the government 2,920 yen as the new salary basis. But this basis was seriously objected to by all the government and municipal workers' unions except the National Railway Workers. Around this issue, the workers were agitated to the point of planning, under the leadership of the All-Communication Workers, another general strike, a nationwide upheaval similar to the general strike of February 1, 1947. This incident is remembered as the *Sangatsu Tōsō* (March Struggle). If the leaders in Zentei (All Communication Workers) believed that they could stage a general strike of that sort in Japan, under the Occupation of the Allied Powers, as indeed it seemed they did, they were naive. This time MacArthur did not move a finger, but a letter written by General William J. Marquat, Chief Aide to SCAP, was sufficient to suppress the entire agitation. The unions had to accept the wage basis laid down in the mediation award of the Central Labor Relations Board, and they did. A general strike was averted, but this did not mean that the situation had improved in the slightest degree. Tension was mounting between the United States and the U.S.S.R., both inside Japan, as seen in the acrimonious debates between the representatives of the two nations on the Allied Council for Japan, and outside, as seen in the friction between the Communist and Democratic unions in the WFTU. This tension was reflected in the changes in the labor policies of SCAP, as will be seen later.

THE MacARTHUR LETTER (MA-SHOKAN) OF JULY 20, 1948, AND THE SEQUEL TO IT

The Mandate of the Letter

In the history of labor in the postwar Japan, if the general-strike plot of February 1, 1947, marked the peak of the wild and wayward behavior of organized workers, the letter that General MacArthur addressed to Premier Ashida on July 22, 1948, may be regarded as the very height of self-restraint exercised by the occupation authority regarding the freedom of action of organized labor under the occupation. The letter marked the end of labor activities free and untramelled by a higher authority; it signaled the beginning of an increasingly strong control of the activities of organized labor. An officer in the Labor Division of SCAP told the representatives of trade-unions at a gathering: "You should know that the honeymoon period for you is now over." Because of the rather fateful character of the letter, it is remembered as *"Ma-Shokan"* (MacArthur Letter), with a sobering, if not entirely ominous, implications.

It was a lengthy letter of more than 4,000 words, and in it, as in the order MacArthur issued to prohibit the general strike of February 1, 1947, one could see how solicitous he was about the true welfare of the workers. It was written, as was the communication on the previous occasion, with great reluctance, though that was not expressed in words this time. It was written in the midst of the July offensive of workers, to restrain the government and municipal employees from overstepping the bounds of their freedom and to suggest that henceforth public servants' strikes should be disallowed. A philosophy of public service was expounded in the letter, and it contained a preachment concerning the ethics that public servants must observe.

Because of its historic nature a few passages will be quoted below. It began:

I have reviewed the conclusions drawn from the joint studies conducted between representatives of your government and this headquarters into the adequacy of the National Public Service Law as a solution to the problems now existing with respect to the Public Service of Japan. I am in general accord with these conclusions as to existing inadequacies which must be corrected.

General MacArthur then took pains to explain the especially

responsible character of public service and why it was necessary for the success of democracy in Japan to insure a proper functioning of public service in the following terms:

It was the purpose of the National Public Service Law to provide for the installation of a democratic and efficient public service in the government of Japan. The plan envisioned a modern type personnel system which recruits public employees from the entire public by competitive test and promotes them on the basis of merit, providing scientific supervision over their classification, compensation, training, evaluation, health, safety, welfare, recreation and retirement. The system provides a grievance procedure for employees and assures them fair and equitable treatment in administration. Enforced by a quasi-judicial administrative authority and supplemented by emergency provisions aimed at immediate reform where urgency demands it, it constitutes a constructive program for dealing with hazards which old bureaucratic practices present to the success of democracy in Japan.

The General took further pains to explain how the Diet, as representative of the sovereign people, should function, and why minority pressures must not be allowed to mar the authority and integrity of the government:

The pattern of personnel administration as here inaugurated views the entire people as exercising sovereignty and control over the employees of government through the National Diet which, functioning through a National Public Service Authority, applies principles of scientific personnel management and standardizes the public service, its recruitment, compensation, discipline, benefits and other factors incident to employment. Such a system, in accordance with democratic concepts, is designed to regard the faithful administration of the law and the efficient conduct of the government's business as a prime duty without yielding to the pressure of politics or privilege.

The studies, now completed, of various laws relating to this subject matter reveal omissions to deal adequately with the situation. They fail to afford positive safeguards against minority pressure upon the authority and integrity of the government and they fail to apply the law to many classifications of governmental employees who clearly are entitled to civil-service benefits and protection and subject to its restrictions. Throughout there is a noticeable failure to distinguish between employee relationships in government and labor relations in private enterprise.

The letter boldly pointed out next that labor in government work has to be treated differently from that in other fields:

The rapid and unprecedented gains labor has made in Japan during the Occupation attest my own awareness of the vital importance of trade unionism in modern life and of the historical significance of the trade-union movement throughout the world in correcting many of the abuses associated with modern industrial economy. In government, however, this movement has but limited application and cannot substitute for or challenge duly constituted executive, judicial and legislative agencies exercising the sovereign power.

The letter went on to stress the supremacy of public interest and to show that under the Constitution the National Diet is "the highest organ of the state power," and that Japan could not have the "responsible government" contemplated by the Potsdam Declaration if any part of the power of government were delegated to or usurped by any private group whatever. "By its very nature, as a private entity the labor union does not possess the attributes of government." This evidently had to be said by SCAP, who saw the danger of the government workers' organizations' taking over the functions of the government, even though it might be only temporarily.

As was to be expected from the tone of the parts quoted so far, in the rest of the letter the General suggested that the rights of organization and of collective bargaining of public servants be subject to limitations. He went on to quote the significant words of "a foremost exponent of labor," former President Franklin D. Roosevelt, on the obligation of public employees, to "serve the whole people, whose interests and welfare require orderliness and continuity in the conduct of their government activities. Their obligation is paramount. Since their own services have to do with the functioning of the government, a strike of public employees manifests nothing less than an intent on their part to restrict or obstruct the operation of government until their demands are satisfied. Such action, looking toward the paralysis of government by those who have sworn to support it, is unthinkable and intolerable."

In making the above quotation, General MacArthur was drawing "a sharp distinction between those who have dedicated their energies to the public service and those engaged in private enterprise. The former are the very instruments used for the exercise by government of the people's sovereign power, and as such owe unconditional allegiance to the public trust imposed by virtue of their employment." The General quoted further from President Roosevelt the following significant words:

All government employees should realize that the process of collective bargaining, as usually understood, cannot be transplanted into the public service. It has its distinct and insurmountable limitations when applied to public personnel management. The very nature and purposes of government make it impossible for administrative officials to represent fully or to bind the employer in mutual discussions with government employee organizations. The employer is the whole people, who speak by means of laws enacted by their representatives in Congress. Accordingly, administrative officials and employees alike are governed and guided, and in many instances restricted, by laws which establish policies, procedures, or rules in personnel matters.

The letter finally stressed at length the "paramountcy of the public interest" and the need for erecting safeguards "to insure that the lawful authority of the government as the political instrument to enforce the people's will as expressed in the body of public law, be only challengeable at the polls as provided by democratic practice," and stated in conclusion: "It is to this end that I feel that a comprehensive revision of the National Public Service Law to bring the same within the framework of the concepts herein discussed should be undertaken immediately. To assist you in this matter this headquarters will continue to be available for advice and consultation."

Effects of the Letter: Government Order No. 201 and Revision of Public Servants Law

The effect of the "letter" couched in such polite terms was devastating. "Devastating," that is, to those people who had cherished ideas of such unrestrained freedom as the working class had enjoyed in Japan in the postwar period until the revisions were made as the result of the general-strike plots of February 1, 1947, and March, 1948. The letter suggested a "comprehensive revision of the National Public Service Law" to be "undertaken immediately." Formal revision of a national statutory law can be made only while the Diet is in session. Because of that constitutional limitation, the government, on July 31, 1948, issued as a temporary measure a decree called "Government Order No. 201," known more popularly as "Potsdam Decree No. 201."

The order prohibited dispute acts of all public servants; they could not even continue bargaining, so that as a result all the mediation cases affecting government services pending at the Central Labor Relations Board were discontinued. Moreover, all the labor contracts (trade agreements) previously entered into by the public servants were set aside as no longer valid. Public servants could no longer engage in collective bargaining with the threat of a strike, slowdown, or other acts of dispute disallowed them. Violators of this ban were liable to penal servitude not exceeding a year or a fine not exceeding 5,000 yen, and discharge.

This action of the government had the effect of separating government workers from those engaged in private industries and of weakening the power of the government workers who had occupied till then a commanding position in the combined movements of organized workers. The National Railway Workers attempted resistance to this action of the government, but their action was futile. The government was carrying out a policy dictated by SCAP.

The necessary statutory action to implement Government Order No. 201 was the revision of the National Public Service Act in December, 1948, accompanied by the enactment of three laws: The Japanese National Railways Act, the Japanese Monopoly Public Corporation Act, and the Public Corporation and National Enterprises Labor Relations Act. By the enactment of these laws, the national public servants (the officials, or white-collar workers, of the central government) and the blue-collar workers engaged in the various enterprises of the government, organized henceforth into "public corporations" or "public enterprises," were completely separated from the jurisdiction of the Central Labor Relations Board. The national public servants came under the jurisdiction of the National Personnel Authority, while the workers engaged in public corporations or in national public enterprises were, in case of labor disputes, brought under the jurisdiction of the newly created Public Corporation and National Enterprise Labor Relations Commission. These laws were supplemented, for purposes of dealing with dispute cases on local or prefectural levels, by the enactment of the Local Public Service Act in December, 1950, and the Local Public Enterprises Act in July, 1952.

How the agencies created by these laws operate will be discussed later.

Government's Program of Labor Education

The significant shift in the occupation's labor policy had an immediate effect on the policy of the Japanese government. This was to be expected if the terms of the Potsdam Declaration and of the Instrument of Surrender are remembered. But that was not all. It must also be remembered that by tradition the government of Japan is a government by an elite, hence a government that leads and directs. Political wisdom in Japan has never taught that "the best government governs the least." The shift in the occupation's labor policy seemed to stir the Japanese authorities, and an active program to "educate" the workers' trade-unions to grow into democratic unions was worked out by the national government.

It will be recalled that in foreign countries, particularly in the United States, there were critics who were unsympathetic toward MacArthur's attempts to turn Japan into a "democracy by directives," and who were skeptical about the outcome. But MacArthur knew the Japanese. For ages, they had been trained to follow the leadership of dedicated men. That was the secret, if there was one, of the rapid modernization achieved by Japan in the early Meiji period. Will Japan succeed in achieving similarly rapid progress in democratization of the Showa period?

In any case, the Japanese government was responsive to the leadership supplied by the occupation. The central government worked out a program of promoting the growth of democratic unions and of democratic relationships between management and labor. A communication of the labor minister, entitled "For Promoting Democratic Unions and Democratic Labor Relations," dated December 22, 1948, was issued to all prefectural governors. The document contained concrete suggestions for drawing up constitutions (and by-laws) of unions and trade agreements. This was followed by another communication dated February 2, 1949, entitled, "The Criteria For Certifications of Unions." It contained the suggestions that (1) nobody who represents the employers' interests should be admitted into a union, and (2) the payment of a salary to a worker who is devoting full time to union activity should be discouraged. There were cases of wages being paid for days that the worker was on strike, also for time spent on union activity during working hours. This communication tried to discourage these practices. In May, 1950, after the revised Trade Union Act went into effect, the Labor Department sent out a communication to all prefectural governors, giving instructions concerning trade agreements. This was an attempt to promote the formation of trade agreements in order to keep unions under agreements as far as possible. Obviously the government in this period was trying to give positive guidance to trade-union workers, following the practices of American unions.

Another notable thing in this period was the effort made by the Japanese government to revise and improve the Trade Union Act and the Labor Relations Adjustment Act. Chief amendments in the Trade Union Act were:

1. Use of violence by trade-unions would in no event be construed as appropriate action. (This was added to the definition of the purpose of a trade-union, Article 2.)

2. The definition of the purpose of a trade-union was narrowed down from what it had been before (Article 1).

3. Qualifications of a trade-union were made more stringent than hitherto; unions failing to meet these qualifications would be denied the certification by the Labor Relations Board that entitled them to participate in the formal "procedures" that the law provides and to avail themselves of the "remedies" provided therein (Article 5). (The "procedures" include the union's participation in the selection of the workers' delegate to the ILO Conference. The "remedies" include the processing by the Labor Relations Board of appeals to redress unfair labor practices of employers.)

4. Unfair labor practices were in the past dealt with directly. Under the amendment, the Labor Relations Board handles the case first and issues orders to grant relief to the complainant after investigation, as is done in the United States.

5. Under the amended law, the term of validity of a trade agreement must be definitely stated. Upon expiration of the term of an agreement, it can be terminated unilaterally by either party. Hitherto, the prevalent interpretation that the agreement was automatically renewable after expiration of the stated term had often placed the employer in an embarrassing situation.

In addition to these amendments in the Trade Union Law, important revisions were made in the Labor Relations Adjustment Law, notably: (1) Some limitations were placed on the exercising of the right of dispute acts after acceptance of the mediation terms of the Labor Relations Board. (2) Limitations were placed on the dispute acts of workers in public utility enterprises after acceptance of mediation terms.

Resentment was expressed by the workers, who considered

these amendments "infringements" on the workers' rights, but the government was resolute in carrying out the measures. On the whole, the government began, in this period, to adopt positive, and even aggressive, labor policies in order to cope with the economic depression that had set in.

Frictions Under Economic Depression

The above-mentioned economic depression was one of the chief factors that compelled the occupation authority, on the one hand, to alter its policy in Japan, and the Japanese government, on the other hand, to resort to drastic measures, which in turn aroused considerable commotion in the country.

To begin with, there was the frightening phenomenon of spiraling inflation. The workers' fantastic plans for general strikes in 1947 and 1948 were, after all, their desperate attempts to rise above the dangers of inflation. During the war, industries had swollen to enormous dimensions. Following the war they had to shrink by disposing of what had become "surplus" labor. In the Japan of prewar years, a mass discharge of workers could have been accomplished without much difficulty. In postwar Japan, not only are the workers strongly organized, but they have learned to resist any "unilateral" action of the employer in matters of personnel administration. The companies that had promptly discharged the large numbers of workers needed only to meet wartime needs were well off; the companies that were slow in acting found themselves in an untenable position. In order to meet the workers' incessant demands for higher wages, they kept borrowing from the banks and running into debt. This created a vicious circle of higher wages—higher prices—higher cost of living. There was no way out of the distressing circle.

To relieve both the employers and workers from this situation the government, in November, 1948, issued for enforcement in all industries the so-called "Three Wage Principles": (1) No bank loan allowed to merely meet the red letter; (2) no price increase allowed for wage increase; and (3) no government subsidy for higher wages. This, as the workers saw, was a sheer "wage-stop" order and nothing else. Such an order in this distressing situation with no thought of relief could result in only one thing—resentment. Critics saw no wisdom in this order. Organized labor contested it vigorously.

This led to the next step, the so-called "Nine Economic Principles," issued by the government under Premier Yoshida at the suggestion of SCAP, with the objective of effecting economic stability. On the premise that Japan must achieve a single exchange rate, as a means of achieving it the government laid down nine principles for faithful observance by the government. They were: (1) a speedy balancing of the budget, (2) an effective taxation plan, (3) loans limited strictly to those that would contribute to economic rehabilitation of Japan, (4) the establishment of a firm program for wage stabilization, (5) further strengthening of the current program of price control, (6) improvements in the control of foreign trade and further control of foreign exchange, (7) improvements in the allocation of materials and the assigning of quotas with a view to enlarging the volume of exports, (8) the increasing of production of important materials and of manufactures, and (9) improvements in the program of assembling of food.

These measures, worked out by the officials under SCAP, for the stability and independence of Japanese economy were a prescription sound in theory but most difficult to implement. Within four months after their promulgation they had to be buttressed by the so-called "Dodge Line."

Mr. J. M. Dodge, director of the Bank of Detroit, was invited by SCAP in March, 1949, to come to Japan to implement the Nine Principles. A series of economic and financial policies were worked out under his direction which came to be known in Japan as the "Dodge Line." For the improvement of the taxation system, Professor Shoup of Columbia University was invited; with regard to foreign trade, the so-called "Logan Program" was adopted. The measures enforced were drastic and thorough. Small-scale industries that had depended on bank loans for their existence crumbled. Widespread unemployment was an inevitable outcome of the application of the austerity economy prescribed at this time. There was suffering on the part of the bankrupted entrepreneurs, and misery for the unemployed workers, but in the deflation that resulted Japan's economy was somehow returned to the more solid and balanced state. Among other things, the rate of 360 yen to the dollar was established and the yen was stabilized. However, the over-all economic outlook for Japan was dismal, to put it mildly; industries were collapsing one after another and unemployed workers were roaming the streets.

Progress of the Democratization Movement and the Birth of Sohyo

One heart-warming item in this period of austerity and gloom was the steady progress of the democratization movement. It arose first as a reaction inside the National Railway Workers' Union, which had been dominated by the Communists, with Ii Yashiro as general secretary. In November, 1947, the Anti-Communist League in the National Railway Workers' Union was formed as the first step. In February, 1948, the Democratization League in the Congress of Industrial Unions (Sanbetsu Minshuka Domei) was organized. In June of the same year, the Sodomei withdrew from Zen Rōren, long before the ICFTU split away from the WFTU in Europe. One might attach a symbolic meaning to Sodomei's withdrawal from Zen Rōren in the throes of the birth of the democratization movement.

Naturally the advent of the ICFTU in Europe in 1949, as the main world stream of democratic trade-unions, furnished much stimulus for the growth of democratic unions in all countries, including Japan, where SCAP was adopting consciously a policy along the line described above. During December, 1949, Sanbetsu Minshuka Domei, mentioned earlier, underwent reorganization and adopted a new name, which it has maintained ever since, commonly abbreviated as Shin Sanbetsu. Though this particular movement has never grown large in membership, it has always maintained a singularly significant role, under the leadership of Hosoya Matsuta. This organization will be discussed later at length.

In the meantime, there arose another movement with a particularly dominant part to play in the labor field in Japan, namely, Sohyo. During March, 1950, a meeting of representatives of seventeen federations with a combined membership of nearly 3,000,000 members was held in Tokyo. It was the organization meeting for the formation of the General Council of Japanese Trade-Unions. It bore fruit; on July 11, 1950, with the participation of twenty-nine federations of unions, with a combined membership of 2,760,000, the General Council of Japanese Trade-Unions (Nippon Rodo Kumiai So-Hyogi Kai, or by abbreviation, Sohyo,) came into being.

Shock of the Korean War

The expression "shock of the Korean War" may sound exaggerated and inappropriate. We venture, however, to use this expression to describe what actually happened. Presumably, military strategists and experts on these questions were not totally unaware of the possible danger of an aggression of this sort by the Communists, but developments on the scene would belie any contention that the Korean incident was foreseen. It is clear, at any rate, that the democratic nations represented by SCAP were utterly unprepared and were taken by surprise by the invasion of South Korea and the actual beginning of the Korean War. This study is not concerned with the military, or even the political, aspects of the issue, but solely with the impact of that war on labor problems in Japan.

The war, which started on June 25, 1950, lasted three long years, North Korea (with "volunteers" of Communist China) on one side and the forces of the United States and of other United Nations on the other. It wrought havoc and untold misery to the thirty million Koreans, with high casualties sustained on both sides. It is true that the United States was the country most seriously involved in the war, with the result that the sacrifices borne by the United States in terms of human lives and war expenditures were unusually high.[22] On closer examination of the picture, one is struck by the irony of the effect of the war on Japan. Up until the year before the outbreak of the devastating incident in Korea, Japan was a land of misery and gloom, under an austerity regime, with bankruptcies and unemployment. The outbreak of the war in Korea suddenly changed Japan into a busy and bustling workshop. The war brought to Japan what seemed like a "boom." There were stock piles of goods and materials, which first the United States and then the United Nations wanted to use in Korea for prosecution of the war. The accumulated stock piles were soon exhausted, but fresh materials were brought in from the United States, huge orders were placed with Japanese manufacturers of munitions, clothing, food, medicine, and what not. Japanese industry had equipment, techniques, skill, and efficiency, upon which the United Nations had to depend to continue the perilous war in Korea. Special orders from the United States to meet the war needs were called *toku-ju,* the abbreviation of *tokubetsu juyō* (special needs), and the temporary boom it brought to Japan was called the *Tokuju Keiki.* Thus, with the spread of the disastrous warfare in Korea, ironically indeed, Japan seemed to enjoy a new prosperity, though one is inclined to wonder whether prosperity under these conditions could possibly be of a sound and durable nature. It will be seen later that the repercussions of the war were not confined to the economic area, but, in fact, extended more significantly to the political area, in which the workers of Japan put up a fight, much to the embarrassment of the governments of the United States and Japan.

CHAPTER VI

From Independence (1952)
to the Present

REPERCUSSIONS OF THE KOREAN WAR

The "Red Purge" and the Decline of Communist Influence

Prior to the outbreak of the Korean War, there were obvious signs that actions deliberately taken by SCAP were directed toward gradual elimination of Communist influence in the Japanese trade-unions. We mentioned earlier that leadership was discreetly supplied, on an entirely voluntary and private basis, by certain individual officers in GHQ of SCAP to promote the "democratization movement" (Mindō, by abbreviation), which was, in fact, another name for anti-Communist movement.

On June 6, 1950, a letter of significance in this connection was addressed by General MacArthur to the Japanese government. Written without any preknowledge of the fateful Korean War that was to come within a few weeks, it suggested, as if in preparation for the imminent crisis, the purging of the extremists from the Japanese government. In effect, the letter ordered the dismissal from public posts of twenty-four members of the Central Committee of the Japanese Communist Party. As subsequent developments showed, the action of SCAP in this instance was the signal for a series of bold and large-scale dismissals of Communists from employment in Japanese industries.

On June 25, the troops of North Korea crossed the 38th parallel and war ensued. Thereupon the purge initiated by SCAP spread all over Japan. The Communists were discharged from government bureaus and private offices, from state and national public enterprises, as well as from private industries. Well over 12,000 Communists or extremists were summarily fired. It should be noted that there were protests by some Japanese critics, who suggested that these dismissals were a violation of the freedom of thought guaranteed by the Constitution (Article 19). However, there was no organized opposition; mere lip service was of no use in the acute situation.

The next stage of the "red purge" was a spectacular one—the government-ordered dissolution of Zen Roren on July 30, 1950. The action of the government aroused public attention, and there were sharp comments then on two accounts. One was that the government, by this action, was taking a definite stand—the anti-Communist stand it had not dared to take previously. As stated earlier, Zen Rōren at its start was the biggest labor organization ever seen in Japan, embracing trade-union organizations of all shades and colors, including notably both Sodomei and Sanbetsu. The WFTU officially admitted Zen Rōren into its fold on January 31, 1949, but on September 28 of the same year a split occurred in the WFTU itself. The unions of the democratic Western nations, led by British, Dutch, and United States unions, quit the WFTU and, at the beginning of the following year, formed a rival organization, the ICFTU (International Confederation of Free Trade Unions). Thereafter the WFTU became a genuinely Communist organization, uniting the Communist trade-unions of the world; in effect, it was the revival of the Profintern of the period prior to World War II. Sodomei saw this drift of affairs and withdrew from Zen Rōren, which had steadily adhered to the WFTU.

The second matter, which aroused no less sharp comments, was the fact that the government, in dissolving the Zen Rōren, had invoked the unpopular Ordinance for Organizations (*Dantai-Tō Kisei Rei*). A furious protest was raised by the native critics and trade-union leaders of all shades when the ordinance was issued in 1949, because it smacked of German Nazism and the Japanese secret police of the prewar and war years. Under this ordinance, a bureau was created to investigate the activities of all organizations. Violators of the ordinance were liable to imprisonment up to ten years and a fine up to 75,000 yen. In the minds of the labor leaders who remembered the tyranny of the Special Higher Police (*Tokkō Keisatsu*) of the prewar Japan, the invoking of this ordinance was like the return of that spectre. It was unfortunate that the government took the course it did in this instance.

On the other hand, a series of frightening criminal incidents took place about this time. The public was led to suspect Communist complicity in those incidents, which in a sense helped the government to justify the severe measures it was taking to suppress Communist activities.

One of those incidents was the mysterious murder of Shimoyama, the governor-general of State Railways, the day after he had announced the government's decision to dismiss 95,000 men from the National Railways. He made the announcement on July 4, 1949; the next day, he disappeared while making a tour by train. His mutilated body was found lying beside the railway track. In protest against the announcement of mass discharge, the railway workers announced their decision "to resort to the use of real force" (*jitsuryoku kōshi*). Naturally, the general public took Shimoyama's murder as evidence of the "use of real force" by the infuriated railway men.

The use of "real force" also involved widespread disruption of rail service by the railway men. In several instances, empty cars (*munin densha*), without driver or conductor, were let loose at full speed, causing loss of life and damage to property near the railway tracks. The so-called "Mitaka incident" and the "Matsu-kawa incident" were examples of "real force" resorted to by workers, presumably under Communist influence. Those found guilty in these incidents were sentenced to long imprisonment, in some cases to death, by the local courts in which they were tried, but all such sentences were objected to by the workers and the cases are still pending. We must refrain from further comment until final decisions are made by the higher courts. However, one thing that can and must be said here is that these acts of terrorism by the extremists did not contribute anything to the cause they undoubtedly meant to serve. The effect was quite the contrary. They contributed, if anything, to the decline of Communist influence among the workers. By nature, the Japanese workers abhor terrorism.

Spread of Junpō Tōsō

When the Korean incident broke out on June 25, 1950, the Allied Forces stationed in Japan were apparently taken by surprise. At all events, they seemed unprepared for a contingency of so catastrophic a nature so near Japan. However, closer examination seems to indicate that somehow, perhaps instinctively, SCAP had commenced to enforce restrictive measures on leftist activities more firmly than ever before. The revision SCAP directed the Japanese government to make in the Public Servants Law, which was made on November 30, was the first important step in that direction. SCAP was of course fully aware of the immediate effect of such a revision. The public servants in Japan had previously enjoyed the rights of organization, collective bargaining, and such collective action as strike and slowdown, as did employees of a private company. The public servants in Japan were strongly organized, constituting a large proportion—well over half at one time—of the organized workers. Moreover, the leadership of many of the public servants' unions was in the hand of the Communists. The revision of the Public Servants Law meant the denial to public servants of the right to conduct any collective action or to engage in strikes or slowdowns. By the revision of the law, the public servants were, on matters of any grievances concerning the conditions of work, removed from the jurisdiction of the Central Labor Relations Board and placed now under the National Personnel Authority of the government. Thanks to this revision, the government was now able to check or forestall the ravages of Communist-led labor disputes in the government, in that if there were grievances, the public servants had to negotiate with their employers first. If the negotiations bore no fruit, the workers would be advised to appeal to the central or local Labor Relations Board for mediation, and if that in turn proved unsatisfactory, their counsel would be to present their appeal to the Diet directly, or to a political party of their own choice, or to the government authority responsible for the matter raised in the union's appeal. They would support the propaganda of the workers by means of leaflets and placards, sandwich men parading in the streets, or as a last resort, organizing a hunger strike, but would insist that actions be "confined to those that do not impede the normal operation of business," since the acts that impede the normal operation of business are, by definition, "dispute acts," which were illegal for public servants and government employees. The leaders insisted that the workers abide by the law.

The honesty and dedication of the leaders who preached the need of abiding by the revised law could not be questioned, but their preachment was effective only where the prevailing conditions were satisfactory to the workers. The workers soon discovered that conditions would not improve unless they found some means whereby the employer could be made to feel the pinch when the workers had grievances. They quickly invented the means. Absolute punctuality, not only in coming to work but in quitting it, was one. Taking annual leave, allowed by law to all workers as a right, was another: if only one or two workers in a department took their leave there was no problem, but when everybody took it at once, that was a disaster. When the workers in postal, telephone, or telegraphic services resorted to these means en masse, although none of them was infringing the letter of the law, the result was a state of anarchy. Thus, the practice of *junpō tōsō*, or "law-abiding struggle," became a feature in this country in those industries in which full-scale strikes are formally forbidden.

To explain more adequately why the occupation authority went so far as to direct the Japanese government to take the stringent legislative measure, the political background of the picture must be provided.

Shortly after the revision of the Public Servants Law, on December 11, 1948, Mr. Chester W. Hepler, chief of the Labor Division in GHQ, issued a warning to the labor leaders of Japan on the need for restraint in their actions. In the meantime, the Dodge Line, mentioned earlier, was in full progress, stiffening the government's measures for deflation. On March 7, 1949, Mr. Dodge gave a warning to the government and people of Japan concerning the need for further tightening of the national economy. It was partly as an effect of this that the ill-famed Ordinance Concerning Regulation of Organizations (*Dantai-Tō Kisei Rei*) was issued on April 7 of that year. These steps were in every instance clearly aimed at curbing the Communist intrigues in Japan. Incidentally, only three days before the ordinance was issued in Japan, the North Atlantic Treaty was signed in Washington by twelve nations of Europe and America, giving birth to the North Atlantic Treaty Organization (NATO). On this basis, one might say that more than a year before the outbreak of the Korean War, the Western nations were lined up, ready for united action. Only in the Far East had the Western nations not succeeded in lining up the nations of the Orient, but steps were being taken by legislative and other means to ensure that the leadership of the workers' movement was firmly in anti-Communist hands.

With these facts in mind, the reason for the birth in Japan of these "law-abiding struggles" might be summed up as follows: Japan was still under Allied Occupation. The government of Japan was "autonomous" nominally, but not effectively in substance. Any action of a Japanese national deemed prejudicial to the interests of the occupation could be subjected to punitive sanction by the occupation authority. This was particularly true after the

"Potsdam Order 201" was issued. The Japanese government had no free choice in the matter. It simply had to follow the line of action indicated by SCAP. There was no room to question the constitutionality of the proposed legislative changes. Nor were the workers free, for that matter. If they had grievances and wished to engage in struggles, their struggles had to be carried on within the framework of the statutory laws. It is only in the political context of Japan during this period that the historic significance of *junpō tōsō* can be grasped.

Needless to say, *junpō tōsō* is an anomalous practice, detrimental ultimately to both the authority of the law that is violated and the dignity of the workers who resort to it. It cannot be stopped by mere infliction of severe penalties. The way out must ultimately be found in a device whereby the workers' grievances are disposed of more expeditiously and by a process in which the workers share responsibility. Of course, we must finally admit that the occupation of the territory of a nation by foreign troops and the subjection of the nation to the rule of a foreign authority is in itself an anomaly.

The Authority of the United Nations Challenged

When the war in Korea broke out in 1950, Japan was still under the Allied Occupation, which was a punitive measure, designed to ensure that the punitive clauses of the Potsdam Declaration would be carried out unaltered and in an orderly fashion. Japan was not an independent nation under these conditions.

To be subject to any sort of punitive measure is humiliating to a nation. Even though MacArthur's occupation was known and acclaimed as a "benevolent" occupation, any such supervision by foreign troops would be distasteful to any proud nation. That would be particularly true of a nation that had prided itself on a history of more than two thousand years, a nation that had never before known invasion or defeat at the hands of an enemy. The occupation had lasted for nearly five years when the Korean War broke out. Five years was a long period for the Japanese people. Japan had longed for a peace treaty, but none was offered. Why was the peace with Japan delayed so long?

For the delay in conclusion of a peace treaty with Japan, there were extenuating circumstances on the side of the Allied

Powers. Credit should be given where it is due, when seeking for the explanation of the delay.

Among the top leaders of the Allied Powers, and particularly in the United States, there were statesmen who remembered how the Treaty of Versailles after World War I failed. It was signed too soon after the hostilities ended. When the treaty of peace with Germany (the Treaty of Versailles) was drafted and presented to the German representatives in 1919, there were burnt cities still fuming and bodies reeking in the battlefields. Enmity and hatred were rife and the prevailing morbid war psychology made it impossible for the draftsmen of the peace treaty to produce a document which would lay sure foundations of a durable peace. Because of that experience, let us say, it was "statesmanship" to delay after World War II the peace-making efforts until the governments on both sides were ready for the calm and dispassionate negotiations.

However, before such a propitious time came, an unfortunate situation arose—namely, the cold war between the two power blocs. Presumably, future historians may have to say that World War III began in the smoldering atmosphere of the cold war in this early period. In the first place, the conclusion of peace with Japan on any durable basis would require hearty agreement between the United States and the U.S.S.R. But, to anyone who remembered how Russia, despite her Treaty of Neutrality and Non-Aggression with Japan, entered the war in its last week, even when Japan was humbly pleading with her for mediation, it was too clear that that country would not easily consent to give Japan a generous or fair deal. For both the security and the honor of Japan, it was safer to delay rather than hurry peace negotiations. This was a tactical consideration on the part of the United States, in favor of Japan, which the Japanese must appreciate to its full value, without raising the question of why anyone on earth other than the Japanese should be solicitous of Japan's security.

In order to grasp the full meaning of a historical event, however, one must be realistic. It was only natural that, besides friendship for Japan, the Allied Powers, including the United States, should be concerned about their own security as well when they decided to restore Japan to her status as an independent nation. The Korean War was a test, indeed a very severe test, of the strength of the United Nations. The UN took the invasion of the troops of North Korea with the aid of the Chinese Communists as a challenge to its authority. The UN did succeed in checking their inroads and in establishing its own authority, but at what cost, and how appalling the sacrifices!

To see what it cost to maintain the prestige of the United Nations, it is necessary to review how the war developed and how it ended. The United States—not the United Nations as such— took action first, immediately after hostilities broke out, sending troops and munitions to Korea to check the aggression. But Seoul, the capital of Korea, fell on June 27. The United Nations would have been unable to take any effective action in the crisis, had it not been for the error made by the U.S.S.R. in boycotting the Security Council by the continued absence of their representative from its meeting. The absence continued from January 12 through August 1, 1950, during which time the Korean incident flared up. It was on the day that Seoul fell that the Security Council of the United Nations passed a resolution, recommending that the member states offer necessary aid to Korea to repel the forces of North Korea and restore peace and security in that country. This resolution was followed by another placing General MacArthur in command of the United Nations forces dispatched to put an end to the war. The same resolution authorized the use of the United Nations' flag for its military operations in Korea.

The job assigned to General MacArthur was none too easy. Reverses were suffered by the forces under the General, who had been known to be "invincible." Much to the surprise of the world, the United Nations forces were pressed, more than once, all the way down to the southern extremity of the peninsula near Pusan. It did not take long to discover that the North Korean troops were equipped with the latest types of weapons of Russian make, often superior to those of the United Nations forces. It was only through the daring and masterly operation of the United Nations forces by General MacArthur, later followed by General Ridgway, that the affair was brought to an end with an armistice signed on July 27, 1953, terminating hostilities after three years and one month of bitter fighting, with enormous losses on both sides.

While we must refrain from giving too many details of the war, we also must admit that a critical review of the principal provisions of the armistice agreement shows that it merely—and barely—halted the fighting. It did not solve the basic issues involved in the unification of the country. Any open-minded critic in these circumstances would wonder whether the United Nations really succeeded in establishing its authority in this test.

SCAP and the Constitution of Japan

Our history now enters a period in which a delicate situation arose affecting the friendly relations between the United States and Japan. This is important here since the organized workers of Japan are seriously involved. An analytical account will be given here, since much of the misunderstanding in the United States and in other countries stems largely from insufficient factual information on the subject. The problem centers around the Constitution of Japan and the scheme of the peace concluded by Japan with the United States, and why the organized workers of Japan have obstinately objected to it. Prior to the conclusion of peace at San Francisco, a whole series of incidents occurred, both in Japan and the United States, that had the unfortunate effect of intensifying the misgivings of the Japanese workers regarding the true intentions of the United States government.

To begin with, one must have a precise knowledge of the Constitution of Japan as promulgated on November 3, 1946, in pursuance of the Potsdam Declaration and of General MacArthur's directive of October 11, 1945. Because of the paramount part played by General MacArthur in the preparation and promulgation of the document, it is frequently called in Japan the "MacArthur Constitution." We give below some excerpts from the Constitution that have given rise to considerable controversy, though in the minds of a large number of the peace-minded Japanese people, the passages quoted here constitute the "soul" of the Constitution.

THE CONSTITUTION OF JAPAN

Preamble:

We, the Japanese people, . . . resolved that never again shall we be visited with the horrors of war through the action of government, do proclaim that sovereign power resides with the people and do firmly establish this Constitution. . . .

We, the Japanese people, desire peace for all time and are deeply conscious of the high ideals controlling human relationship and we have determined to preserve our security and existence, trusting in the justice and faith of the peace-loving peoples of the world. We desire to occupy an honorable place in an international society striving for the preservation of peace. . . .

Chapter II. *Renunciation of War*

Article 9. Aspiring sincerely to an international peace based on justice and order, the Japanese people forever renounce war as a sovereign right of the nation and the threat or use of force as means of settling international disputes.

In order to accomplish the aim of the preceding paragraph, land, sea, and air forces as well as other war potential, will never be maintained. The right of belligerency of the state will not be recognized.

This Constitution of Japan, containing these striking passages, was promulgated on November 3, 1946, and went into force six months later, on May 3, 1947. The Japanese nation accepted this Constitution, often called "The Peace Constitution" because of the passages quoted above, with enthusiasm and genuine, if naive, faith in its authority, because the Japanese were the first nation to suffer the damages of an atomic bomb and had fully tasted the bitterness of modern war. Never again did they wish to be visited with the horrors of a war.

A matter of significance in this connection, which is clearly remembered by the thinking people among the Japanese, are General MacArthur's words of blessing and exhortation in his New Year's Message to the Japanese people on January 1, 1950. He concluded his message with the following words:

Some contemporary cynics deride as visionary Japan's Constitutional renunciation of the concept of belligerency and armed security. Be not overly concerned by such detractors. A product of Japanese thought,[1] this provision is based upon the highest of moral ideals, and yet no constitutional provision was ever more fundamentally sound and practical. . . . In this historic decision, you are the first. The opportunity therefore is yours to exemplify to mankind the soundness of this concept and the inestimable benefit resulting from the dedication of all energy and all resource to peaceful progress. In due course other nations will join you in this dedication, but meanwhile you must not falter. Have faith in my countrymen and other peoples who share the same high ideals. Above all, have faith in yourselves!

Let it be remembered that General MacArthur, who made this significant public pronouncement concerning the Peace Constitution of Japan, was an American; it will presently be seen what America, so friendly to Japan, had to do for Japan before the pen with which he wrote this memorable message was dry.

The Dilemma of the Peace of San Francisco

As has been noted, the Korean War was a severe test of the strength of the United Nations forces, which were for the most part United States forces. Why should American boys be fighting in Asia? Why did not the Asians settle their own affairs? How about the youths of Japan, whose bravery was so well known through *kamikaze* bombers? These were the questions asked and discussed widely in American newspapers in the critical period of the Korean War and soon a body of opinion emerged that Japan should be put on her own feet again at the earliest moment. The need for restoring Japan to an independent status was urged strongly among the leading journals in the United States. Secretary of State John Foster Dulles played the predominant role in concluding the peace with Japan.

As the shape of the peace scheme contemplated by Mr. Dulles became gradually clear, however, severe criticism began to be addressed to him in Japan from among the ardent and loyal, if naive, supporters of the "Peace Constitution." The fact should not be overlooked that those supporters of the Constitution comprised the liberal or progressive elements, including the socialists and trade-union leaders, who had learned to hate militarism and war and had become zealous believers in democratic freedom and peace. It was they who voiced misgivings about the motivation of the proposed peace. They feared that Japan might be required to rearm and be involved in the current war and in any future wars. As matters progressed, unfortunately the apprehensions of the ardent supporters of the Constitution seemed confirmed.

The Conference to sign the treaty was called at San Francisco on September 9, 1952, while the war in Korea was raging. The governments of the nations that had fought against Japan in World War II were invited to send their plenipotentiary delegates for signature of a treaty of peace with Japan. Only India, under Premier Nehru, declined the invitation on the ground that the proposed scheme of peace would hardly put Japan on an equal footing with other nations, even though the peace treaty might restore to Japan nominally independent status. Forty-nine nations signed the peace treaty, but neither the U.S.S.R. nor the People's Republic of China (Communist China), were among them. This was precisely the situation that those Japanese people who were opposed to the peace of San Francisco had wished to avoid.

The Peace Treaty was signed during the forenoon on September 5. Technically speaking, Japan was not yet an independent nation, since the Treaty would not become effective until a certain number of the signatory powers had ratified the Treaty. However, that was a question of mere formality. Arrangements had been made for a representative of the independent Japan to proceed immediately to sign another treaty, the Mutual Security Treaty with the United States. That signature took place several hours later, late in the afternoon of the same day. Japan's Prime Minister Yoshida Shigeru, who had signed the Peace Treaty with other fellow plenipotentiary envoys of Japan, went alone to sign the Mutual Security Treaty.

The objection of the socialists and liberal trade-union leaders was focused on this Treaty, which, in their view, was unmistakably in the nature of a military alliance, concluded in violation of the Peace Constitution. Further, a series of questions arising from this pact constituted more serious grounds for their objection. Because the pact raised so many controversial questions, the original text of the Security Treaty is given below:

SECURITY TREATY BETWEEN JAPAN AND THE UNITED STATES OF AMERICA

Japan has this day signed a Treaty of Peace with the Allied Powers. On the coming into force of that Treaty, Japan will not have the effective means to exercise its inherent right of self-defense because it has been disarmed.

There is danger to Japan in this situation because irresponsible militarism has not yet been driven from the world. Therefore Japan desires a Security Treaty with the United States of America to come into force simultaneously with the Treaty of Peace between Japan and the United States of America.

The Treaty of Peace recognizes that Japan as a sovereign nation has the right to enter into collective security arrangements, and further, the Charter of the United Nations recognizes that all nations possess an inherent right of individual and collective self-defense.

In exercise of these rights, Japan desires, as a provisional arrangement for its defense, that the United States of America should maintain armed forces of its own in and about Japan so as to deter armed attack upon Japan.

The United States of America, in the interest of peace and security, is presently willing to maintain certain of its armed forces in and about Japan, in the expectation, however, that Japan will itself increasingly assume responsibility for its own defense against direct and indirect aggression, always avoiding any armament which could be an offensive threat or serve other than to promote peace and security in accordance with the purposes and principles of the United Nations Charter.

Accordingly, the two countries have agreed as follows:

Article I

Japan grants, and the United States of America accepts, the right, upon the coming into force of the Treaty of Peace and of this Treaty, to dispose United States land, air, and sea forces in and about Japan. Such forces may be utilized to contribute to the maintenance of international peace and security in the Far East and to the security of Japan against armed attack from without, including assistance given at the express request of the Japanese government to put down large-scale internal riots and disturbances in Japan, caused through instigation or intervention by an outside power or powers.

Article II

During the exercise of the right referred to in Article I, Japan will not grant, without the prior consent of the United States of America, any bases or any rights, powers or authority whatever, or transit of ground, air or naval forces to any third power.

Article III

The conditions which shall govern the disposition of armed forces of the United States of America in and about Japan shall be determined by administrative agreements between the two governments.

Article IV

This Treaty shall expire whenever in the opinion of the Governments of Japan and the United States of America there shall have come into force such United Nations arrangements or such alternative individual or collective security dispositions as will satisfactorily provide for the maintenance by the United Nations or otherwise of international peace and security in the Japan area.

Article V

This Treaty shall be ratified by Japan and the United States of America and will come into force when instruments of ratification thereof have been exchanged at Washington.

In witness whereof the undersigned Plenipotentiaries have signed this Treaty.

Done in duplicate at the city of San Francisco, in the Japanese and English languages, this eighth day of September, 1951.

For Japan: Shigeru Yoshida
For the United States of America: Dean Acheson

In comparison with the Peace Treaty, which was an elaborate document consisting of twenty-seven articles, accompanied by a Protocol and a Declaration, the Security Treaty was an extremely simple document, consisting of only five articles, with no appendix of any sort. Simple in form, but the questions it raised were far from simple.

Besides the baffling question of the constitutionality of the Treaty in that it seemed to involve Japan in a military alliance requiring Japan to rearm, there was the second question that it was a unilateral or unequal treaty. Under the treaty, Japan would offer her territory to United States troops and the United States could, but was nowhere *required* to, use her troops stationed in Japan to defend her. Whether or not to deploy the United States troops for the defense of Japan in an emergency was, as far as the provisions in the Treaty were concerned, optional to the United States. There was a third question. Under the Treaty, the bombers of the U.S. Air Force might take off from their bases in Japan to attack a third power without the knowledge of Japan. This would be an invitation for enemy planes to bombard Japan at any time that the United States was engaged in hostilities with a third power. This, in the minds of those who objected to this Treaty, was too big a risk for Japan to take. These and a few other provisions that were targets of attack finally led the governments of the United States and Japan to revise the Treaty completely in 1960. By the revision, most, if not all, of the objectionable points in the Security Treaty were either removed or considerably modified. The foregoing brief account of the Treaty is given here to explain how serious objections to the Security Treaty arose in Japan.

As stated above, most of the technically objectional provisions in the Security Treaty were removed by the revision in 1960, but it must be borne in mind that, fundamentally, the governments of the United States and Japan are faced with a dilemma as long as they believe in and rely on armed security. Seeking for security and peace in and around Japan, the government in Washington might succeed in turning Japan into an effective military ally, but will that success mean a victory for the cause of democracy in the long run, in Japan or in this part of the world?

Re-entry of Japan into the ILO

Whether or not this item should come under "Repercussions of the Korean War" is doubtful. In any case, however, as a matter of historical sequence, it should be mentioned here that Japan's return to the ILO was discussed at the thirty-fourth session of the ILO Conference in June, 1951, and approved by that conference.

The decision of the conference became effective on November 26, 1951, and since then Japan has been a member of the ILO. It is interesting to note that re-admission of Japan into the ILO was decided by the conference before the Peace Treaty of San Francisco went into force.

As one of the ten "states of chief industrial importance," Japan occupies a permanent seat on the Governing Body of the ILO, and the representative of the Japanese government sits in that seat. The employers' representative of Japan has been a deputy member of the Governing Body since 1954, while the representative of Japanese workers was elected a deputy member of the Governing Body in 1957 (but not thereafter). Occupancy of so many seats on the Governing Body by Japanese representatives is a postwar development and shows the increasingly responsible share that Japan has in the administration of the ILO.

Also, on the staff of the secretariat of the ILO, the International Labor Office, there were as late as December, 1963, as many as five Japanese members permanently employed. When we recall that before the war, there were only one or two Japanese staff members at the Geneva Office, this is definitely an expansion, though the number is still far below the quota for Japan.

When Japan officially withdrew from the ILO in 1938, the Tokyo Branch Office was closed down, but on Japan's re-entry as a regular member state, it was re-opened. It was first called "Correspondent's Office," and the Correspondent was Ogishima Toru, formerly a staff member of the Geneva Office. In 1955, the rank of the Tokyo office was restored to that of branch office. Sakurai Yasuemon, formerly governor of Tochigi Prefecture, who, incidentally, was a secretary of the Permanent Japanese Delegation Office in Geneva, was appointed director of the Tokyo Branch Office.

As a consequence of the recovery of Japan as an industrial power, with the rise to power of employers' and workers' organizations, the volume of work of the Tokyo office has multiplied greatly in recent years.

INDEPENDENCE OF JAPAN
AND HOW IT AFFECTED LABOR

Rise of Sohyo to Power

If a student of labor problems were asked to name one event of paramount importance in postwar Japan, quite likely he would not hesitate to mention the rise of Sohyo to power. Sidney and Beatrice Webb, when they wrote their classic work *A History of Trade Unionism*, in 1894, in describing the growing strength of workers' unions in England, pointed out that they were assuming the shape of a "state within state." A similar statement could well be made in Germany today with reference to the German trade-union federation DGB (Deutscher Gewerkschafts Bund) and in Japan with reference to Sohyo. Sohyo is an abbreviation of the long official title Nippon Rodo Kumiai So-Hyogi Kai (General Council of Japanese Trade-Unions). It was inaugurated less than a month after the outbreak of the Korean War, on July 11, 1950. At the time this body was formed, it comprised twenty-nine unions with a total membership of 2,760,000.

As explained earlier, the unions which had been opposed to leftist or Communist domination were united under the leadership of the men who had advocated the "Democratization Movement" (Minshuka Domei or Mindō by abbreviation) in February, 1948. One of the leaders was Takano Minoru, at one time a leader of the left-wing faction of Sodomei. Born in Tokyo in 1901, he was trained for work in applied chemistry at Waseda University. He did not finish college, however, but, at twenty-four, quit his studies to enter leftist union work when he was appointed chief secretary of the Amalgamated Trade-Unions of Toshima in Tokyo. After twenty-five years of experience in trade-union work he was elected secretary-general of Sohyo in 1950. He was then nearly 50 years old, a trenchant orator and trained debater.

Associated closely with him at the start of Sohyo was another able leader, Hosoya Matsuta, the same age as Takano, but with a career perhaps more becoming a labor leader. Born in a family of very modest means in the impoverished prefecture of Yamagata, Hosoya was unable to go beyond primary school. He was apprenticed first as a glassmaker, but he disliked the job, and became for some years a merchant sailor. During this time he joined the Seamen's Union. For illegal acts as a labor leader (in the days when practically all union activities were a violation in one way or another of the Public Peace Police Act), he was imprisoned several times before the war. After the war, Hosoya was elected director of the headquarters of the National Congress of Industrial Unions. After the fiasco of the February first general-strike plot, Hosoya headed a campaign to oust the Communist leaders from the industrial union movement. This led to his expulsion from the union, but, on the other hand, he took the leading part in founding the National Congress of Industrial Unions (better known as Shin Sanbetsu). As director of the political division of the National Congress, Hosoya was engaged in the delicate work of steering the political activities of the Congress. During the years of the occupation, Hosoya came into contact with officers of the Labor Division engaged in educational work for democratization of workers' unions. It was through the help of these officers under SCAP that Takano and Hosoya were able to organize Sohyo. Actually, those officers were performing the midwifery that eventually gave birth to Sohyo.

Incidentally, there were two circumstances outside Japan which helped the birth of Sohyo. One was the split that occurred in the WFTU in 1949. The unions in Britain, the United States, and the Netherlands first broke away from the WFTU and formed a world federation of democratic unions, namely, the International Confederation of Free Trade-Unions (ICFTU). The other circumstance was the Korean War. The occupation authorities did everything possible to induce the Japanese unions to leave the Communist-dominated WFTU and join ICFTU. Sohyo was born in this period, a godchild of the occupation.

The Four Peace Principles

The authorities under SCAP had fully expected Sohyo to behave like their docile godchild. Nobody was more disappointed or surprised than they when they discovered that Sohyo had led the opposition against the peace of San Francisco. As a matter of fact, Sohyo led the movement among the rank and file of organized labor while the Socialist Party did the same in the political circles. During the spring of 1951, both the Socialist Party of Japan and Sohyo adopted the so-called Four Peace Principles as a slogan. The Four Principles were:

1. Over-all peace i.e., the conclusion of peace, not unilaterally with the United States and the Western democracies, but bilaterally—or multilaterally—with such others as the Soviet Union, the Peoples' Republic of China, and the countries under the Communist regime.

2. Absolute neutrality (i.e., siding with neither of the conflicting ideologies).

3. No military bases in Japan (i.e., allowing no military, naval, or air force base of any country in Japan).

4. No rearmament (i.e., no rearming of Japan, under whatever justification, in violation of the Peace Constitution).

The fourth principle was an addition; before it was included the Socialist Party and Sohyo had advocated the Three Peace Principles.

Sohyo adopted the Four Peace Principles at its National Convention in March, 1951. The Socialist Party had adopted the Three Peace Principles two months earlier, on January 19.

It would be wrong not to mention the controversy that arose among the rank and file before these principles were formally adopted. At the convention, a highly vociferous minority took a realistic view of the political exigencies of the times and advocated adoption of the peace scheme of San Francisco. Some of the men who took this stand were more "patriotic," concerned more with national interests than the humanitarian. Some of them were more informed about the dangerous reality of the international situation. This can be better understood when we recall that about this time the United Nations forces in Korea under the command of General MacArthur were experiencing "reverses," and the General was on the point of taking drastic action in the emergency. The plan contemplated by MacArthur led to his summary dismissal by President Truman and the appointment of General Matthew Bunker Ridgway to replace him. General Ridgway, as Supreme Commander for the Allied Powers, saw fit to restrict the licentious display of the power of organized workers in Japan. He forbade, for example, the use of the Imperial Plaza for the May Day celebration, since he could not brook the thought of the tens of thousands of workers assembling at the Imperial Plaza and parading in front of the General Headquarters with placards advocating the Four Peace Principles.

As stated above, there were those, both in the Socialist Party and in Sohyo, who opposed the adoption of these slogans. Some, if not all, were realists ready to support rearmament or even war "for defense." Although these men constituted numerically a minority, it was a group of no small importance. That group in Sohyo finally withdrew from the main body and, in September, 1951, formed Minroken (Minshu Rodo Undo Kenkyu Kai, or the Democratic Labor Movement Study Group). What this subsequently grew into will be discussed later.

The effect of the division of opinion in the Socialist Party on the adoption of these principles was more immediate and symptomatic. A deep and ultimately fatal cleavage developed, though it did not actually split the party, as it did Sohyo. What must be remembered about the Socialist Party in this connection is that the majority of the party had always taken the idealistic rather than the realistic stand, supporting the letter and spirit of the Constitution, upholding the Four Peace Principles to this day.

Laws Restricting Labor's Freedom

Strange as it may seem at first sight, the workers in Japan, after their country regained the status of independence, seem to enjoy not more but actually less freedom than under the Occupation of the Allied Powers. This is the resentful sentiment expressed by some casual observers, and seems to be substantiated by two laws passed by the Diet over the furious protests of the working class. How does one account for this paradoxical phenomenon?

Any researcher carefully studying the matter of personal freedom in countries that have acquired independence after long subjection by colonial powers may opine that this phenomenon is not confined to Japan. Nor is this the place to philosophize on general questions of this sort. The subject may be dismissed by stating simply that life is replete with paradoxes of this nature. The purpose here is to discover how these laws, objected to as restricting labor's freedom, came to be adopted after Japan became independent.

As was seen in the preceding section, peace was achieved by the signing of two treaties, the Peace Treaty and the Security Treaty, on November 28, 1951. These treaties came into effect half a year later, on April 28, 1952. Japan thereupon became an independent nation; however, long before she became independent she had been formally admitted—on April 16, 1951—to the United Nations. Looking back on the political situation, both inside and outside Japan, it can be seen that at least two factors contributed to the decision of the government to tighten its control of labor's activities. One was the increasing sense of uncertainty among the people concerning international relations surrounding Japan. Superficially, the Peace Treaty signed by fifty nations served to establish peace on a firmer basis than ever. At the same time, however, the Security Treaty, under which the Soviet Union was the potential enemy, could not serve to promote amicable relations with that great nation, nor with any other nation under the Communist regime. Fortunately the peace offensive launched by the Soviet Union was gaining momentum, so that any chance of a major war seemed now further removed than at any period in the past. Nevertheless, measures for "defense" were being taken in the four islands of Japan on a vast and awe-inspiring scale by the United States. In pursuance of the Security Treaty, military, naval, and air bases—over 490 of them at one time—were being constructed in the islands.

Unfortunately, the construction of so many bases in these small islands of congested population often involved the expropriation of farmlands of peasants who had inherited them from their forefathers. Parting with the land bequeathed them by their ancestors was an unbearable hardship to the peasants, brought up in the tradition of ancestor worship. When their land was virtually taken over by troops, the peasants would sit down in protest on their farmlands and remain there even as target practice was scheduled to commence. They were often aided by students belonging to Zen Gakuren, who opposed the rearmament of Japan. Demonstrations were staged, often accompanied by incidents of violence. Occasionally pranks and even well-meant but mistaken action on the part of young soldiers added to the embarrassment of both the government of Japan and the U.S. troops. Presumably the Communists capitalized on these incidents to form hostile sentiments among the youths. Naturally, under the circumstances the government sought to curb any excesses on the part of the workers.

On the other hand, the Japanese government was steadily engaged in strengthening its defense potential, pursuant to the terms of the Security Treaty. Previously, there had been in Japan the Reserve Police Corps, which was, as the prime minister explained to the Diet, "a force without fighting strength" (*senryoku naki guntai*). The Constitution forbade the government to maintain "land, sea, or air force and other war potential." After the ratification of the Security Treaty, the government was emboldened. Among the constitutional lawyers of Japan were some who would argue that a treaty with a foreign country takes precedence over the constitution of a country. If the rearmament of Japan is an infringement of the Constitution, according to those lawyers, the government should abide by the Security Treaty in the first instance. Consequently, what, out of timidity, was previously called the "Reserve Police Corps" came to be called the

"Self-Defense Force," and was equipped openly with the instruments of warfare, including missles of the latest design. This transformation of the Reserve Police Corps into a Self-Defense Force as a consequence of the Treaty was a process which no one anywhere except in Japan would hesitate to call "rearmament."

It should be noted in this connection that the annual budgetary expenditure of the Japanese government for the Self-Defense Force is still "small" compared with that of other major powers like the United States, the U.S.S.R., and so on. This subject will be discussed later. It should also be noted that the government, in 1953, appointed an important commission, with Dr. Takayanagi Kenzo as chairman to "investigate" the Constitution. The critics interpreted the appointment of this commission as an attempt on the part of the government to turn the *de facto* rearmament of Japan into a *de jure* rearmament by either the elimination (which obviously would be most difficult) or emasculation of Article 9 of the Constitution. Obviously, this is the reason the "naive" Socialists and trade-union leaders who had faith in the practicability of the "Peace Constitution" were raising most serious objections to the drift of things after the Peace Treaty of San Francisco went into effect.

It is against the background described above that the significance of the two laws restricting workers' freedom will be discussed.

The first of the two laws is generally known by the abbreviated title *Ha-bō Hō* (for *Hakai Katsudō Bōshi Hō*, or "Destructive Activities Prevention Act"), promulgated June 21, 1952. It may be recalled that the most unpopular law in prewar Japan was *Chian Iji Hō* (Public Peace Maintenance Act) of 1925. The *Ha-bō Hō* was considered among the workers as the postwar version of *Chian Iji Hō*. Both the prewar and postwar laws were clearly aimed at suppression of subversive acts of the Communists. There was no mistaking the avowed objective of the law. What the Socialists and trade-union leaders feared was the possible, or probable, abuse of the law to infringe on the workers' normal trade-union activities. In view of the furious opposition of the workers all over the country, the government, before the promulgation of the law, issued a formal and public announcement to the effect that (1) the law would not unduly infringe on the people's rights or liberty, and (2) the law would not restrict proper trade-union activities. Whether or not the assurance given by the government had the effect of calming down the excitement of the workers, we are unable to ascertain. In any case, the law was enacted despite the furor of opposition.[2]

The second law restricting workers' freedom enacted in this period was also known by an abbreviated title, *Suto Kisei Ho* (Strike Restriction Law). As happens occasionally, the abbreviation was inaccurate and misleading, though the justification for the abbreviated name was that the official title of this law was inordinately long. It might be literally translated as a "Law Concerning the Regulation of the Methods of Dispute Acts in Coal Mining and Electrical Industries." Amidst an uproar of protests, this law was rushed through the two Houses of the Diet. It prohibited, as a dispute act, the withdrawing of the guards stationed at designated posts in coal mines for safety reasons. In the electrical industries, the law prohibited, as dispute acts, the workers letting the water run off at the source (the dam), and the switching off of the electrical current.

This legislation was the result of the commission of these very acts in previous years by the coal miners and electrical workers. The workers' unions were indulging in these acts, and the government considered it necessary to have a special law to deal with them. The law was severely criticized as another repressive law of the *Gyaku Kōsu* regime, but the government was firm and did not budge in the face of the protests, except that it consented to provide that the law should be in force for only three years, as a trial. In 1956, when the three-year period expired, the Diet decided not to terminate but to retain the law for an indefinite period. This was a case in which the firm attitude of the government proved sound and satisfactory and won the approbation of the Diet.

Workers' "Peace Offensives"

The Peace Treaty of San Francisco went into force on April 28th, 1952. Japan thereupon regained the international status, the dignity and honor of an independent nation. An anomalous event that embarrassed the government marked the start of Japan's independent state. On May Day, only three days after the treaty went into force, well over 200,000 workers in Tokyo took part in demonstrations known as *Chi-no Mei Dei*, or "Bloody May Day."

In Russia, in 1905, long before the Bolshevik Revolution, there was the sad story of the "Bloody Sunday," which was in a sense the eve of the Russian Revolution. It was unsuccessful but it contributed to the weakening of the medievalism of Imperial Russia and led finally to the downfall in 1917 of the Czars' despotic dynasty. We read in history that on January 22, 1905, workers demonstrating peacefully under Father Georgi Capon, singing the national anthem, were fired upon suddenly and dispersed, with a death toll of about one thousand. The snow on the ground in front of the Czars' palace was stained red with the blood of the victims and the plaza was strewn with bodies. The incident augured ill for the Russian empire. How are we to divine the meaning of the unhappy incident of Bloody May Day, 1952, in Japan? No *divination* will help here. We must *understand* the meaning.

It will be recalled that during the previous year, General Ridgway, Supreme Commander for the Allied Powers succeeding General MacArthur, forbade the use of the Imperial Plaza for the May Day celebration. Japan was still under the occupation. The Supreme Commander at that time deemed it necessary and wise to issue the order as he did. Once Japan had gained her independence, the workers had freedom, and they chose to use the Imperial Plaza in front of the Palace for their demonstration.

In order to understand the situation, the reader must be aware of the increasingly combative mood of the Japanese workers in 1951 and thereafter. On January 26, 1952, Sohyo staged a mass meeting in Tokyo to protest the repressive laws mentioned in the preceding section. On April 12 there was a nationwide work stoppage protesting those "iniquitous" and "repressive" laws, with more than 300,000 participating in street demonstrations. As time went on, the protest gained momentum. Sohyo launched strike waves involving 1,070,000 participants. The May Day demonstration was in the nature of an interlude. The third wave of strikes came on June 7, with 3,200,000 participants. The number of participants kept multiplying.

Several factors, political, psychological, and economic, contributed to the combative mood of the workers. We have dealt with the political aspect at some length, explaining that the leaders of trade-unions and socialist movements were opposed to the peace plans of the San Francisco treaty, which would turn Japan into a munitions workshop, a military base, a rearmed military nation. This opposition was evident from the inscriptions on the placards and banners carried by the demonstrating workmen. "Yankees, go home" was one characteristic slogan. As has been repeatedly pointed out, the Japanese workers were not against the American people. The GIs were quite popular among the people generally. What they were against was rearmament and militarization of Japan. With the advance of the measures taken under the Security Pact, there was an increase of tangible and visible signs of "defense" and, proportionately, there was an increase of tangible and visible signs of social unrest.

The economic factor that entered into the picture of unrest must not be underrated either. The Korean War brought a transient boom to Japan, but it could not and did not last long. The usual postwar slump was hard on both the enterprises and the workers. This caused an increase of demands for higher wages. Previously, the wage demands of the Japanese unions had been based on minute computations of *Current Population Survey* and *Consumer's Price Index*. They discarded those bases of calculation. Takano Minoru, who had visited England and had seen the salutary effects, advantageous to the workers, of the "market-basket formula" used among the British unions, transplanted the formula to Japan; Sohyo, under Takano's guidance, presented a demand in their "fall offensive" of 1952 for a monthly take-home pay of 25,000 yen and a flat minimum of 8,000 yen as the initial pay for an eighteen-year-old youth entering employment. This was intended to be the new basis of the workers' demand for a national minimum wage pressed for at a later stage. The economic hardship experienced by the Japanese workers in the period after the Korean War deserves fuller treatment, but it cannot be discussed at this stage.

The third factor contributing to the unrest at this period was psychological. Trade-union leaders will probably consider the writer as lacking in sympathy with the cause of trade-unionism for making this blunt and forthright statement, but it must be said in order to clarify the issue. The leaders of the organized workers were inevitably growing conscious of their influence and power, but were not sufficiently conscious of the excesses they were committing in the exercise of their power. "Scheduled demonstrations," "scheduled strikes," "spring and fall offensives," and so on were being launched in the unions with little restraint. The incident of May Day, 1952, is relevant to the subject.

As on other May Days, the writer went out to observe the demonstrations. Literally hundreds of thousands of demonstrators marching through the main boulevards of Tokyo were streaming finally into the vast plaza in front of the Imperial Palace. Frenzied scuffling broke out between the police force and the demonstrators not long after the latter entered the Plaza. Exactly how the shooting began could not be ascertained, but the writer was an eye-witness to the firing of revolvers by the police force, lined up in a formation apparently previously laid out in order to minimize the violence and excesses of the demonstrating workers. Scores of men were wounded; fortunately none were killed, presumably because the police had no intent to kill any one, their sole object being to maintain order. The demonstrators overturned many automobiles parked beside the deep moats surrounding the Palace and the Plaza. Cars parked in front of the Dai Ichi Building, which had been the General Headquarters of the Supreme Commander for the Allied Powers, apparently were considered as belonging to United States officers, and every one was subjected to the same treatment. Obviously, the police had every justification for resorting to force in order to restrain the demonstrators. The shooting and fighting could not have lasted more than fifteen or twenty minutes, but innumerable young men were wounded; some were being carried, others were leaning on the shoulders of their comrades. A stranger, also an eye-witness to the scuffling and bloodshed, accosted the writer, saying, "Is this the eve of a revolution in Japan?" None of the Tokyo papers reporting on the incident the next day approved of the excesses committed by the workers. It was clear that the scene of the "Bloody May Day" put the workers' movement in an unfavorable light before the public. Leaders of mass movements in this country must learn that the Japanese people, as a race, are passionate and behave themselves passionately or recklessly at times, but, basically, they honor the wisdom of serenity and calm, undisturbed by passion. Bloody May Day, for this reason, was definitely a low point, bringing discredit to the leaders responsible for the incident. In Japan, "peace offensives" of organized workers have the support of the masses, but "peace offensives with violence" do not.

Birth of Zenrō

Sohyo, the "godchild of the occupation authority," and, if not all-powerful, certainly the most powerful of all union federations in Japan, had certain weaknesses that were inherent in the very formation or structure of the organization itself. Because of these weaknesses, the influence of Sohyo had begun to wane noticeably by 1953. In the view of the critics at that time, one unmistakable symptom of the declining strength of Sohyo appeared early in 1953, when Min-Ro-Ren (Federation of Democratic Trade-Unions) was formed. This led to a split in the federation, with important consequences, which must be explained in some detail.

From the outset, there were in Sohyo two groups of unions, dissimilar and heterogeneous in character, though not necessarily hostile to each other. One group included the unions of workers in public corporations or government-owned enterprises. In Japan, the government is engaged in various enterprises on a national scale, in industries which may or may not be in the nature of public utilities. When there was profit in an industry, even though the goods produced or services rendered might have nothing to do with public welfare, the government would take over the industry and monopolize it. When that happened, the workers employed thereupon by the government would be subjected to certain restrictions in the exercise of their trade-union rights. Whenever Sohyo wanted to engage in tactics of some sort on a national scale, this proved a hindrance to the exercise of full liberty by the unions in government enterprises. On the other hand, the workers belonging to the unions in private industries had no such difficulty. Because of this difference, there were signs of chafing among the leaders of the two groups.

Those who have watched with sympathy the development of Sohyo might contend that the difficulty mentioned above is not as great as some others, and that it may in fact be more imaginary than real. In any case, however, no one would deny that the tactics of Sohyo have had to be ironed out, always bearing in mind the character of the heterogeneous groups constituting the organization.

To many leaders in Sohyo, *junpō tōsō* is fundamentally obnoxious; it is a sham, carried out under false pretenses. They are in favor of *jitsu ryoku kōshi*, i.e., the exercising of real strength. They would urge the workers to take *issei kyūka* (leave of absence) en masse. They would encourage workers to resort in unison to *chōkin kyohi* (refusal to work overtime). In essence, this is the same as *junpō tōsō*, because the workers have legal rights to resort to these practices. Therefore, in urging the rank and file to adopt these tactics, the leaders were now heading definitely and outspokenly for more belligerent policies. However, these tendencies on the part of the main stream of Sohyo were not approved of by the leaders opposed to undemocratic lines of thought and action.

The element that was opposed to the dictatorial or undemocratic leadership in Sohyo finally asserted itself openly when Min Rōren (Federation of Democratic Unions) was organized in February, 1952. This faction grew rapidly in prestige and influence in the following years. A strong move to give it shape and a definite place in the labor movement in Japan arose in April, 1954, when the representatives of Sodomei met with the leaders of Zensen Domei (All Textile Workers' Federation) and Zen Nippon Kaiin Kumiai (All Japan Seamen's Union), and Zen-ei En (All Film and Theatrical Actors' Union) in Tokyo and founded Zenrō Kaigi (Congress of All Trade-Unions). Takita Minoru, president of Zensen Domei, was elected chairman of the Congress Zenrō, an organization that, in the minds of the authorities on social and labor questions of Japan, is destined to play a significant role in the labor movement of Japan in the coming years.

Some mention should be made of the training and personality of Takita at this stage. He was born in 1912, the son of an artist. His father, a painter of recognized standing in Toyama Prefecture, wanted his son to become an artist in the family tradition, so Takita was sent to a school of industrial arts. Takita himself never dreamed of becoming a labor leader. However, after graduation, at the age of twenty, Takita was employed as a mill operative in a textile mill. He discovered himself to be more adept at handling human affairs than spindles or weaving looms. When World War II ended, and Sodomei came to life again under the leadership of Matsuoka Komakichi, Takita was thirty-four years old. Matsuoka found in Takita the "stuff" to make of him a leader in the resurgent movement of textile workers. In 1948, Takita was duly elected president of the Textile Workers' Union; and as mentioned already, it was Takita who led the textile workers and assumed leadership in forming Zenrō.

Because Zenrō came into being as a reaction to Sohyo, it is to be expected that in the charters, by-laws, and programs of action of the two organizations fundamental differences are to be found. Zenrō stresses realism based on the realities of national and international economics. It is openly anti-Communist and oriented strongly toward the democratic ICFTU. On practically all questions confronting the organized workers of Japan, quite the opposite of Sohyo's philosophy and tactics are found in Zenrō. It will be recalled that Sodomei, the traditional mainstay of moderate and prudent trade-unionism, took early steps to help organize and join Zenrō.

The Textile Workers Union, which Takita has always led as president, has been known as one of "bread-and-butter" type, a steady organization on the British trade-union pattern. We have already pointed out that the seamen—who along with Sodomei and the textile workers, form the "tripod," as it were, in Zenrō— were unique in the matter of their relations with shipowners. They have always maintained an intimate relationship with them, having set up a "Joint Maritime Commission," and have always taken pride in abiding by the standing trade agreement into which they entered voluntarily.

Other features in the organization of Zenrō will be discussed later.

THE STEADY RECOVERY OF JAPAN AND HOW LABOR CONTRIBUTED TO IT

Signs of Steady Economic Recovery

The writer visited Europe shortly after World War I and lived in Switzerland for fifteen years thereafter. One thing that impressed me most during that time was the amazingly rapid recovery of Germany, after her complete defeat in that war. The intention of the Allied Powers at Versailles in 1919 had been to keep Germany from recovery, or at least to keep her from recovering sufficient military strength to wreak vengeance on the Allied Powers. However, ten years after Versailles, Germany had regained sufficient industrial and military strength under the Nazis to challenge and wage battles against the Allied forces.

The recovery of Germany after World War II has been strangely reminiscent of the experience of the previous war. Whoever visited Europe after World War II must have heard the expression, "the miracle of Germany's recovery." This was used particularly in reference to the amazing increases in industrial and mining production and in exports. The same is true of another country defeated in the same war, namely Japan. The figures of manufacturing and mining in Japan after the war suggest that Japan, ten years after surrender, was not only definitely recovering, but was in fact on the road to prosperity and affluence undreamed of in prewar years. How is this to be accounted for? What effect has it had on the industrial relations in the country? Has it exerted a steadying influence on organized labor in Japan?

The expression "the miracle of Germany's recovery" referred to the situation that obtained in that country for about ten years after the end of World War II. As statistical bulletins of the United Nations reported, Germany was leading the Western nations in the rate of recovery of mining, manufacturing, and exports. In 1956 the U.S.S.R. caught up, and, in the following year, outran Germany, but in the years thereafter the UN figures showed that still another country had outstripped all the rest. That country was, and still is, Japan.

Ten years after surrender in World War II, a phenomenon called *sūryō keiki* (quantity boom) occurred in Japan. In that it was without precedent in the entire span of 2,600 years of Japanese history since Jimmu, the first emperor, it was called more commonly *Jimmu Keiki*. Limited space will not permit a comprehensive or detailed analysis of it; on the next page, however are two tables that illustrate the statements made above. One is a table of industrial production in the major countries of Western Europe and outside, in index figures, down to 1955. The other is a table showing the rapid rise of the average monthly living costs of urban families in Japan, bearing out the statement made earlier that after the war Japan began to emerge as an "affluent" nation. The former is taken from the *United Nations Monthly Bulletin of Statistics*, and the latter from the Statistics Bureau of the Prime Minister's Office, Tokyo.

How, one may ask, can the phenomenal recovery of Germany and Japan be explained, when both countries were thoroughly defeated in the last war?

Though Germany offers data that are stimulating indeed, we must concentrate on Japan; even for Japan, we must refrain from displaying the statistical and other materials from which our conclusions are drawn, except where they are considered indispensable.

Table 34, on industrial production, takes the year 1948 as the base (100) for the comparative index figures. As the table shows, Germany in Europe and Japan outside of Europe showed star-

TABLE 34

INDUSTRIAL PRODUCTION IN MAJOR COUNTRIES OF
WESTERN EUROPE AND OUTSIDE, IN INDEX FIGURES
(1948 = 100)

	1937–1938	1948	1952	1953	1954	1955
WEST EUROPE						
Belgium	102	100	115	115	124	135
France	100	100	128	126	136	149
W. Germany	192	100	233	253	284	331
Italy	99	100	147	162	176	189
Netherlands	88	100	130	141	156	170
Sweden	68	100	112	113	119	125
United Kingdom	84	100	116	122	131	139
OUTSIDE						
Canada	55	100	118	126	125	134
U.S.	59	100	119	129	121	133
U.S.S.R.	—	100	200	220	255	280
India	89	100	119	125	135	149
Japan	210	100	215	265	285	310

SOURCE: United Nations. *Monthly Bulletin of Statistics.*

TABLE 35

AVERAGE MONTHLY COSTS OF URBAN FAMILIES IN
JAPAN; LIVING EXPENDITURES

Year	Persons per family	Food	Housing	Fuel & light	Clothing	Miscellaneous	Total
1950	4.79	6,880	547	596	1,473	2,484	11,980
1951	4.80	7,828	651	854	1,954	3,208	14,389
1952	4.82	9,134	866	982	2,579	4,277	17,838
1953	4.92	10,374	1,165	1,167	2,838	5,837	21,381
1954	4.91	10,995	1,224	1,200	2,695	6,564	22,678
1955	4.84	10,891	1,331	1,215	2,717	7,056	23,211
1956	4.61	10,786	1,625	1,225	2,920	7,402	23,958
1957	4.56	11,368	1,819	1,331	3,096	7,994	25,608
1958	4.57	11,898	2,239	1,353	3,135	8,546	27,171
1959	4.56	12,260	2,660	1,396	3,376	9,270	28,902
1960	4.56	13,000	2,790	1,597	3,755	10,134	31,276
1961	4.35	13,842	3,399	1,731	4,326	11,031	34,329
1962	4.29	15,063	3,951	1,906	4,933	12,734	38,587

SOURCE: Japan. Statistical Bureau at the Prime Minister's Office, *Family Income and Expenditure Survey.*

tlingly rapid recoveries. John Stuart Mill pointed out[3] long ago that it is a general rule in history that the nations that suffer defeat and destruction in a war rise, if they rise at all, more rapidly than the nations which won the war. The case of Japan, however, would seem to deserve a special observation.

It has been noted that immediately after Japan's surrender, there was a short period during which some manufacturers and entrepreneurs of the nation were accused of being in a state of stupor (*kyodatsu jōtai*), but that was only momentary. Before long they picked up courage and devoted their efforts to rehabilitation. The sympathetic attitude of the occupation under SCAP at this stage was a positive factor for rapid rehabilitation. Besides the food, clothing, and medicine that American friends supplied to the Japanese people through LARA and CARE programs, the Supreme Commander demonstrated both generosity and foresight in seeing to it that materials necessary for rebuilding residences and factories were to some extent made available to Japanese manufacturers. Furthermore, while certain powers were pressing for reparation of damages caused by the Japanese troops in the war, the United States took the leadership in encouraging Japan to recover by providing both material and moral help. The importance of this factor should not be underestimated.

The industrialists of the nation were painfully conscious of how the disastrous war had retarded the technology of Japan's industries. Every effort was conscientiously made by them in order that Japanese industry might catch up to and outrun the former rival nations of the West. The traditional Japanese virtues of saving and thrift seemed to have been lost in the few years immediately after the war, but those virtues had fortunately not completely died out. On the contrary, savings in banks have not only returned to the prewar levels but have far surpassed them in recent years. Moreover, the savings of the people have not taken the form of copious hoarding, but, instead, have followed the Keynesian economics of investment.[4] Comparative statistics on the proportion of equipment-investment to total national production show that the Japanese people are "enterprise-minded" and that this national characteristic has proved to be a tremendous help to Japan in achieving its remarkable recovery. The following figures show the equipment investment as a percentage of the total national production (column 1) and the rate of economic growth (column 2) by country:

	(1)	(2)
United States	6.3	3.0
United Kingdom	8.3	4.5
France	8.3	4.5
West Germany	11.5	10.8
Italy	13.4	10.6
Japan	16.7	11.2

Effects of Urbanization and Shrinking of War Industries

Another factor which must not be overlooked is the one that sociologists call "urbanization." Urbanization is a "program" in many countries, and this is so in Japan. The sudden influx of population into cities and towns is creating congestion and conditions of anarchy in some cities. That is the dark side of urbanization. But there is also the bright side that comes from the industrialization that urbanization involves. Japan, with 40 per cent or more of the population engaged in "primary" industries of which agriculture plays the dominant part, has long been baffled by the problem of where to send the second, third, and other boys born into farming families. This was particularly true in the days when the time-honored system of primogeniture was in force. Since the MacArthur Revolution, the system of primogeniture has been abolished and the parents' property, including farm land, is now distributed equally among the children, but because of the small size of the farm, in spite of the new system of land distribution, the youths in the agricultural districts are leaving the countryside to seek jobs in urban areas. In other words, in Japan, urbanization has involved largely the shifting of the labor force from the primary industries into the secondary, and that process is continuing at the present time.

The foregoing account might give the impression that land reform did not benefit the farming population. Such an impression is wrong and should be corrected at once, for, as a result of the land reform, the proverbially impoverished tenant farmers became landowners, in most cases with greatly increased incomes, and this resulted in the widening of the domestic market for the products of industry.

This situation also means that the agricultural element in the population of Japan, which had constituted the "reservoir" of labor force in the past, had proved to be a real asset in the period of economic growth, though how long Japan can take advantage of this "reservoir" remains to be seen. In the past, the countries that have had attained something like "full employment" have experienced difficulty in achieving economic growth because of lack of manpower reserves.

The increased strength of the trade-unions can be interpreted in two ways. If the ideology of the major unions were such as to produce more conflicts and impede economic expansion, the effect would be only negative. However, an increase in union strength normally means a higher purchasing power for the laborers who constitute the consuming public. In any case, it is granted that higher purchasing power resulted from union activities.

One item that must not be overlooked in postwar Japanese industry is the vast amount of technological innovation. As an eminent authority on these questions remarked, the period from 1956 through 1959 was one of "unprecedented technological innovation which included the introduction of large, efficient equipment for steel production, and the development of synthetic textiles, synthetic resins, petrochemicals, and electronics. Progress in these and other related fields of production was made at a rate Japan had never experienced before."[5]

Finally, there is a factor of a tremendous importance that beyond all doubt has helped Japan achieve the amazing industrial expansion of the postwar years. That is the new Constitution, popularly called the "Peace Constitution," whereby the nation has been relieved of heavy expenditure for "defense." Previous to 1940, for instance, as much as 63.8 per cent of national expenditure was on goods and services for war purposes. The major powers of the world, led by the United States and the U.S.S.R., are continuing to do what the military government of Japan was doing during the last disastrous war. No one is so naive as to imagine that under the "Peace Constitution" Japan has no arms and no expenditure for armament. Under the Mutual Security Treaty (called "The Treaty of Mutual Cooperation and Security between Japan and the United States of America" after its revision in 1960), Japan is obliged to maintain a gradually increasing amount of arms, but the expenditure for defense in the strict sense has amounted to barely 1.5 per cent of national income in recent years.[6] When the national income was small, it once rose to 1.8 per cent. For further details, see Table 36.

This means that Japan has been able to turn the money that might have been expended for the manufacture of nonproductive munitions into meeting civilian needs, for manufacturing consumer goods, or for expanding investment. It has already been pointed out that private, fixed investment as a percentage of the gross national product had increased from 8.8 per cent of the average in 1946–1951 to 16 per cent of the average of 1959–1960.[7] Let us look at the outcome of these phenomenal increases.

"The Emergence of An Affluent Society" is the title of a revealing article by the Tokyo correspondent of the *Financial Times* in London, reporting on Japan's postwar recovery and

TABLE 36
DEFENSE EXPENDITURES FOR 1956–1963
(100 million yen)

	1956	1957	1958	1959	1960	1961	1962	1963
Defense (a)	1,429	1,436	1,485	1,556	1,600	1,835	2,137	2,412
se Ministry	1,000	1,000	1,198	1,354	1,513	1,744	2,040	2,293
d Force	539	502	576	605	668	735	830	931
Force	228	219	256	322	370	430	482	518
Force	200	256	327	387	431	528	672	779
sidiary	33	30	40	40	43	51	56	65
se Disburse-ment	406	402	261	176	60	61	64	81
se Equip-ments (b)	23	26	26	26	27	30	33	38
al Exp. Budget	10,897	11,846	13,381	15,121	17,652	21,074	25,631	28,500
nal Income (c)	76,276	82,859	85,190	100,373	119,037	141,176	153,200	166,500
per cent)	13.11	12.12	11.10	10.29	9.07	8.71	8.34	8.46
er cent)	1.87	1.73	1.74	1.55	1.43	1.30	1.39	1.45

SOURCE: *Japan's Finance for 1963*, p. 275.

prosperity. In this article, the correspondent mentions that there are now more than fifteen million television sets in Japan, served by nearly two hundred stations. He says further that "one out of every two houses has an electric washing machine and nearly 40 per cent of Japanese homes are equipped with electric refrigerators. Tokyo's streets are clogged with private cars, and Scotch at £12 a bottle sells so fast that dealers can't keep up with demand."

The same article continues: "Nor is this a sign merely that a small segment of the Japanese population is enjoying the benefit of higher living standards while the vast majority languish in

Oriental squalor. The improvement in living standards has spread virtually throughout every class and segment of Japanese society." As he points out, in Tokyo one frequently sees thousands of young people lined up in long queues to buy tickets for a forthcoming visit of, say, the Berlin Opera, at prices ranging from 2,000 to 10,000 yen a seat. "Taxis are often air-conditioned and carry transistorized TV sets for the delectation of their fares."[8]

TABLE 37

DEFENSE EXPENDITURE AS PERCENTAGE OF NATIONAL INCOME OF MAJOR POWERS (1961–1963)*

	National Income	Defense Exp.	Percent-age
Japan (1)	16,650	2,412	1.5
United States (2)	4,567	526	11.5
United Kingdom (3)	21,557	1,745	8.1
West Germany (4)	2,408	129	5.4
France (5)	2,332	178	7.6
Italy (6)	185,574	7,849	4.2

*Figures are given in hundreds of thousands of (1) yen, (2) dollars, (3) pounds, (4) marks, (5) francs, and (6) lire.
SOURCE: *Japan's Finance for 1963*, p. 276.

The *Financial Times* correspondent contends that whereas these manifestations of prosperity are obvious to a casual observer, and might be considered superficial, there is indeed a vast change in the Japanese way of life resulting from rising living standards. He argues that "whereas in Britain a rising standard of living is a matter of kind. Before the onslaught of the 'affluent society,' traditional Japanese customs and manners which survived the great upheaval of the Meiji Restoration in the middle of the last century, and the depression of the 1920s and World War II are now beginning to crumble. Japanese society itself is being reshaped to cope with the modern world, and no one seems to be sure what form it will finally take—or even what form they want it to take."

The "Energy Revolution" and the Miike Coal Dispute

The description of the bewildering rates of economic growth in the preceding sections might easily induce one to conclude that Japan's economy is returning, if it has not already returned, to normal, even to firmer foundations than ever. However, one is warned against any hasty conclusion of that nature, because of the tormenting effects of the "energy revolution" on the industrialists of this country, much as in many Western nations. There is little sign of improvement in the pattern of management-labor relations, at least in the coal industry, which has been most adversely affected by the increase in hydroelectric and other sources of heat and power besides coal. No attempt will be made here to trace how coal is being replaced by other sources of power, but the way in which labor has reacted to the change, generally called the "Energy Revolution," will be recounted briefly.

The story concerns the behavior in 1959–1961 of the coal-mining workers at the Miike mine, one of the most important coal mines in Kyushu, belonging to the giant Mitsui firm. The coal-mining workers' union at Miike belongs to Tan Rō (Coal-Mining Workers' Union), which had a membership of some 200,000 in 1959–1960. The long history of tension and struggle between the Mitsui firm and the coal-mining workers assumed serious dimensions when a dispute arose in 1959 at the Miike mines, which then had 48,000 employees. The workers presented a demand for a 2,000-yen raise in monthly salary of all workers. The demand was flatly rejected with a so-called "zero reply." Moreover, the company reported, it was in debt to the amount of 1,900 million yen, and, in order to cope with the distressing situation, was planning to carry out a "reconstruction of the industry" involving the necessity of asking 6,000 mining workers "to volunteer to retire." The workers were fully aware of the company's sad plight. There was a vast stock pile of coal amounting to 12,000,000 tons. The Central Labor Relations Board had already been advised of this situation early in the spring of the year, and Chairman Nakayama of the Board had attempted to ease the tension through conciliation, but his efforts had proved fruitless.

In October, 1959, workers of the Miike mines staged a 24-hour strike, which was followed by a series of "scheduled work stoppages." The company posted appeals for volunteers to retire from employment. The striking workers organized teams to tear the appeals from the bulletin boards. The union of the Miike mining workers announced its decision to expel from membership anyone who volunteered to retire. Then, as often happens in the course of a protracted strike, a "second union" was born, consisting of men who had become weary of the prolonged dispute. The situation grew worse as the company named a list of men to be discharged during December, 1959. Moreover, on January 25, 1960, the company declared a lockout. In the meantime, the membership of the second union had increased rapidly to 4,000, while that of the first union had fallen off to 10,000. During the desperate attempt of the workers belonging to the second union to break through the picket line of the first union, the company took advantage of the opportunity to rush loads of armed men to the scene. This led to the death of one man and serious injuries to many others who were guarding the picket line. The incident horrified the public.

Shortly after this tragic incident, the Central Labor Relations Commission, under its new chairman, Professor Fujibayashi Keizo, without a request from either party but on its own authority intervened in an effort toward conciliation. On April 6, 1961, seventy-three days after the lockout, the conciliation terms of the Central Labor Relations Board were transmitted to the company and the union. The company was to withdraw its list of men to be discharged, and the men whose names were on the company's list were to be treated as having "retired voluntarily"; the company was to pay these men 10,000 yen in addition to the amount announced earlier as "retirement allowance," and were to make every effort to find employment for them elsewhere, or to re-employ them in the company itself; finally, the two parties were to put an end to the dispute through peaceful negotiation.

Conciliation terms have no legally binding force; the parties are free to accept or reject the terms. The company accepted the terms, but the attitude of the union was negative, and that meant that the conciliation efforts of the Central Labor Relations Board were abortive. The dispute continued till the Board intervened a third time in August, four months later. In the meantime the damages caused by the protracted dispute were alarming.

The expenditure of the Miike Mining Company directly connected with the dispute rose to 3,000 million yen. Since the banks refused any further loans, the company had to ask its major clients for "advance payments" for coal to be delivered in the future. Such advances rose to the stupendous figure of 1,100 million yen. The company was already in debt to the amount of 10,000 million yen—a fabulous sum, even for the fabled Mitsui family. As a matter of fact, the *Zaibatsu* has been demolished by the occupation authority.

For waging this historic battle, Sohyo, with which Tan Rō (the Coal-Mining Workers' Union) is affiliated, carried out a fund-raising campaign to support the striking mining workers, asking the help of each member in raising 648 million yen. Failing to raise the whole amount, Sohyo borrowed from the Workers' Bank, and was paying interest at the rate of 100,000 yen a day.

Still more appalling was the extent of violence which the excitement of the dispute had aroused: 1,754 men were injured and one man was killed. During the whole period of the strike, which began in January, 1961, a total of 700,000 men stood in picket lines, and 530,000 policemen were dispatched to suppress violence. In the annals of Japanese labor, no dispute had ever before risen to such dimensions.

The active Labor Minister, Ishida Hirohide, in the Ikeda Cabinet, newly formed on July 19, 1961, called upon both parties to end the disturbance. Thereupon the Central Labor Relations Board again decided to intervene on "its own authority." The intervention took the form of conciliation; two prominent experts, Professor Fujibayashi Keizo and Professor Nakayama Ichiro, former chairman of the board, acting as conciliators.

The conciliation procedure, with a virtual order for a truce, was accepted after a week of further rioting by the workers, during which there were more injuries. Public hearings began on July 27, and, on August 10, carefully drawn conciliation terms were presented to the parties.

In order to understand the nature and actual content of the conciliation terms, the reader must realize that in the final stage of the long-protracted dispute, the question had centered on the proposed dismissal of the 1,200 mining workers listed by the company. Furthermore, as an emergency measure, an extraordinary thing had been done. The conciliators had requested a "blank consignment" of the case, which the parties had conceded prior to any action by the conciliators. Therefore, this was virtually arbitration.

The conciliators in their award set a period of one month during which the men listed by the company could "volunteer" to retire. Those who volunteered to retire would receive 50,000 yen of compensatory allowance in addition to the sums formerly offered by the company, while those who did not volunteer but chose to let the period expire would be "retired" (not "discharged") and would receive 20,000 yen in addition to the sums previously fixed by the company. The government and the company were urged by the conciliators in their award to take adequate measures to relieve the retired men from the privation of unemployment, by providing them with professional retraining or guidance and actively seeking placement for them. The company was advised to set up a joint council of the representatives of the company and of the workers for resumption of production.

The company readily accepted these terms; the mining workers, represented by the Central Strategy Committee, remained somewhat skeptical for a while, but eventually they also gave in, as indeed they had to.

Was this the "end" of the historic coal strike? As far as the Miike mine was concerned, one might say it was, but it would be much more realistic to state that there is no end to the coal dispute in Japan, because, as suggested already, the underlying cause of the coal disputes lies deeper than the questions of wages, hours, and treatment; it lies in the "Energy Revolution" previously alluded to. Only the government can, and must, lay out a program through the Diet, a practical program to deal with the problem arising from the increasing dependence of industries on water power, natural gas, oil, and sources other than coal for fuel. In practice, this will mean that both capital and manpower must be redistributed so as to reduce to a minimum the disturbance and suffering such a transition entails.

Growth of the Gross National Product and the Expansion of the Labor Force

Reference has been made to Japan's unusually high rate of economic growth in the postwar years. It is known that the chief explanation for the growth lies in the technological changes occurring in Japan's industries. No matter how one explains it, it is unquestionably a striking phenomenon. During the six years from 1955–1961, the average rate of economic growth for Japan was 10.5 per cent, whereas it was 2.2 per cent for the United States, 2.5 per cent for the United Kingdom, 4.2 per cent for France, and 5.9 per cent for Italy. Even Germany fell below Japan in this respect, with a figure of 6.3 per cent. Looking back on the prewar years in Japan, it was 2.9 per cent per year for the period 1930 to 1939. The peak in the early postwar years was 9.6 per cent in 1946. How strikingly rapid has been the rate of growth in more recent years can be seen in these few figures; in such a situation, an analysis is needed to see how the growth affected labor as regards employment, wages, and labor-management relations.

First to be noted is the sudden expansion of the labor force. As shown in the table below, while the total number of workers increased by 3,579,000 during the period from 1950 to 1955, during the following five-year period, 1955 to 1960, it increased 4,536,000.

TABLE 38

INCREASE OR DECREASE OF LABOR FORCE BY CATEGORY OF WORK (1950–1960)
(in thousands)

	1950–1955	1955–1960
Total working force	3,579	4,536
Self employed	153	338
Primary industries	403	32
Secondary industries	78	150
Tertiary industries	405	221
Family employees	274	1,466
Primary industries	660	1,547
Secondary industries	91	40
Tertiary industries	297	120
Employed workers	3,867	5,660
Primary industries	59	17
Secondary industries	1,557	3,307
Tertiary industries	2,375	2,524

SOURCE: Japan. Cabinet Statistics Bureau, *National Census Report.*

The employed workers (as opposed to those working in family enterprises) multiplied enormously, while family employees, who had always been on the decrease, shrank noticeably. Further, among the employed workers, while the increase for the period 1950–1955 was more marked in the tertiary industries (commerce, service industries, banks and insurance offices, public welfare enterprises, and public servants), the increase in the period 1955–1960 was far more accentuated in the secondary industries, which comprise more modern and large-scale enterprises (mining, manufacturing, and transportation). Why did the family employees decrease so rapidly? This was due, of course, to the decline of the primary industries.

The effect of economic growth is seen also in the steady increase in the number of workers employed as full-time and permanent employees rather than as part-time or temporary employees. This is particularly the case in construction, manufacturing, transport and communication, and fuel and light industries. One exception is mining, in which the decrease has been drastic. Statistics on this subject are omitted here to save space for other matters, but they show that the increase of the employed workers slowed down in 1961 and 1962. There were two reasons: one was the tighter policy adopted by the banks in that year, and the other was the diminishing supply in the workers' reserve, yet with no decrease in the demand for workers. When the statistics are examined more closely, they show that the largest increase of manpower was in the manufacturing industries, which claimed well over 60 per cent of the freshly recruited workers, and of that number, again, over 60 per cent were for the metal or mechanical engineering works. Obviously, the explanation of this phenomenon was to be found in the high growth rate, for which technical innovations in this country were responsible.

Now, what factor made such enormous expansion possible in Japan? This question is often addressed by inquisitive economists from abroad to the industrialists of this country. There is no secret miracle; as a matter of fact, the answer lies in simple economics, and is explained briefly in a recent publication of *Nippon Rodo Kyokai*.[9]

The problem can be approached from various angles. First, take the factory where, through technological change, automation has been introduced widely in a section of the manufacturing process. Automation is seldom or never applied to the entire process. For example, a certain electronic factory had installed, in 1956, five transfer machines, two for one process and three for another. Installation of the former machine, operated by one worker, enabled the firm to displace six men operating outmoded machines; the latter, operated by one man, involved the displacement of nine workers. Thus, as far as this part of the process was concerned, the firm was able to achieve a considerable saving in work force. Moreover, adoption of the automated machinery resulted in a 130 per cent productivity increase by 1960. However, because there was no comparably efficient and labor-saving machinery for certain other tasks, the same firm had to engage twice as many laborers to perform these tasks using standard methods and equipment. Additional personnel were necessary to transport and handle the increased quantity of material incident to the increase in productivity. The net result was an increase in the work force of approximately 50 per cent! In other words, although the technological change itself did mean considerable saving as far as labor was concerned, still, as long as there was a widening market, production grew on a greater scale and the factory's need for manpower kept increasing instead of shrinking.

Second, take industry as a whole. Technological innovation calls for bigger equipment investments, which means an increase of orders in engineering industry as a rule. Statistical reports of the Economic Planning Agency show that there has been a steady unusual increase in orders for machinery. In 1959, there was an increase of 44.6 per cent over the previous year; in 1960, 47.7 per cent; and in 1961, 34.4 per cent. It fell to 25.3 per cent in 1962 because of the policy adopted by the government "to adjust the boom." However, the general trend is toward expansion of equipment investment. It happens that of all the manufacturing industries, engineering work requires relatively the largest increment for each unit increase of the product. "Marginal employment coefficient" is the term used to indicate the value of the increased labor divided by the increment in production. Below is a table of the coefficients computed on the basis of the industrial statistics of the Ministry of International Trade and Industry. This was worked out by ascertaining the number of workers actually required to increase the product by one million yen per unit. This incidentally shows that for growth in mechanical or engineering and electronic industries, there is a larger demand for work force than in any other industry.

Third, take the national economy as a whole from the viewpoint of its reproductive structure. Machine and engineering industries are most closely tied up with other industries. The increased production of machinery, for example, creates an immediate need for increased production of iron. In building factories and installing machinery, active construction work will be called for. Who buys machines? What for? When we inquire into this, we discover that there will be further production until the point where the primary product reaches the final consumer. "Investment calls for investment" is the axiom that applies here. It is clear that investment has three effects, which constitute a cycle. The primary effect is that it will require the necessary manpower for each unit of production in the industry concerned. This is the marginal employment coefficient alluded to above. The secondary

TABLE 39
INDEX OF PRODUCTIVITY AND EMPLOYMENT IN MANUFACTURING INDUSTRY (1955–1961)

	United States		United Kingdom		W. Germany		France		Italy		Japan	
	Prod.¹	Emp.²	Prod.	Emp.	Prod.	Emp.	Prod.	Emp.	Prod.	Emp.	Prod.	Emp.
1955	100.0	100.0	100.0	100.0	100.0	100.0	100.0	100.0	100.0	100.0	100.0	100.0
1956	103.0	102.1	98.7	101.7	107.7	105.5	109.9	102.7	106.7	100.8	123.4	109.6
1957	103.1	101.7	101.8	101.8	114.6	109.4	124.0	105.3	115.0	102.9	146.4	123.1
1958	94.8	94.4	101.2	101.4	118.5	111.2	131.4	106.4	119.2	99.8	143.8	128.5
1959	108.2	98.7	107.3	101.3	126.9	114.1	133.9	104.0	132.5	101.3	174.2	142.7
1960	111.3	99.3	115.9	105.0	140.8	120.4	148.0	105.0	151.7	109.6	218.8	165.0
1961	112.4	96.4	116.1	106.3	149.2	124.6	155.4	106.0	168.3	116.6	262.4	182.7

¹ Productivity, in index figures.

² Employed workers, in index figures.

SOURCE: Index figures for production from *UN Monthly Bulletin of Economic Statistics*; Employment index from *ILO Statistical Supplement of International Labor Review*. Figures for Japan are from Ministry of International Trade and Industry for production index; from Ministry of Labor for employment index. Borrowed from Nippon Rodo Kyokai, *Rodo Keizai No Aramashi*, p. 23.

effect is that each unitary production in industry A will provide stimulus to industries B, C, and so on, which furnish materials or services. These industries, in turn, will then require more manpower. The tertiary effect is that the increased production in industries B, C, and so on, will in their turn provide stimulus to industry A, resulting in further need for manpower in industry A. Fourth, consider the repercussions of increased income. The level of productivity and wages in machine and engineering industries happens to be higher than in most other industries. Sudden increase of employment in these industries means a general rise in wages and incomes, inducing a rise in other related industries and, in consequence, a rise in the general purchasing power. Such a rise in purchasing power is bound to affect the tertiary industries, inducing further employment.

The explanation given so far has been taken from Japanese experience, but one might assume that it is applicable to other nations as well. The table below shows unmistakably how closely the rise in industrial (i.e., manufacturing) production was related to the rise in employment in the experience of the major industrial powers within the past decade. Incidentally, we might note here that in West Germany, where the manufacturing industry has a remarkable record of expansion, shortage of manpower is beginning to make itself felt. We might note further that how long Japan can count on her "reservoir" of manpower remains to be seen.

Rise in Productivity and in Wages

The picture of Japan's spectacular economic growth is incomplete without reference to the benefits the working class has received in the form of higher wages. Without going into too many details, we might look over the rates of wage increase in the postwar years.

It will be recalled that, during the early years of the postwar period, there was a tide of inflation that drove the workers to engage in desperate struggles to raise wages. In 1948 there was an average rise over the previous year of 174.2 per cent for all industries, and 177.2 per cent in the manufacturing industry. In 1949, as the "Dodge Line" economy was enforced, the increase rate was tempered down to 73.8 per cent, and in 1950 it fell to 19.3 per cent. The following year, however, the outbreak of the Korean War brought a temporary boom to Japan, and the rate of increase rose

again to 27.0 per cent. Only through the stiff financial retrenchment policy adopted by the government for the second time in
1955 was the nation enabled to keep some stability; the wage
increase rate was restricted to around 5 to 7 per cent per year. But
in 1961, reflecting the effect of the tremendous expansion of total
national production, which registered a nominal increase of 23 per

TABLE 40

YEARLY INCREASE OF WAGES (1948–1954)

(per cent)

Year	All investigated industries	Manufac- turing industry
1948	174.2	177.2
1949	69.6	73.8
1950	19.0	19.3
1951	24.8	27.0
1952	18.7	16.6
1953	15.2	12.1
1954	6.5	5.4

cent and a real increase of 16 per cent, the total wage increase
again rose to 11.8 per cent. The government made an attempt to
enforce retrenchment for the third time, but the wage increase in
1962 over the previous year was still 10.6 per cent. Was this
healthy and normal, or was something wrong? For details, see the
table below.

TABLE 41

YEARLY INCREASE OF WAGES (1955–1962)

(1955 = 100)

Year	All investigated industries		Manufacturing industry	
	Index	Percentage over previous year	Index	Percentage over previous year
1955	76.1	5.3	74.5	3.9
1956	81.8	7.5	81.4	9.3
1957	85.6	4.6	84.2	3.4
1958	88.2	3.0	86.2	2.4
1959	93.5	6.0	92.6	7.4
1960	100.0	7.0	100.0	8.0
1961	111.5	11.5	111.8	11.8
1962	123.3	10.6	123.0	10.0

SOURCE: Ministry of Labor, *Maigetzu Kinro Tokei* (Monthly Labor
Statistics).

TABLE 42

INCREASE IN REAL WAGES (1955–1962)
(1960 = 100)

Year	All investigated industries		Manufacturing industry	
	Index	Over previous year (per cent)	Index	Over previous year (per cent)
1955	82.1	6.3	80.4	5.1
1956	88.0	7.2	87.5	8.8
1957	89.3	1.5	87.8	0.3
1958	92.4	3.5	90.3	2.8
1959	96.9	4.9	96.0	6.3
1960	100.0	3.2	100.0	4.2
1961	105.9	5.9	106.2	6.2
1962	109.6	3.5	109.3	2.9

SOURCE: Japan. Ministry of Labor, *Monthly Labor Statistics.*

As to the question whether these high increases were healthy and normal for Japan, or unhealthy and abnormal, the following explanation given in a publication of Nippon Rodo Kyokai is worthy of notice.[10]

Among the factors that have contributed greatly to the rise of wage levels in recent years is first, the high initial salary that graduates of schools and colleges command on entering into employment in the period of continued boom. There is sharp competition among firms to recruit young graduates. One might say it is the employers who are contributing to the higher wages in this instance. On the other hand, it is the high figures of "base up" which the workers' unions are demanding in their "spring offensives" every year. We have already mentioned the special circumstance of the public servants and the employees of the government enterprises who present their wage demands in the spring before the government formulates the budget for the following year. We have also noted incidentally that the public servants and government employees constitute a heavy proportion of the organized workers of Japan. When newly employed workers start their work with high initial salaries, or when the public servants and government employees set the example each spring with demands for higher wages, it is only natural that the wages tends to rise higher as a consequence.

Had it not been for the wave of tremendous economic growth that has visited Japan in recent years, it is conceivable that the demand for higher wages would not have produced such effects as it has. However, we must not overlook in this situation that the "surplus" of manpower, which was a problem for Japan in the past, is rapidly diminishing. At the same time, we should note that the remarkable rise in the productivity of labor resulting from technological improvements and also the awakening of the employers to the need of improved conditions of work are doubtless contributing to the rise in recent years of nominal and real wages in Japan. See Tables 42 and 43 for the rise of real wages and a comparison between productivity of labor and wages.

TABLE 43

RISE IN PRODUCTIVITY AND WAGES (1955–1962)
(1960 = 100)

Year	Labor productivity		Wages	
	Index	Over previous year (per cent)	Index	Over previous year (per cent)
1955	75.4	5.3	74.5	3.9
1956	84.9	12.6	81.4	9.3
1957	89.7	5.7	84.8	3.4
1958	84.3	6.0	86.2	2.4
1959	92.0	9.1	92.6	7.4
1960	100.0	8.7	100.0	8.0
1961	108.3	8.3	111.8	11.8
1962	111.4	2.9	123.0	10.0

SOURCE: Japan. Ministry of Labor, Monthly Labor Statistics.

FREQUENCY OF LABOR DISPUTES AND THE SYSTEMS OF DISPUTE SETTLEMENT IN JAPAN

Recent Strike Propensity of Japanese Workers

The story of the economic growth of Japan would not be complete without a discussion of the extent and frequency of labor disputes, and also of how those disputes are settled.

To provide the background, let us recall that when General MacArthur took office in 1945 as Supreme Commander for the Allied Powers in Japan, he took urgent measures to promote unionization of workers. The effect was immediate and far-reaching. Starting from practically nothing when the war ended, union membership rose within a few months to more than a million, and within two years to five million. In 1946, under the direction of the Supreme Commander, a new Constitution was adopted, containing, as already mentioned, a solemn renunciation of the right to wage war. It was by the same Constitution that the basic rights of workers were guaranteed, including the right to organize, to engage in collective bargaining, and to take collective action, i.e., to strike (Article 28). Results of these constitutional measures are seen in the increase of frequency of labor disputes involving collective action in the form of strikes. The story of the rapid growth of union membership will be told in the next section; only the question of frequency of labor disputes will be taken up here.

The government and people of Japan are mindful of world opinion. They are anxious to live up to the expectations of the "free world" and to guarantee the "democratic freedom" of the worker. A glance at the brief comparative statistics of labor disputes occurring within the major industrial powers of the world (the United States, the United Kingdom, West Germany, and Japan), will not fail to impress anyone with the great extent to which the workers of Japan are exercising their constitutional right of collective action—the strike.

Table 44 gives statistics for four nations, two of which won in the last war and two of which lost. The comparison is striking in more than one respect. As the United States had been leading the world of democracy, it would not be surprising if that country led, as indeed it does lead, in the exercise of workers' democratic freedom in the conduct of labor disputes. A nation with the highest per capita wealth, endowed with natural resources and abundant capital, the United States may be able to "afford" the enormous economic losses resulting from the high degree of worker participation in strikes and the tremendous number of man-days lost. Britain nominally won the war but suffered more losses than most other powers that participated in the war. Whether she can afford those high strike figures is questionable, although that is not our present concern. Germany obviously decided that she must not "indulge in the luxury" of freedoms resulting in such wastage. The Germans are determined that their nation must undergo the severest austerity, must discipline themselves and learn to work together for rapid recovery. Hence their famous Co-determination Law (*Mitbestimmungs Gesetz*) and the extraordinarily low figures for both labor disputes and workers participating in the disputes. We see that the figures

TABLE 44

LABOR DISPUTES OF MAJOR INDUSTRIAL NATIONS (1957–1961)

Nations and years	Number of disputes	Number of participants	Man-days lost (1957–1961)	Number of disputes per 1000 workers*
USA[a]				
1957	3,673	1,390,000	16,500,000	Average for
1958	3,694	2,060,000	23,900,000	1947–1957
1959	3,708	1,880,000	69,000,000	
1960	3,333	1,320,000	19,100,000	15,190
1961	3,300	1,450,000	16,500,000	
UK[b]				
1957	2,859	1,359,000	8,412,000	Average for
1958	2,629	524,000	3,462,000	1947–1957
1959	2,093	646,000	5,270,000	
1960	—	818,000	3,024,000	2,260
1961	2,648	765,460	3,021,000	
W. Germany[c]				
1957	86	45,000	1,071,846	Average for
1958	1,484	202,000	782,000	1947–1957
1959	55	22,000	61,825	
1960	—	17,065	37,723	920
1961	121	21,000	64,350	
Japan[d]				
1957	830	1,557,000	5,652,000	Average for
1958	903	1,279,000	6,052,000	1947–1957
1959	887	1,216,000	6,020,000	
1960	1,063	918,094	4,912,000	7,680
1961	1,371	1,640,000	5,271,000	

[a] For the United States, figures for 1957 exclude Hawaii and Alaska, also disputes involving fewer than six workers and those lasting less than a full day or shift.

[b] For the United Kingdom, disputes not connected with terms of employment or conditions of labor are excluded; also disputes involving fewer than ten workers or lasting less than one day are not included unless a loss of more than 100 working days is involved.

[c] For West Germany, West Berlin is excluded, and also strikes lasting less than one day except when a loss of more than 100 working days is involved.

[d] For Japan, excluded are workers indirectly affected and also disputes lasting less than four hours.

* The figures for man-days lost per 1,000 workers have been taken from O. D. Foenander's *Industrial Conciliation and Arbitration in Australia*. Foenander has drawn his figures originally from ILO sources.

SOURCE: ILO, *Year Book of Labour Statistics*.

of man-days lost are impressively high in Germany compared with the number of cases of disputes. We imagine that this is due to the self-restraint of the workers, who will not easily enter into a strike but, once they have entered it, will stick to it till they win.

So much for other nations. Can Japan afford the loss of so many man-days? Despite the "phenomenal economic growth" of Japan, we must remember that the figures are only relative and Japan has far to go yet before she reaches the economic level of the United States.

A close examination of the statistics shows that the definition of "labor dispute" is not the same for all countries, as is indicated in the footnote. This results in a distortion of the picture to be drawn from the comparative statistics, though it does not destroy the value of a general comparison. We must also keep in mind the difference in the actual size of the working population from one country to another. A large number of participants in labor disputes in one country may or may not mean a high propensity of workers to strike. It must be checked by comparing it with the total working force of the nation concerned. Suppose the working population of the United States were about twice as large as that of Japan. Suppose further that the number of participants in labor disputes in the United States was twice as large as that of Japan. In such an event, as far as the figures indicated, one might conclude that the strike propensities of workers of the two countries were about the same.

To provide a fairer picture of the workers' proneness to strike in the various countries, we have added to the accompanying statistics comparative figures showing the number of participants in disputes per 1,000 workers; these comparative figures are taken from a study made by O. D. Foenander, an Australian scholar.[11] The study was made for the years 1947–1957 and, for that reason, it might be considered a little out of date, but the average experience during the eleven-year period after the war should be regarded as sufficiently respectable and helpful for us still.

Foenander's study has shown that the strike propensity of Japanese workers (7,680 per 1,000 workers) compared with that of American workers (15,190 per 1,000 workers) was only half as high during the period under review. But the figures after 1957 show that there was a large increase in the number of Japanese workers engaging in strikes. In 1957, and again in 1961, the actual number of workers participating in strikes was higher in Japan than in the United States. Someone looking at these figures recently remarked: "The United States has been leading the world of democracy in everything, including notably in the exercise of democratic freedom. But on sufferance of the United States, Japan is now leading the world in matters of labor disputes." But is Japan's high number of participants in labor disputes a sign of "democratic freedom" and of progress on which Japanese people should be congratulated?

Space does not permit us to discuss in detail the implication or social and economic consequences of these disputes. Such discussion must be reserved for another study. For the time being, we must content ourselves with a glance at the causes of the disputes, shown in Table 45, covering the recent eight-year period 1955–1962. The figures reveal that it is largely the pressure of economic needs that gives rise to disputes in Japan, rather than social, quasi-political, ideological, noneconomic, or other motives. During the eleven-year period, from 70 to 80 per cent of the disputes arose from wage issues, and included demands for raises, opposition to reduction of pay, demand for wage payment at fixed periods (because certain employers failed to observe the legal requirement in this respect), and demands for payment of bonuses and other nonperiodical cash allowances. These items accounted for 71.1 per cent of the issues in 1955, and this rose steadily to 83.4 per cent in 1962.

On the other hand, the issues centering on management and personnel affairs represented 17.2 per cent in 1955. This percentage steadily decreased from year to year, and fell to 9.1 per cent in 1962. Recognition of a union or of union activities is no longer an issue because of the wide diffusion of knowledge among the employers about legal provisions in the Trade Union Law. The demand for welfare provisions represented 8.0 per cent of the causes of disputes in 1955, but it had fallen to 0.1 per cent in 1962. Other demands of workers, as far as the statistics show, are of minor or negligible importance. Taken as a whole, it can be argued, as it has been argued by the leaders of the union movement, that the activities of the unions in Japan are increasingly in the economic rather than the noneconomic fields, and that the occasional disputes into which they are drawn are serving steadily to raise the standard of wages and other conditions of work.

TABLE 45

WORKERS' MAJOR DEMANDS IN LABOR DISPUTES (1955–1962)

	1955	1956	1957	1958	1959	1960	1961	1962
tal demands (Index)	100	100	100	100	100	100	100	100
(actual number)	(1,538)	(1,419)	(1,768)	(1,874)	(1,711)	(2,222)	(2,566)	(2,313)
cognition of union, etc.	1.2	1.3	1.4	1.8	2.0	1.4	1.3	1.6
nclusion of contract	4.8	4.3	4.4	3.7	3.4	2.5	2.7	1.9
ages, allowances, etc.	71.1	72.3	72.4	59.6	67.4	70.0	80.9	83.4
Wage increase	17.4	25.0	29.5	22.9	27.3	36.2	43.0	48.7
Objection to wage cut	1.8	0.9	0.1	0.6	0.6	0.3	0.4	0.2
Regular payment	7.3	3.0	2.4	2.2	1.4	0.6	0.4	0.8
Other wage demands	4.2	3.3	4.0	1.3	1.6	1.5	3.4	1.3
Bonus	32.7	33.5	31.3	28.4	32.3	28.7	31.6	30.4
Layoff allowance	3.2	1.8	1.9	2.3	1.5	0.5	0.4	0.1
Retirement allowance	4.6	4.8	3.2	1.7	2.6	2.2	1.7	1.9
nditions of work	3.3	2.5	4.8	3.7	2.6	1.8	3.2	1.6
Working hours	1.0	0.4	2.5	1.4	0.8	0.7	1.5	0.7
Vacations, holidays	0.9	0.4	0.2	0.2	0.2	0.5	0.5	0.2
Other conditions	1.4	1.6	2.1	2.1	1.6	0.6	1.1	0.6
ect of collective contract	0.8	1.3	0.5	0.6	0.7	0.4	0.2	0.2
nagement, personnel	17.2	16.8	14.9	18.4	12.6	6.9	7.3	9.1
Participation in mgmt.	0.1	—	0.1	—	—	—	0.1	0.2
Objection to work curtailment	1.7	1.8	1.5	1.4	1.3	0.7	0.9	0.8
Dismissal, restitution	12.4	11.4	9.2	11.6	8.4	4.2	4.6	5.9
Other personnel matters	3.1	3.6	4.2	5.3	2.9	2.1	1.8	2.1
lfare provision	0.8	0.8	1.0	1.0	0.5	0.4	0.3	0.1
her	0.7	0.7	0.7	11.3	10.8	16.6	4.1	2.2

SOURCE: Japan. Ministry of Labor, *Rodo Sogi Tokei* (Labor Disputes Statistics), for 1963, pp. 394–395.

Evolution of Dispute Settlement Machinery

The Trade Union Act of 1945 set up a system of permanent, tripartite commissions to settle labor disputes of all workers on land and at sea, including public servants and workers employed in government enterprises as well as in privately owned industries. It was shown in an earlier chapter that a severe test of the strength of the system followed quickly after it came into legal force, before the members of the central and local Labor Relations Commissions either on land or at sea had had time to get really acquainted with the mechanism of the system. The test came from the inflation that swept the Japanese economy, resulting in a drastic fall of real wages and mounting economic difficulty for the workers. It was noted that workers in state railways, telephone, telegraph, and postal services and in other national or local public utility works, were strongly organized in trade-unions, as were teachers in public schools, who were employees either of the central government or of local public authorities. These workers were all demanding higher wages and better treatment. The Law for Adjustment of Labor Relations, enacted in 1946, supplementing the Trade Union Act as regards the work of dispute settlement for public utility workers, had provided for a thirty-day cooling-off period, which meant that those workers were able to launch a strike only upon the expiration of thirty days after they had served notice of the strike action with the public authorities. Instead of weakening the public utility workers, the provision of a cooling-off period only served to strengthen them, because they were willing to bide their time. They had satisfied this legal requirement and were free to engage in a spectacular strike action, involving at least two and half million workers, when the general strike to take place on February 1, 1947, was planned.

We recall how the showdown was averted by the intervention at the eleventh hour of Supreme Commander MacArthur. We saw how this incident led to the issuance of the famous or fateful *"Ma-Shokan"* which suggested, or, rather, enjoined the Prime Minister of Japan to take measures to treat public servants and the workers engaged in various public enterprises separately from the workers in private industries. Furthermore, the same letter enjoined the prohibition of dispute acts of public servants and workers in public enterprises.

The action immediately taken by the government by an executive order (Order No. 201, July 31, 1948) giving effect to SCAP's letter had to be formalized subsequently by a series of legislative acts of the Diet. The legislative acts included the following:

1. Revision of the National Public Servants Act, December, 1948.

2. Enactment of laws governing the public corporations of national railways (1948), government monopolies (1948), and tele-communications (telephone and telegraph) (1952).

3. Enactment of Public Corporations and National Enterprises Labor Relations Act, December, 1948.

4. Enactment of Local Public Servants Act, December, 1950.

5. Enactment of Local Public Enterprises Labor Relations Act, July, 1952.

Changes in the systems of dispute settlement brought about by these legislative actions will be explained very briefly in the following sections.

Apportionment of Dispute Settlement Work

The foregoing enumeration of the laws enacted in this country seems bewildering, especially in the complexity of the mechanism of labor legislation. However, a careful analysis will show that the mechanism is not nearly so complicated as it seems at first sight. Under the revised system or systems of dispute settlement, Japanese workers can be divided into three categories, according to the degrees of trade-union rights which they enjoy. In order to deal with these different categories of workers, about as many different government agencies have been set up.

If we take as workers' basic trade-union rights the four rights of organization, collective bargaining, trade agreement, and dispute acts (strikes, slowdowns, etc.), there is at one extreme the category of such workers as policemen, firemen, prison guards, and men in maritime police work. To these workers all the four rights are denied. At the other extreme are workers who are enjoying all four rights. To this last category belong the vast majority of workers employed in privately owned enterprises. Between the two extremes are the white-collar public servants of the national or local governments and the workers employed by public corporations and various national or local public enterprises. In addition, forming a special category, are the workers employed in public utilities not necessarily owned or operated by government or public authorities, but which are of great public importance, because of which the worker's rights are somewhat restricted.

With the exception of the policemen, firemen, prison guards, and men in maritime police work, all workers are free to form or not to form, and to join or not to join, unions, and to engage in collective bargaining, but the right to enter into collective agreement is denied national public servants. Workers in public corporations and in national public enterprises may conclude trade agreements on certain limited items, but are prohibited from engaging in dispute acts (strikes, picketing, slowdowns, and so on). Details will be explained later.

Government Agencies of Dispute Settlement

There are five government agencies or authorities responsible for personnel administration and the settlement of disputes.

The first and the most important of the government agencies is the National Personnel Authority (*Jin-ji In*) created by the National Public Servants Act 1947. This Act forbids policemen, firemen, and prison guards to exercise any trade-union rights. The same Act forbids white-collar national public servants to enter into collective agreements or to engage in any dispute act. These workers are outside the jurisdiction of the Trade Union Law, the Labor Relations Adjustment Law, the Labor Standards Law, and the Mariners' Law. Their working conditions come under the Regulations of the National Personnel Authority.

Since all workers in Japan, with the exception of policemen, firemen, prison guards, and maritime police, are free to organize and bargain collectively in one way or another, all staff in national public services are organized, though the rights to have collective agreements with the government authorities or to engage in dispute acts is denied to them by this law.

Of the 8,359,876 organized workers in Japan on June 30, 1961, 287,748 were national public servants, belonging to 281 unions. They represented 3.4 per cent of all organized workers.

Second in order among the government agencies are the local governments (city, town), which employ workers covered by the Local Public Servants Act. They have the right to organize, to bargain collectively, and to enter into collective agreements, but are forbidden to engage in dispute acts. In 1961, there were 1,315,813 local public servants organized, representing 15.7 per cent of the total organized workers. They belonged to 3,440 unions. This shows how big an employer the government (including central and local governments) is and how embarrassed the government could be if the workers had, as they did at first, the right to engage in work stoppages and other dispute acts.

The third of the government agencies set up for the purpose of disposal of labor relations problems is the Public Corporations Labor Relations Commission, created under the Public Corporations and National Enterprises Act. The workers in public corporations and national public enterprises have the rights to organize, to bargain collectively, and to enter into collective agreements, but may not engage in dispute acts. In 1961, there were 953,012 workers organized, belonging to seventy-seven unions. They represented 11.4 per cent of the total organized workers.

The fourth government agency to deal with the labor relations problems of the local public enterprises is the Local Labor Relations Commission of each prefecture, set up originally under the Trade Union Act. So-called "local public enterprises" include local (i.e. intra-prefectural) railways, tramways, automobile haulage, electricity, gas, water, and so on, and the workers engaged in these services are forbidden to engage in dispute acts, though they have all other trade-union rights. No new government agency was created to deal with these workers. While the public servants in national or local governments and workers in national or local public enterprises were released from application of the Trade Union Law and came under separate laws creating new agencies to deal with their problems, here an exception was made. It was arranged to keep the workers in local public enterprises under the jurisdiction of the Local Labor Relations Commissions created by the Trade Union Act. Normally, the work of the Central and Local Labor Relations Commissions is to deal with workers in private enterprises. This exception was made here because of the small number of workers coming under this category. In 1961, there were 154,285 workers, belonging to 396 unions. They represented 1.8 per cent of the total organized workers.

The fifth government agency dealing with labor relations problems on the grandest scale is the Central Labor Relations Commission, together with the Local Labor Relations Commissions, created under the Trade Union Act. They deal with the labor relations problems in all private industries on land. Last come the Central and Local Maritime Labor Relations Commissions, also created by the Trade Union Act, to deal with the labor relations problems of workers at sea. In 1961, there were 5,649,018 members belonging to 20,048 unions, and representing 67.8 per cent of all organized workers covered by the Trade Union Act and the Labor Relations Adjustment Act.

The accompanying table of dispute settlement agencies, unionization, and union rights gives a synoptic view of the principal current laws, the government agencies created under these laws for administration of personnel and adjustment of labor relations problems, the extent to which the workers of the

TABLE 46
DISPUTE SETTLEMENT AGENCIES, UNIONIZATION, AND UNION RIGHTS (1961)

Applicable principal laws*	Administering agency	Number of unions	Number of members*	Association	Collective bargaining	Collective agreement	Dispute acts
Trade-Union Act Labor Relations Adjustment Act	Central & Local Lab. Rel. Comm. Central & Local Maritime Labor Rel. Comm.	20,048 82.7%	5,649,018 67.6%	Yes	Yes	Yes	Yes
Public Corporations & Public Enterprises Act	Pub. Corp. Labor Rel. Commissions	72 0.3%	953,012 11.4%	Yes	Yes	Yes	No
Local Public Enterprises Act	Local Labor Rel. Commissions	396 1.6%	154,285 1.8%	Yes	Yes	Yes	No
Local Public Servants Act	Local Govs. & Local Public Authorities	3,440 14.2%	1,315,813 15.7%	Yes	Yes	Yes	No
National Public Servants Act	National Personnel Authority (Policemen; Jailors; firemen; etc.)	281 1.2%	287,748 3.4%	Yes	Yes	No	No
		0	0	No	No	No	No
Totals		24,237 100%	8,359,876 100%	—	—	—	—

*SOURCES: for material in these columns are *Rodo Hakusho* 1961, p. 204, and *Roppo Zensho*, 1963.

various categories are organized in trade-unions, and the various trade-union rights enjoyed by these workers.

Work Record of the Labor Relations Boards

As already explained, the functions of the labor relations boards are to examine the qualifications of unions and to certify them, and to deal with unfair labor practices. As far as these functions are concerned, they are to some extent similar to those of the National Labor Relations Board in the United States.

However, unlike those in the United States, the labor relations boards in Japan have, in addition, the functions of conciliation, mediation, and arbitration in labor disputes. The following three tables show to what extent labor relations boards of Japan have carried out their assigned functions.

Besides the figures for the labor relations boards concerning workers in private industries, there are statistics for maritime workers and also for public servants and employees in public corporations. However, because of space limitation, we cannot provide statistics other than those in Tables 47, 48, and 49.

TABLE 47

EXAMINATION OF UNION QUALIFICATIONS (1950–1961)

Year	Cases brought in	Modifications counseled	Withdrawn	Qualification approved	Qualification denied	Examination completed
1950	7,082	2,268	636	6,164	74	6,874
1952	4,858	621	306	4,475	8	4,789
1954	3,918	381	242	3,440	6	3,688
1956	3,700	422	311	3,228	3	3,542
1958	3,324	418	349	2,844	4	3,194
1960	3,027	388	366	2,539	2	2,907
1961	2,812	430	361	2,184	3	2,548
Total	48,731[a]	7,522	4,415	43,823	200	48,450

[a] Totals are for the twelve-year period, 1949 (June to December) to 1961.
SOURCE: *Rodo Iinkai Nenpo 15*, p. 155; figures supplied by the Labor Ministry.

THE PRESENT STRENGTH OF ORGANIZED LABOR AND PROBLEMS OF ORGANIZATION

Numerical Strength of Organized Labor

This history deals with labor in Japan, which is at the stage of industrial evolution where organized labor plays a crucial role

TABLE 48

EXAMINATION OF UNFAIR LABOR PRACTICES CASES
(1950–1961)

Year	Cases brought in	Unfair labor practice				Unions' appeals[b]	Cases handled	Relief provided (R)[c]
		No. 1	No. 2	No. 3	No. 4			
1950	526	453	74	110	—	193(37)	499	21
1952	320	272	35	126	1	169(53)	335	45
1954	445	355	67	215	4	312(70)	443	43
1956	367	288	91	172	6	282(71)	350	26
1958	443	329	100	239	7	351(79)	442	40
1960	392	256	130	203	4	339(86)	375	51
1961	491	361	135	234	7			
Total[a]	5,185	4,053	1,015	2,211	52	3,490(74)	4,991	133

[a] Totals are for 1949 (June–December) to 1961.

[b] In parentheses are the percentages of union appeals against the total.

[c] Relief provided (R) is computed as follows:
$$R \ \ total \ relief \ cases \times 2 + part \ relief \ cases$$
$$Orders \ issued \times 2$$
In this condensed tabulation, we have omitted the detailed figures of orders issued by the Labor Relations Commission for: (1) total relief, (2) part relief, (3) no relief ordered, (4) appeal rejected. We have also omitted the figures of "non-acceptance" of the Commission's final decisions.

TABLE 49

DISPUTE SETTLEMENT WORK OF LABOR RELATIONS
COMMISSIONS (1946–1961)

Year	Conciliation		Mediation		Arbitration		Totals	
	Cases	Per cent	Cases	Per cent	Cases	Per cent	Cases	Per cent
1946	136	72.3	40	21.3	—	—	188	100
1948	1,087	76.8	318	22.7	6	0.5	1,414	100
1950	887	79.6	227	20.4	—	—	1,114	100
1952	889	84.5	162	15.4	1	0.1	1,052	100
1954	931	91.0	90	8.8	2	1.2	1,023	100
1956	984	95.5	43	4.2	3	0.3	1,030	100
1958	1,108	94.1	66	5.6	3	0.3	1,177	100
1960	1,157	96.4	37	3.1	7	0.6	1,201	100
1961	1,719	94.0	98	5.4	12	0.6	1,829	100
Total[a]	15,808	—	2,150	—	50	—	18,092	100

[a] Totals are for the sixteen-year period 1946–1961; here the table has been condensed and the figures given here do not add up to the totals.
SOURCE: *Rodo Iinkai Nenpo 15*, p. 253.

in the economic and industrial life of the nation. We saw that there was a phenomenal growth of organized labor immediately after the MacArthur Revolution began, both in the number of unions and of union members. That expansion continued steadily during the postwar years, as Table 50 shows. This steady expansion of trade-unions was interrupted only by the outbreak of the Korean War, which caused a temporary setback.

In 1962, total union membership was nearly nine million, representing 36.2 per cent of the total employed workers; this

TABLE 50

INCREASE OF UNIONS AND UNION MEMBER-SHIP (1945–1962)

Year	Unions	Members	Organized percentage
1945	509	380,677	3.2
1946	17,266	4,925,598	41.5
1947	23,323	5,692,179	45.3
1948	33,926	6,677,427	53.0
1949	34,688	6,655,483	55.8
1950	29,144	5,773,908	46.2
1951	27,644	5,686,774	42.6
1952	27,851	5,719,560	40.3
1953	30,129	5,927,079	38.8
1954	31,456	6,075,746	37.6
1955	32,012	6,285,878	37.8
1956	34,073	6,463,118	35.4
1957	36,084	6,762,601	35.5
1958	37,823	6,984,032	34.4
1959	39,303	7,211,401	33.9
1960	41,561	7,661,568	33.8
1961	45,096	8,359,876	36.1
1962	47,812	8,971,156	36.2

SOURCE: Ministry of Labor (*Rodo Kumiai Kihon Chosa*). Omiya Goro, *Rodo Keizai No Aramashi*, p. 107.

compares favorably with West Germany (35.0 per cent) and the United States (32.0 per cent), though Japan is still behind the United Kingdom, which leads the world, with 44.0 per cent. The aim of the organization as provided by the Trade Union Law was "to enhance the status of workers by enabling them to stand on an equal footing with the employers in their bargaining process." One could well imagine that the tremendous growth in the numerical strength of organized labor served to raise the status of workers.

However, owing to the haste with which the organization grew, the outside influence of the occupation authorities, the stresses of Japan's position between the cold war camps, and the so-called "dual structure" of the Japanese economy—to be explained later in detail—the trade-unions of Japan present features unfamiliar to the industrialized nations of Europe or America. One of these peculiarities is that a very large majority, indeed more than 95 per cent of the unions, are "enterprise unions," organized along the lines of enterprise, rather than of craft or industry. Pure craft unions or industrial unions, which are common in Western countries, are rare in Japan. Moreover, in the big enterprises employing 500 or more workers, including government and municipal offices, organized workers represent around 90 per cent. On the other hand, in those enterprises with from 30 to 90 employees, it is around 9 per cent, and in the small shops of less than 30 employees, it falls to 3 per cent. This means that the activities of organized labor are concentrated in big enterprises. Clearly, medium-sized and small enterprises have tended to be neglected.

This tendency arises from the "dual structure" of the Japanese economy and at the same time constitutes the factor that perpetuates the dual structure.

As for the "enterprise unions," we should note that by the nature of their organization, they contribute to the stability of relations between management and workers. The union is interested in the financial or business success of the enterprise and is likely to co-operate with management. The members of the enterprise union are, in a sense, "serving two masters," the enterprise and the union. It cannot be denied that they are equally concerned with the interest of the union members and with the continued good business of the enterprise in which the workers are employed. For this reason, there is a sort of dualism in the loyalty of the members. Therefore, in the case of a protracted dispute involving members of unions in big enterprises, it is most difficult to continue a united action to the end. From the theoretical point of view, it will be argued that the workers in smaller enterprises should be urged to join the unions of workers of big enterprises for the sake of solidarity and to ensure the improvement of general working conditions. However, in practice, the workers in small or medium-size enterprises are left out.

However, this does not actually mean that the enterprise

TABLE 51
TYPES OF ORGANIZATION AND THEIR MEMBERSHIP
(1962)

	Unions	Percentage of total	Members	Percentage of total
Enterprise unions	22,404	90.0	7,228,660	80.6
Industrial unions	933	3.7	977,909	10.9
Craft unions	1,219	4.9	361,312	4.0
Local or regional	141	0.6	120,332	1.3
Other forms	202	0.8	282,943	3.2
Total	24,899	100.0	8,971,156	100.0

SOURCE: Ministry of Labor (*Rodo Kumiai Kihon Chosa*). Omiya Goro, *op. cit.*, p. 108.

TABLE 52
MEMBERSHIP OF MAJOR NATIONAL LABOR FEDERATIONS
(1962)

Unions	Membership	Percentages
Sohyo (Nihon Rodo Kumiai So-Hyogi Kai)	4,122,099	45.9
Domei Kaigi (Zen Nihon Rodo Sodomei Kumiai Kaigi)	1,202,696	13.4
Zen Nihon Rodo Kumiai Kaigi	798,621	8.9
Zen Nihon Rodo Sodomai	406,378	4.5
Zen Nihon Kankoshoku Ro Kyogi Kai	39,062	0.4
Shin Sanbetsu (Zenkoku Sangyo Betsu Rodo Kumiai Rengo)	56,779	0.6
Independent unions	1,335,392	14.9
Others	2,276,749	25.0
Total	8,971,156	100.0

SOURCE: Ministry of Labor (*Rodo Kumiai Kihon Chosa*). Omiya Goro, *op. cit.*, p. 109.

unions remain within the walls of the enterprises. They have formed loose federations or councils along industrial or regional lines, which in turn have grouped together in national federations or councils. As the above table shows, there are actually three big national federations: Sohyo (Nihon Rodo Kumiai So-Hyogi Kai, General Council of Japanese Trade-Unions), which has an aggregate membership of 4,122,099, representing 45.9 per cent of all organized workers; Domei Kaigi (Zen Nihon Rodo Sodomei Kumiai

Kaigi, All Japan Congress of Trade-Unions), with a total membership of 1,202,696, or 13.4 per cent; and Shin San-Betsu (Zenkoku
Sangyo Betsu Rodo Kumiai Rengo, National Federation of Industrial Unions), with 56,779 members, representing 0.6 per cent.

The nature of the formation and problems of these federations will be explained later. Meanwhile, we must look further into
the "dual structure" of the Japanese economy and the extent of the
problems of medium-sized and small industries peculiar to the
Japanese economy, and which hamper the expansion of workers'
unions.

Problem of "Dual Structure" of Japanese Industry

A brief explanation was given above of the "dual structure" of
Japanese industry as a factor hampering the growth of a more
sound and powerful union movement. What is meant by "dual
structure" and how it came about will now be discussed.

Japan's modern economy started late, as compared with the
Western industrial powers. Efforts were made to catch up within a
brief period; the introduction of the machinery and techniques of
the more advanced Western nations with the use of very limited
capital resulted in the modernization of only a limited sector of
Japan's economy and industry. The large enterprises consequently
reached the highest productivity and the best conditions of
employment. Workers engaged in medium-sized or small-scale
industries which did not have the necessary capital had to content
themselves with lower wages, longer hours, and less satisfactory
conditions of work because of the inferior productivity of their
workplaces. Such was the situation that persisted before the war.
The war ruined Japan's industries. Her techniques suffered from
long retardation. The efforts of the big enterprises after the war to
catch up with the advanced nations of the West produced once
more the conditions which had given rise to the dual structure.
Forces were working relentlessly in this direction before the
government or the trade-unions realized it fully.

One result of the dual structure was a distinct difference
between the labor practices of big enterprises with abundant
capital outlay and modern equipment and those of the small
enterprises without such benefits or amenities. The former, in
looking for necessary manpower, will not depend on recruitment
in the general labor market, because they can avail themselves of
the best graduates of the colleges and technical schools more

readily than the small enterprises. They give the necessary training to the newly appointed personnel and keep them as lifetime employees. "Life employment," with periodical or annual increments in wages, has evolved in the big enterprises as one of the features of Japanese economy. However, this applied only to the big enterprises, since small enterprises could not afford these practices. The result is that while workers occasionally drop out from the big enterprises and move into small enterprises, the reverse (moving from small to big enterprises) seldom happens. In these conditions, the labor market in big enterprises is in a sense a "blocked market."

Another characteristic of the dual structure is that it has perpetuated the chronic pool of unemployment, or "disguised unemployment." In the large number of medium-sized, enterprises, and more particularly in the small ones with little capital, inferior equipment, and lower productivity, the opportunity for employment is very limited. The wages are low, the hours long; often family members return and threaten the small number of outsiders who are employed. As a result there has always been and always will be the danger of unemployment, disguised unemployment, or underemployment in the smaller enterprises.

One new factor that has entered the economic scene is the lively growth, spurred on by the adoption of technological innovations, of the gross national product (GNP) in Japan since 1955. During the years 1955–1961, the annual average growth was 10.5 per cent for Japan, while the figure for the United States was 2.2 per cent, for the United Kingdom 2.5 per cent, France 4.2 per cent, Italy 5.9 per cent, and even West Germany only 6.3 per cent. Thus, the rate of economic growth has been even more brisk than in the years 1946–1954, when the growth per year was generally regarded as very high—9.6 per cent. Such a phenomenal change in GNP is bound to affect the labor market, and for that reason no hasty conclusion should be made; nonetheless, it must be noted that the dual structure of industry has been a perplexing problem in this country.

Problems of Small and Medium-sized Enterprises

In the laws relating to banking or financial matters, enterprises employing 300 or less employees or those with a capital of 10 million yen or less are treated as *chū-shō kigyo*—small or medium-sized enterprises, but in common practice, those with 500 or more employees are treated as big enterprises and all the rest as medium-sized or small; for practical reasons, we shall follow that practice here also. How large a proportion enterprises of various sizes occupy in the total picture of Japanese industry is shown below:

TABLE 53
PROPORTION OF ENTERPRISES ACCORD-
ING TO SIZE (1960) (per cent)

Workers employed	Enterprises	Workers
1	12.1	0.6
2–4	23.2	3.4
5–9	25.8	8.5
10–29	26.5	21.2
30–99	9.6	23.5
100–499	2.4	22.7
500 or more	0.4	20.1
Total	100.0	100.0

SOURCE: Statistical Bureau at Prime Minister's Office, *Report on Statistical Investigation of Enterprises*, 1960.

Low Rate of Union Organization.   One thing we must not overlook in this connection is that in small industries the rate of organization of workers in trade-unions is quite low. The smaller the enterprise, the lower the rate of organization, as shown in Table 54.

TABLE 54
RATES OF ORGANIZATION ACCORDING TO THE SIZE OF
ENTERPRISES IN PRIVATE INDUSTRIES (1960)

Size of Enterprise (number employed)	Total Employees	Organized Employees	Number of Unions	Rate of Organization (percentage)
Over 500	4,670,000	3,228,290	8,995	69.1
499–100	2,180,000	839,431	6,170	38.5
99–30	2,990,000	264,771	5,834	8.9
29 or less	7,810,000	250,168	3,418	3.2
uncertain	uncertain	(61,558)	1,330	—
Total	17,680,000	4,644,218	25,747	26.3

SOURCE: Japan. Ministry of Labor, *Basic Inquiry of Trade Unions*, 1960.

We saw earlier that the rate of organization of all Japanese workers was 34.5 per cent and that this compared favorably with the advanced Western industrial powers (e.g., the United States, 35.2 per cent; West Germany, 37.4 per cent; the United Kingdom, 43.3 per cent), but when we look more closely into the situation of small private enterprises, we find that the rate falls to 8.9 per cent in enterprises employing from 30 to 90 employees and to 3.2 per cent at workshops with 29 or fewer employees.

Since space will not permit further statistical evidence to substantiate the general statement, we must content ourselves with the conclusions drawn from the statistics of frequency of labor disputes in the smaller industries, demands presented by workers in disputes, duration of strikes, wages, hours, and the extent of welfare work provided in the smaller industries.

Labor Disputes in Small Enterprises. Comparing the frequency of labor disputes in the large and small enterprises, we find that in recent years the rate has been rising much higher in the small than in large enterprises. Thus, if 1955 is taken as the base year, with an index figure of 100, for enterprises of 1,000 or more employees, the figure rose to 270 in 1961, whereas for enterprises of less than 100 employees, the figure was 410. We must also note that in the smaller industries, disputes are accompanied by work stoppages and other dispute acts more often than in big industries. Thus, for enterprises with less than 100 employees, the rate rose from 100 in 1955 to 540 in 1960 and to 766 in 1961, whereas for big industries with from 500 to 999 employees, the figure rose to only 135 in 1961. For the bigger enterprises of 1,000 or more employees, the figure dropped from 100 in 1955 to 22 in 1961.

The nature of the demands presented by the workers in smaller enterprises and by workers in larger enterprises also differ. In the former case, the workers are still demanding recognition of their unions or their union rights—a demand which has practically disappeared in recent years in big industries. So-called "negative demands," which include opposition to the closing down of a firm, opposition to dismissals, demand for re-employment of the workers who have been dismissed, and the like, are more or less common in the small enterprises, but are rare or are rapidly diminishing in the large industries.

As to the duration of the disputes, they last almost as long in the small industries as in big industries, if not longer. In 1961, for example, as the table below shows, at workshops with less than 100 employees, 35.2 per cent of the disputes lasted 31 days or more, while at the large enterprises of 1,000 or more employees, 33.6 per cent of the disputes lasted 31 days or longer.

TABLE 55
DURATION OF DISPUTES BY SIZE OF IN-
DUSTRIES (1961)
(per cent)

Employees	Number of disputes lasting		
	−10 days	10–30 days	+30 days
−100	41.5	23.3	35.2
100–499	36.0	27.5	36.5
500–999	33.4	35.5	31.5
+1,000	30.4	36.0	33.6

SOURCE: Japan. Ministry of Labor, *Labor Disputes Statistical Report.*

Wages and Hours in Small Enterprises.   While we must, for the sake of brevity, omit any statistics on wages, we can say that in small enterprises, the wage level is quite low compared with that in larger enterprises. If we take the cash income in the manufacturing industry, and take enterprises with 500 or more employees in 1961 as the base (100), the figure for enterprises of 100–499 employees was 74.5; for enterprises of 30–99 employees 61.7; and for smaller enterprises of less than 30 employees, as low as 49.3. This means that the worker in a small enterprise is actually earning less than half as much as a worker in a big enterprise.

The same trend seems to apply to working hours. Statistics show that in enterprises employing 5,000 or more workers, 56.9 per cent of the workers work a seven-hour day, and only 1.1 per cent are working an eight-hour day. On the other hand, in smaller enterprises with from 30 to 99 employees, the proportion is reversed: 78.2 per cent of the workers work an eight-hour day while only 3.4 per cent of the workers work a seven-hour day. Since, as a rule, the working hours are longer at smaller enterprises, there is need for practical measures to protect the welfare of the workers in smaller enterprises.

Welfare Provisions in Small Enterprises.   Finally, as regards welfare provisions, anyone uninformed about the emphasis laid upon welfare provisions by both employers and the unions of Japan will be agreeably surprised to see the statistics on the subject. Indeed, welfare provisions might be considered as constituting an outstanding feature of Japanese factories. As Table 56 shows, in 1962, 82.9 per cent of the enterprises had welfare provisions of one kind or another—among them housing accommodations for employees, provisions for medical care and pharmaceuticals, provisions for hygiene and health, accommodations for providing food (mainly lunch), sales at the company store at cost or at reduced prices, education, recreation, and athletics.

TABLE 56

WELFARE PROVISIONS IN JAPANESE ENTERPRISES (1962)
(per cent)

		Workers employed		
Welfare Provisions	Average	30–99	100–499	+500
Enterprises with welfare provisions	82.9	78.5	93.8	99.5
Housing accommodation	63.0	56.6	77.4	94.7
Medical and pharmaceutical	15.1	5.2	33.6	83.9
Hygienic	40.0	31.8	58.2	81.7
Baby-feeding	0.7	0.2	0.5	9.4
Meal provision	20.1	15.3	29.9	50.5
Sales	5.5	1.2	12.0	46.0
Education, recreation	20.2	12.3	35.5	73.0
Sports, athletic	23.3	14.7	40.9	76.4

SOURCE: Japan. Ministry of Labor, Statistical and Investigation Division, *Inquiry into Welfare Work Directly Undertaken by Enterprises,* December, 1962.

Now, while the general picture presented by this statistical table is interesting enough, a close examination reveals at once a striking difference between large and small enterprises. The smaller enterprises apparently cannot afford to extend welfare provisions to their employees, and this is certainly one of the important factors leading to the restiveness of the workers and the disputes between the workers and their employers. At small enterprises, welfare work is more often the product of the thinking of a single man, the employer; as a result the plan often lacks steadiness or continuity. Often more interest is shown in cultural, educational, and sport activities; provisions for hygiene and health are apt to be neglected. For example, a characteristic deficiency among the small enterprises is the absence or inadequacy of retirement plans for workers who have served long in the enterprise. This is a matter about which government authorities and trade-unions are seriously concerned, yet nothing has been proposed to improve the situation.

TABLE 57

MEMBERSHIP OF MAJOR FEDERATIONS OF LABOR
UNIONS (1961–1962)

	1961		1962		Increase
Major federations	*Number*	*Per-centage of total*	*Number*	*Per-centage of total*	*over previous year*
1. Sohyo (General Council of Jap. Trade-Unions)	3,968,123	47.5	4,122,099	45.9	153,976
2. Domei Kaigi (Jap. Confed. of Labor)	(1,107,867)	(13.3)	1,202,696	13.4	94,829
Zenrō (Jap. Trade-Union Congress)	(751,497)	(9.0)	798,621	8.9	47,124
Sodomei (General Fed. of Labor	356,370	4.3	406,378	4.5	50,008
Kanko Shoku Ro	——	—	39,062	0.4	39,062
3. Shin San-betsu (National Fed.)	42,847	0.5	56,779	0.6	13,932
4. Unaffiliated Unions	1,124,217	13.4	1,335,392	14.9	211,175
5. Others	2,133,119	25.5	2,276,749	25.4	143,630
Total	8,359,876	100.0	8,971,156	100.0	611,280

SOURCE: Ministry of Labor (*Rodo Kumiai Kihon Chosa*).

N.B. There are unions which are affiliated with two or more national federations. For this reason, the figures of the various federations do not add up to the total figures given at the bottom. The figure for Domei Kaigi in parentheses for 1961 indicate the number that belonged to Zenrō in that year. The figure for Zenrō in parentheses in 1961 indicate the number that belonged to Zenrō, except those members that belonged to Sodomei.

The Japan Institute of Labor (Nihon Rodo Kyokai) published recently a series of booklets dealing with various problems of labor in Japan. In one of these, which we have used very freely in this section of our study,[12] the writer, Professor Yoshitani Yoshio, has made an analysis of the whole problem of medium-sized and small-scale enterprises, and mentions the four basic difficulties of small enterprises in Japan. The first is that in the small enterprises the separation of capital from management has not taken place as yet. The problem lies in the fact that, as a rule, the employer is the owner, a capitalist; he may be one of four types—a dictator, a moralist, a patriarch, or a tyrant. Difficulties are inherent in each of these types. The second difficulty lies in the fact that the employer-worker relationship in a small enterprise is apt to be too intimate and human, which can lead to an unmanageable *impasse* when a dispute arises. Third, in a small firm the employer usually resorts to "pre-modernistic" methods of employment, in which relatives of the employer are apt to be favored, and which are apt to lead to other abuses and a peculiar sort of inequality among employees. If the worker is employed through a channel such as a public employment agency, he need not entertain feelings either of inferiority or of a special bond with his employer. Lastly, productivity is lower at small enterprises than at the large ones, as has already been pointed out.

Orientation of Major Labor Federations

General Remarks. The three major national labor federations, Sohyo, Domei Kaigi, and Shin Sanbetsu, have already been noted. The primary objective of this section is to set forth the main characteristics of these three organizations. By way of introduction, it will be helpful to point out a few general features particularly noticeable in the federations of Japanese trade-unions.

First, it is a "divided" rather than a "united" front that the workers of Japan have at present. The United States has AFL-CIO, a remarkable alliance brought about by the merger in 1955 of the AF of L and the CIO. Samuel Gompers was completely against disunity, hence the motto he adopted: "United we stand; divided we fall." The ADGB (Allgemeiner Deutscher Gewerkschafts Bund) of Germany was split with the division of Germany, but West Germany has a united DGB (Deutscher Gewerkschafts Bund) and England has the TUC (Trades Union Congress) organized in 1868—the first year of the Meiji. No matter what the reason for it is, no one can deny that the divided front spells weakness.

Second, as already pointed out, compared with other industrialized nations, the rate of organization of workers in trade-unions in Japan is not low (36.2 per cent), but when it is recalled that the total number of employed workers was nearly 25 million (24,782,199) in 1962 and the number of organized workers was 8,971,156, the question arises as to why the rest are not organized. Moreover, those who belong to Sohyo, Domei Kaigi (including Zenrō) and Shin Sanbetsu total only 5,381,574, or 59.9 per cent of the organized workers. This means that over 40 per cent of the organized workers are "independent," or unaffiliated with any national federation. This is anomalous, if not unhealthy, in the opinion of anyone interested in trade-union movement. The leaders of the movement in Japan are endeavoring to improve this situation, about which both the ICFTU and the WFTU are seriously concerned. This means that in a few years' time the structural shape of national federations in Japan may be somewhat different from what it is now.

Third, in connection with the point raised above, it should be noted that the dominant type of national federation is similar to what the British call the "general unions." In Sohyo, which comprises half of the organized workers, there are national and local public servants, teachers, and the employees (both white and blue collar) of the national railways. Numerically, these workers constitute two thirds of the total membership of Sohyo. The fact that these workers are either servants in national or local public authorities, or employees in public corporations, inevitably influences the policies and practices of Sohyo. There are problems inherent in the formation and structure of Sohyo that have given rise to difficulties, which will be discussed later in connection with the orientation of union federations.

Fourth, it should be noted that all national federations of labor in Japan are increasingly turning their attention to the problems of smaller enterprises and the enterprise unions, which are in many ways a hindrance to the growth of healthy and robust trade-unionism in this country. Minimum wages, productivity, hours, social security, and, lastly, the ILO Convention No. 87, are among the major questions to which all federations of labor are directing their attention.

In concluding these general remarks, we venture to add that with the exception of the brief setback experienced during the years of the Korean War and shortly thereafter (1950–1953), the membership of trade-unions in this country has been steadily increasing from 3 to 4 per cent per year, and one may assume that as they are growing in maturity they are gaining the confidence of the public.

Before turning to the description of the orientation of the three national federations, the reader should glance over Table 57, which gives the membership of the major federations of labor.

Platform and Orientation of Sohyo. The General Council of Japanese Trade-Unions (Nihon Rodo Kumiai So-Hyogi Kai), known generally in Japan and abroad by the abbreviated name Sohyo, was founded on July 11, 1950, as a loose federation of twenty-nine unions with a total membership of 2,760,000. Earlier in these pages it was shown how a democratization movement, with the moral support of the occupation authority, had started during February of the previous year. The movement was led by Hosoya Matsuta, who had formed the Democratization League in the Congress of Industrial Unions (Sanbetsu Minshuka Domei), and Takano Minoru, who was the chief figure in the left wing of Sodomei. It was a healthy and vigorous reaction against the domination of the Communist leaders in the trade-union movement; in fact, that was how Sohyo was born. The outbreak of the Korean War supplied the impetus for the growth of the newly formed Sohyo. Many unions in the federation, led by the example of the National Railwaymen's Union, joined the newly organized ICFTU, and this undoubtedly helped Sohyo gain international status. The rise of Sohyo to power was, as we have seen, spectacular.

The character of Sohyo was shaped at the start, when its platform, or "Basic Program," was adopted at the foundation meeting on July 11, 1950. The first paragraph of that document, which could be called a "Preamble," reads as follows:

> The General Council of Japanese Trade-Unions intends to maintain or improve the working conditions of workers through the combined strength of all free and democratic unions of Japan, to raise their political and economic status, to promote the democratic revolution in Japan and at the same time establish a socialist society, thereby contributing to the founding of a human society in which freedom, equality, and peace are assured, by attaining economic expansion and independence of the nation.

It should be noted that the aim, as stated here, was to promote democratic revolution, to establish a socialist society, and to attain independence of the nation. There is nothing startling in these items for Japan of today. "Independence of the nation" was inserted at this time since the Japanese people did not know, when the declaration was adopted, how long the Allied Powers intended to occupy Japan.

In order to promote the above-mentioned basic ideas, this document enunciated five principles. Given below is the gist of the principles of the Basic Program.

1. A trade-union is a self-organized body with the purpose of maintaining or improving the common economic or social interests among the workers and is totally different in functions and character from a political party, which is organized with the direct objective of the acquisition of political power based on a specific political idea. Therefore, the trade-union must categorically reject any control or intervention from outside such as the government, management, and so on, and at the same time must be completely free and independent from any political party.

However, under the present condition of domination by the capitalist class, it is not possible to confine all activities of trade unions to the economic sphere. Their activities must of necessity extend to the political sphere.

Sohyo has been and is still severely criticized for its political propensities. This was for Sohyo a matter of principle from the outset.

2. Stability of livelihood is the basis for restoration of productivity and the condition of economic stabilization. As regards any reactionary attempt to bring about stability of capitalist economy through exploitation of workers, . . . we fight to the bitter end, exercising the rights of organization, strikes, and all other powers that trade-unions have at their command.

However, economic activities of trade-unions must in all cases be carried out constructively. . . . No movement of the destructive, extreme leftists which runs counter to the constructive should be tolerated.

The principle enunciated above should be noted because Sohyo, particularly, has been criticized for its leftist tendency in the conduct of disputes.

3. The interests of the working class are fundamentally opposed to those of the capitalist class. This is true through all history. . . . On the other hand, the interests of workers should basically be in agreement with one another. . . . Therefore, the workers' unions should co-operate with one another on a basis of sincerity and fraternity, believing that the interests of workers' unions are fundamentally united.

The first two lines here remind us of the declaration of the IWW, the historic syndicalist movement in the United States, while the line "This is true through all history . . ." is reminiscent of Marx's *Communist Manifesto*. However, we notice that what is stressed here is not the necessity for a proletarian or Communist revolution, but a close co-operation among the workers' unions.

4. For the emancipation of the working class, it is important to secure political power in the hands of the working class. However, the acquisition of political power must in any case be done through constitutional means. For this reason, the workers' unions must advance through the orderly channel of Constitution and laws.

In this section of the Basic Program emphasis is laid on constitutional and legal procedures. People have had misgivings about the leftist leaning of Sohyo, but we may rest assured that fundamentally Sohyo is a law-abiding organization declaring its respect for the Constitution and laws of the country.

5. In order to maintain permanent world peace, it is necessary to have recognized in different countries democracy based on economic welfare and freedom of the toiling masses, who constitute the majority of the people in each country. Autonomy and independence of all nations must be respected and guaranteed on the basis of mutual understanding, trust, and brotherliness. It is the power of international organization of democratic trade-unions which will pave the way for world peace.

As shown here, Sohyo stressed from the outset the need for maintenance of permanent world peace, and it was in accordance with the principle enunciated here that Sohyo took the most active, even aggressive, stand in favor of peace. Its naive behavior even proved embarrassing to the occupation authority in some cases.

In addition to the Basic Program, Sohyo adopted on March 12, 1951, a more concrete Program of Action, consisting of eleven items. We list the main points of the Program below, since it must be recognized that during the past twelve years, Sohyo has not failed to carry on activities designed to realize these points: (1) Opposition to low wages; demand for a minimum-wage system and for full employment. (2) A demand for the repeal of oppressive laws. (3) Opposition to collective bargaining agreements that infringe upon labor's basic rights. (4) A demand for the expansion of unemployment insurance and a more comprehensive social security system. (5) Equal pay for equal work. (6) A demand for the reduction of taxes. (7) Democratization of management; socialization of basic industries and of banks. (8) Reorganization of trade-unions on industrial lines. (9) Co-operation with democratic political parties for promoting democratic revolution in Japan. (10) Co-operation with ICFTU. (11) Emphasis on the "Four Principles of Peace": over-all peace, maintenance of neutrality, opposition to rearmament, and opposition to the use of Japanese territory as military bases.

Platform and Orientation of Domei Kaigi.   Until April, 1962, Zenrō (Japanese Trade-Union Congress) was the second largest national federation of trade-unions in this country, but the situation has changed since the formation of Domei Kaigi (Japanese Confederation of Labor) on April 26, 1962. A brief account of how the new organization appeared on the scene follows.

The organization of Zenrō in 1954, already described in some detail, by Sodomei, Zensen Domei (All-Textile Workers' Federation) Kaiin Kumiai (Seamen's Union), and Zen-ei En (Screen and Theatrical Workers' Union) was in many ways a prelude to the emergence of Domei Kaigi. These four union organizations had parted from Sohyo in protest against what they regarded as extremism in the conduct of the leaders of that organization. When Zenrō was organized, its combined membership was around 800,000. But this number multiplied rapidly in the following months to 1,400,000 with the affiliation of new members or new unions.

While this increase in the number of members was encouraging, the leaders realized that there was now need for reorganization of the entire body, especially since the structure of Sodomei and that of Domei Kaigi needed readjustment. In the meantime, among the unions of government workers and of employees of public corporations that had belonged to Sohyo, there were those who had misgivings about the conduct of Sohyo and who ultimately organized Zen Nihon Kanko Shokuro Kyogi Kai (National Council of Government and Public Corporation Workers' Unions) in 1959, splitting away from Sohyo. When this National Council was formed, aiming at democratization of the unions of government and public corporation workers, it was natural that Zenrō, Sodomei, and the newly formed Zen Kanko come together to organize a united front to promote democratic trade-unionism.

Meetings of the three organizations took place, and they formed on April 26, 1962, Zen Nihon Rodo Sodomei Kumiai Kaigi (Domei Kaigi, by abbreviation; Japanese Confederation of Labor, in English).

Platform of Domei Kaigi. The platform of Domei Kaigi adopted on the day of its inauguration was as follows:

1. We regard the realization of progress, prosperity, and social justice under democracy as the principle of free and democratic trade-unions. Domei Kaigi will consist of such free and democratic unions as its constituent members.

2. We will engage in positive struggles against the forces that try to restrict the rights of workers or destroy trade-union organizations, the totalitarian forces of the right and left, and all other antilabor movements, and will work for workers' organization within the country that enables us to advance our struggles effectively.

3. We will secure full employment, and promote various measures to safeguard the rights of labor in order to raise the living standard and increase workers' welfare; we will work for improvement of conditions of work, shortening of working hours, increasing of leisure, establishment of a minimum-wage system, and expansion of social security.

4. We will promote the modernization of industry in order to bring about continuous prosperity of our national economy, and endeavor to establish a thoroughgoing industrial democracy by working out effective plans for raising productivity and actively participating in the inplementation of those plans.

5. We will promote the necessary social or political activities to enable the trade-unions to carry out their functions fully in the economic sphere, and to co-operate with political parties that agree with this purpose.

6. We will reject forces that tend to destroy democratic parliamentarism, uphold various principles of democracy that contribute to the endeavors for reform of present conditions, and work for the establishment of a society where man's freedom and equality are realized and the capacities of each individual are given the fullest play by the establishment of a welfare state.

7. We will co-operate with international labor organizations having common aims with us, and will contribute to permanent peace based on international justice, opposing communism, fascism, militarism, colonialism, racial discrimination, and all other reactionary tendencies, through an international organization of free and democratic trade-unions.

Program of Shin Sanbetsu (National Federation of Industrial Unions). For comparison, we give below the program of Shin Sanbetsu adopted in December, 1949, at its foundation meeting:

1. Establishment of fundamental workers' rights of organization and of collective bargaining; removal of restrictions on the right to strike.

2. Eight-hour day (six hours, in underground work).

3. Opposition to low wage policy; establishment of minimum-wage system; removal of sex discrimination in wages.

4. Establishment of social security system borne entirely by the government and the capitalists.

5. Opposition to munitions production, inflation for rearmament, and taxation of the masses.

6. Freedom of speech, assembly, and organization.

7. Repeal of public peace ordinances and other repressive laws.

8. Establishment of industrial democracy; nationalization of banks, electricity, coal, steel, and other vital industries.

9. Opposition to unemployment; promotion of peace and independence.

10. Thorough neutrality and over-all peace.

11. Opposition to rearmament and military agreements.

12. Opposition to all restrictions of trade, and establishment of economic independence.

13. Establishment of militant unionism, a united front of fighting unions.

14. Formation of a class political party of the masses; strengthening of united action between peasants and workers.

15. Fight against all Fascist movements and revolutionary tactics of the Communist Party.

16. Co-operation with the movement for independence of Asian Nations; co-operation with the world's peace forces.

IS A UNITED FRONT FOR JAPANESE UNIONS FEASIBLE?

A divided front spells weakness. This is a truth anywhere in the world, and Japan is no exception. It was pointed out earlier that the Japanese workers' unions presented a divided or disunited front. Is a united front feasible in this country? In this respect, the movement of organized labor in Japan is facing, at this writing, a crucial test. The key question at this point is the relationship of Japanese unions to the ICFTU. As the question is somewhat complicated, it will be examined at some length.

Sohyo and ICFTU

It will be recalled that Sohyo was formed in 1950 by the unions that had split away from the Congress of Industrial Unions (Sanbetsu Kaigi) in protest against the domination of the Communists in that organization. The new organization was designed to join in and co-operate closely with the ICFTU, which was started in the previous year. However, considering that there were still more unions withdrawing from Sanbetsu Kaigi, in order to enable all those unions to join the ICFTU in a bundle, the leaders considered it wise not to have the entire body of Sohyo affiliate immediately with the ICFTU, but to allow individual unions to take steps to affiliate separately for the time being. It was for this reason that such industrial unions as Zensen (Textile Workers' Union), Kaiin (Seamen's Union), Nikkyoso (Teachers' Union), Kokutetsu (National Railwaymen's Union), and Zen Nichiro (Casual Workers' Union) took steps to affiliate with the ICFTU. Sodomei was the only organization in the form of a national center that was affiliated with the ICFTU, while all others were admitted temporarily, as it were, being industrial unions. The intention of Sohyo to co-operate with the ICFTU was clearly declared in its Basic Program. However, despite the solemnly announced program, not only did Sohyo abandon its effort to have more unions join the ICFTU, but it began to enter into closer relations with the WFTU. That was why the unions in Sohyo eager for democratization of the workers' movement withdrew from it and formed Zenrō in 1954.

Zenrō and ICFTU

Zenrō, as we saw, was organized from the outset as a national center, designed to affiliate with the ICFTU. The unions which came under the aegis of Zenrō took immediate steps for Zenrō to apply for admission to the ICFTU in 1954. The application was rejected by the ICFTU because of an objection raised by the member unions of the ICFTU. At the time that Zenrō applied for admission, its structure was that of a national center, though its total membership (700,000 in 1954) was lower than that of the industrial unions in Sohyo belonging to the ICFTU (over 1,000,-000). If the matter were left as it stood then, it would mean that an organization formed as a national center for the purpose of affiliation with the ICFTU was rejected and unaffiliated, while several industrial unions were affiliated. In order to amend this anomalous situation, President Becu and Secretary-General Oldenbrock of the ICFTU visited Japan in 1954. The outcome of the visit was to continue to recognize the affiliation of individual unions as a temporary measure. But what resulted from the "temporary measure"?

Intervening Confusion

The outcome of the temporary measure since 1954 has proven disappointing, for there were more withdrawals of Japanese unions (affiliates of Sohyo) than new adhesions (of unions joining Zenrō), so that the total membership of unions belonging to the ICFTU decreased from 3 million to only half that number. The unions that withdrew were Nikkyoso (Teachers' Union, 550,000 members), Kokutetsu (National Railwaymen's Union, 400,000), Shi Tetsu (Private Railwaymen's Union, 150,000), and Zen Nichiro (Casual Workers' Union, 500,000, which was dissolved). As agaist this, there were unions joining Zenrō, including Zensen (textile workers), Den Roren (electricians), Kaiin (seamen), Jidosha Roren (auto workers), and Zen Ei-en (screen and theatrical workers) representing a total of 780,000, and they were affiliating individually instead of as a group. In any case, the balance sheet for the nine-year period unquestionably showed a loss for the ICFTU, which grew out of the confusion resulting from the "temporary measure."

Birth of Domei Kaigi and After

An event which occurred in 1962, and which is expected to alter the situation somewhat, was the birth of Domei Kaigi and its application for admission to the ICFTU. On receipt of this application, Secretary-General Becu of the ICFTU saw the gravity of the problem involved and came all the way to Japan in order to work out some formula satisfactory to both the unions under Sohyo affiliated with the ICFTU and Domei Kaigi, which would enable all to affiliate with the ICFTU in a group. Apparently the headquarters of the ICFTU was convinced of the need for such a compromise, since the unions belonging to Sohyo had again raised an objection to the affiliation of Domei Kaigi, on the ground that the unions of workers in the government and public corporations belonging to Domei Kaigi are "second unions"—i.e., undesirable turncoats that had deserted the mother unions, which had remained in Sohyo. To this charge, the leaders in Domei Kaigi retort that the ICFTU was a "second union" for the WFTU, Sohyo was a "second union" for Sanbetsu, and Zenrō was a "second union" for Sohyo. How long will the ICFTU overlook and permit the ill-advised action of the elements in the organization that results in rejection of other unions that are genuinely working for free and democratic unionism? The leaders in Zenrō and Domei Kaigi are asking if such a situation will not be detrimental in the end to the interest of the ICFTU and be of help to the WFTU, which is seeking to destroy democratic forces in the workers' movements of the world.

The visit to Japan of Secretary-General Becu of the ICFTU in October, 1963, did not result in any concrete action. The question of admission of Domei Kaigi is still pending at this writing. Experience since Meiji has shown time and again how powerful is the impact of forces exerted from outside on Japan. Is it realistic to hope that after a convenient formula is worked out for admission of all Japanese workers' unions into the fold of the ICFTU the much-desired united front for the workers' movement of Japan will result?

As to what will happen in the distant future, no prediction is possible; but for the near future, the answer will have to be based on the stern reality of the present. The world's working-class movement itself is divided today. The ICFTU must not err by being unrealistic, seeking unity where there is none. What Japan badly needs at the present crucial period is a stronger formation of democratic forces, and that is why Zenrō was, and Domei Kaigi at present increasingly is, looked upon as the hope of free and democratic unionism in this country.

Japan in the Limelight at the ILO

This history has revealed how pervasive the influence of the ILO has been in this country, particularly as regards labor legislation, labor administration, and the growth of democratic trade-unionism. We close with an account of a problem because of which Japan again stands in the limelight at the ILO. This is significant because it shows how meaningful the impact of the ILO continues to be for Japan. The story centers on a convention of the ILO (Convention 87), which the Japanese government has not ratified to date (December 30, 1963). For the delay in ratifying this Convention, the Japanese government is literally being "grilled" at present. Why should any government be criticized at the meetings of the ILO, as the Japanese government is, concerning a convention which it has decided either not to ratify, or to ratify only after taking certain measures involving some delay? This rather complicated problem calls for a historical analysis and explanation.

The Constitution of Japan and the Position of Workers Employed in Public Corporations.   It will be recalled that under Article 28 of the Constitution of Japan, all workers of Japan were given the rights of organization, collective bargaining, and collective action. The right of collective action is understood to imply primarily the right to strike. However, by virtue of the laws stemming from the policy of SCAP, set forth in MacArthur's letter of July 20, 1946, notably the Revised Public Servants Law (1949) and the Revised Public Corporations Labor Relations Law (1949), public servants and the workers engaged in public corporations were deprived of the constitutional right to strike. Moreover, by virtue of a special provision (Article 4, paragraph 3) of the Public Corporations and National Enterprise Labor Relations Act, it is only the workers who can be members or officers of a union in that particular corporation. Violating this provision of the law, however, three top officers of the All Communication Workers' Union took a leading part during 1958 in a strike of the communication workers. Thereupon the corporation discharged the three men as the representatives of workers in the corporation. On the other hand, however, the union insisted on its right of collective bargaining, asserting that it is a constitutionally guaranteed right of all workers in Japan. Controversy on this point was mitigated subsequently when the union made a slight concession by electing other men. Basically, however, it was the controversy between the union and the corporation that hindered earlier steps of the government toward ratification of Convention 87. Why? Because, in the event that the convention in question were ratified, the government, in order to conform to the terms of the convention, would have to alter the existing law or laws and recognize the workers' right to enter into collective bargaining "through representatives of their own choosing," regardless of whether the men chosen by the workers as their representatives were, or were not, the employees of the public corporation concerned.

Revision in the Constitution of ILO.   As conceived originally by the men who drafted the Labor Part (Part XIII) of the Treaty of Versailles, which became and still is the Constitution of the ILO, the ILO consisted of sovereign states and was not a superstate. As far as this concept is concerned, the ILO remains the same as when it started in 1920.[13]

As regards the conventions adopted at the ILO conferences, the member states were and still are free to decide for themselves whether or not they should ratify any of the conventions. The sole obligation the member states had was to bring the conventions adopted at the ILO Conference before the "competent authority" (or authorities) of the country within a stated period of time for the enactment of legislation or other action. If the competent authority gave its consent the member state had to communicate the formal ratification of the conventions and take such action as was necessary to make effective the provisions of the ratified conventions. However, if the consent of the competent authority was not obtained, no further obligation remained with respect to the unratified conventions.

An important change occurred on this last point in 1946 when a revision was made in the Constitution, with the addition of paragraph 5 (e) to Article 19. According to this revision:

(e) if the Member does not obtain the consent of the authority or authorities within whose competence the matter lies, no further obligation shall rest upon the Member except that it shall report to the Director-General of the International Labor Office at appropriate intervals as requested by the Governing Body, the position of its law and practice in regard to the matters dealt with in the Convention, showing the extent to which effect has been given, or is proposed to be given, to any of the provisions of the Convention by legislation, administrative action, collective agreement or otherwise and stating the difficulties which prevent or delay the ratification of such Convention.

Were this all, the matter might not have been so difficult for the Japanese government as it proved to be, because there was no system of questioning any government. There were no teeth, so to speak, to coerce or embarrass the governments.

Action of WFTU and ICFTU. Workers' movements of the world were not slow to perceive this, and teeth were put into the above provision by the actions taken successively by them through the channel of the Economic and Social Council of the United Nations, in March, 1947, and after. There was a request adduced to the council by two powerful workers' organization: The American Federation of Labor (AF of L) and the World Federation of Trade Unions (WFTU). This took place before the anti-Communist unions in the latter split away in 1949 and organized the International Confederation of Free Trade Unions (ICFTU) in 1950.

The Economic and Social Council discussed the "guarantees

for the exercise and development of trade-union rights." This item was taken up by the Council because of the action of the two workers' organizations, which were the "non-governmental organizations" recognized by the United Nations. In a memorandum submitted by the WFTU, it was pointed out that:

Since World War II, in certain countries such interventions were being made as would demolish the foundations of trade-union rights; trade-union movement was impeded by mass dismissals of workers in trade-unions, the arrest of active union members and leaders, seizure of union offices, dissolution by the government of agencies democratically set up by the unions, appointment by the government of union's officers, prohibition of unionization by colored or native workers, ban on national or international federations of trade-unions, etc.

These attacks on trade-union rights were made because of the survival in certain countries of the pernicious ideologies that had plunged the world into disaster. In these circumstances, trade-union rights must be internationally safeguarded as essential factors for ensuring peace and co-operation among the nations.

Adoption of Conventions 87 and 98 by ILO.   As a result of discussion of the above-mentioned item the Economic and Social Council adopted a resolution whereby the ILO was requested to place on the agenda of the next session of the General Conference the question of trade-union rights, and to report to the Economic and Social Council the result of deliberations of the conference. There was, previous to this, an agreement between the United Nations and the ILO, which was in fact the basis on which this request was addressed to the ILO. The Governing Body of the ILO took up the matter without delay, and consequently the 30th session of the ILO Conference, held in July, 1947, had on its agenda the question of "Freedom of Association and Industrial Relations." The discussion at the conference on this agenda resulted in the adoption of a "Resolution concerning Freedom of Association and Protection of the Right to Organize and to Bargain Collectively."

It should be noted here that it was the former half of this resolution that was taken up by the Conference in 1948, and which resulted in the adoption of the "Convention concerning the Right to Organize" (Convention 87). The latter half of the same resolution was taken up by the Conference in 1949, resulting in the adoption of the "Convention concerning the Application of the Principle of the Rights of Organization and of Collective Bargaining" (Convention 98).

When we trace the sequences of events, it is clear that it was primarily the pressure of the workers' movements, national and international, that led, after the revision of the Constitution of the ILO, to the adoption of the two conventions concerning the rights of organization and collective bargaining.

Fact-Finding and Conciliation Commission on Freedom of Association. So far we have traced the origin of the two conventions and have seen also how the Governing Body of the ILO might request the director-general to receive from time to time reports from various governments on the law and practice on matters dealt with in the unratified conventions, and statements on the difficulties preventing or delaying the ratification of such conventions. It is necessary to note further that another important step was taken early by the ILO Conference, acting on the proposal of the WFTU and the AF of L, urging the creation of a permanent organ to internationally supervise the exercise of trade-union rights. That step was the "Resolution concerning International Machinery for Safeguarding Freedom of Association." The Governing Body, which was enjoined to study how to implement this resolution, worked closely with the Economic and Social Council and, finally, at its session in January, 1950, decided to set up within the framework of the ILO an organ called "Fact-Finding and Conciliation Commission on Freedom of Association." This decision of the Governing Body was formally approved by the Economic and Social Council in February, 1950, and the ILO Conference in June of the same year.

Creation of such machinery for international supervision may be justified on various grounds. Only after ratification of a convention is a member state subject to the supervision provided by the Constitution of the ILO. A member state that fails to give full freedom of association is liable to hesitate to ratify in order to escape the supervision. Consequently, supervision is all the more necessary for members of the United Nations that are not members of the ILO. There is no obligation under either the Constitution or any convention of the ILO. How can the right of association of the peoples of such member states be assured? It is clear that the degree of freedom of association will be influenced by the extent to which such general civil rights as the rights of speech, assembly, and press are enjoyed. Now these civil rights come under the jurisdiction of the United Nations. Consequently, creation of such machinery in co-operation with the United

Nations will greatly facilitate the disposal of cases relating to civil rights. Furthermore, creation of a joint organ of this sort between the United Nations and the ILO will serve to strengthen the bond of co-operative relations between the two organizations.

This organization, a product of much thought, known as the "Fact-Finding and Conciliation Commission on Freedom of Association," was finally set up during 1950, consisting of nine members, all distinguished men of high authority as judges or with attainments as jurists. The Commission was empowered to treat complaints alleging infringements of trade-union rights. However, in order to minimize the objections of governments to the delicate work of the Commission, despite the opposition of the workers' delegates, it was decided that the complaints could be referred to this Commission only when consent of the government concerned was obtained. It is reported that no government has ever given its consent since the Commission was set up, and as a result, the actual work of fact-finding is carried out, not by the Commission itself, but by the "Commission on Freedom of Association," which was created originally by the Governing Body to determine whether or not there was need to refer certain complaints to the Fact-Finding Commission.[15]

Awkward Position of the Japanese Government. The foregoing account has shown, briefly, the complexity of the problem—a problem which has become particularly embarrassing for the Japanese government.

As explained earlier, as the result of revisions to the Public Servants Law and the Public Corporation Labor Relations Law (particularly the provisions in Article 4, paragraph 3 of the latter), the Japanese government was not in a position to ratify Convention 87. It first decided, therefore, not to ratify the Convention in question.

Considering the traditional "family spirit" that is still alive in Japan's industries, even if there were no legal difficulty of this sort, it is understandable why the Japanese government as an employer should be reluctant to be bound by an international convention to recognize the workers' unqualified right to enter into collective bargaining through representatives of their own choosing, regardless of where the representation might be employed. In any case, at first, the position of the government concerning ratification of Convention 87 was decidedly negative.

However, the government perceived early that it could not

long maintain its negative attitude. The pressures of the labor movement and of public opinion as expressed by the Rodo Mondai Kondan Kai, an advisory group of scholars surrounding the Minister of Labor, were so strong that the government finally yielded and the then competent minister announced the intention of the government to ratify the Convention in due course.

In view of the fact that more than five years have elapsed since this first assurance that the government would ratify Convention 87, and that the same assurance has been repeated on at least twelve occasions, questions may well be raised as to why the Convention remains unratified—why this procrastination? The answer may be summarized as follows:

It is neither lack of interest nor of good faith on the part of the Japanese government: it is rather the contrary. However the government considers it, it is necessary before ratifying the Convention to make certain adjustments in current practices or revisions in the existing laws on points other than those involved in the act of ratification. The government considers it necessary, for instance, to prohibit or restrict the prevailing practice of workers' serving as union officers on a full-time basis while continuing to receive wages from their employers. The proposal was made also that the employers should discontinue the practice of "check-off," which has become almost universal in Japan in the postwar years. There were a few other proposals which tended also to limit or restrict the rights and privileges hitherto enjoyed by the workers in this country.

Naturally, these proposals of the government (or of the Liberal Democratic Party, which is the government party) were seriously objected to by the socialists and trade-union leaders. The efforts of the government to reach a compromise with the trade-union and socialist leaders on these points led to further delay in the steps toward ratification.

On account of the delay in ratification of the Convention, as the dispatches from Geneva reported to Japanese press, the Governing Body has served "for the fifteenth time" a note to the Japanese government, recommending a more expeditious handling of the matter. Indeed, in the whole history of the ILO, few governments have received the amount of publicity that the Japanese government has on matters of this sort. From the last report received during November, 1963, we must conclude that the ILO Committee on Freedom of Association might proceed to request the Japanese government to give its consent to having the whole matter referred to the Fact-Finding and Conciliation Commission on Freedom of Association. Naturally, that would be unwelcome to the government of Japan, because it could seem that the government, despite everything it has done so far, were failing to fulfill an obligation which it had incurred as a member state of the ILO, and this is the very situation which every effort has been made to avert.

Outlook

In conclusion, two things must be done. First, the current problem should be looked at in the perspective of history.

Seventy years ago, Sidney and Beatrice Webb in their monumental work (*A History of Trade-Unionism, 1894*) described the structure and power of trade-unions in Great Britain by the pregnant phrase: "a state within a state." Seventy years later, in Japan, the organized workers of this country have come to assume the position occupied by the workers of Britain, as described by the Webbs. Likewise, elsewhere in the world, organized workers wield powers equal to those of states. We will have to admit candidly that it is the power of workers organized in the WFTU, the ICFTU, and others that has focused attention on Japan at the world's tribune of labor, the ILO, at Geneva. One might affirm that under the Constitution of the ILO, no country is legally obliged to ratify a convention that the competent authority in the country deems it unnecessary or unwise to ratify. Morally, however, the states can now be placed in a situation where they have no choice but to ratify. No doubt, it behooves our government to reflect and take hereafter a more full account than ever of the "a state within a state," national or international. Failing to do so, the government can again be put in an embarrassing position, even when, legally speaking, what it has or has not done was perfectly correct.

Second, let us admit frankly that the impact of the ILO on Japan has always been salutary and of tremendous help to the healthy growth of organized labor. Let us hope that by the same token the difficulty the Japanese government is currently experiencing regarding the Convention on the workers' rights of organization and of collective bargaining will prove helpful in furthering democratic freedom in the industrial relations of this country.

NOTES

CHAPTER I

1. Lord James Bryce, *American Commonwealth*. 2 vols. (New York: Macmillan, 1926); André Siegfried, *America Comes of Age* (New York: Harcourt and Brace, 1927); André Siegfried, *America at Mid-Century* (New York: Harcourt, 1952); Alexis de Tocqueville, *Democracy in America* (New York: Appleton, 1904).
2. Sir George Sansom, *Japan: A Short Cultural History* (New York: Appleton-Century, 1943); also his *The Western World and Japan* (New York: Knopf, 1950).
3. Edwin O. Reischauer, *The United States and Japan* (Cambridge: Harvard University Press, 1950); Chitoshi Yanaga, *Japan Since Perry* (New York: McGraw Hill, 1949); Hugh Borton, *Japan's Modern Century* (New York: The Ronald Press, 1955); Harold Scott Quidley, *Japanese Government and Politics* ("The Century Political Science Series") (New York: Century, 1932).
4. W. H. E. Griffis, *Mikado's Empire* (New York, Harper, 1913); Henry Dyer, *Dai Nippon* (New York: Scribner's, 1904); Walter Dickson, *Japan* (Edinburgh and London: W. Blackwood & Sons, Ltd., 1869); J. Ingram Bryan, *The Civilization of Japan* (London: Williams and Norgate, Ltd., 1927).
5. Lafcadio Hearn, *The Writings of Lafcadio Hearn* (New York: Houghton Mifflin, 1923).
6. Solomon B. Levine, *Industrial Relations in Postwar Japan* (Urbana, Illinois: University of Illinois Press, 1958); James C. Abegglen, *The Japanese Factory: Aspects of Its Social Organization* (Glencoe, Illinois: Free Press, 1958).
7. Warren S. Hunsberger, "Lessons from Japan's Development," *SAIS Review*, Autumn, 1961, p. 9.
8. W. W. Rostow, *The Stages of Economic Growth: A Non-Communist Manifesto* (Cambridge: Cambridge University Press, 1961).
9. *The Oriental Economist* (Tokyo), January, 1962, p. 27. Here we draw heavily on this article.
10. The situation was modified during 1963.
11. U.S. Congress. Joint Economic Committee. Subcommittee on Foreign Economic Policy. *Japan in United States Foreign Economic Policy*, by Warren S. Hunsberger. 87th Cong., 1st sess. (Washington, D.C.: GPO, 1961).
12. In passing we might note that occasional rumors arise of receiving from Japan cans filled with pebbles instead of fish or other food

that was ordered. Credence is given these stories by people who believe that a nation can rise to a position of prestige in this world by fraud or trickery. Even if such a practice were in fact discovered in a case or two out of hundreds of thousands, no one need be overly disturbed.

13. Robert A. Scalapino, "The United States and Japan," in *The United States and the Far East* (New York: Columbia University Press, 1956), p. 11.

14. The late President Kennedy did much to improve the situation. His loss is regretted by the world all the more.

15. COCOM (Co-ordinating Committee) and CHINCOM (China Committee) were both formed as subsidiary organs of C.G. (the Consultative Group), created originally by the Western nations to co-ordinate and control the export of strategic goods to nations under the Communist regime. CHINCOM was organized September, 1952, after the Korean War, in order to render more strict the control of export of strategic goods to China, quite apart from control by COCOM. Fifteen nations belonging to the C.G., including the United States, Great Britain, France, and Japan, joined CHICOM. When it started, the list of banned export articles to China included ninety items in addition to those in the COCOM list. The COCOM list consisted at first of three categories: (1) items completely banned, (2) items subject to limitation as to quantity, and (3) items subject to supervision or inspection. The COCOM list at first had a little over 300 items. Reduced by degrees, the list is said to contain 165 items as of March, 1965.

CHAPTER 2

1. Tokugawa Iyeyasu, the founder of the Tokugawa Shogunate, was given the title of Shogun by the Emperor Goyazei in 1603. Tokugawa Yoshinobu, the fifteenth shogun, tendered his resignation as shogun to the Emperor in 1867, when the Shogunate came to an end.

2. Expression used in the old *Constitution of the Great Japanese Empire, of 1889,* Article 1.

3. The term widely used by Japanese scholars for the Restoration is *i-shin,* which means "completely new," though another expression, *wo-sei fukko,* "return of the emperor's rule," is also used.

4. For a full account in English of the peasant uprisings and their effect on the feudal economy of Japan, see Hugh Borton, "Peasant Uprisings in Japan of the Tokugawa Period," *The Transactions of the Asiatic Society of Japan,* XVI (May, 1938), 16.

5. A *sangi* in the early Meiji government was a councilor of semi-ministerial rank.

6. Toyama Shigeki, *Sonno Joi to Zettai Shugi* ("Revere the Emperor, Expel the Foreigner" and Totalitarianism) (Tokyo: Hakujitsu Shoin, 1948), pp. 48–50.

7. The First International was founded in 1864, and came to an end

in 1876. The Second International was organized in 1889, which was the twelfth year of the Meiji.

8. Cf. Kato Hiroyuki, "Waga Kokutai to Kirisuto Kyo" (Our National Policy and Christianity) in *Kokutai Shin Ron* (Tokyo: Inada Sahei, 1875).

9. "Luddites" is a name supposed to have derived from the name of the leader of the movement, Ned Ludd. After a violent uprising in 1799, the movement reached its peak in 1812, but it died out as the workers began to appreciate the futility of a movement to oppose progress.

10. Tokugawa Nariaki, the Lord of Mito, to whom this expression was attributed, was a sturdy leader of antiforeign movements.

11. Takao Tsuchiya, *Ishin Sangyo Kensetsu-shi Shiryo* (Materials for the History of Establishment of Industries at the time of the Restoration) (Vol. I, Tokyo: Kogyo Shiryo Kanko-Kai, 1943; Vol. II, Tokyo: Maruzen Publishing Co., 1944), pp. 97, 108. Accounts in considerable detail on the development of industries in the early Meiji period are found in this work of Tsuchiya. We have made free use of this material for these pages.

12. *Kōbu Shō Enkaku Hōkoku* (Report on the Historical Development of the Ministry of Industry and Communications), pp. 96–149, quoted by Takao Tsuchiya, *op. cit.*, p. 103.

13. The records show that when Perry started on his mission to Japan he had no clear idea as to who was the ruler of Japan, or to whom the presents should be submitted. The designation "Tycoon" was used.

14. Since the adoption by the ILO of the convention prohibiting the use of white phosphorus for match manufacture, Japan's adherence to that convention has completely eliminated the evil mentioned here.

15. S. Uyehara, *The Industry and Trade of Japan* (London: P. S. King, 1926) has a good chapter on capital investment, pp. 26–35. We have made here a free use of this chapter.

16. G. D. H. Cole, *A Short History of the British Working Class Movement 1789–1927* (New York: Macmillan, 1927), p. 3.

17. We have already suggested that the prospect of a war on the continent supplied the impetus for speedy completion of the railway from Tokyo to Shimonoseki.

18. Hitherto foreigners were allowed to reside only inside the settlement areas. In July, 1899, that restriction was removed.

19. Arahata Kanson: *Nihon Shakai Shugi Undo Shi* (The History of the Socialist Movement in Japan), pp. 28–29.

20. Suehiro Izutaro, *Nihon Rōdō Kumiai Undō Shi* (History of the Trade Union Movement) (Tokyo: Chuo Koron Shu, 1954), p. 28.

21. The drafting of this document is attributed to Abe Isoo, one of the founders of the party. Cf. Ishikawa Kyokuzan, *op. cit.*, p. 78.

22. The meaning of this last item will be made clear in the following pages.

23. Kishimoto Eitaro, *Nihon Zettai Shugi no Shakai Seisaku Shi* (His-

tory of the Social Policy under Totalitarianism in Japan) (Tokyo: Yuhi Kaku, 1955), p. 67.

24. This was *Chian Keisatsu Hō* (Public Peace Police Act), March 10, 1900, Law No. 36.

25. This decree was *Gyosei Keisatsu Kisoku* (Administrative Police Regulations), dated March 7, 1875.

26. This was *Ikei-zai Shokketsu Rei* (Order for Summary Disposal of Police Offenses), dated September 24, 1884.

27. Dated June 6, 1900, Law No. 84.

28. Cf. Suehiro Izutaro, *op. cit.*, p. 32. Kada Tetsuji, *op. cit.*, pp. 73–75, 88–89.

29. E. W. Clement, *A Short History of Japan* (Chicago: University of Chicago Press, 1915) (Tokyo: Kyo Bun Kan, n.d.), p. 56.

30. Hugh Borton, "Peasant Uprisings in Japan of the Tokugawa Period," *The Transactions of the Asiatic Society of Japan,* XVI (May, 1938), 16.

31. Borton, *op. cit.*, p. 62.

32. Some might very well object to this statement on two grounds: (1) that the outflow of the rural population to industrial centers in this period was temporary and limited mostly to young women who went to textile and other mills, chiefly to earn their dowry; and (2) that the temporary exodus of the rural population served to enrich the rural peasantry rather than to impoverish them, because the young people recruited to the factories were earning money which they sent home. These objections are not unfounded, and yet the fact remains that the government's policy of favoring industrial expansion at the expense of agriculture had the effect of depopulating the countryside and of hastening the increase of urban population and the lopsided accumulation of wealth in industrial centers. In this connection, it is interesting to see what Goldsmith himself wrote to Sir Joshua Reynolds, to whom the poem was dedicated: "I know you will object (and indeed several of our best and wisest friends concur in the opinion) that the depopulation it [*The Deserted Village*] deplores is nowhere to be seen and the disorders it laments are only to be found in the poet's own imagination. To this I can scarce make any other answer than that I sincerely believe what I have written; that I have taken all possible pains, in my country excursions, for these four or five years, to be certain of what I allege...." (Oliver Goldsmith, *The Deserted Village,* London: Parmstadt, 1924.)

CHAPTER 3

1. Are the Russians wholly and strictly Caucasian and white, and are the Japanese wholly Mongolians? These questions could be discussed at some length, but we must avoid controversial and irrelevant digressions.

2. For a description of the incidents and the statistics of the disputes that occurred during the period covered here and in the following

section, we depended largely on Kyocho Kai, *Saikin no Shakai Undo* (Recent Social Movements) (Tokyo: n. p., 1929), a voluminous work.

3. Kyocho Kai, *op. cit.*, p. 43.

CHAPTER 4

1. The Carnegie Endowment for International Peace, *The Origins of the International Labor Organization* (New York: Columbia University Press, 1934), Vols. I–II.

2. Replaced later by Mr. Robinson. Professor James T. Shotwell joined later.

3. Mr. Harold B. Butler acted as substitute for Mr. Barnes.

4. M. Arthur Fontaine, Director of Labor in the Ministry of Labor, and M. Leon Jouhaux, president of C.G.T., joined later as substitutes.

5. This is the story as it was told by Suzuki himself, to the writer, who had the opportunity of visiting with Samuel Gompers at the AF of L Convention at Atlantic City, N.J., in 1919, in company with Suzuki. Suzuki passed through the United States on his way back from the Paris Peace Conference.

6. Carnegie Endowment, *op. cit.*, Vol. I, pp. 313–314.

7. As a matter of fact, in presenting the motion, Mertens did say that the workers' delegates had decided not to object to the admission of the man chosen as workers' delegate from Japan (though there were irregularities in the procedure of his selection). While neither Masumoto nor any other delegate from Japan had fully understood the text of the motion which practically censured the practice of the Japanese government, it was sufficient to frighten the entire Japanese delegation. For further particulars, see League of Nations, International Labor Conference, Proceedings of the First Annual Meeting (French edition) (Washington, D.C.: Government Printing Office, 1920), p. 49.

8. *Ibid.*, p. 155.

9. Carnegie Endowment, *op. cit.*, p. 314.

10. Dr. Adachi always spelled his name this way.

11. It is recorded that as early as 1905 a small gathering to commemorate May Day was held each year at the publication office of *Heimin*. Sakai Toshihiko, Ishikawa Sanshiro, and Kinoshita Naoe were among the socialist leaders present. It was a quiet meeting without any special incident.

12. During the confusion caused by the great earthquake of 1923, besides Osugi and his wife, there were other active leaders suspected of belonging to the anarchosyndicalist faction who were also murdered. One such unfortunate incident was the arrest and murder of Hirasawa Keishichi and several other trade-union leaders at Kemedo Police Station in the north of Tokyo. The incident is known as *Kemedo Jiken* (the Kemedo Incident).

13. Notice that this was *Minshū* (people) and not *Minshu* (Demo-

cratic). The latter word came to be applied only in the next stage.

14. Phrases used by Frederick Harbison and Charles A. Myers in their *Management in the Industrial World* (New York: McGraw-Hill, 1959), chap. 1, pp. 3–20.

15. The writer has particularly in mind G. D. H. Cole, *A Short History of the British Working Class Movement.*

16. Serious and scholarly studies on this subject have been made by both Japanese and foreign scholars. Works of Kita Teïkichi (*Minzoku to Rekishi*, or Race and History [Tokyo: Misuzu Shobo, 1919]), Takigawa Masahiro (*Nippon Shakai Shi*, or Social History of Japan [Tokyo: Tōkō Shoin, 1928]), Yanagita Kunio (*Iwayuru Tokushu Buraku no Shurui*, or Kinds of So-called Special Villages), James Murdock (*A History of Japan* [London: Kegan Paul, 1926]), and others, contain the results of valuable studies. A relatively brief but remarkable work is that of Ninomiya Shigeaki, entitled "An Inquiry Concerning the Origin, Development, and Present Situation of the Eta in Relation to the History of Social Classes in Japan," *Transactions of the Asiatic Society of Japan*, Second Series, X (December, 1933). There is a good chapter devoted to the subject in Kyocho Kai, *Saikin no Shakai Undo*, pp. 471–486. We have made a very free use of these sources, particularly the works of Ninomiya and of Kyocho Kai.

17. We have adopted here Ninomiya Shigeaki's translation.

18. Carnegie Endowment, *op. cit.*, pp. 195–196.

19. For a full treatment of the subject of *giri* and *ninjo*, see Nitobe Inazo, *Bushido: The Soul of Japan* (New York: Putnam, 1905).

20. After withdrawal from the League of Nations proper, Japan remained in the ILO, but finally withdrew also from the ILO in 1938. Japan re-entered the ILO in 1951, as will be explained later.

CHAPTER 5

1. Soviet Russia officially entered the war, in accordance with the Potsdam Agreement, on August 8, 1945, exactly one week before Japan surrendered on August 15.

2. An authoritative and readable account of the Potsdam Conference is Herbert Feis, *Japan Subdued: The Atomic Bomb and the End of the War in the Pacific* (Princeton: Princeton University Press, 1961).

3. Edwin O. Reischauer's *The United States and Japan* is a highly recommended work. There, the term "Potsdam Proclamation" is used, but we use here the more popular term, "Potsdam Declaration."

4. C. A. Willoughby and John Chamberlain, *MacArthur 1941–1951* (New York: McGraw-Hill, 1954). John Gunther, *The Riddle of MacArthur* (New York: Harper, 1951). Courtney Whitney, *MacArthur: His Rendezvous with History* (New York: Knopf, 1956).

5. As a matter of fact, according to a more authoritative source, the flag used on the battleship *Missouri* was the one that was hoisted

on the White House on the fateful day of the Pearl Harbor assault. The same flag was unfurled in Casablanca, Rome, and Berlin, commemorating each time the victorious entry of the American forces. This should not mar the beauty of the legend for anyone who believes that each victory of the American forces means victory for freedom and for the rights of man. See Kase Toshi Kazu, *Road to Missouri* (New Haven: Yale University Press, 1950).

6. Whitney, *op. cit.*, p. 213.

7. Whitney, *op. cit.*, p. 216.

8. Edwin O. Reischauer, *The United States and Japan*, pp. 31–32.

9. Robert A. Fearey, *The Occupation of Japan: Second Phase: 1948–1950* (New York: Macmillan, 1950), p. 8.

10. Reischauer, *op. cit.*, p. 48.

11. W. Macmahon Ball, *Japan, Enemy or Ally?* (New York: John Day, 1949), p. 33.

12. There was, however, one important difference in the procedure of drafting the Labor Standard Act which should be mentioned especially, to give credit where it is due. In drafting the law, Miss Golda Stander, an expert in the Labor Division of SCAP, rendered special help to Mr. Terada Kyusaku, director of the Labor Administration Section in the Ministry of Labor, who had been assigned the task of drawing up a preliminary draft of the law.

13. In this and the following sections, I have made free use of material in Suehiro Izutaro, *op. cit.*, pp. 147–148.

14. Suehiro, *op. cit.*, pp. 130–131.

15. We found out in no time that this was in fact a "warming-up" instead of a "cooling-off" period, hence the revision of the law in 1949.

16. Miriam S. Farley, *Aspects of Japan's Labor Problems* (New York: John Day, 1950), p. 153.

17. *Ibid.*, p. 153.

18. Tokuda Kyuichi, who was a member of the Central Labor Relations Commission, during a tea at which the writer sat with him, casually remarked to the writer, "I believe the total number of members of the Bolshevik Party that won the Revolution of 1917 was a little over 70,000. We now have in our Party in Japan over 100,000 members." What he implied in making this remark was not made clear during the conversation.

19. Including purely tenants and part-owner and part-tenant farmers. Percentages of total farming families.

20. Robert A. Fearey, *op. cit.*, pp. 97–98.

21. On the negative side of the government's policy on the problem of surplus population in the rural areas, there is the positive leadership taken by the government since 1952 in family planning, or birth control practices. Japan seems to have succeeded in this line of social policy.

22. From the United States alone, a total of 5,720,000 men served in

the war, and 157,530 casualty cases were reported, including men killed, missing, and wounded.

CHAPTER 6

1. For some years after the Constitution was promulgated, questions were raised as to the actual authorship of this document. It is now general knowledge that the body of the Constitution was originally drafted in SCAP, GHQ, but the passages relating to the renunciation of the right of belligerency were inserted at the request of the then Prime Minister Baron Shidehara. As a matter of fact, the Japanese government did prepare first a Japanese draft of the Constitution at the behest of SCAP and submitted it for approval. However, there was a delay in the submission. SCAP returned to the Prime Minister some days later a text drafted at GHQ instead of the one prepared by the Japanese government. The text received from GHQ was acted on by the Diet and became the Constitution of Japan. However, the thought expressed by Baron Shidehara had been incorporated in the Constitution as it now stands. Hence this expression by General MacArthur: "A product of Japanese thought. . . ."

2. It is only fair to give here an explanation of the terms of the law, to see what was meant by "destructive activities" that were liable to prosecution. By "destructive activities" the law meant: (1) civil war; preparation, plotting or aiding of civil war; inviting or inciting of aid to be given to foreign invasion; printing, distributing, publicly displaying, communicating or broadcasting of literature or pictures urging the justification or necessity of invasion; and (2) rioting, arson, use of explosives, the disturbing or overturning of trains or tramcars, manslaughter, robbery, disturbance of performance of police duties; preparation, plotting, inciting or abetting of the above-mentioned acts.

3. John S. Mill, *Principles of Political Economy* (London: J. W. Parker, 1848), chap. 5.

4. How much the rate of economic growth of Japan has been helped by investment in industrial equipment can be seen by the comparison of the proportion of equipment-investment against total national production with the rates of economic growth in the major industrial nations of the world. The figures are for 1957.

5. Nakayama Ichiro: *Industrialization of Japan* (The Centre for East Asian Cultural Studies, 1963), p. 17.

6. *Ibid.*

7. *Ibid.*, p. 10.

8. Peter Robinson in the *Financial Times*, July 22, 1963.

9. Nippon Rodo Kyokai: *Rodo Keizai no Aramashi*, by Omiya Goro, 1963. We have made a very free use of the valuable material contained in this pamphlet, particularly pp. 14–23.

10. Nippon Rodo Kyokai, *op. cit.*, pp. 48–50.

11. O. D. Foenander: *op. cit.*

12. Nihon Rodo Kyokai: *"Chushō Kigyo no Ro-shi Kankei,"* a study contributed by Yoshitani Yoshio (November, 1962).
13. The first session of the General Conference of the ILO was held in 1919 at Washington, D.C., but officially the League of Nations, of which the ILO was part, came into being only in February, 1920.
14. In this and following sections, the writer has made a very free use of the excellent work of Kaite Shingo and Toda Yoshio: *ILO*. We acknowledge our indebtedness to the authors of that helpful material.
15. Kaite and Toda, *op. cit.*, p. 216.

INDEX

Date Due

MAY 9 '68			

Demco 293-5